Arden/D'A... D'Arcy/Arden Plays: One

The Business of Good Government, Ars Longa Vita Brevis, Friday's Hiding, The Royal Pardon, The Little Gray Home in the West, Vandaleur's Folly, Immediate Rough Theatre

The Business of Good Government, a nativity play written for performance in the church of Brent Knoll, Somerset in 1960 was the first of a series of vivid and effective experiments in community drama for D'Arcy and Arden. *Ars Longa Vita Brevis* continued the experiment with a framework for performance or a basis for free improvisation. *Friday's Hiding*, a mime piece, is a comedy representing certain features of country life and *The Royal Pardon* is about order and anarchy, illusion and reality and is a plea for an unfettered, vital drama. *The Little Gray Home in the West* is a fast-moving satirical melodrama, black and hilarious by turns, drawing out the tangled web of the still continuing Irish conflict. In *Vandaleur's Folly* 'Arden and D'Arcy have the gift for writing a heightened prose that shades almost imperceptibly into song and ballad' (Michael Billington, *Guardian*). *Immediate Rough Theatre* is a series of improvised, topical plays put on in houses, pubs, streets and meetings in the West of Ireland in the 1970s.

Margaretta D'Arcy is Irish and has worked with improvisational and theatre techniques since the fifties. Her work with Arden includes *The Business of Good Government* (1960), *The Happy Haven* (1960), *Ars Longa, Vita Brevis* (1963), *Friday's Hiding* (1965), *The Royal Pardon* (1966), *Muggins is a Martyr* (1968), *The Hero Rises Up* (1968), *The Island of the Mighty* (1972), *Keep the People Moving* (for radio, 1972), *The Non-Stop Connolly Show* (1975), *Vandaleur's Folly* (1978) and *The Little Gray Home in the West* (1978). Her play *A Pinprick of History* was performed at the Almost Free Theatre, London in 1977. She is a member of Aosdána (parliament of Irish artists), and she runs the only women's radio station in Ireland.

John Arden was born in Barnsley, Yorkshire, in 1930. While studying architecture at Cambridge and Edinburgh universities, he began to write plays, four of which have been produced at the Royal Court Theatre: *The Waters of Babylon, Live Like Pigs, Serjeant Musgrave's Dance* and *The Happy Haven*; while a fifth, *The Workhouse Donkey*, was produced at the Festival Theatre, Chichester. For a year he held an Annual Fellowship in Playwriting at Bristol University, and Bristol Old Vic produced *Ironhand*, his free adaptation of Goethe's *Goetz von Berlichingen*. *Armstrong's Last Goodnight* was first produced at the Glasgow Citizens' Theatre and later at the National Theatre. *Left-Handed Liberty* was specially commissioned by the Corporation of London to commemorate the 750th Anniversary of Magna Carta and was produced at the Mermaid Theatre. He is married to Margaretta D'Arcy, with whom he has collaborated on several plays. Arden's first novel, *Silence Among the Weapons* (1982), was short-listed for the Booker-McConnell Prize for Fiction. His other novels are: *Books of Bale* (1988) and *Cogs Tyrannic* (1991).

ARDEN/D'ARCY
D'ARCY/ARDEN

PLAYS: ONE

The Business of Good Government
(Arden/D'Arcy)
Ars Longa Vita Brevis (D'Arcy/Arden)
Friday's Hiding (D'Arcy/Arden)
The Royal Pardon (Arden/D'Arcy)
The Little Gray Home in the West
(D'Arcy/Arden)
Vandaleur's Folly (D'Arcy/Arden)
Immediate Rough Theatre
(D'Arcy/Arden and group collaboration)

Methuen Drama

METHUEN WORLD DRAMATISTS

This collection first published in Great Britain in 1991
by Methuen Drama, Michelin House, 81 Fulham Road, London SW3 6RB
and distributed in the United States of America by HEB Inc,
361 Hanover Street, Portsmouth, New Hampshire NH 03801-3959.

The Business of Good Government first published in 1963 by Methuen & Co
copyright © 1963, 1983 by John Arden and Margaretta D'Arcy
Ars Longa Vita Brevis first published in 1965 by Cassell & Co Ltd
copyright © 1965 by John Arden and Margaretta D'Arcy
Friday's Hiding first published in 1967 by Methuen & Co
© 1967 by Margaretta D'Arcy and John Arden
The Royal Pardon first published in 1967 by Methuen & Co
copyright © 1967 by John Arden and Margaretta D'Arcy
The Little Gray Home in the West first published in 1982 by Pluto Press Limited
copyright © 1982, 1986 by John Arden and Margaretta D'Arcy
Vandaleur's Folly first published in 1981 by Eyre Methuen Ltd
copyright © 1981 by Margaretta D'Arcy and John Arden
Immediate Rough Theatre copyright © 1991 by Margaretta D'Arcy
and John Arden
The authors have asserted their moral rights.

A CIP catalogue record for this book is available from the British Library

ISBN 0-413-64940-7

The front cover is a detail from 'Moses' (1945) by Frida Kalo and the slide was
provided by the Women Artists Slide Library.

Printed and bound in Great Britain by
Cox & Wyman Ltd, Reading, Berkshire

Contents

Chronology

Introduction

When I was a little girl we had a children's book called *101 Things To Do For a Rainy Day*. One of the chapters was headed, 'Let's Do A Play'. My mother had just made each of us a new summer-green nightdress with short puffed sleeves. So if we Did A Play, it would be an opportunity to wear our nightdresses during the day. We put together our story in our sitting-room, to present to our mother, a story about four princesses – but were they who they thought they were? My eldest sister was the dramatist, of the Artaud school, with a taste for the sinister. My youngest sister, a toddler, walked off in the middle of the piece and sat on mother's lap, and no harm was done to the drama.

In this volume, I realise that all the plays (except for *Vandaleur's Folly*) do in fact re-create that same spirit from my childhood. Let's do a play! in our own room, with our neighbours, friends, and families. In 1959, having children of my own, and yet keeping on working, gave me a choice – child-minding and worry and at the end of the week being no better off because all my wages would have gone to the child-minder, or staying at home and making theatre there, which the children could be part of.

And also: where to live? Stay in London with babies and no money, trying to find flats? Or move out to a rural village and rent a place that would be both cheap and damp? I chose dampness and cheapness, because it meant freedom from landlords or property-companies with agents sniffing around poking their noses everywhere. The country in fact meant creating one's own entertainment. To the superficial glance of an urban dweller the only rural culture at that time in England was county-tory/anglicanism; however, with a bit of scratching-around, the underside was revealed, the ancient folklores, the old mother-goddess still breathing her message of randomness, chaos, anarchy, anathema to the military-industrial complex. Moving into a village just because the rent was low was a bit arrogant – what had *we* to offer, as we had no money, no status, no land, and an ingrained aversion to the local squirearchy and its values?

But had J. Arden and I sorted out *our* values, in relation to each other, in relation to the way we thought theatre ought to be made, in relation to the relation between theatre and life? It was easy for me, because I had been in the theatre since the age of fifteen and had knocked around a lot; I had already decided I wanted theatre but not the arbitrary cruelty of the professional stage. But Arden was just 'stepping out', hovering excitedly on the lip of the dragon's mouth. His whole family background (with a strong reverence for 'the professions') was pushing him toward conventional hierarchic success. My mongrel Irish background based its values on dissidence and positive rejection of the petty-minded gombeen hypocrisies of my country – I believed we should be praised for what we did, not for who we were. I gained my strength from the old rural generosity and traditions of open house, open entertainment, including good conversation and controversial politics – the political starts with the personal – where everyone would come in and do their bit for the sake of good company and a good night.

As I was the one who had initiated the change in *my* life, which Arden followed, even though he was now the sole wage-earner, it had to be my values that were brought into the new life to reveal the richness of reality which Arden knew (from books) that he had been deprived of. It took about a year for us to get to know the people in the village and for them to trust us. And at the end of the year *The Business of Good Government* came into being.

I was expecting a baby that Christmas, and having difficulty with the utilitarian NHS bureaucracy and its ingrained prejudice that any Irish woman without money who wanted children rather than contraception must be a rampant Catholic, so my personal preoccupation fell in naturally enough with the seasonal story. (We were lucky to live beside the village church; we were lucky to have a vicar who was interested in theatre; we were lucky to find Mr Hodge, an old retired shepherd, who still had his father's traditional Somerset smock, crook and cider-firkin, which he insisted on bringing into the play like an actor from a 14th-century guild-mystery.)

I suppose I can say that all the other plays in this book sprang out of equally direct and personal experiences of double-think in my own life and circumstances. Take, for instance, the two children's pieces, *The Royal Pardon* and *Ars Longa Vita Brevis*. *The Royal Pardon* reflected the superior way in which professional theatre people in London assumed that any play that didn't go on at the Royal Court (or somewhere similar) with a professional cast, could not be important; and that my excitement in telling them about the 12-year-old Girl Guides in Yorkshire who knocked on my door one evening and wanted us 'to do a play with them' was totally unaccountable and irrelevant. They did not realise how those girls fought tooth and nail to put on *Ars Longa Vita Brevis* the way they did – they were assailed on all sides by criticisms – it wasn't *a real play*, there was no curtain, they made up their lines instead of having to learn them, wearing masks and wearing make-up was unsuitable for young females – but their joy in ridiculing the military-industrial complex and overturning all the taboos of family and thrift remains a delight in my mind, and has been more valuable to me over the years than all the stodginesses and corruptions of the London theatre.

By the early '70s, in the west of Ireland, we were living in a highly-charged political arena, our subject-matter had changed accordingly, and so had the State's attitude toward the plays; although the actual process of discovering stories and making plays in the house remained the same.

The first presentation of *The Little Gray Home in the West* (then called *The Ballygombeen Bequest*) was a reading in a house in the Connemara countryside where bailiffs were imminently expected to evict the family (the immediate place and situation, in fact, that had inspired the play to start with). The first *acted* performance took place in a teachers' training college in the Falls Road, Belfast, with a regular battle outside between the IRA and the British Army – we could hear the gunshots throughout the show. The students in the cast had been stopped by the Army while attending rehearsals, harassed, searched, their scripts riffled through in the open street and publicly despised by the soldiers – who the hell were they to put on a play, they were nothing but ignorant Teagues?

Vandaleur's Folly has an odd history. It sprang from our *Non-Stop Connolly Show*, because we found that Connolly had used the Ralahine Co-operative in his writings as an emblematic beacon of light for Irish Socialism. The late Eamonn Smullen came out of an English gaol to the Corrandulla Arts and Entertainment in our house ten miles from Galway, and we gave a reading of his play

(*The Terrorists*) about agrarian rebellion in the Ireland of the
1830s. He wanted to set up a left-wing theatre, and so created the
conditions for us to present the Connolly plays in Dublin: then he
wanted to bring a play to Cuba. The three of us mulled over
various subjects and decided on Ralahine. That dream was never
fulfilled because of political and financial complications: so our
script ended up in the hands of the English 7:84 company.

This was not a happy experience, as the political climate in
England had become highly coercive and scary. There was the
perennial IRA bombing campaign which only added to the
intimidating effect on our Irish actors of Irish anti-terrorist and
censorship laws, compounded by the even more intimidating
effect of the British Prevention of Terrorism Act when they came
to work in England. Their agents would warn them against
taking part in political plays. You would think you had a cast,
and then mysteriously the next day a phone call would come
saying this or that actor had had to drop out for all sorts of
plausible reasons. The play dealt with a historical shift from
revolution to reform and reflected a similar shift in both Britain
and Ireland; and therefore did not go down very well with the
left. It also reflected parallel contradictions within the left-wing
theatre companies themselves, which came out into the open
when the actors collectively removed (from the decor) relevant
posters which highlighted what was happening in the Six
Counties, the H-block protests in particular. This meant that
when we played in Belfast I had to stand outside the theatre
handing out leaflets about the prisoners while the actors disowned
my presence. In the end my actions got me into gaol at Armagh
and the company continued with the play without letting anyone
know where I was. In fact, a healthy experience for me:
professional actors, after all, go into the state-subsidised theatre
primarily to earn their living and make a career, not to put
themselves on the line against the military-industrial complex.

The other play of this collection which does not bring me very
happy memories is *Friday's Hiding*. Its techniques came out of the
work done by the Girl Guides in *Ars Longa*. The story was based
upon a brother and sister whom we knew in Yorkshire. The
Edinburgh Lyceum company commissioned a mime-play (a genre
new to us), and we wrote it, expecting to be asked to go to
rehearsals and explore the technique in practice. We were neither
invited nor even told when the production was to commence. So
the memory of the script vanished into history; until our affection

for it was revived in 1990, when Dr Lamice El-Amari of Oran University invited us to Algeria to examine her students of English who were preparing Arabic translations of *Friday's Hiding* and *The Business of Good Government*. *Friday's Hiding* proved especially appropriate to the rural society of a Muslim country.

When I consider these plays it is like looking through a family album of photographs, letters and keepsakes.

M. D'Arcy, 1991

In the early 1940s, in the middle of World War 2, I would be about ten or eleven years old, at a private boarding school in Yorkshire, and discovering the excitement, the exploration, the unbelievable personal extension of making up stories in all sorts of different voices, telling them to my friends, receiving attention and response and laughter and sometimes flat dissent as rude as it could come ('Oh no I don't believe *that*, Arden, far-fetched, Arden's far-fetched, tell him to shut up, put the cork in, fizzle! – whoever's in the next bed, tell him! nobody believes *that*!'); all this in the dormitory, after lights-out, and very strictly out, the blackout pulled back from the windows to give us air, so that any light shown would immediately signal the Luftwaffe as well as the school staff.

Talking itself was anyway forbidden. Telling stories with any sort of dramatic climax – shouts, screams, cackles of laughter, volleys of what we presumed to be oaths, associated vocal sound-effects of blood, bombs and burst – was very highly dangerous. Has it ever been so dangerous since? If we were heard the headmaster would flagellate our bare behinds with a flat-backed varnished wooden hairbrush, or a stick like a Regency buck's walking-cane. Voluptuous peril gladly risked for the sake of nightly narrative-drama; indeed almost *welcomed*, for reasons of a characteristically 'English' middle-class psycho-cultural complexity which we did not perhaps fully understand until several years later. The stories I told, under threat not so much of censorship as total restriction of communication (a direct flouting, were it to happen today, of Article 19 of the UN Charter of Human Rights, 'the right to free exchange of information'), dealt almost entirely, and some would say significantly, with perverse anti-heroes, thoroughly improper objects of bardic empathy, German naval officers, national enemies – I can remember their names to this day – Glueck, von Kellermann, Herz, Klatt . . .

malignant yet grotesque, terrible yet teutonically ridiculous, winning all their imagined battles except (we assumed) the *last* one.

There was another boy, his name was Paul and he eventually became, I think, a Church of England clergyman, who had a similar cast of characters, led by the torpedo-bearded leather-jacketed *Kapitaen zur See* Goburg. Sometimes we told stories about each other's people, or mixed their adventures together. In daylight, on wet afternoons in the recreation-room, we drew pictures of episodes in the stories, and worked up, within a small community of close friends, little plays of vehement nautical disaster, shipboard mutiny and peculiar eruptions of the ghoulish supernatural.

I suppose for two years or so I lived more intensely within the haunted heart of the Nazi navy than ever in the school itself, perhaps all of us did – or if the others' imaginations gripped them less fiercely than mine did me, I was not made aware of it. The plays brought together in this book have had much the same effect. They were all 'home-made', told and acted-out as between friends and neighbours . . . and in more than one case (as M. D'Arcy explains above) under conditions of some insecurity – *The Little Gray Home in the West*, for example nearly disappeared altogether as a result of the 'headmasterly' approach adopted towards it by General Tuzo (in command of the British troops in the north of Ireland), the Arts Council of Great Britain (which penalised 7:84 by taking away their grant), *The Daily Telegraph*, and the libel courts. I believe, in hindsight, that the whipping headmaster hovers within the scripts as well as behind them – the constable in *The Royal Pardon*, the interrogator in *The Little Gray Home*, Herod in *The Business of Good Government*, the demon who will stop the story if he can; and if he can't, then he must be *part of* it, a U-boat thug in a gold-braided cap to drown or be drowned, disintegrate his enemies or be blown up himself, yelping his rage in defiance against those who defy his power.

J. Arden, 1991

A word about the 'notation of joint-authorship'. This volume is called **Arden and D'Arcy**; but also (on the title page) **D'Arcy and Arden**: and most of the plays in it are individually headed **D'Arcy and Arden**. We are told that **Arden and D'Arcy** should remain on the front cover because of cataloguing and

bookshop/library shelf arrangements, a commercial expedient
which we regret; but otherwise, which name is printed first
indicates which one of us was the principal driving-force behind
the play in question, and the shaper of the overall structure of the
story. There has been some inconsistency of attribution in earlier
printings; but we intend this edition to be definitive.

If we were asked which play has had the most to teach us as
playmakers, we would answer *Ars Longa Vita Brevis*. We would
think of the Girl Guides in Kirkbymoorside, of Albert Hunt and
his students in Shropshire, of Robert Leach at Birmingham using
five different groups of actors all interpreting it and improvising
in different ways at the same time. We met a woman from
Yugoslavia who told us of a production in that country in which
she and her brother had taken part in the glorious heady days of
student rebellion. It was broadcast into Greece to topple the
Colonels' junta (which we like to think it did). And its ingredients
contain the seeds of an entire ideology which we have since
arrived at in fuller and more rational form – the recognition of
women's invisible work, women's power subverting the military-
industrial complex, spectators' power to subvert the power of the
actor where all activate and none are passive, everyone becoming
their own script-writer, director, performer.

We developed this latter aspect in our *Immediate Rough Theatre
for Citizens' Involvement*, and have taken it one stage further with
Gerard McLaughlin and Catherine Couvert in Belfast, where a
regular gathering of artists has met since 1987 under the name of
Dúchas Na Saoirse ('the nature, culture, or heritage, of liberation').
Dúchas also derives from Galway Women's Entertainment as set
up by M. D'Arcy in 1982 and then (with Janet Watts) developed
into a radio now known as Radio Pirate-Woman – an unlicensed
uncensored women's neighbourhood transmitter linking and
making waves with women in struggle all over the world. The
medium of the airways is particularly important at present, for
the State everywhere is clamping down on freedoms of speech
and exchange of information, striving at all points to control
knowledge for its own purposes – as we can see by the growth of
censorship on radio and TV; in Ireland Section 31; in Britain its
mirror-image, the banning of what is deemed to be 'Sinn Féin'
even to the extent of cutting ancient speeches by Eamonn De
Valera out of documentaries and refusing to allow the script of

Star Trek to look back from the future to an Ireland without British troops in it; in the United States the 'Five Forbidden Words'. Without knowledge there can be no freedom, without freedom there can be no power.

Footnote
If professional companies wish to present either *The Little Gray Home in the West* or *Vandaleur's Folly*, we would like them to cast women to play the male characters – we feel it is time that men were enabled to see their role in society (especially as regards the 'military-industrial complex') as it is seen by women, and deliberate cross-casting is one way to bring it about. Let us assure sceptical readers that it can be done and easily done, both of these plays have been acted in New York under such a proviso; and in both cases we are informed it worked excellently.

M. D'Arcy & J. Arden
Galway, 1991

The Business of Good Government

A Christmas Play

1960

John Arden

and

Margaretta D'Arcy

Music

The songs sung in the course of the play will all fit existing and easily available tunes. The three carols –

> 'I saw three ships'
> 'As Joseph was a-walking' (The Cherry Tree Carol)
> 'Down in yon Forest' (The Corpus Christi Carol)

– are medieval in origin and have their own proper melodies. The other songs may be sung to tunes from the *Penguin Book of English Folk Songs* as follows –

> Shepherd's Song, 'I came to town' ('The Grey Cock').
> Shepherd's Lullaby, 'Go to sleep, little baby' ('Long Lankin').
> Farm-Girl's Song, 'The Seed was set' ('John Barleycorn').

The following tune for the remaining song – the Shepherds' Round – was specially composed by Alexander Robertson:*

Three Part Round by A. Robertson

Who'll lend me six pence   all I want is six pence

To buy a pair of red leather boots   a wide black hat and a new blue jack-et

If you lend him six pence I   swear to you you'll soon regret it

* Reproduced by kind permission of the composer.

Characters

ANGEL
KING HEROD
HIS SECRETARY
THREE WISE MEN
THREE ATTENDANTS
THREE SHEPHERDS
HOSTESS OF THE BETHLEHEM INN
JOSEPH
MARY
MIDWIFE
FARM-GIRL

This play was written specially for the village of Brent Knoll in Somerset and was performed there in the Church of St Michael during the Christmas season, 1960. I would like to thank the Vicar of Brent Knoll, the Parish Church Council, and all those who took part in the play or in any way assisted its production.

John Arden

The play begins with the stage empty.

All the characters except MARY *and* JOSEPH *enter through the audience in procession, in the following order:*

> ANGEL
> SECRETARY
> HOSTESS *and* MIDWIFE
> FARM-GIRL *and* SHEPHERDS
> WISE MEN (*and* ATTENDANTS, *if convenient*)
> HEROD

As they enter, they sing the carol 'I saw three ships':

> I saw three ships a-sailing in,
> A-sailing in, a-sailing in,
> I saw three ships a-sailing in
> On Christ's Sunday at morn.
>
> They sailed in to Bethlehem,
> To Bethlehem, to Bethlehem,
> Saint Michael was the steersman,
> Saint John sat in the horn.
>
> Joseph did whistle and Mary did sing,
> Mary did sing, Mary did sing,
> And all the bells on earth did ring
> For joy our Lord was born.
>
> And all the bells on earth did ring,
> On earth did ring, on earth did ring,
> A welcome to our heavenly King
> On Christ's Sunday at morn.

HEROD *does not sing, and he does not, in fact, make his entrance until the rest of the procession has reached the stage and grouped themselves – the* ANGEL *in the pulpit, the rest lined up to face the audience.*

ANGEL (*as soon as the singing is finished, from the pulpit*). Behold, I bring you tidings of great joy, which shall be unto all people. Glory to God in the highest, and on earth peace, goodwill towards men.

> HEROD *now comes rapidly through the audience.*

HEROD. Goodwill, great joy, peace upon earth – I do not believe they are altogether possible. But it is the business of good government to try and make them possible.

> *As he comes up on to the stage the other characters withdraw from him as though in alarm, and take their seats as quickly and quietly as they may.* HEROD *turns and addresses the audience.*

Herod the King. Herod the Great. Ruler of Judaea. To the west, the Roman Empire. To the east, the Persian Empire. In the middle, a small country in a very dangerous position. If I lean towards the east, I am afraid of invasion from Rome: if I lean towards Rome, then I shall be called upon to fight Persia. I would prefer to choose neither. But I had to choose Rome, because Rome rules Egypt, and it is from Egypt that we buy our corn. We are not self-supporting. *I* am not self-supporting. I have Roman officers in my army, Roman advisers in my palace, Roman spies in every department of state . . .

> *The* SECRETARY *rises from his seat and moves towards* HEROD. *He notices this and immediately changes his tone to one of insincere political rhetoric.*

The enormous friendship and generosity shown by the Roman people to the people of Judaea can only be repaid by our continued loyalty and vigilance. The historic alliance between our two great nations must be for every citizen an eternal inspiration. Peace, prosperity, goodwill: one man carries them all upon his back. If he falls down –

ANGEL (*interrupting him in the tone of a palace official*). King Herod. There are three visitors to Jerusalem asking for an audience.

HEROD (*casually*). Where do they come from?

ANGEL. Persia.

HEROD (*in alarm*). Eh? Where is my Secretary?

SECRETARY. Sir?

HEROD. What's this about Persia?

SECRETARY. They are not an official delegation. They said they want a private audience. They would not state their business. One of them is an African. Sir: I think we had better be careful. . . . Do you want to see them?

HEROD. Ah? Yes, I'll see them. But just you stay in the corner and listen to what they say. You may have to send a report to Caesar to keep my name clear. Do you understand?

SECRETARY. Yes. . . .

The WISE MEN *have risen and the* SECRETARY *beckons them forward.*

The king is waiting, gentlemen. Will you come this way?

They present themselves on the stage in front of HEROD. *The* SECRETARY *steps back a pace towards his seat, but does not sit down.*

HEROD. Good morning.

WISE MEN. Your Majesty.

They make a formal bow. HEROD *considers them carefully.*

HEROD. Gentlemen . . from Persia, I believe.

BLACK WISE MAN. The Empire of our Great King encloses more than one land.

HEROD (*a little irritated by this enigmatic answer, but attempting the same tone*). The greatness of a king may be measured less by his lands than by the devotion of his subjects.

YOUNG WISE MAN. Better five men of righteous life than a multitude of evildoers.

BLACK WISE MAN. Evil is more of the mind than of the actions. The slothful man is in many ways found worse than the murderer.

OLD WISE MAN. If we can say that we live, then surely we must die. Who shall number the self-deceivings of the human heart?

The WISE MEN *silently congratulate themselves upon the fluency of their precepts.* HEROD *looks at them sideways.*

HEROD. Deceit is not always plain to see. To be wise, the honest man must often put on an appearance of falsehood. (*He suddenly thrusts a question at the* OLD WISE MAN.) What does the King of Persia want?

OLD WISE MAN (*not disconcerted*). The mind of the Great King is not always penetrable to the thoughts of his subjects, otherwise how should he be called Great?

HEROD (*trying the* BLACK WISE MAN). It is written, is it not, out of Africa comes always something new? You, sir, be so good as to tell me, what is your novelty?

BLACK WISE MAN (*in genuine surprise*). Novelty, your Majesty? But we have come to *you* to find it.

HEROD (*equally surprised, but concealing it*). Indeed. A poor kingdom here: little food, little land, many people, a great deal of danger. I am sorry, my politics are quite without novelty.

BLACK WISE MAN (*knowingly*). Politics and philosophy are not incompatible. Who knows but we discover both in the one revelation?

HEROD (*in annoyance*). Eh, what? Enough of this. I do not understand you.

ANGEL (*quietly*). King Herod, perhaps *they* do not understand *you*.

YOUNG WISE MAN (*complacently*). We understand nothing. All that we do is to read the stars – as some read history books, or as others read geometry.

OLD WISE MAN. The stars have said: 'King Herod.'

YOUNG WISE MAN. 'Jerusalem.'

BLACK WISE MAN. 'The birth of a child.'

HEROD (*bewildered*). Child.

BLACK WISE MAN (*knowingly*). Why not? Great kings have many wives. Many wives have many children. (*Obsequiously.*) Permit us to visit the young prince and his mother.

HEROD (*trying to control the situation*). Visit? . . . What for?

YOUNG WISE MAN. We have been told by the stars that when we see him we shall know.

OLD WISE MAN. Until then, you see, we must be bewildered. Please show us the child.

YOUNG WISE MAN. Please.

WISE MEN. Please, sir, show us the child.

HEROD *steps aside from them, beckoning the* SECRETARY, *and speaks urgently to him in a whisper:*

HEROD. What are they talking about? Everybody knows I have had no children.

SECRETARY. There must be a mistake.

HEROD. Whose mistake? Mine? What has this to do with Persia? Each of these men dangles from the King of Persia's fingers.

ANGEL. Be careful.

HEROD. I will be careful . . . (*He returns to the* WISE MEN, *his tone now more confident.*) Gentlemen, we are not at one. Your stars have deceived you.

BLACK WISE MAN (*shocked*). That is not possible.

HEROD. Then you have misread them. Study them again. Come back next week. I regret at the moment I have no statement to make.

He and the SECRETARY *return briskly to their seats and sit down. The* WISE MEN *look at each other in some confusion.*

BLACK WISE MAN (*knowingly*). For reasons of state, the king has no statement.

YOUNG WISE MAN (*shakes his head disapprovingly*). Deceit is not always plain. Next week information may be more available.

OLD WISE MAN. He may not have understood.

YOUNG WISE MAN (*sharply*). *We* may not have understood. Gentlemen, we must reconsider our calculations. Politics and philosophy are becoming confused.

BLACK WISE MAN. Yes.

OLD WISE MAN. The interview has been inconclusive. We will repeat it next week.

They return to their places and sit down.

The YOUNG SHEPHERD *rises from his seat, mounts the stage, and walks about blowing on his hands to keep them warm.*

ANGEL. There were shepherds, abiding in the field, keeping watch over their flocks by night.

YOUNG SHEPHERD. Ah, and a cold night – you should say that.

The other two SHEPHERDS *come up on to the stage and sit down on the far side from the pulpit, well downstage, as though they are warming themselves over a fire.*

Have we got a good fire there? We'll want to thaw out a bit after all this.

SOLID SHEPHERD. Are there any of the sheep missing?

YOUNG SHEPHERD. No, I don't think so—I'll have another count.

*He goes through the motions of counting sheep.**

Hana mana mona mike
Barcelona bona strike
Hare ware frown venac
Harrico warrico we wo wac
Hana mana mona mike – *etc.* . . .

SOLID SHEPHERD. Comes in any worse than this, we'll be losing a few of 'em. (*A little noise, off – like a distant cry.*) Wait up – what's that?

They get to their feet and listen, afraid.

YOUNG SHEPHERD. Sounds like wolves to me. (*To the sheep.*) Easy, easy now – don't you be feared of it. . . .

SOLID SHEPHERD. Whatever it was, it was over the hill – no call to be feared of it.

They resume their positions.

OLD SHEPHERD. You certain it was a wolf? Sounded to me it might be a man making out to be a wolf. There's a lot of outlandish folk about here these days. I seen 'em on the roads.

He gets up again uneasily. The SOLID SHEPHERD *reassures him.*

SOLID SHEPHERD. Coming in for the tax-gathering, that's all. . . . You registered your name yet?

OLD SHEPHERD. Did it this morning. . . . Tax-gathering or not, some of 'em could be bandits.

YOUNG SHEPHERD. That's true, you know – they could. I seen soldiers on the roads. Now why'd there be soldiers if they hadn't heard word of bandits?

* This little jargon is a traditional shepherd's counting system appropriate to the play's original West-Country production. Other such systems from other parts of England may be found in the *Oxford Dictionary of Nursery Rhymes* and may be preferred – or if not liked, may be replaced by ordinary 'one two three', *etc.* . .

OLD SHEPHERD (*doggedly*). Call 'em soldiers, call 'em bandits –
I don't see no difference. You get these soldier-boys up here,
they wouldn't mind taking a beast or two on a dark night.

SOLID SHEPHERD. That's the truth all right, ah, true, true. . . .

The YOUNG SHEPHERD *walks about again, listening.*

YOUNG SHEPHERD. Seems all quiet enough now. . . .

OLD SHEPHERD (*wrapping himself more closely in his blanket*).
Ah. . . .

YOUNG SHEPHERD (*stops walking as a thought troubles him*).
Hey – about this tax-gathering. I've not put my name down
yet.

SOLID SHEPHERD. You'd better do it, son, quick. They'll
be on to you for sure.

YOUNG SHEPHERD (*doubtfully*). I don't like giving up my
name to these fellers.

SOLID SHEPHERD. You'd better do it. They'll run ye in, you
know.

YOUNG SHEPHERD. I thought it was only for householders
and that.

SOLID SHEPHERD (*soberly*). Ah no. You'd better do it.

OLD SHEPHERD. Where were you born?

YOUNG SHEPHERD. Why, Bethlehem, of course – same place
as you – you know that very well.

OLD SHEPHERD. All right, then: you go down to Bethlehem
tomorrow, give in your name, that's all you've got to do.
You do it quick, and they'll leave you alone.

YOUNG SHEPHERD. Ah . . . I don't like giving up my name.
Are they making us pay money?

SOLID SHEPHERD. Not yet they're not.

OLD SHEPHERD. They will. Ha ha. You're not telling me
they'll let us get out of it without paying. I know 'em better
nor that.

They all laugh a little bitterly.

SOLID SHEPHERD. There aren't any of the flock missing, are there?

YOUNG SHEPHERD. No, I just counted.

OLD SHEPHERD. The old one with the broken horn?

YOUNG SHEPHERD. She's there.

SOLID SHEPHERD. We're all right, then.

OLD SHEPHERD. Sit down, lad, keep warm. Here, take a drop o' this.

The YOUNG SHEPHERD *sits down with them and the* OLD SHEPHERD *passes his flask. They each take a drink appreciatively, yawning. The* OLD SHEPHERD *starts to sing, more to himself than at large.*

> I came to town to see my true love
> But I found her gone and far away
> Deluded by an Irish sailor
> Who took her off on a rainy day—

YOUNG SHEPHERD. That's a sad one, isn't it?

OLD SHEPHERD. Ah . . . it's a sad world. Cold enough, anyways. . . . All right, then, we try another: let's warm it up for us.

He sings another song.

> Who'll lend me sixpence?
> All I want is sixpence.

To the SOLID SHEPHERD

Now you.

SOLID SHEPHERD (*singing*).

> To buy a pair of red leather boots
> A wide black hat and a new blue jacket.

OLD SHEPHERD (*to the* YOUNG SHEPHERD). You.

YOUNG SHEPHERD (*singing*).

> If you lend him sixpence
> I swear to you you'll soon regret it.

OLD SHEPHERD. All right, not bad: now we sing her in a round.

> *They sing the song again as a three-part round, and continue singing it until, one by one, they yawn, stop singing, roll themselves up in their blankets, and fall asleep on the stage – well to one side to allow room for the next action.*
> *The* HOSTESS *leaves her place and comes forward with a broom, sweeping busily, talking to the audience as she does so.*

HOSTESS. It's not as if they were all paying for their rooms neither – half of 'em come here with a piece of yellow paper – 'A Government chit, madam, it'll be charged to your credit from the beginning of the next Revenue Period – take it to the Town Hall.' The way my house is at the moment, you'd think *I* was running the Town Hall. Civil Servants . . . Then there's the Military – *they* don't pay neither. 'Haw haw, landlady, I want accommodation for a corporal and thirteen men of Number Eight Detail, three nights altogether, breakfasts and suppers, find their own dinners: but you'll have to provide cooking facilities. . . . Oh yes, and covered storage for the transport. See the place is clean.' Oh, I could lie down and die! To say nothing of the rest of 'em. 'Have you got a room, please?' 'Could you let us have a bed, missus?' 'Just a corner, just a mattress, just a bit of straw – every house in the place is full, we've been all round the town.' I know very well they're full. *I'm* full! No vacancies! Not any more. I mean it. Why should I have my premises made a scapegoat for administrative incompetence? – and I don't care who hears me!

ANGEL (*sternly*). Madam, be careful. The decree has gone out from Caesar Augustus.

HOSTESS (*shaking her broom at him angrily*). I am perfectly aware of it, young man. That's exactly what I mean. All done as usual with no thought whatever for the convenience of individuals . . . Where was I?

ANGEL. Administrative incompetence.

HOSTESS. Oh there's more to it than that, you know. It's not just incompetence – it's the downright inhumanity that makes me so upset.

As she says this JOSEPH *and* MARY *enter through the stage entrance and come out from behind the pulpit. She half turns and points them out to the audience.*

This poor girl from the north – all that long way in such terrible weather and the baby due any minute. . . . What do they expect me to do? I haven't a room in the house. (*She turns and speaks to* MARY.) What do you expect me to do, dear? I don't know whether I'm on me head or me heels – just look at the place, all chockablock and I'm run off me feet! You'll have to find somewhere else.

She resumes her sweeping, angrily.

JOSEPH (*worried but obstinate*). The fact is, we've tried everywhere.

HOSTESS (*doubtfully*). What about outside the village – there *are* one or two farmhouses where they sometimes take people. I could give you the addresses—

JOSEPH (*considering this pessimistically*). Outside? I don't know about that. It says Bethlehem, you see, black and white, down on the document—(*He shows her an official paper which he takes from his pocket.*) Look. I very much doubt if the authorities would allow . . . (*He looks indecisively from the* HOSTESS *to* MARY.) Besides, I don't know that we dare waste any more time. She ought to be under a roof and that's the plain truth.

HOSTESS (*obviously disturbed*). Oh, yes, I know. I can see. I do understand – oh dear, oh dear . . . (*An idea strikes her, but she hardly likes to suggest it.*) Look, would it be all right if I was to put you in the stable? (*She goes on with a rush in case of objections.*) I mean, just for tonight, till we can get a bit of space organized. It won't be too bad in there; there's plenty of straw and that, and we can keep the animals separate – I could give it a clean-out first.

JOSEPH (*much relieved*). We're not ones to grumble, ma'am; anything at all, you know – we'd be very very grateful – oh no, we're not choosey—

HOSTESS (*embarrassed*). Yes, yes, well – over here, you come along, my dear, you take my arm, that's right – (*She takes* MARY *by the arm and leads her upstage to the central rostrum.* JOSEPH *makes to follow, but she firmly prevents him.*) Oh no – you stay here. (*She settles* MARY *down on the rostrum, which need only be raised a few inches from the main stage level.*)

JOSEPH, *after a moment of indecision, comes downstage and sings, quietly, towards the audience, from underneath the pulpit.*

JOSEPH (*singing*).
> Joseph was an old man
> And an old man was he
> When he married Mary
> In the land of Galilee.

The HOSTESS *suddenly stands up and comes down from the rostrum, looking about her anxiously.*

HOSTESS. I'd better get the midwife – where's the midwife?

The MIDWIFE *stands up in her place.*

MIDWIFE. Do you want me, dear?

She comes downstage. The HOSTESS *takes her by the arm.*

HOSTESS. Yes, quick, come to the stable!
MIDWIFE (*shocked*). The stable!
HOSTESS (*embarrassed*). It's the best I could do. . . . *She leads the* MIDWIFE *up to* MARY.

JOSEPH (*singing*).

> As Joseph was a-walking
> He heard an angel sing
> This night shall be born
> Our heavenly king.

MARY, *seated on the rostrum with the* HOSTESS *and the* MIDWIFE *bending over her at each side, speaks to the audience.*

MARY.

Nine months we sit and wait and dream.
Quiet in dreams and quiet in fear.

ANGEL (*to audience*).

Young wives of honest men:
The time is near.
Your work is made
That will be yours no longer.
Say good-bye. Let go.

MARY.

What we have made
We learn to leave alone.
What we now know
From now must live unknown.

She folds her hands across her belly.

Good-bye, good-bye.
I have come to let you go.

She bows herself down on the rostrum.

JOSEPH (*singing*).

> He neither shall be born
> In housen nor in hall
> Nor in the place of Paradise
> But in an ox's stall.

He neither shall be clothed
In purple nor in pall
But all in fair linen
As were babies all.

He neither shall be rocked
In silver nor in gold
But in a wooden cradle
That rocks on the mould.

The HOSTESS *and the* MIDWIFE *have moved aside and are waiting, looking towards* MARY, *who kneels alone with her back to the Audience. When* JOSEPH *has finished singing he sits down at the base of the pulpit, on the small step that should be provided there.*

The ANGEL *leans out of the pulpit and suddenly shouts across the stage at the sleeping* SHEPHERDS *in a vigorous urgent voice:*

ANGEL. Who's awake! Hey-ey, shepherds, up up, who's awake!

They wake, startled and confused. The YOUNG SHEPHERD *staggers to his feet.*

YOUNG SHEPHERD (*dazed*). Eh, what, what is it?
ANGEL. Wake up, wake up!
YOUNG SHEPHERD. What's the matter? Where are the sheep?

He wanders vaguely about, looking for them. The other SHEPHERDS *also pull themselves to their feet. Throughout this passage they must not appear to see the* ANGEL.

ANGEL. Safe and sound. All safe where you put them.
YOUNG SHEPHERD. Who are you? I can't see you. Who is it calling?
SOLID SHEPHERD. Who is it?
OLD SHEPHERD. What's the matter – where are the sheep – wolves – bandits. . .?

The SHEPHERDS *move about in confusion, getting in each other's way. The* ANGEL *now speaks to them in a quieter but no less urgent voice.*

ANGEL. Fear not.

SOLID SHEPHERD (*restraining the other two*). Wait. Listen!

The SHEPHERDS *stand still. They listen, but do not look directly up at the* ANGEL.

ANGEL. Fear not. For behold, I bring you good tidings of great joy, which shall be to all people. For unto you is born this day in the City of David a Saviour, which is Christ the Lord. And this shall be a sign unto you; ye shall find the babe wrapped in swaddling clothes, lying in a manger.

The SHEPHERDS *cluster together, astonished.*

SOLID SHEPHERD. Here, I don't like this –

YOUNG SHEPHERD. Did you hear what it said?

SOLID SHEPHERD. Somebody's having a game with us. They're trying to make us fools—

OLD SHEPHERD (*doubtfully*). Why don't we go to the town and see?

SOLID SHEPHERD. See?

YOUNG SHEPHERD. Why don't we go there?

SOLID SHEPHERD. What do you mean, go there?

YOUNG SHEPHERD. Down to the town.

OLD SHEPHERD (*regretting his impulse*). No. No. I don't think I like to.

ANGEL. Glory to God in the Highest, and on earth peace, good will towards men.

YOUNG SHEPHERD. Come on, I'm going –

The ANGEL *now continues to repeat his last line, which – if convenient to the production – may be picked up and augmented by voices from different places round the building out of sight of the audience. This repetition of the 'Glory' continues in crescendo throughout the ensuing dialogue. The* YOUNG SHEPHERD *tugs vainly at the sleeve of the* SOLID SHEPHERD.

Come *on*!

Giving up the SOLID SHEPHERD *as a bad job, he leaves him, jumps down from the stage, and sets off rapidly round the hall to the back of the audience.*

OLD SHEPHERD. Wait, hey, wait for me—

He comes down from the stage and hobbles after the YOUNG SHEPHERD. *The* SOLID SHEPHERD *remains alone in an agony of indecision.*

SOLID SHEPHERD. Why don't they leave us alone! We were doing a job of work, that's all – you've got no right to meddle with the lives of working men! (*He calls after his colleagues.*) Hey, wait, wait for me – wait—

He, too, jumps from the stage and runs after the others. When they reach the rear of the hall they wait there quietly for their next cue. The ANGEL'S *'Glory' now comes to an end.*

MARY *stands up and turns to face the audience. She is holding a baby in her arms. She starts to walk downstage, the* HOSTESS *and the* MIDWIFE *coming with her on either side.* JOSEPH *rises and helps her to sit down on a stool, which he can fetch unobtrusively from behind the pulpit.*

JOSEPH.

> He came all so still
> Where His mother was
> As dew in April
> That falleth on the grass.

He came all so still
To his mother's bower
As dew in April
That falleth on the flower.

As he speaks this verse, the SHEPHERDS *slowly advance through the audience. They stop at the foot of the stage steps.*

SOLID SHEPHERD. Why, it *is* a baby.
YOUNG SHEPHERD. That's right.
SOLID SHEPHERD. A little boy?

They climb up on to the stage.

We didn't dream it.
YOUNG SHEPHERD. No.
OLD SHEPHERD. Can we have a look at him, missus?
MIDWIFE (*bossily*). Now be very careful, don't breathe too near him. Quietly, young man, quietly, don't make such a disturbance with your great big boots now – *careful!*
HOSTESS (*fussing about*). Now you're not to upset the poor young lady, she's very very tired. If you don't want them in, dear, you just say so to me, and I'll send them straight out.
MARY (*listlessly*). No, they can come.

They come nearer with clumsy consideration and bend to see the baby.

OLD SHEPHERD (*holding out his hand*). Hey, you hold my finger, boy – can you do that? Clutch it? Ah, that's the feller – he knows how to make an effort, don't he now? You look at him – strong! He likes me! Now you go to sleep now, and let your mam have a bit of rest . . . mind if I sing to him, eh?

He sings, quietly.

Go to sleep, little baby, and then you will see
How strong grows the acorn on the branches of the tree.

How tightly it lives in the green and the brown
But the strong storms of autumn will soon shake it down.

The deeper it falls then the stronger will it tower
Bold roots and wide limbs and a true heart of power.

Though the oak is the master of all the trees on the hill
His heart will be mastered by the carpenter's will.

SOLID SHEPHERD. Build a roof for your house, boy, the oak
tree will – keel and planks for your boat if you want to
go a voyage, cradle for you to sleep in – you grow up as
strong as that – oh you'll be the rare master!

YOUNG SHEPHERD. Hey, missus, do you know, we heard
this in a dream? We all dreamed it, you see, all three of
us. . . . 'In the City of David, a Saviour which is Christ
the Lord. And lying in a manger.'

OLD SHEPHERD. That's right. It said that.

SOLID SHEPHERD. We don't know what to think, missus. Do
you think it could be true?

MARY.
Nine months ago I dreamed a dream:
A white fish swam into my heart.
I took my hand and pulled it out:
But the hands of the strong men tore the little fish apart.

JOSEPH. Believe it to be true and celebrate it. All these things
will be known, in good time. Here is the baby: here is his
mother . . . your sheep are left out on the hills. You had
better go back now and look after them. If it was a good
dream: then you will dream it again one day. If it wasn't –
well, the world has to carry on turning. There are trees
must be cut down and the timber to be shaped, there are
houses to need roofs, the ships to need their frames, there
are always the cradles will need to be rocked. And each one
of these works will call for its true attention . . . Thank you
for coming.

MARY. Thank you.

MIDWIFE (*bossy again*). Now I think that's enough, I'm sure you've had enough, dear – (*She feels* MARY'S *brow.*) Yes, we're getting rather tired – you'd better go now, quietly, quietly, thank you very much – it's very important at this stage, lots of rest and quiet – *thank* you.

THE SHEPHERDS. God give you good health and strengthen the child.

> *They withdraw quietly, and take their original places in front of the pulpit, below the stage. As soon as they are gone, the* MIDWIFE *and* HOSTESS *gather in on* MARY. *The* HOSTESS *picks up the baby.*

HOSTESS. You'd better let me take him now, dear.

MIDWIFE (*sharply*). Not too long for the first time.

HOSTESS (*to* MARY). We've got to conserve our energies, haven't we ? (*Sharply, to* MIDWIFE.) *I* know, dear – I've had four of 'em myself. . . . There, there, the little lamb, there, the little precious – oh he's a lovely boy, dear, he's going to make you so happy – don't you carry on now, about all those rough fellows trampling in. I think they'd all had a drop too much, if you ask me—

> *The* MIDWIFE *butts in again, pulling the* HOSTESS *by the elbow.*

MIDWIFE. She ought to be moved, you know. We can't have her lying in a stable *now*.

HOSTESS (*worried again all of a sudden*). But I haven't a room in the house.

MIDWIFE (*decisively*). Then she'd better come to my place. . . . You'll come to my place, dear, won't you ? You can have my bed, you see, and I can sleep in the kitchen.

JOSEPH (*worrying*). But we couldn't put you out like that—

MARY. Thank you, you are very kind.

HOSTESS (*glad to be rid of the responsibility*). Don't talk, dear, don't exhaust yourself—

MIDWIFE. That's right, there we are—

> *The* HOSTESS *and the* MIDWIFE *help* MARY *away and install her on a seat beside the* MIDWIFE'S. JOSEPH *follows and stands beside his wife – they are partly concealed by the pulpit and remain out of the action for a while. The* HOSTESS *and the* MIDWIFE *resume their seats.* HEROD *rises and comes forward.*

HEROD. Those three from Persia – they should be here today. Where are they?

SECRETARY (*rising and coming up to him*). They are waiting to see you, sir. Shall I bring them in?

HEROD. If you would be so good.

> HEROD *takes his stance downstage, confidently. The* SECRETARY *beckons to the* WISE MEN, *who rise and come to the king.*

Gentlemen, good morning.

WISE MEN. Good morning, Your Majesty.

> *They bow, formally.*

HEROD (*genially*). I owe you an apology. On your previous visit, I was unaccountably obtuse. Although the blame must to some extent lie with my advisers. I had not been supplied with the necessary information. Had I?

SECRETARY (*playing the comedy*). No, sir, you had not. Gentlemen, may I, too, apologize for the inadequacies of his Majesty's staff. We entirely regret the misunderstanding.

> *The* WISE MEN *bow politely.*

HEROD. When you spoke of a prince, I naturally concluded you were referring to a member of my own household. Alas, Heaven has graced me with no recent issue.

WISE MEN (*formally*). Alas.

HEROD (*echoing their manner*). Gentlemen, alas . . . But— (*He looks keenly at them and adopts a sharper tone.*) But to ascertain the truth from the stars, it is necessary to remember the recurrent cloudiness of the firmament. As no doubt you have realized.

OLD WISE MAN (*waiting for what is coming*). In science, even yet, there is no complete certainty.

HEROD. Nor is the possibility of human error ever to be underrated. As no doubt you have realized.

BLACK WISE MAN (*slyly*). Yet it is written: even in the depth of dark winter, the sun may sometimes be descried shining with unlooked-for brilliance.

YOUNG WISE MAN (*sardonic*). It is also written that the flowers brought forth to greet such winter sun are likely to fade and die in the frost of the evening.

OLD WISE MAN (*checking his colleague with a slight gesture*). This is perhaps beside the point: for, Your Majesty, *we* have yet to see any sign of the sun at all.

HEROD (*enjoying himself*). Aha, is that so? Wise men from the east? There are wise men in Jerusalem. I have been asking them some questions since our last meeting. . . . (*He has turned his back casually: now he whips round to startle them.*) Gentlemen: Bethlehem!

WISE MEN (*surprised*). Bethlehem?

HEROD *takes an impressive scroll which the* SECRETARY *is holding in readiness for him.*

HEROD (*reading with emphasis*). 'And thou, Bethlehem, in the land of Judah, art not least among the cities of Judah, for out of thee shall come a Governor that shall rule my people Israel.' . . . A history lesson, gentlemen. (*He finds a different place in the scroll, as pointed out by the* SECRETARY, *and reads further.*) 'Abraham begat Isaac, and Isaac begat Jacob, and Jacob begat Judah – and his brethren – and

Judah begat Phares, and Phares begat . . .' (*He skips a bit.*) . . . 'Begat – one, two, three – seven generations: and the seventh was Obed, and Obed begat Jesse, and Jesse begat David the King!' (*He looks at them significantly over the scroll.*) Now David the King was begotten in Bethlehem, and I must confess to you, gentlemen, that I myself am not among his posterity. So, therefore, any prince liable to find loyalty in Israel, who does not spring from Herod, will in all probability spring from the seed of David; and according to the logic of prophecy – which I am sure you will understand – you must look for him in Bethlehem. Jerusalem is no good. I am sorry to have wasted your time.

The WISE MEN *are somewhat disconcerted.*

OLD WISE MAN. Your Majesty, will you excuse me while I confer with my colleagues ?

> HEROD *nods graciously, and the three of them get into a huddle and whisper rapidly together.*

YOUNG WISE MAN. Your Majesty, would you permit us to study the documents ?

> HEROD, *enjoying himself, hands the scroll to the* SECRE-TARY, *who gives it to the* YOUNG WISE MAN. *They return to their huddle and study it. While they do so* HEROD *addresses them genially.*

HEROD. The information is taken from the prophetic books of Israel. I can assure you it has been collated for me under conditions of the most exhaustive scholarship.

> THE WISE MEN *come to a unanimous decision, and turn to face the king.*

OLD WISE MAN. Your Majesty, we will go to Bethlehem. This could be an occasion of the utmost importance.

HEROD (*pleasantly*). You will inform me directly, whatever you find ?

OLD WISE MAN. Your Majesty, without fail.

They are about to bow and make their farewell. HEROD *interrupts them, casually.*

HEROD. One further point. The stars. How long have you been observing this new revelation ?

BLACK WISE MAN. It has been visible for two years. It took us a year to calculate the significance, and then the preparations for the journey, the travelling itself, the—

HEROD (*cutting him short*). Thank you, gentlemen. I understand. Good morning. I look forward to your news.

Before they quite realize it, the audience is over, HEROD *and the* SECRETARY *have returned to their seats, and they are left alone on the forestage.* HEROD *and the* SECRETARY *do not sit down, but stand there with their backs turned.*

WISE MEN (*a little put out by this abruptness*). Thank you, Your Majesty. Good morning. . . .

They bow towards the place where he stood, and then leave the stage and walk in a stately manner up the hall to the rear of the audience.
HEROD *walks back across the stage, and the* SECRETARY *sits down.* HEROD *looks up and catches the* ANGEL'S *eye.*

HEROD (*irritably*). It was necessary to tell them. If I had pretended I had heard nothing about any prophecies, they would have found out I was lying, and in the end they would still have gone to Bethlehem. The difference would have been they would never have come back to tell me what they found. . . . (*He is troubled in his mind.*) Supposing a Son of David *should* have been born: and supposing he is demonstrated to carry some Divine Marks of Royalty – or whatever the book says ?

ANGEL (*deadpan*). The situation should be within your control. Are you not the king?

HEROD (*petulantly*). I am not trained to understand prophecies and superstitions! Those that do understand them have assured me that it is very unwise to ignore their political importance. Here are the King of Persia's men, looking for what might well be a claimant to the ancient line of Israel. If Persia determines to recognize such a claimant, Rome will punish *me*.

ANGEL. How?

HEROD. How do you imagine? They will send in an army to secure their Legitimate Interests. A Roman Governor will be appointed in Jerusalem. If I am lucky, I may be permitted to wash up in his kitchen.

ANGEL. And if not?

HEROD (*making a despairing gesture*). Ah. . . . Wheresoever the carcass is, there will the Eagles be gathered together.

ANGEL. Surely your loyalty to Caesar will not so easily be doubted?

HEROD (*bitterly*). My loyalty to Caesar is continually being doubted – and not without some reason. . . . (*He speaks now with great sincerity.*) I am not primarily concerned with my own personal fortunes. The object of my life is the integrity of my kingdom. What am I to do?

ANGEL. You had better wait and see what the three gentlemen discover.

HEROD. (*He suddenly looks up sharply, puzzled*). Who *are* you?

> The ANGEL *shrugs unhelpfully.*
> HEROD *glares up at him with defiance.*

Do you want to see Jerusalem with not one stone left upon another, and in the Temple which *I* built, the Abomination of Desolation standing where it ought not?

ANGEL (*firmly and simply*). No.

HEROD. Then pity the king: and pray for his policy.

He turns sadly away and sits down in his place.

ANGEL (*addressing the audience with sadness*). Not one stone shall be left upon another. . . . Ye shall hear of wars and rumours of wars. And nation shall rise against nation, and kingdom against kingdom: and there shall be famines and pestilences and earthquakes in divers places. (*His voice rises in a torrent.*) And there shall be signs in the sun and in the moon and in the stars, and upon the earth distress of nations, with perplexity; the sea and the waves roaring; men's hearts failing them for fear and for looking after those things which are coming on the earth: for the powers of heaven shall be shaken! (*He seems for a moment afraid of his own vision: then his voice quietens and he delivers his next lines with sober stillness.*) And then they shall see the Son of Man coming in a cloud with power and great glory. Verily I say unto you: this generation shall not pass away till all be fulfilled.

After his words there is a silence, broken by the WISE MEN *approaching the stage through the audience.*

YOUNG WISE MAN (*mounting the stage*). Bethlehem.

The other two join him, and they look around them.

BLACK WISE MAN. I think this is a place that should answer the description.

OLD WISE MAN. Possibly.

BLACK WISE MAN. A small town or large village, agricultural population, one principal hostelry, decidedly third-class—(*He frowns doubtfully.*) Gentlemen, is it likely, do you think, that the king's information can be correct?

OLD WISE MAN. Possibly.

BLACK WISE MAN. Possibly? Oh yes, yes, possible. But I said, is it *likely*? I confess I have my doubts.

YOUNG WISE MAN. You are of the opinion that the king has deceived us?

BLACK WISE MAN. No . . . no . . . I hardly mean quite that.

OLD WISE MAN. The king impressed me as very definitely a man of high intelligence, genuinely understanding the responsibilities of power and with an enlightened attitude towards philosophy and science. I cannot believe that he would wish to deceive us.

BLACK WISE MAN. We could have been mistaken. Are we not all fallible?

YOUNG WISE MAN (*firmly*). The stars are not fallible. (*He looks up at them, and is suddenly transfixed with excitement.*) Look! Look at the Great Bear – and then look at Orion!

They follow his gaze and are infected with his excitement.

OLD WISE MAN. The Dog Star has retreated!

YOUNG WISE MAN. Yes, but consider the passage of the Moon!

BLACK WISE MAN. Let me see the chart.

The OLD WISE MAN *fumbles in his satchel and produces a rolled-up chart, which he clumsily unfurls.*

YOUNG WISE MAN (*assisting him hastily*). Calculating forward from her last presence in Scorpio—

BLACK WISE MAN (*thrusting between them and snatching the chart*). Let me see the chart!

They all three crowd round it, getting in each other's way.

OLD WISE MAN. Why should we find the Dog Star diminished, yet Mars is still flamboyant?

BLACK WISE MAN (*decisively*). Look, gentlemen: look at the chart, and look again at the Heavens! The king has *not* deceived us. *We* have been blind. It *is* here, in Bethlehem, that our treasure will be found. Let us go forward, and see!

The MIDWIFE *rises and comes forward hesitantly.*

MIDWIFE. Who are these gentlemen?

ANGEL. They have come from a far country. They are here to see the baby.

MIDWIFE (*nervously*). Political gentlemen?

ANGEL. No, not exactly. Scientific and philosophical. Very wise, very important. . . . So, sirs, you have arrived. What do you expect to find?

The WISE MEN *draw themselves up authoritatively, but have no very clear answer.*

BLACK WISE MAN. We – we have brought gifts.

YOUNG WISE MAN. We are certain, without doubt, that a new age may well be at hand.

OLD WISE MAN. We must be ready to welcome it. We must not be left behind.

BLACK WISE MAN. Gifts, we have brought. We chose them symbolically. . . . Madam, if you please: may we see the Child?

If the cast allows of the WISE MEN *having* ATTENDANTS, *the* OLD WISE MAN *at this point signals towards the rear of the hall and the three* ATTENDANTS *come through the audience, each carrying his master's gift. These gifts should be elaborate caskets of some size. If the* WISE MEN *have to carry their own gifts, they can be smaller, and can be carried in satchels. In such case the satchels should appear to be made of rich materials – not any old bags.*

The MIDWIFE *now turns and beckons forward* MARY, *who comes, carrying the baby.* JOSEPH *is behind her, and assists her to sit down on the same stool as she used to greet the* SHEPHERDS. *The* WISE MEN *seem a little unsure of themselves and give the impression of having expected something very different.*

OLD WISE MAN (*looking vaguely from* MIDWIFE *to* MARY). The mother? Which is she? Is the mother not here?

BLACK WISE MAN (*addressing* MARY, *once she has sat down*). Dear lady, our congratulations. (*They bow to her politely. The* ATTENDANTS (*if any*) *have ranged themselves on the stage, kneeling, and holding up their gifts.*) For the child, we have brought gifts.

> *Each* WISE MAN *in turn takes his gift from the* ATTENDANT *and holds it up to the audience, describing it; and then turns and presents it to* MARY – *or rather, holds it up to her and then lays it on the stage at her feet.*

Gold. Gold speaks of power. Where there is power there lie the benefits for the future generations.

YOUNG WISE MAN. Frankincense. Frankincense speaks of religion. As men of science, we cannot but recognize those great forces in our lives we do not fully understand.

OLD WISE MAN. Myrrh. Myrrh speaks of death, and no one can escape it. Yet in a well-governed land the good work of one man will be continued by his successors. (*A slight pause. The* WISE MEN *look at one another, and at* MARY *with the baby. The* OLD WISE MAN *clears his throat and offers a general sentiment on behalf of the others.*) We are confident that this Son of David, to whom we bring our gifts, will prove a notable descendant of his most notable forefathers: it is, in fact, so written in the ordering of the constellations. Hence our visit – we thank you—

> *He glances at his colleagues, and they pick up their cue.*

WISE MEN. We thank you for permitting us to welcome your son. You have given us an experience of the utmost importance.

MARY. Thank you.

> *The* WISE MEN *bow and withdraw a little.*

WISE MEN. Good day, dear lady. Thank you.

They bow again. MARY *and* JOSEPH *withdraw, the* MID-WIFE *follows, carrying the gifts. The* WISE MEN *turn their backs upon them, and confer, facing the audience.*

BLACK WISE MAN. Well.

OLD WISE MAN. Well?

YOUNG WISE MAN. I do not understand it.

OLD WISE MAN. Of course, it *is* the Son of David, the stars have made it clear, the mother did not deny it. But the significance? Why, I had expected—

BLACK WISE MAN. I too had expected . . . These people obviously have nothing to do with politics. And I see no connexion either with religion or with prophecies, or with anything else. Except that—

YOUNG WISE MAN. Except that we were *told*. Except that *we* were told. And *what* have we been told?

BLACK WISE MAN. No, I do not know. . . . And even if this *is* a true Prince of Israel—

ANGEL (*he offers his remarks like a prompter, and the* WISE MEN *accept them into their conversation without realizing who is speaking*). Even if this *is* a true Prince of Israel?

YOUNG WISE MAN (*thoughtfully*). It will do him little good for us to declare it.

OLD WISE MAN (*sharply*). Herod?

ANGEL. Herod. Yes, Herod.

BLACK WISE MAN (*quickly*). Do you think—

OLD WISE MAN. I think—

ANGEL. I think you would be best advised—

YOUNG WISE MAN. I think we would be best advised to leave the country quietly and forget the whole business.

BLACK WISE MAN. Yes, very true: I think that *is* wisest.

ANGEL. You had better go home.

OLD WISE MAN (*hurrying down from the stage*). We had better go home!

The other two follow him and they hasten one after the other through the audience towards the rear of the hall.

BLACK WISE MAN. Yes. Quickly. Now!

YOUNG WISE MAN. Don't look behind you! We might be being followed!

OLD WISE MAN. Quick, quickly, home, we have got to get home!

They run out of the hall without stopping – if there are ATTENDANTS, *these follow them in equal panic. The door slams, and their shouts and footsteps die away outside. There is a moment of quiet as the* ANGEL *looks keenly towards the door; then, without turning his head, he beckons to* JOSEPH.

ANGEL. Joseph, come here. (JOSEPH *comes forward and stands by the pulpit in some surprise.*) Are you afraid of the great men of the world?

JOSEPH. No, sir, I am not. I am a carpenter and a good crafts-man. I stand firm by my trade – good joints in good timber.

ANGEL. You have married a dangerous wife.

JOSEPH (*stubbornly*). I married who it was my concern to marry. I do not know why you should be commenting upon it.

ANGEL. There are thousands of carpenters in the provinces of Egypt. Too many for anyone to ask what sort of wives they have, there.

JOSEPH (*thinking hard*). Or what sort of children. . . . The question about danger. How close?

ANGEL. Tonight.

JOSEPH (*in consternation*). Tonight?

ANGEL. She is well enough to travel?

JOSEPH. I think so—

ANGEL. Very well then. Go!

MARY *has come quietly forward and catches the last few words of this dialogue.*

MARY (*to the* ANGEL). I can see that you have made my husband afraid. He is not a timorous man. What have you told
him ? What is to happen ? Who are they going to kill ?

ANGEL.

The King, if they can.
The axe will drive into the timber
And the leaves are not yet green.

JOSEPH.

What are you talking about – King ?
King Herod, do you mean ?

ANGEL.

Green leaves for that one ?
No, sir, he is red and he is gold
And he will fall. On which day
And in which year has not yet been foretold.
But there is to be time for the next King to grow,
Short time, narrow time, time enough to know
That the night will be over
And the day will be wide
And as wide as the world.

MARY.

Let the waters be beaten so yet the ship will sail,
Let the wind be driven, but the house yet hold its roof,
Let the timbers only be seasoned under the strong dry sun.

ANGEL (*disturbed*).

So that they may hang, and creak,
And grind, and bear against the strain ?
Run to Egypt in the dark
And then come slowly home.

> *They turn away from the* ANGEL *and walk about the stage
> for a turn or two. The* FARM-GIRL *comes from her place
> towards the front of the stage. She walks up and down, going
> through the motions of sowing corn from a sack, and singing
> as she does so.* MARY *and* JOSEPH *stop, as though to rest by
> the roadside, further upstage.*

FARM-GIRL (*sings*).

> The seed is set into the ground
> At the darkening of the year,
> When the rain runs down in the cold kirk town
> And the roofs are hung with fear.
>
> The grain is scattered on the land
> At the side of Egypt's road.
> God send the proud young harvesters
> A full and golden load.

She looks up and sees JOSEPH *and* MARY.

You seem to be lost. Can I show you the way?

JOSEPH. We were on the road to Egypt, but I don't know whether we are going right – can you tell us, please?

FARM-GIRL (*looking hard at them*). Surely, why not? You go straight ahead, you see, keeping to the west and the south, you cross over that river, and there you are in Egypt.

JOSEPH. Thank you. . . . I wonder – if anyone comes after us – I mean – anyone to be afraid of – you won't tell them you've seen us?

FARM-GIRL (*suddenly hostile*). Afraid of? You mean soldiers? You mean you're in trouble? Look, my father's farm stands right by the frontier. We have to take care what we say to soldiers. If they ask me the truth, I daren't tell 'em any other. How do I know you've not been sent to spy, so they can burn down our house? Go on, go to Egypt – if they ask me anything I shall have to tell 'em true!

MARY. Joseph, this way, she said west and then south, quick, quick, hurry to the river. . . .

She and JOSEPH *hasten out by the stage door.*

FARM-GIRL (*appealing to the audience*). They burn houses. I've seen them. Kill my husband, kill the children, take all the last harvest stored in the barns. What about my father?

He's been ill in bed all the winter. They say there's not a farm on the frontier lasts more than twenty years. I've seen some burnt three times in two years. We have to take care.

> HEROD *and the* SECRETARY *come from their places and the* FARM-GIRL *retreats in alarm to the base of the pulpit.*

HEROD. Straight away from Bethlehem—

SECRETARY. By the least-frequented road—

HEROD. Without one word to me!

SECRETARY. They are over the frontier and back half-way to Persia.

HEROD. What did they find?

SECRETARY. Not necessarily anything.

HEROD. Not necessarily? Of course they did. Rabbit holes under my walls.

SECRETARY. Rabbit holes?

HEROD. Yes. Burrowing in. Scrabbling. Put traps in the holes . . . Inform my officers I want a complete investigation. The unity of this kingdom has been thrust into peril— (*The* SECRETARY *goes and sits down:* HEROD *shakes his arm at the* ANGEL.)
Don't you tell me to be careful! I *am* being careful!

ANGEL. Careful: and afraid.

HEROD. Of course I am afraid.

ANGEL. Tell me what of.

HEROD. The end of my world. The end of peace of life. The end of good order. . . . The king must rule his human subjects by means of his own humanity. And naturally, within his rule must be comprehended such difficult extremes of good and of evil as may be found from one end to the other of his unfortunate kingdom. . . . (*He assumes a rhetorical posture, and addresses the audience.*) Citizens! Patriots! Through the years I have been your leader I have kept you free from war and provided unexampled prosperity. You are richer and happier than ever you have been! Your children are receiving opportunities for education and advancement that your own fathers could not have imagined in their wildest dreams. Dare you see this prosperity destroyed in one night? You answer me – no. You answer me – King Herod, do what you believe to be necessary and we your faithful people will follow you as always in loyalty and trust! (*To the* ANGEL.) You understand – I am putting a very particular mark against my name in the history books, and I know it, and I am not afraid. It is fitting that the honour of one man should die for the good of the people. (*He beckons to the* SECRETARY, *who rises in his place and takes a step forward.*) Send out an instruction to my officers. They are to put to death all the children that are in Bethlehem and in all the coasts thereof from two years old and under, according to the time which I diligently inquired of the Wise Men. It is the only safe way. See that it is done. (*The* SECRETARY *bows and remains standing with lowered head. To the* ANGEL.) I suppose you will tell me that even this in some way fulfils some sort of prophecy.

ANGEL. Yes. The Prophet Jeremiah, chapter 31, verse 15. Do you want to hear it?

HEROD. I have not got time. (*To the* SECRETARY.) Have you done what I told you?

SECRETARY. Sir, it has been done. Your officers have received the orders, and are carrying them out.

> *The Massacre is indicated by a sudden clash of cymbals, and a loud wailing cry which should proceed from different places all around the hall. The actors still on the stage can take part in it. This cry dies away as suddenly as it has arisen.*

ANGEL. From the Prophet Jeremiah, chapter 31, verse 15: 'In Rama was there a voice heard – lamentation and weeping and great mourning. Rachel weeping for her children and would not be comforted, because they were not.'

HEROD. Very well. I can carry it. All upon one man's back. . . .
   Is it finished?

SECRETARY. Sir, it is finished.

   HEROD *is about to return to his seat.*

ANGEL (*in the voice of a palace official*). One moment. King
   Herod – a message for my lord the king. From the captain
   in command of the road leading south from the city of
   Bethlehem. A man and a woman carrying a young child were
   seen to pass on this road half an hour before your orders
   were received. A patrol has been sent after them: but they
   have not yet been caught.

HEROD. They have gone towards Egypt. They must be held
   before they get there. I know the road to Egypt. There
   are too many secret ways for them to slip across the frontier
   – for instance, this farm. Who does it belong to!

   The FARM-GIRL *comes forward, terrified.*

FARM-GIRL. Lord, this is my father's farm. My husband
   works it for him and I help him to do it. How can we serve
   you, lord?

HEROD. A man and a woman, carrying a young child. Did they
   pass? Did you see them?

FARM-GIRL. Yes, lord, I saw them.

HEROD. When?

FARM-GIRL. Not long since – I'm not certain—

HEROD. *When?*

FARM-GIRL. I was sowing that field; it can't have been more
   than—

HEROD. This field?

FARM-GIRL. Yes, lord—

HEROD. Are you certain of that?

FARM-GIRL. Why, yes, lord, I swear it – I told them I
   couldn't hide them. I always respected the law. I never told
   a lie to the soldiers, not in all my life—

HEROD (*cutting her short in disgust*). This corn has been growing for a couple of months. If anyone crossed here, it's nobody to interest *me*. Hold your noise, woman: you won't suffer any harm. But just you be certain that you and your family always behave. It's not very safe to do anything else.

FARM-GIRL. No, lord, I know. Thank you, lord, thank you. . . .

She shrinks again to one side. HEROD *takes no more notice of her.*

HEROD. I think I have missed them. We followed the wrong road. If it was them at all. I do not know. Nobody knows. I hope it is finished. All of you here; pray for the king and pray this may be finished.

He returns to his seat. The FARM-GIRL *timidly comes forward again.*

FARM-GIRL. That corn grew in one hour. It *was* the right field. How could I tell lies to *him*? Soldiers – he's worse than soldiers – he was the *King*! . . . Oh my Lord God, it grew in one hour. (*She bends down as if examining blades of corn.*) It – it seems to be ordinary corn . . . if we cut it and threshed it and ground it into flour – I don't know that we dare. I don't know how anyone dare eat this piece of bread, without they know first who it was went across it – and who it was, was carried. . . .

She retires to her place and sits down.

ANGEL. And the Prophecy continues. From the Book of the prophet Jeremiah, chapter 31, reading from the sixteeenth verse: 'Thus saith the Lord: 'Refrain thy voice from weeping and thine eyes from tears. For thy work shall be rewarded, saith the Lord, and they shall come again from the land of the enemy.' (*The cast on the stage now stand, and line*

up along the stage front. They are joined by the WISE MEN
through the stage door.) 'And there is hope in thine end,
saith the Lord. Thy children shall come again, and dwell in
their own border.'

*The actors on the stage now conclude the play by singing the
Corpus Christi Carol.*

Down in yon forest there stands a hall:
The bells of Paradise I heard them ring.
It's covered all over with purple and pall:
And I love my Lord Jesus above anything.

In that hall there stands a bed:
The bells of Paradise I heard them ring.
It's covered all over with scarlet so red:
And I love my Lord Jesus above anything.

At the bedside there lies a stone:
The bells of Paradise I heard them ring.
Which the sweet Virgin Mary knelt upon:
And I love my Lord Jesus above anything.

Under that bed there runs a flood:
The bells of Paradise I heard them ring.
The one half runs water, the other half blood:
And I love my Lord Jesus above anything.

At the foot of the bed there grows a thorn:
The bells of Paradise I heard them ring.
Which ever blows blossom since he was born:
And I love my Lord Jesus above anything.

Over the bed the moon shines bright:
The bells of Paradise I heard them ring.
Denoting our Saviour was born this night:
And I love my Lord Jesus above anything.

While they are singing MARY *and* JOSEPH *with the* BABY *come in by the stage door and take their places behind – then the cast opens to let them through, and they lead the procession out of the hall, the* ANGEL *bringing up the rear. The carol should be timed so that all the actors are clear of the hall before they stop singing.*

Ars Longa Vita Brevis

A Theme for Variations

1964

Margaretta D'Arcy

and

John Arden

This little piece is not exactly a play, nor is it anything else in particular. If we must call it something, it might well be termed 'A Theme for Variations'.

This script is intended to be used as a framework for a performance.

The dialogue is of two kinds –

(a) Long and complicated speeches, which could be learnt off by heart but are not really intended for that purpose. It would be better if the content of these speeches were to be broken down and used as a basis for free (and up-to-date) improvisation. There is no reason, for instance, why the Headmaster's speech in Scene One should not be interrupted by remarks from the Governors or from the members of his speechday audience. The scene between the Art Master and his Wife is written in a very formal Victorian manner and might well be played straight: it could also be developed into a freely improvised scene in which the props (tea-things and so forth) could play a large part.

(b) Entirely token speeches, allotted to no particular characters, intended to give the general line of the scene, around which again all manner of elaboration can be constructed. Scene Six and Scene Seven are examples of this. There are also two passages of verse in these scenes which ought to be rendered as they are written.

These are scenes which have hardly any dialogue and which are intended as opportunities to develop stage effects and business round certain costumes, props, and situations. The behaviour of the Children in the art class is one of these – while the Art Master is speaking, the actual arrangement of his class, first as a class, then as a drill squad, and finally as a regular battle, can be as elaborate and as complicated as the actors wish to make it. Similarly, the arrival of the Territorials in Scene Four, and the dressing up of these as trees in the wood is barely indicated in the text and allows a great deal of imaginative variation. What happens to the Art Master's Wife in the last scene may also be the subject of very free improvisation.

M. D'A. & J.A.

Characters

HEADMASTER
SCHOOL GOVERNORS
(no fixed number, can be male and/or female)
ART MASTER
ART MASTER'S WIFE
OFFICER OF TERRITORIALS
LANCE-CORPORAL OF TERRITORIALS
PRIVATE OF TERRITORIALS
TERRITORIALS (any number)
SCHOOL CHILDREN
(any number, boys and/or girls)

The action of the play takes place somewhere in England, next
year or the year after.

Scene One

HEADMASTER, GOVERNORS.
The HEADMASTER *makes his formal speech-day speech.*

HEADMASTER. Mr Chairman, Governors, Ladies and
Gentlemen, on this our annual speechday and prize-giving at St
Uncumbers, it falls to me as Headmaster to present my usual
report upon the work of the school during the past year, and to
offer up to you in public some predictions prophecies
suggestions intentions plans plots devices designs confederacies
conspiracies collations collections confidences and pious hopes
for the succeeding twelve months until the next speechday
which will be (God willing) in exactly twelve months time
from today, when I hope as many prizes will be awarded to as
many deserving pupils. It has been a very good year and we
have all made a lot of money and I think we may safely
congratulate ourselves upon that. Very good. Now what has
not been so good? Football successful; hockey successful;
cricket successful; nature-study very successful; school
orchestra both successful and harmonious, school meals
excellent – I have eaten some of them myself – scholarships
obtained all over the shop; the health of the pupils has never
been better; their spiritual improvement has been very well
looked after; and their carpentry and metal working classes
have been filled to capacity by aspiring carpenters and
blacksmiths? fitters? plumbers? One point, one point, however,
upon which I am not so complacent. The continued absence of
an Art Class in the school. It may be objected that the Art Class
is not necessary, I have heard it said that it would produce a
number of would-be Beatniks – as I believe they are called. In
my young days we used to say bohemian. But whatever the

name the result is the same – untidy, lazy, dirty, verminous, drunken, drug-addicted, people with beards, need a haircut, need a wash, need a disinfectant, need a good sensible old-fashioned housewife to scrub them, boys and girls, black stockings, appalling sweaters, jeans, guitars, coshes, flick-knives, bicycle chains, what has happened to the old-fashioned figure of the policeman, a fatherly character with a benevolent moustache, the Man in Blue, to knock their heads together, give them a good hiding and no questions asked, no nonsense about all this psychology then, none of this Z-cars, foolish weakness about Ombudsmen, Civil Liberties, CND, sitting down in the rain and keeping a very fine body of men away from their week-end leave in an irresponsible antic manner, and then complaints about violence: absurd, absurd, ridiculous, not wanted at St Uncumbers, under no circumstances – NO! But, and I repeat, but: this is not an inevitable corollary. An appreciation of art is very important these days if we want our children to be accepted upon equal terms in the wide world of business politics technology housewifery orthography archaeology psephology pseudo-psephology ecclesiology and the organisation of bingo. We must move with the times: dig it: be with it: in the groove: in not out: U not non-U; hep and not square, hip? Hup? Hup two three as they used to say in the Army. Hip? Hip. Let us return to our theme. Art Classes. Yes. An Art Master has been appointed. He will take up his duties next term. I am quite sure there will be no nonsense of any sort from him. He is called Mr Miltiades. I am informed that despite the odd sound of his name, Mr Miltiades is in fact exceedingly English, he has very good references. I have no doubt he can be trusted to keep all our aspiring Picassos, Matisses, Rembrandts, Giulio Romanos, William Ettys, Bouguereaus, Aubrey Beardsleys, Gauguins, Bouchers and Goyas upon very much the straight and narrow. That's all I have to say at the moment about Mr Miltiades. I will shortly be according him an interview with a view to confirming his appointment. Shall we adjourn for refreshments? A hearty vote of thanks to myself and to the Governors to the parents and all the pupils, St Uncumbers for ever, three cheers in the traditional manner of the school, School, Hip Hip Hip Za Huzzah Huzzah etcetera. . . .

Scene Two

HEADMASTER, ART MASTER.

HEADMASTER. Mr Miltiades, how do you do? I hope you are, yes, very satisfactory, references, and are you married? Married? Married? I always like to think a teacher is married. Gives him a backbone or even a root. Ideas? Your ideas? What are they?

ART MASTER. Ideas, Headmaster?

HEADMASTER. Yes, your intentions, programme of work, views upon education, curriculum?

ART MASTER. No free expression.

HEADMASTER. None?

ART MASTER. Not to start with. Highly perilous. Undesirable. Loosens, weakens, disintegrates, softens the foundations, carries away the moral fibre, shreds it, unravels it, scatters it abroad.

HEADMASTER. I am very glad to hear you say so. Just what I myself have always held. Discipline essential.

ART MASTER. Firm groundwork in drawing. Set a few pots, oranges, a still life, an old mangle, a newspaper, a bowler hat, a can or bucket, a tin of peaches, on a table. Make them draw it. Then after that progress to plaster casts. Heads of Caesar, Alexander, Young Augustus, Venus de Milo –

HEADMASTER. Head only.

ART MASTER. Head. No arms. Arms quite available anyway from various other works. There's an Athena, in a tunic, helmet, shield, very suitable. Make them draw it.

HEADMASTER. In pencil.

ART MASTER. Exactly. Give them paints and they splash. Draw also with instruments, I like them to do that.

HEADMASTER. Geometry.

ART MASTER. Squares, cubes, tetrahedrons, parallelograms, triangles, cones, conic sections, hexagons. Very invigorating to the spirit: learn at once some sort of regulated dimension.

Scene Three

ART MASTER *and Class*.

ART MASTER. We will start off this morning, boys and girls, with hexagons. Hexagons. And octagons, and when they are thoroughly accomplished, we will proceed to our first still life which will consist of this octagonal vase, this hexagonal ashtray and three cubical boxes. One two three, arranged so, against a background, so, of a square piece of hardboard, divided into squares, so. I want you to draw on graph paper. Above all I want an absolute accuracy. Precise. With your rulers, and your T-squares, no freehand, no expressionism, impressionism, futurism, abstractism; constructivism the only permissible abstraction, but realism the keynote. No laxity, keep to purity of the forms, the line is rigid, the corners acute or obtuse or rectangular, and every pencil sharp sharp sharp as the point of a bayonet. Pencils invariably 4H if you please. Draw. No, I am not satisfied. There are rhythms appearing in your work that I find profoundly disturbing. Under no circumstances can I permit the line to waver. Rulers must be held in the left hand, so – and the pencil in the right. Hands up those who cannot distinguish their left hands from their right, right hand up. Left hand up. No. Try again, smarter. Left hand up. Right hand up. Left hand right hand left hand. Right. Left. Left hand up. Left right left right. Right right right, left. Left hand up. Left hand down. NO! Left, right, left, right, left! It is evident you are in need of drill. Let us see you do some drill. All out here,

quickly. One two three. Hup. You, the right marker. Class,
upon the right marker, fall in. Take your distances two three.
Standing easy. Class, stand at ease. Two three, call the time,
count a pause. As you were. Easy. Stand at ease. Two three.
Class, class, shun. Right turn. By the right, quick march.
About turn. About turn. Right wheel. Right incline. To the
right salute. About turn. Eyes right. Eyes front. As on pay
parade salute. Two three. Pay-and-paybook-correct-sir. Squad
halt. Stand at ease. Watch it. Watch it. Watch that dressing.
One two three. By the right number. Somebody's scratching
his bottom. I see him, he knows who he is. Lazy idle
nonconformist man. He knows who he is. You're idle, lax,
loose, unbuttoned, you're a bum, you're a beatnik, what are
you? Yes you are, say it say it say it. Good, so you are. That's
better. Now then, we seem to have learnt a little drill, not
good, but not so bad, we must put ourselves to a practical use
with our improved knowledge. Warfare, fighting, combat,
conflict, battle, fight for our rights, fight to be right, fight to be
mighty, might out of right, might indeed is right, strength
through new unity. Two three. Delicious. Remember
Dunkirk.

El Alamein	Bannockburn
Waterloo	The Glorious First
Fontenoy	of June
Agincourt	Thermopylae
Inkerman	Salamis
Remember Navarino	Austerlitz
Marengo	Mohacz Field
Remember Bull Run	Fort Apache
Pearl Harbour	Cat Coit Celidon
Little Big Horn	Cat Goddeu
Cannae	Badon
Zama	The Battle of
Chaeronea	Camlann
The Battle of Lake	THE BATTLE OF
Trasimene	CAMLANN.

The Battle of Camlann at which King Arthur fell. Struck to the heart by his own flesh and blood. But yet what a battle. You're Arthur, you're Mordred, Mordred, the false nephew, stole his wife, in rebellion, thousands of men involved, the great round table man for man, fallen in Lyonnesse, remember the tactics. First the long-drawn-out infantry manoeuvrings, slow stolid pacing across bog and heath and rocky hillside, keep it slow, keep it solid, a heavy fire of arrows. Now then the ambush, all the light armed skirmishers run out of the trees, where are the trees? Here they are, you're in ambush. Advance, charge, try again, ambush, I want a really furtive ambush, kill every man that comes along the trail. Excellent, excellent – no time to pick up the wounded now. We come to the main shock of the battle. Heavy cavalry dismounted because of the boggy ground, you are heavy cavalry, remember, you're in armour, thirty forty pounds every man on your shoulders, slowly, painfully, through the bog advance. Met by pikemen, on foot, stand firm, push of pike against broadsword and shield. Push hack parry shove heave kick thrust thump bang wallop hit knock topple 'em over. Where is Arthur? Where is Mordred? Stand forward, the two enemies, hate each other, deadly, poison, murder, you have stolen his wife and stolen his kingdom. You meet in the mellay. You don't know what a mellay is? I'll make you a mellay. Here you are, I've made it. Lost an eye, lost a tooth, lost a foot, lost a lung, that's as it should be, this is a battle. You recognise one another. Uncle against nephew. Honour against treason. Order against chaos. Kill each other kill each other kill each other KILL!

The HEADMASTER *intervenes.*

HEADMASTER. Your methods –

ART MASTER. Tried and trusted, tried and trusted, sir. Forged in the fire of experience.

HEADMASTER. Why not join the Territorials? I am afraid we have no Cadet Corps here.

The HEADMASTER *dismisses the class to their next lesson which is French, Divinity, or Nature Study.*

Scene Four

ART MASTER *and his* WIFE.

ART MASTER. Is my tea ready?

WIFE. No it isn't.

ART MASTER. Why not?

WIFE. You're home early.

ART MASTER. Not very early.

WIFE. Yes you are. Half an hour early.

ART MASTER. Things were a little difficult at school today.

WIFE. Oh Antiochus, and your first day too.

ART MASTER. It's not my fault. I told the Headmaster and he
    seemed to agree with me. It is essential, I told him, that
    discipline be preserved.

WIFE. Of course it's essential, Antiochus. You must preserve
    discipline. Did you not preserve it, my love, my chick, my
    chuck, my piggiesnye, my little apple dumpling, my sweet
    cake, my cherry tart, my pretty little Christmas tree? Did the
    children misconduct themselves?

ART MASTER. They did not. Why should you imagine they
    did, Rowena? Have I not always been able to control them,
    have I not always commanded?

WIFE. Of course you have, my delight, my heart, my hinny and
    my dove: you are a man of iron, my God you are a Prussian,
    and I worship you, my treasure.

ART MASTER. No no. Where's my tea?

WIFE. Never mind your tea now, you must tell me your
    troubles.

ART MASTER. I want my tea.

WIFE. What happened at the school, Antiochus?

ART MASTER. My tea, Rowena –

WIFE. No. Tell me!

ART MASTER. Rowena, I am hungry. I would like a large pot of Indian tea, a small jug of milk, a medium jug of hot water, seven lumps of sugar, and three toasted teacakes.

WIFE. You shall not have them.

ART MASTER. What?

WIFE. Not until you tell me the full story.

ART MASTER. It's too unpleasant. I fear I have so aggravated the Headmaster that I must lose my employment unless he has a change of mind before tomorrow. Is this not enough for you, that you should withhold from me my tea into the bargain?

WIFE. No no no, you must tell me. Wait for your tea, you glutton, you sot, you stewed infusion, wait until I hear the truth – and then, if you still have stomach for it, I daresay you may eat.

ART MASTER. Three toasted teacakes, madam, on the instant, if you please.

WIFE. I will not be given orders as though I were the servant girl. I would never have married you if I had known that I was not to share your trials and disappointments, your crimes and your ineptitudes: and by sharing them alleviate them, or, it may be, go some distance towards pardoning them – though completely to forgive, alas, that is not possible. What is it you have done wrong today?

ART MASTER. I have done nothing wrong. I am hungry, that is all. I am hungry and I am thirsty. Had I not married you, I would have enlisted as a soldier, I would have submitted myself to the glories of discipline and the beautiful discomforts of khaki serge. I would have enjoyed the manly companionship of the barrack room, the glowing brutalities of non-commissioned officers, and the rigours and delightful hardihood of the early morning drill parade. Art has failed me. Education has failed me. Marriage has failed me. Life has failed me. The world is unlaced, Rowena, unlaced, unbraced, and falling apart, at every button hole. We must preserve rigidity, we must remember that unless we can subordinate ourselves wholeheartedly to the enthusiasm of total control we shall distintegrate. Did the great artists of the past disintegrate?

WIFE. Far too many of them – yes.

ART MASTER. Far too many, now you mention it. Look at Leonardo da Vinci – he painted the Last Supper and it fell off the wall. Why? Because he had forgotten that once he had been a military engineer. The precision and the unity, the mathematical and rectilinear beauty of his work was allowed to collapse beneath the insidious infiltration of liberty and licence, I mean curvature of line and sensuality of colour. I do not believe there is one man on this earth that understands what is necessary to save our civilization – except myself. I do not believe there is one man on this earth as unhappy as myself.

The TERRITORIALS *march past, their band playing 'The British Grenadiers'. The* OFFICER *calls for recruits.*

OFFICER. Join the Territorial Army. I can assure you, sir, it is a man's life in the Territorial Army. Enjoy yourself, improve yourself, learn a trade and learn a skill. Make yourself a master of all the latest weapons, the products of technology. Facilities for recreation, sport and social life, and week-end training centres, swimming baths, gymnasia and polo. Look at this young man, he has already, after three years in his Territorial battalion, attained the rank of Lance-Corporal, and a very fine rank it is too, carrying with it as it does not only extra pay and family allowances but also a family to go with the allowances and next year he will be full Corporal and have two wives and next year no doubt a Sergeant and have no less than three!

LANCE-CORPORAL. All the girls want to walk out with me when they see the stripe on my sleeve, they understand the straightness of my backbone.

OFFICER. Of course they do and why not? Come on, young man, put on the khaki, leave the dreary domestic round and fears of unemployment.

ART MASTER. What about the discipline?

OFFICER. What about the discipline? Oh well, of course we have to have it. . . .

ART MASTER. Of course, of course, I want it!

OFFICER. You what? But don't think that by discipline we mean what you might call 'Bull' – our discipline is positive. In itself. It is a skill and indeed a technology. Here's a soldier: he knows, he understands.

SOLDIER. Electronic and radio-magnetic artificer, me: five year part time course at the Army School of Electronics and Radio-Magnetics – at present employed superannuating the nuclear deficiencies in magnetic and radio-co-ordinated prediction equipment.

OFFICER. For a job like that you most certainly need discipline.

ART MASTER. I didn't want to be a technician exactly, I was brought up to be an artist, all I want to be is a –

OFFICER. Ah you are no use to us, young fellow – all you're fit for is soldiering!

ART MASTER. But that's all I want to do –

OFFICER. Strike up the drums, advance banners in the name of St George, company, set forward to the onset!

They march around and the band plays 'Over the hills and far away'.

ART MASTER. Please take me with you, oh you gallant soldiers, don't leave me behind!

WIFE. Don't leave *me* behind – Antiochus, I am your wife!

ART MASTER. Scold, shrew, termagent, harpy, you keep my tea from me, but your own fat stomach is full – no no no I will follow the drum. Besides, it's only at the weekends.

He follows the drum.

Scene Five

The ART MASTER *puts on the uniform.*
   The OFFICER *addresses the men.*

OFFICER. Today we have manoeuvres, in the woods. We are
   going to disguise ourselves – camouflage, blend with nature.
   Dress yourselves up as trees.

   The soldiers dress themselves up as trees. When they have done this,
   they group themselves in the wood.

OFFICER. All trees? Very good. Now silence and stillness,
   expectancy and danger. Wait for the words of command.

Scene Six

HEADMASTER *and* GOVERNORS *come to the woods to shoot.*
They converge and now and then shoot at small game.

THEIR CONVERSATION. I understand that one may quite
   often shoot more than pheasant in these woods. Wild deer are
   frequently to be seen. The Lord Lieutenant has very kindly
   accorded us permission to shoot any that we see. Venison is
   very good to eat. Who knows how to cook a venison pasty?
   And upon a Sunday too, what especial pleasure it is to be able
   to shoot animals and birds instead of going to church.
   There are a great many rustlings in the forest today. The place
   is alive with deer. I wish I could see them.
   Are you sure they are not men? I thought I heard one swear.
   No no they are deer.

A QUIET VOICE AMONG THE COMPANY. *I* know they
   are men, but I do not wish these others to know that too,
   because it would be a good joke to see how long it takes them
   to tell the difference between a tree, a Territorial, and a deer.

THEIR CONVERSATION. Aha, there is more than a rustling, there is most definitely a deer, behold the beauty and spreading strength of his antlers.

THE HEADMASTER. Look I will shoot him, and wear his horns upon my head.

The shot kills the ART MASTER.

ART MASTER.
Oh delight of my life
I did not dream in vain
I put on the khaki to stifle my pain
I went to the manoeuvres
But endured the coarse laughter
Of those who believed that the life of the soldier
Was no more for glory ferocity and steel
But was only the achieving of a poor bourgeois skill.
Technology is confounded and art takes its place:
For here I have received a real bullet in my face.
Hardihood and discipline,
Straight lines and repression
Have today found their old true expression:
I die for my duty and I die with a smile
The Territorial Army has proved itself real.

He dies.

GOVERNORS. Who did this terrible thing? It does not matter, the Chief Constable is of our party and the woods are the Lord Lieutenant's. Who will comfort the widow?

Scene Seven

WIFE *and* GOVERNORS.

WIFE. Alas, he is dead.

GOVERNORS. But a subscription has been raised and you are not to go unsupported.

HEADMASTER. He died in the knowledge that he was fulfilling his vocation. He was so still that we were certain he could only be a stag; had he moved we would have known he was a man.

A QUIET VOICE AMONG THE COMPANY. I knew all the time he was a man, but I thought it best to keep quiet. Now I think it even better, though I am the Chief Constable.

HEADMASTER. Here is the money, Mrs Miltiades. You should be proud of your husband.

WIFE. Thank you very much. Now I can have all those things that I was unable to enjoy before because of the poor pay of the teaching profession.

With the money she buys clothes, food, wine, a new house and she enjoys herself in fast cars with innumerable young men, all more handsome and less confused than her late husband. In the middle of her enjoyment, she meets his funeral on the way to the graveyard.

WIFE.
I shed a tear upon his bier
Because to me he was ever dear.
But I could not follow him in all his wishes
I prefer the quick easy swimming of the fishes
Which sport and play
In green water all day
And have not a straight line in the whole of their bodies.

Friday's Hiding

An Experiment in the Laconic
1965

Margaretta D'Arcy
and
John Arden

We were asked to write a 'play without words' – in fact, this little play does contain some spoken passages (indicated by italics), because it seemed impossible to establish the plot without them. If they can be eliminated in the action and replaced by sufficiently expressive mime, we would raise no objections; though probably the opening expository speeches should remain and the song at the end ought not to be omitted. We would also recommend musical (or, at least, percussive) accompaniment, reflecting the rhythms of the action.

A group of students performed some improvisations round the theme of this play while we were writing it. They were:

Maurice Burgess

Frank Challenger

George Dorosh

Delia Jones

Mary Saunders

Linda Watkins

– all of the School of Art, Shrewsbury. We are most grateful for their assistance, and also that of their drama director, Albert Hunt.

M.D'A. & J.A.

Friday's Hiding was first produced at the Royal Lyceum Theatre, Edinburgh, on 29 March 1966 with the following cast:

JOHN BALFOUR, *a Farmer*	Callum Mill
MISS LETITIA BALFOUR, *His Sister*	Lennox Milne
EDDIE ⎱ *Labourers*	David Kincaid
WILLIE TAM ⎰	Brian Cox

Directed by Sheila Ronald and Tom Fleming

The scene is a Farm (both within doors and out) in the Lowlands of Scotland.

The time is the present.

MISS BALFOUR.

There was an auld dour skinflint of a farmer
His name was John Balfour
He lived with nae wife but a weary auld sister
   Her name was Elspeth Letitia
              That's me
   They call me Aunt Letty.

Forbye he was rich eneuch to marry a Laird's dochter
Forbye he was rich eneuch to pay his farm-hands better.

   Twa young men he had
                   That's Eddie and Willie Tam
   But they're young men nae langer
   They've dug and delved John Balfour's land
   Seventeen year wi' never a rise in wages
   And they're lucky to get what they do get

For every Friday
         That's pay-day
He gangs to the bank in the forenoon to draw out the money
But in the afternoon whaur is he? Whaur does he meet them to pay
   them?

EDDIE.

Dear goodness he meets us in nae place
But he hides awa, fast, like the wee man he is,
In the house or the barn or the yard or the field
             or under the bank of the burn or
                       awa yonder on the fell
             or onywhere else I canna think of nor tell
For Friday for Balfour is nocht but the day he's in hiding
And before we get paid we maun find him.
Has he been to the bank yet?

WILLIE TAM.

He hasna come back yet.
We maun wait in the yard and waylay him.
He'll be wanting his dinner within.

Aunt Letty in the kitchen lays out John Balfour's dinner.

MISS BALFOUR.
I want my money too.
I canna buy the man meat without it.
He willna even gie it to his ain sister, consider it!

ALL THREE OF THEM. *Dear goodness, what a man!*

John Balfour, hame frae the bank, looks into the yard
he sees his two labourers on the watch, he retires.
    The pair of them, weary with waiting, bring out their bread
    and kebbuck, contrive to keep an eye on the gate, but grow
    careless.
John Balfour throws a stone, it goes over their heads,
hits the wall on yon side of them, they turn toward it –
suspicious –
then creep over there and watch, their backs turned towards his
entry.
    Which he makes, concealed in a haycock.

    The Haycock sneezes.

    They turn at the noise.
    There is nocht but a Haycock.
    Whaur the hell did that come from?
    They look at it – dubious –
a dog barks beyond the house, distracts their attention, they
swing around and run over there.

    The Haycock moves again.

    This time, when they turn back to continue their watching and
    waiting and eating
    it is that degree nearer the porch of the house.
Willie Tam observes this but doesna care to tell Eddie
lest Eddie think him daft.
But unobtrusively he paces the distance between the Haycock and
the house and Eddie sees him do it.
    Eddie does it himself.
    By God it *is* nearer.
They are not at all sure they want to meddle with this.
    if Mr Balfour should choose to walk home inside a Haycock

it is not for the likes of them to interfere with his fancy.
But none the less they want their money.

They retire to consider the possibilities of some action.
As they whisper together the Haycock moves
They see it move
                                       and run forward
                                                              but too late
    It is at the door.

    Mr Balfour is in his ain kitchen
    And the Haycock's whisked awa.

John Balfour, safe at last where they canna get after him
without breach of etiquette
transfers the weekly money
counts out certain banknotes – these into a cashbox
(lock it, put it away, lock the cupboard, carefully replace both
keys on the end of his watchchain into the watchchain pocket) –
these notes, till now retained under a careful stern thumb, go in
their turn, wrapped in an old fold of dry paper,
    into his wallet.
    a worn wallet, tight, fastened with farmer's twine, into the
    inner breast pocket, button it up. Good.
Sit down to your dinner, mean old devil.
Poor Letty serves it up. She's had hers already. Sit sideways to
table, eat potatoes off your knife, heavy movements with your
eating irons, vulgar old devil, aye, ye *would* read the *Farmer's
Weekly* propped up on the salt-cellar.
    What's the matter with her? She's got her fingers on the edge of
    the table, tap-tapping there like a leaf against the window.
    Rap her on the knuckles with the back edge of your knife.
    No, you'd better not, she is your ain sister.
    What the de'il is she after?

MISS BALFOUR.
Housekeeping money, John, Friday . . . ?

Bedamned to that. He's wanting his cup of tea.
Are ye no gaun to pour it out, woman? That's better. Aye, ye can

drink a cup yersel. Set down to it and gie ower demonstrating
your damned fidgets.

He lights up his pipe with a great deal of profound hesitation.

> Willie Tam and Eddie at their dinners in the yard
> are slow over bread and kebbuck,
> dry it is, slow between the teeth.
> Get up and gie the auld woman your can to be filled.
> She takes it in at the back door and hands it back full of tea.
> She gives them one or two significant looks.
> She's telling them, ye ken, he has the money frae the bank,
> But lockit up,
> > lockit,
> > > ye canna get it yet.
> Ach, awa wi' that, they'll drink their tea and bide their time.

EDDIE.
Seventeen year I've dug and delved his fields
He's offered me ne'er a raise in wages.
Nor you neither? Aye, aye, nor you neither:
Begod this very day I'm gaun to make shift and ask him.

WILLIE TAM.
Ye'll never dae it.

Aye aye but Eddie will, but he'll have to catch him first. Mean
auld devil and they glare at his back door.

He's finished his tea and reconsidered the front page of the
Farmer's Weekly (having read the whole paper from front to back
first), reconsidered the middle page, thought seriously about
something else upon the back page, folded it up, once, twice, and
again, to about the size of a flatiron, then carefully places it on one
end of the mantelpiece on top of last week's issue and sixteen
weeks before that.

A great deal of profound hesitation once again with his pipe that
has to be knocked out and drawn upon and generally supervised,

Then a slow trudge to the door
taking no notice of the auld sister,
stand in the door, meeting the regard of the two labourers.

They look wages at him, grind their teeth in wages,
shuffle wages with their feet (to which they are risen)
But he takes no damn notice.

Only indicates the dungforks
they are to work with this afternoon and away he goes from
them.
Minding his own business, minding it severely.
His own business is a hoe. He selects it,
And all upon his own with a hoe upon his shoulder he leaves
them
     alone in the yard.

Once out of their sight he runs.
Aunt Letty clears the table and clears herself off.
She has a sad thought about the cash box
lockit up and awa – eh deary me . . .

Dungforks up, dung on the dungforks,
swing it up, the pair of ye, slow swings but experienced
from the midden to the cart, loading it up.
This'll no get us our wages.
But it's little good to rush it. Fork a bit further.
Whaur the hell's he gone?
He took a hoe, he's in the Lang Field,
Eddie's awa to find him.

Willie Tam's dubious,
  but Eddie's the boy,
                    angry,
                         he wants his siller,
           he's awa.
Willie Tam stacks the forks, gangs after, not happy.

Into the Lang Field, where Balfour sets his cold eye
considering the furrows and the work of his hoe;
commences his slow bend, drives his weapon,

all upon his own and a mile from the house.
Finishing the first row, he looks up
                              and there they are

   The pair of them glaring.
   Good God they want their money.

Up to the head of the second row, let them follow if they want
to.

   They want to.

Stoop again, hoe again, he's all upon his own,
neither word nor look given to acknowledge their existence.
The three of them together move, backwards, down the field.
End of the second row,
                      Good God they're still beside him.

So up the field again to the head of the third.
   A pair of daft bridesmaids grinning ingratiation.
   Ah well, John Balfour's no such a bad fellow at heart.
   He cracks a wee smile in return, leans on his hoe,
   hand to his pocket, slowly slowly slowly
   does he mean to pay them already?
                      he does not.
   He has tobacco in his pocket
   and a great deal of profound hesitation
   toward replenishment of his pipe.

WILLIE TAM.
It's a grand afternoon, Mr Balfour.

EDDIE.
It's Friday afternoon, Mr Balfour.

   Aye, so it is, it's a fine time of day for the enjoyment of a pipe.
   Then the hoe propped on its end in the furrow
   is somehow transferred from John Balfour to poor Eddie,
   who, mollified by the humanity of the farmer's rare smile
   and the contentment expressed by the farmer's humane pipe,
   cannot, as a Christian, do other than take the hoe
      and commence the third row.

At the end of each row Eddie smiles at the farmer
but fails to speak.
Backwards and forwards he works. John Balfour takes his ease.
Willie Tam is silly Willy, fidgeting and grinning.
He minds the dungfork labour has yet to be concluded,
bobs his apologies and trudges to conclude it.
   John Balfour looks after him,
                          considers,
                                    calls him back,
    they are all three of them to work at the hoeing, after all,
        so Willie Tam must trudge and fetch a pair of hoes.

Eddie finishes his third row, smiles and comes to his master,
smiles again, opens his mouth –

EDDIE.
Friday . . .

    John Balfour didna hear him, he says it again,
    He meets John Balfour's eye and pretends he hadna spoken.
   · To them baith returns Willie Tam,
       one hoe for himself
                    and another for the master,

    Thus we have three men stooping
    Working together backwards,
    Two of them wondering when's he going to give them their
    money
    One of them wondering how the devil to avoid giving it,
    And he works in the middle.

So they swop glances, (that would be nudges, were they nearer)
across his bended back, Eddie gives vent
to certain dismal menaces, swinging up his hoe
and feigning to bring it down on the devoted head of Balfour,
thereby he terrifies the gentle soul of Willie Tam,
continuing as he does with a pantomime of cruel violence,
first: to hoe John Balfour's head – then: to jump upon his body –
then:
to stamp down upon his vitals and rifle his waistcoat pocket.

There is such exaggeration in the finale of this mime
that Willie Tam begins to laugh and John Balfour hears him
laugh,
looks rapidly up at him and then up at Eddie
who at that moment is executing his dance of triumph
to celebrate his rehearsed rapine
and is forthwith compelled by the cold eye of the master
to turn the dance into the pursuit with hoe and hand
of a non-existent wasp, which he murders
just in time to save John Balfour from a non-existent sting.
   John Balfour is not grateful and shows that there are many
                                        furrows yet to hoe.
But Willie Tam is more amused by the discomfiture of Eddie
and laughs
and laughs
and laughs
            across John Balfour's back.

   Eddie thereupon rages within him
   and there are serious signs that he really will attack
   Balfour
   and if Willie Tam isna careful he'll catch a bang as well –
   here's a hunk of a boulder that would pulverise John
                                        Balfour's brain pan
   and here's a hob-nailed boot-toe for his quick emasculation.

Eddie stops his work.

He is at the end of a row.
Balfour comes backward towards him,
when he reaches him, by God, there is about to be
a terrible conjunction of crisis – look at the hoe,
how it is gripped in Eddie's angry hand.
Look how he signals Willie Tam to stand by him and
look how Willie Tam in great fear would dissuade him –

   and backwards comes Balfour,
                        unaware,
                              stooped,
                                    vulnerable.

He works right up to the boot of Eddie
                              and he stops.
He doesna get up but contemplates the weed penultimately
dislodged
considering maybe that he would have done better to have
dislodged it deeper . . .

EDDIE.
Friday. Mr Balfour, it's Friday.

If he were to look up now he would see the two men
– there they stand – about to beat him and to shake their money
out of him.
But without lifting his body one hand's-breadth
                          he runs away sideways
                          dropping his hoe
                          away over furrow and ditch
                          out of the field-gate
before either Eddie or Willie Tam are even aware he has gone.
How stupid they stand there.

EDDIE.
Awa, man, let's get him!

Seventeen years of suppressed oppressed hard labour
are running after Balfour and God kens what they'll dae to him –
supposing they should catch him.

                          For the first time ever

John Balfour is afraid of his men.
And yet for Godsake they would never be so violent
as to actually damage him –

                          oho though would they not!
And he looks out from behind a thorn hedge and sees them come
running
across the clayey ridges, their hoes in their hands,
he dodges round the bush, he is quicker than they are,
they think they have him surrounded but he dodges round again,
then he's off and out of sight and they stand and look stupid.

Then after him again
and he seeks for bush after bush
using each one for cover until
he is flushed out of it,
dodging hither and thither
but never in a panic,
using his intelligence,
which, he is ever confident,
is more than twice as sharp as theirs.

Down into a ditch and he pulls a bush over him,
they leap the ditch without noticing
find nobody beyond it, cast in different directions around,
draw together again frustrated, and take counsel
at the very edge of the ditch where he lies.

Their fury is more than a bit abated.

Eddie pulls out tobacco and papers to roll himself a wee smoke
                and one for Willie Tam.
Willie Tam strikes a match, the wind blows it out.
Willie Tam strikes another match, blown out in like manner.
He has but the one more match left to him in the box:
He strikes it,
                and endeavouring to conceal it from the wind
                succeeds with it in burning the tips of his fingers.
                Curses it
                Drops it.
                Through the leaves in the ditch
                On to Mr Balfour's face.
                Mr Balfour cries out
                (not very surprisingly)

And they see who it is and they pull the bush off him.
He slithers out unabashed
    but he kens what to do.
    Before they can assess their own attitude toward him
    he has his own matchbox out and
        has offered them a light

Gracious goodness but now they are under an obligation to the man.

They must accordingly help him to his feet and dust him down
they must replace the odds and ends that are falling out of his
pockets
they must pretend with great embarrassment
that they meant no more than rough humour.
He's a crude carl himself, he will understand their notion of a joke
and he appears to understand it for he laughs with them
                accommodatingly.
                But keeps his hand
                (as it were by accident)
                pressed hard on his wallet-pocket.

He minds their purposes yet, which they seem to have
forgotten.
But not for aye – they've remembered them now,
for here in Eddie's helpful fist is the loose dangle of John's
watchchain
with the cashbox keys upon it.

John Balfour sees he sees them,
he kens the clicketty-click in Eddie's slow brain –

EDDIE.
Friday . . . Why, Friday, it is . . .

And Balfour's awa again,
shot from his grasp and running like a weasel,
stuffing chain and keys within him as he runs,
and where does he run to?
This time clear of ploughland hedge and ditch
deep into the thickets – whinbush bramble blackthorn,
and the pair of them after him
struggling falling cursing.
                They have him
                and they've lost him.
Eddie gets a strong hold of him
but he drags himself clear and by force of his dragging
throws himself across to the nervous grab of Willie Tam
knocks Willie in the belly, rebounds clear towards Eddie
dodges Eddie, knocking Eddie with his foot under the chin,

Eddie falls backward, Willie Tam's already fallen,
John Balfour's foot went too much upward,
he dances back upon one leg
he's no a stork, he's a man, he canna sustain it,
he's arsy-versy over in the matt of the blackthorn.

And the pair of them are up and jump in upon him terribly.

They grab him up, he slumps under,
they hoick his feet, his arms hang heavy,
they stoop and lift his head, they shake it and it lolls.

Good God have they murdered him?
It looks damn well like it.

They are stricken men.

They are all in a fluster with penitence
and hang above John Balfour's body
slapping his cheeks and feeling his bone-joints
and attempting many contradictory forms of resuscitation.
Then with a look from one to the guilty other
they hoist him up betwixt them
and hump him home to his house.
His head hangs like a dead head
and their remorseful steps as they carry him
are as heavy as lead . . .

Aunt Letty in the kitchen, doing a bit of dusting,
Hears their slow tramp as it comes across the yard
and she looks through the window in a passing curiosity
see what there it to see
        drops her duster in horror and flies out to meet them

assailing the cortège with weeping and wailing
and ungirdled reproaches and strikings at their heads.
She pulls John Balfour in more or less in spite of them
and has him sprawled upon a sofa
and hot water and cold water and poultices and compresses
and smelling-salts and iodine and all the other condiments
rushed in and applied in a fury of commiseration.

But she's no sae simple, Aunt Letty.

In a frenzy of grief she may be but she minds her proper interests
and in all the whirlpool muddle of sickbed assiduities
she cunningly unhooks her brother's keys
from the end of his watchchain and
         slips them in her apron pocket

Eddie and Willie Tam, distracted, fail to notice.
There is no sign of life from the prostrate master of the house.
And sorrowfully, inch by inch, his kinswoman and in his dependants
accept and recognise the inevitability of death.

He was all that *she* had
And who will employ *them* now?
And a cloth is drawn across his face
And they turn away in gloom.

MISS BALFOUR.
I'll mak ye a cup o' tea.

And she begins this necessary work of mercy and consolation
with heavy heart.
But the keys in her apron jingle-jingle some small reassurance.

Of course the man's not dead at all,
(this is a comedy)
and after a while he lifts back the cloth
peeps out, sits up. They're all at their tea.
Not one of them to bother to look around at him.
What in the de'il's name's been happening?
And who for Godsake put this cloth upon his face?
With a shrug he pulls out his pipe
and is about to strike a match and light it
when he recollects
         at last he recollects
that there had been some sort of nonsense about the men's wages.
In his pocket is his wallet, he takes it out – quietly –

subtracts the folded paper with the banknotes within it
puts the wallet into the pocket – quietly –
and sets the money on the mantelpiece
                    in two careful piles

            and nobody's noticed.

   Then he strikes the match for his pipe.
   Ho ho they notice now.

   But being of a sombre northern race they do not respond
                                    to miracles.
   Eddie and Willie Tam do however respond to the fact
   that they are sitting in the master's kitchen chairs
   without the master's express invitation
   and they get up in a hurry and flatten themselves against the
   walls.

Aunt Letty, frozen and angry that her grief was so premature
thrusts a cup of tea at John Balfour and sits down again, her back
turned.
He takes the cup to the table and sits and drinks it, smoking.

   Willie Tam is edging his way to the door when his eye lights
                    on the mantelpiece
                    and he sees what is to be seen there.
                    He nudges Eddie.
                    Eddie sees it too.
                    They clear their throats.
                    John Balfour takes no notice.
                    Eddie takes the money –
   He appreciates the convention that it should not
   be acknowledged as being there at all, thereby
   saving all and sundry from expressions of gratitude
   for what is after all only due to them by right,
   and he pockets his own pile and hands Willie Tam his.
   They nod their heads and knuckle forelocks in a perfunctory
   manner.
   John Balfour takes no notice.

Aunt Letty takes no notice
                              her back to all three of them.
So the two men work themselves bashfully towards the door.

At last *they have been paid* and one more Friday's toils are over.
                    Or are they?
                    Willie Tam thinks so.
                    But Eddie recollects.
                    He stops short in the doorway,
                    obstructing Willie Tam.
                    He clears his throat.

EDDIE.
A rise . . .

WILLIE TAM (*restrainingly*).
Na na . . .

EDDIE.
Ah, ah, a rise in wages – seventeen year . . .

Eddie is gey determined and courage fills up his demeanour.
He strides across the room to Mr Balfour's foursquare back
And claps him hard upon it.

EDDIE.
A rise, a rise, Mr Balfour, I mean to ask ye for a rise.

John Balfour heard him the first time and has sat struck rigid with
pipe and tea-cup
now he spills his tea and drops his pipe in the puddle.
Aunt Letty too, half-risen, can scarce believe her ears,
while Willie Tam would like to creep under the teapot.
      John Balfour turns and stares.
      This is beyond his comprehension.
      Slowly he rises up.
      He paces the room, so slowly,
      back and forth in amazement
      three times altogether paces the room,
            then he stops.
            He puts his face before the quailing face of Eddie
            till the noses are all but touching.

BALFOUR.
What for!

> Eddie can think of no answer.
> Aunt Letty thinks of it for him.

MISS BALFOUR.
John, the cost of living. He's a man with a family . . .

> John Balfour, in furious contempt at this,
>   dances and spins,
>   laughs, whirls his arms,
>   seizes the *Farmer's Weekly*
>   and dashes it on the ground.

> Eddie, the miserable coward, implicates a poor neutral.

EDDIE.
Willie Tam wants a rise too.

> Willie Tam is now spun upon by the dervish John Balfour,
> he retreats in bewildered terror,
> then, gripped on the elbow by Eddie,
> remembers he's a man and stands up for his rights.

WILLIE TAM.
Aye aye aye – we baith want a rise . . .

> John Balfour flings him from him and spins and whirls
>   saucers
>   his coat tails fly, his watchchain leaves its moorings
>   Then he stops.
>   Then he crouches.
>   Then he advances upon Willie Tam,
>   thrusting up at him a trembling finger,
>   his knees are bent double beneath him
>   his eye is like a pitchfork point.

BALFOUR.
You! Why, you're a single man!

Then he throws himself upon the table, sits there cross-legged
and cackles with rage, dominating the whole kitchen.

Old gnome, he reassembles the dishevelled ends of his
accoutrements
including
                 his watchchain
                             which he finds
                                    has no keys on it.
                                    Where are the keys?
                                    Aunt Letty has the keys.

                 And furthermore she has, for the first time, her
                 own appropriate rage.

She throws herself utterly upon these sordid men
and brandishing the keys and brandishing a toasting fork
she clears them all from the kitchen
tumbling one over the other head over heels to avoid her
                                       out into the yard.
   When the door is fast bolted, she is left alone within.
   So she opens the cupboard and then opens the cash box.
   She takes out all the money – and there is a fair quantity too –
   she sits down at the table and enjoys her *coup d'état*.

Also in the cupboard is John Balfour's personal whisky.
She fills up a tea-cup and she sits and she drinks.
She picks up the *Farmer's Weekly* and the other cups and so
forth
and clears them all away.
   Then somehow she's no sae blithe.
   She's got one cup and saucer before her
   and heretofore there has always been at least one other.
   She sets a second one out again and looks at it . . .
Then she bethinks her of something that was said.
Then she bethinks her of an auld kist that lies behind the door.
She pulls it out and opens it.
                 She takes out of it
                 (wrapped and camphored)
                 what must have been
                 her mother's original wedding dress
                 long kept in vain for herself.

It's a large full-skirted Edwardian garment,
far too large for her dried-up wee body
and it goes on very easily on top of her ordinary clothes.
She holds it up against her,
                    and then she puts it on.
                    Then she sits down again
                    and broods on possibilities.

    John Balfour is the first of the three to attempt to get in
    again.
    He forces the catch of the window with a bent bit of wire
    and with a great deal of difficulty puts his head through it.
    Two moonlike faces in the aperture behind him
    are Eddie and Willie Tam,
                        who goggle at the wedding dress.

John Balfour considers the pros and the cons.
Suppose she were to marry Willie Tam?
To pay for the pair of them would no doubt come even cheaper
than to pay them both separately as he has to do now.
He calculates this on his fingers out there in the yard.
Then, very carefully, he scrambles
                            through
                                the window.
He tiptoes to his sister and clears his throat, carefully,
She doesna turn upon him, so he emboldens himself.

And he opens the door and beckons in Eddie and Willie Tam.
Willie Tam bethinks him of something that was said
And he willna come in so Mr Balfour has to pull him.
Once he's in, John Balfour makes an effort to improve his
appearance,
Sprucing him up, quickly, and thrusting a cauliflower
in at his button-hole to give the semblance of a bridegroom
then, playing the Best Man, he leads him grandly up
to majestic Aunt Letty
and presents him, with deference.
        She accepts him.
        She embraces him.

Willie Tam can make no protest,
so large and preposterous is her embracement.
And she gives John Balfour back his keys.

Then John Balfour pours out whisky
  into everybody's cup
  with leaping generosity,
  back-smacking, laughing hugely,
  the whole bottle is lavishly emptied,
  he grabs another bottle from the inside of the cupboard
  and he pours that out as well.

He kisses his sister's cheeks and slaps her on the hurdies
and he sits them all down and indicates Liberty Hall.
He himself, the gracious host, the indulgent brother-in-law
presides as is fitting, patriarchally, in the middle.
  Yet at the same time, unobtrusively,
  he puts all the money back
  into the cash box, locks it up,
  and he puts the cash box back
  into the cupboard, locks it up,
  and he puts the keys back
  on to his watchchain and he puts that back
                              into his waistcoat pocket.

Then he resumes his ease amongst the party,
where Eddie is highly delighted and Willie Tam is making the
best of it
and only Aunt Letty is beginning to wonder how much longer
this foolishness will go on. She mops up spilled whisky.
  John Balfour raises his voice in song.
  The tune was once the tune of a metrical psalm
  but the words are his own and the men join in the refrains.
  If they thought about it twice they would not, but this is a
  party.

BALFOUR.
The devil sure had done his work
And put us all in misery

But now concordance is restored
And here we sit and we agree.

CHORUS.
And we agree and we agree
And we agree in harmony.

BALFOUR.
What was a while turned up-side-down
Is now once more turned right-side-up
The master has his blessing gien
And poured y'all out a cheerful cup.

CHORUS.
And poured us out and poured us out
The auld white ewe has a strong black tup.

BALFOUR.
Then let us drink and never think
We can ourselves improve our life
Unless the master take the lead
We shall find nocht but grief and strife.

CHORUS.
We shall find nocht we shall find nocht
Till every man controls his wife
Till every fork lies under the knife
Till every plate kens its place in the larder
And every slate sticks to the rafter
And one gangs first and the rest gang after
That's what we call restoring order.

The last refrain, being longer than the others, takes on the quality of a round song. And they sing it and sing it until the whisky restores its own sort of order and God kens how much work will be done in the fields this Saturday . . . Aunt Letty kens all right. She takes off the wedding dress and folds it up as neat as ever it was and lays it back in the kist and puts the kist back behind the door and sits down again in patience, mopping up spilled whisky and watching that the cups do not get broken.

The Royal Pardon

or

The Soldier who became an Actor
1966

John Arden
and
Margaretta D'Arcy

The Royal Pardon was first performed at the Beaford Arts Centre, Devon, on 1 September 1966, under the direction of the authors, with the following cast:

LUKE (A Soldier)	Roger Davenport
Strolling Actors	
THE CLOWN	Nigel Gregory
ESMERALDA	Martha Gibson
MR CROKE	Philip Sayer
MRS CROKE	Maureen Lipman
WILLIAM	Timothy Craven
Villagers	
THE CONSTABLE	John Arden
THE UNDER-CONSTABLE	Frank Challenger
MRS HIGGINBOTTOM (His Wife)	Lesley Joseph
The English Court	
LORD CHAMBERLAIN	Frank Challenger
THE KING	Tamara Hinchco
THE PRINCE	Mark Wing-Davey
The French Court	
AN OFFICER	Nigel Gregory
AN ACTRESS	Lesley Joseph
AN ACTOR	Frank Challenger
THE KING	Rupert Haverbrook
THE PRINCESS	Tamara Hinchco
A COOK	Nigel Gregory

Stage Managed by Valerie Beer
Music composed and played by Boris Howarth and
Russell Howarth
Décor and costumes by Margaret Hogg and Sanny Yen

The action of the play is set in England and France
The period is legendary rather than historical

Act One

The Actors' stage is already set up. It is little more than a small curtained booth with bunting and other cheap decorations. The ACTORS *are heard singing behind it.*

SONG.

> Sun and moon and stars and rainbow
> Drum and trumpet, tambourine,
> A greedy king or a haughty beggar
> A virgin slut or a painted queen –
> Put your boots on, mask your faces
> Heave your cloaks and swing your swords,
> Laugh and weep and stamp with anger,
> Kick your jigs and strut the boards,
> All is painted, all is cardboard
> Set it up and fly it away
> The truest word is the greatest falsehood,
> Yet all is true and all in play –
> Sun and moon and stars and rainbow
> Drum and trumpet, tambourine.

The CLOWN *enters, followed by the* 'DRAGON' [ESMERALDA], *who nips and worries him as he addresses the audience.*

CLOWN. Ladies and gentlemen, ladies and gentlemen, ladies gentlemen – get-aht-of-it, you've split me breeches –
   (*He removes his loose trousers which the* DRAGON *has torn, revealing another pair underneath.*)
   Keep him off me, keep him off me – he'll stop the show before we've started – get-aht-of-it, get in – (*He drives the* DRAGON *behind the curtains.*)
   Puts you off, dunnit ?

Why, I was going to give you a prologue . . . oh yes, here
we are . . .

> Our little play this afternoon,
> Not too early, not too soon,
> Is the glorious story of bold St George
> And how he choked the Dragon's gorge . . .

He didn't hear that, did he? He don't know what's in store
for him, does he? It's all right, it's all clear . . . I'm safe
for a few minutes more . . .

> In days of old this Dragon roamed the land,
> Not one man brave enough against him for to stand.
> The King and all his People were in fear
> For every day the Dragon would appear
> Consuming all in horrible flaming fire.

(*Enter* 'KING' [MR CROKE] *and* 'PRINCESS' [MRS CROKE].)

> Here is the King, here is his lovely Daughter,
> And here's the brutal monster, tearing a'ter –

The DRAGON *comes in again and chases them all off and
round about the stage. After a while the* KING *and* PRINCESS
are left alone.

KING.

> My child, I have spoken to many wise men
> Both north, east, west and south:
> And only one answer have they given to me
> How to stop the Dragon's mouth.
> They say that I must sacrifice to him
> Whatever I hold most dear:
> And that, my dear, I sorely fear,
> Is you, it doth appear.

PRINCESS.

> Oh father, such a horrid fate
> I did not dream nor contemplate.

KING.

> Weep not, faint not, the dragon is so quick

He'll gobble you up in half a tick.
I doubt very much if you'll feel any pain.

PRINCESS.

But father, I shall never see you again.

KING.

Which is so sad indeed, I know not what to say.
But here I must tie you up till the dragon should pass
this way. (*He binds her.*)
My child, it is for your country and your King
That you must suffer this abominable thing.
There we are, safe and sound . . .
I hear his footsteps beat and pound!

KING
PRINCESS } *together*

Oh {daughter / father} such a horrid fate,
I did not dream nor contemplate.

Exit KING.
Enter 'ST GEORGE' [WILLIAM].

ST GEORGE.

Why, what is here, as though for sale displayed?
Tied like a parcel, a beautiful young maid?
Speak if you can! She weeps, she cannot utter.

Enter CLOWN.

CLOWN.

Watch out, he's on his way, I see his head!
He's coming for his slice of bread.
Do you want to be the butter?

ST GEORGE.

Who, what, where, when, how?
Do you talk of a dinner or a feast?

CLOWN.

I'm talking of the dreadful scaly beast

Who'll eat you up, lungs, liver, lights and gall!

ST GEORGE.

Aha! I am St George and dragons I appal.

Enter DRAGON.

DRAGON.

A lovely girl, a strong young handsome boy:
Which of the two shall I the best enjoy?

ST GEORGE.

Fight for your life!

DRAGON.

Struggle and strife,
I fight for my dinner!

ST GEORGE.

I fight for my wife!

He kills the DRAGON *after a good deal of business.*
The KING *enters and cheers.*

KING.

Did I hear you say 'wife'?
First we shall have to see whether you suit her social
status.

CLOWN.

Another couple of minutes and this creature would
have ate us –
Such consequential fortitude
Deserves a bit of gratitude.
Go on then, let them wed,
Get the blankets on the bed

KING.

That's quite enough of that –*

---

* This line is spoken 'out of character' – i.e. CROKE is rebuk-
ing an irregular gag by the CLOWN and raises his mask briefly for
the purpose.

Sir, you are so brave and glorious,
So splendidly victorious,
That if you want her, you must have her.
Of course, I do suppose I'll have to ask her mother.
Yet am I not the King?
So, with the greatest pleasure,
I render you my treasure.

PRINCESS.

This is too much.
Oh father dear, I never thought –

KING.

Ah not at all,
I expected something of the sort –

CLOWN.

Take her by the hand
Kiss her on the cheek
And you shall have a lovely honeymoon
That'll last you all next week –

(*As he jumps around he steps near the supposedly dead* DRAGON, *who nips him in the rear. His trousers split again revealing yet another pair on underneath.*)

Ow, I've split me breeches, look, they've gone again, I thought you told me he was dead –

The CONSTABLE *comes forward out of the audience.*

CONSTABLE. Right, that'll do. That is the second occasion in this deplorable performance that vulgar and indecent behaviour has taken place. I've got it down in me notebook, it is incontrovertible. Twice, no less, was breeches mentioned and each time they was removed: to the scandal of the populace. Whatever you might get away with in London, we do *not* allow that sort of thing round here. Close your show at once and take yourselves out of this town.

The ACTORS, *crestfallen, remove their masks.*

CROKE. And who, sir, do you think you are? Choosing to address me with such, er, with such, er . . . er, h'm . . .

CONSTABLE. I'm the Constable, that's who. We had a warning about this performance, I may tell you, and my worst fears have been justified. Why – children might have been present. Sickening, I call it. Go on, get out of here before I run you in. Rogues, vagabonds, dirty-minded hooligans.

Enter LUKE.

LUKE (*addressing the audience, while the* ACTORS *sadly pack up their gear*). I wouldn't go quite so far as that meself – dirty-minded, to my mind, is piling it on a bit strong. But they are a slovenly baggagey lot and if they'd been let continue long enough to pass around a hat, they'd ha' got nowt from me in it, I can tell you that plainly. Tearing his pants off – *twice*! Well, did anybody laugh at it – did you? *I* didn't. And what about St George? There was a man, if they'd had the intelligence, to look out a proper play about him, there was a man that could *call* himself a man.

> His sword was strong, his heart was clear;
> Inside his stomach he knew the claws of fear.
> But he fought them first and then he fought again
> The claws of the dragon and the fire and the raving
>   pain,
> And he brought it through to a finish
> And he took the lady by the hand
> And he said 'How dare they offer so frail a sacrifice on
>   this strand?
> The King himself should ha' stood here to defend his
>   ravaged land.
> Coward that he was he must now defend it from me:
> The dragon being dead and his daughter being free,
> I take my stand and I stake my claim.
> Fight me,' declares St George, 'Or forever bear the
>   the blame

That you've lost your crown and your daughter
And your old respected name.'

And so he should ha' fought him and St George should ha'
won, and your useless King done-for, and then you'd have
had a play and a marriage worth celebrating – but as for all
this, it's just rubbish and insulting – I haven't got patience.
Go on, Constable, get rid of 'em, there's no two ways.

CONSTABLE. Ho, indeed, is that so? I'll attend to *you* in a
moment . . .

(*To the* ACTORS.) Come on then, aren't you ready yet? Now
I'm giving you just two more minutes and if you're not on
the move by then –

WILLIAM. Oh be quiet and leave us alone, you dreary little
jack-in-office!

CONSTABLE. What did you say?

WILLIAM. I said –

CONSTABLE. I heard what you said. Abusive language I heard,
to an officer of the law in pursuance of his duty!

(*He blows his whistle. Enter* UNDER-CONSTABLE.)

Ah there you are, Higginbottom. And not before time. Is
this what you call being upon instant readiness in the service
of public order?

UNDER-CONSTABLE. I'm sorry, Mr Hopkins, but my good
wife was just on the process of pitching up a statch, I mean
statching up a pitch, I mean, well, she's yet at it – I mean she
can't discern the eye.

CONSTABLE (*notices his bare legs*). What eye? Your –

UNDER-CONSTABLE (*who is in his underpants*). Trousers. It's
what I'm telling you. She's trying to get the thread into the
needle at this identical moment, but being as you know a
little bit dim-sighted – there you are, you see, look at her.

Enter MRS HIGGINBOTTOM, *trying to thread a needle.*

CONSTABLE. Higginbottom, you are a-casting upon me
mockery and confusion in the very presence of these male-

factors. Just look at 'em there – laughing! You can run this
fellar in. Put the cuffs upon him – sharp!

(WILLIAM, *who is laughing the loudest, is suddenly handcuffed
by the* UNDER-CONSTABLE.)

Now then, anybody else require any persuading? Or do you
do what I tell you and get that clobber on the road!

CROKE. Yes, Officer, just so – no more trouble. We're all going
quietly. Hurry up, my dears, don't waste any time. We're
not wanted here so we might as well be off.

ESMERALDA. But what about poor William?

WILLIAM. Hey, yes indeed – what about me?

CROKE. My dear William, you *were* rude. You were very rude
to the Officer. Most injudicious, my dear boy. There's nothing we can do, you know. We can't *all* be arrested. Well, can
we? Good lord, can we?

ESMERALDA. Yes, of course we can, why not?

MRS CROKE. Why not? Why, of course not – we have a responsibility to our public, Esmeralda, which we cannot
discharge from prison. Do not be ridiculous, my dear, I beg
you – this is no time for foolish jokes.

ESMERALDA.

A foolish joke
To Mrs Croke
Is altogether foolish
And true, when all is said and done
It gets quite hard to see the fun
Of being set upon the run
By all the cops in every town
From Bude to Ballachulish.

(*She sings, with tambourine. The* CLOWN *joins in, and the*
ACTORS *all file out, lugging their dismantled gear.*)

Close the show, we're a lousy lot of layabouts,
Close the show, we're obstructing in the street,
Our jokes are blue, our noses too,
Our cash is few, we've stinking feet –

Keep your kids away from danger
Keep your wives away from vice
Never let your husband talk to an actress
For what she does is not quite nice . . .

MRS CROKE. Esmeralda, will you *please* help me to carry this hamper and try not to make worse what was bad before already!

ESMERALDA (*resignedly lifting the load and staggering out with a swirl of her tambourine*). Oh, unjust expulsion, and unprovoked peregrination – I come, I come, reluctantly, I come . . .

CONSTABLE (*once they have all gone*). I will considerately take no action upon that last impertinence, but it's written down, you know – they're noted, in the book!

LUKE. I've just been reading a different book – in Flanders – broken bones and rotted limbs, puddles of blood, a chopped-off skull in a black ditch with· a rat that played peep-bo through either eye-socket – let them exercise their responsibility to that class of public and we'd see who laughed the loudest. Do you know what I'm talking about?

MRS HIGGINBOTTOM. Talking about – no. But I'll tell you what I think –

UNDER-CONSTABLE. Not when we're on duty, Mabel: Mr Hopkins does the thinking here.

CONSTABLE. Mr Hopkins' cogitations at the moment are upon an improperly dressed subordinate. I am about to request you, Higginbottom, to perform a routine function and I want those legs concealed!

UNDER-CONSTABLE. Yes, Mr Hopkins. Come on, don't you hear him – is it threaded yet or isn't it? You can mend it while I'm wearing it. You make me proper ridiculous.

He puts on his torn trousers and MRS HIGGINBOTTOM *starts to sew them up.*

CONSTABLE (*to* LUKE). Flanders? It's a long way. And you've come here upon foot. With no apparent occupation nor yet means of support. Who are you, what's your business?

LUKE.

> I am a soldier of the King returned from the war
> And here in green England I will live for evermore.

CONSTABLE. Carry on then, give details. We've had enough rhyming clap-trap for one afternoon.

LUKE. I was Adjutant's Ancient in the Second Battalion of the Twenty-Third Regiment, otherwise known as the Royal Loyals or the Grin-and-bear-it Grenadiers. I am furthermore the only survivor of the disastrous expedition – to the Low Countries – against the French – last year – do you remember? But we didn't meet no French. We met fever, we met starvation, pouring rain and flooded country. A third of us was dead already and another third too poorly to put one foot before the other. And then the French did come. Horse, foot, guns. In the early stages of their onfall I got a blow from a partisan on the corner of my forehead – here: observe the scar. When I recovered my senses I found myself alone among a great field of dead men. The entire English army. And there were some French and all. . . . So I came home. All alone and being sought for. I got across the sea, even. I was fortunate – there were smugglers, who took no heed to either party in a war that didn't concern them, but were ready and willing to carry a man that had gold. Don't ask me where I got that gold. There are inevitable deeds have been performed in Flanders this last year that no decent man should inquire after. But I paid them all I had and they brought me; here I am. I am on my way to London to obtain my discharge from the Army in a regular fashion.

CONSTABLE. And no doubt to get a pension.

LUKE. I have hopes.

CONSTABLE. Ah. But have you papers? What's your proof of your identity?

LUKE. Proof? Papers? Look, my friend, I am a man of many

trials, I have had experiences, I have told you what they were, I thought I saw you listening! And yet you ask of me for papers. Of course I've not got papers!

CONSTABLE. Then you're a vagrant. It's not allowed. I'm afraid I have no alternative but to ask you, as a purely routine matter, just to answer a few questions, you understand, and to assist the police, and finally, to accompany me, and my subordinate here, with as little fuss as possible, into the lock-up.

(*During the pauses for punctuation in the above-speech, the* CONSTABLE *and* UNDER-CONSTABLE *have punched* LUKE *in the stomach with their truncheons, slapped him with the edge of their hands across the back of his neck, tripped him at the ankles, twisted his arms behind his back, and generally reduced him to a state of semi-consciousness. Taken by surprise and winded, he has made small resistance.*)

There we are, Higginbottom, fasten him in.

He and the UNDER-CONSTABLE *set about constructing a gaol round* WILLIAM *and* LUKE *until they are surrounded.* WILLIAM'S *handcuffs are removed. The ensuing dialogue continues during this business.*

WILLIAM. Hey, wait a minute, you can't treat him like that.

CONSTABLE. Can't we? We have.

MRS HIGGINBOTTOM. They have.

WILLIAM. I'm a witness. I saw it. You just knocked him down and stamped on him.

CONSTABLE. I'll stamp on you too.

MRS HIGGINBOTTOM. He'll stamp on you too.

WILLIAM. It's a gross abuse, it's brutality. I'm quite certain it's not allowed.

CONSTABLE. Vagrancy's not allowed. Performing filthy plays is not allowed neither.

MRS HIGGINBOTTOM. No, it's not, neither.

The gaol is now completed by the addition of a barred door.

CONSTABLE. So there you are, in.

MRS HIGGINBOTTOM. In.

CONSTABLE. And there you will stay until an opportunity arises to haul you both forth and present you to the magistrates. Did you take off his cuffs, Higginbottom?

UNDER-CONSTABLE. I did.

CONSTABLE. Come on then, where are they – we may want them for someone else? It's our red-letter day by the look of it today, we don't want to be held up in any further good work by the lack of essentials, what did you do with 'em, lad?

UNDER-CONSTABLE. I'm not entirely sure, I think I put them –

MRS HIGGINBOTTOM (*holding them up*). Here!

CONSTABLE. Right, we'll leave 'em to it.

(*He and the* HIGGINBOTTOMS *retire to the side of the stage.*) Now you set down and keep your eyes upon 'em. Don't stand no nonsense, comply with no requests. We've not had many regular prisoners in before, so don't let your ignorance of correct procedure be took advantage of. In the meantime I shall make a tour of inspection of the parish and its boundaries: if there's any more misconduct, as it might be, infected by the bad examples we've already had, I shall know how to deal with it.

Exit CONSTABLE.

LUKE (*recovering his senses*). Oo – ouf – stamped upon . . . Kicked . . . Truncheoned in the gut . . . Oh: you're here as well, are you – bold St George for Merry England. Well, they say every blessed country gets the patron saint it deserves. I only hope your holiness is satisfied with the reception you're afforded.

WILLIAM. Really, you know, there is no need to taunt me. At least I was arrested trying to do a job of work, while all you were doing was –

LUKE. Begging – to be frank – vagrancy – quite true.

I gave all my filthy lucre
To the captain of the hooker
For a trip across the tide.
I couldn't ha' done worse
If I'd stayed on the far side.
At least in the midst of a war
A man whose clothes are tore
And whose legs are muddy
And his hands all bloody
Is greeted by the populace
With a degree of some respect.
They give you what you ask for, there,
So long as you ask for it direct
And when you've taken what you want to,
Off they scapa, double pronto.

I've got a cavern inside me – how's it going to get filled?
Do we get no rations, Mister, while we're stuck in your –

UNDER-CONSTABLE. No. I've no authority. Anything you've
got to say can be said before the magistrates.

MRS HIGGINBOTTOM. Unless, I suppose –

UNDER-CONSTABLE (*as she prompts him in a whisper*). Unless,
I suppose, you are prepared to make a statement. I believe
that's important, and I fancy that betwixt us, we could get
it written down.

MRS HIGGINBOTTOM. We could get it written down.

LUKE. Statement? Written down? Here we go then. Are you
ready? Got your notebook? Got your pencil?
(*The* HIGGINBOTTOMS *search frantically to assemble these
materials.*)
I, being of sound mind and both sober and responsible for
my actions, am also – are you with me – am also downright
hungry, and I'd be very much obliged if you'd –

UNDER-CONSTABLE. Oh no, that's not a statement.

LUKE. Yes it is.

MRS HIGGINBOTTOM. No it's not.

UNDER-CONSTABLE. No it's not. That's not a statement. That's Anything to Say, that, and it can be said before the magistrates, whom you will confront in – what is it?

MRS HIGGINBOTTOM. Due course.

UNDER-CONSTABLE. Don't you see? Mr Hopkins has a book, it's got rules in –

MRS HIGGINBOTTOM. Rules in. We're the Law.

UNDER-CONSTABLE. You've got to do like what we tell you. (*Enter* ESMERALDA *with a parcel.*)
This is private. Go away. Mr Hopkins says it's private.

MRS HIGGINBOTTOM. Yes he does, it's private.

ESMERALDA. Please –

UNDER-CONSTABLE. Oh no – it won't do – oh, look at her, love, she's crying –

MRS HIGGINBOTTOM. Oh dear, what a shame – poor girl, who can she be?

ESMERALDA. Please, your honour, my poor brother – I've followed him for miles and miles, I've been sent by my dear mother to bring him home to an honest life again, oh, William, my dearest William, how can you fall so low! Oh, William, leave this dreadful theatrical career and come home unto your dear ones, come home with me, William, today, for all has been forgiven!

MRS HIGGINBOTTOM. Oh my poor child, this is so sad and so true, he has fallen very low indeed.

UNDER-CONSTABLE. Is this lady your sister?

WILLIAM. My what?

UNDER-CONSTABLE. Is she your sister?

WILLIAM. Well, er, yes, if she says so.

UNDER-CONSTABLE. Then I hope you are ashamed to have brought her down to such a state.

WILLIAM. Oh yes, it's quite mortifying, I really am struck dumb.

ESMERALDA. Come home, then, come home with me – William, come home – don't just stay there but come!

WILLIAM. Esmeralda, do be practical – how on earth can I come home?

ESMERALDA. But I am sure they will let you go when I tell them that all has been forgiven. His poor mother has forgiven him everything, sir, everything, even the theft of the family pawntickets, which – poor boy – he didn't mean to take, only that he needed a little morsel of dry bread for his journey. Please let him come!

UNDER-CONSTABLE. I shall have to ask Mr Hopkins.

ESMERALDA. Do you think he will be lenient? But of course he will, if you will plead for us. Oh, Mrs –

UNDER-CONSTABLE. Higginbottom.

ESMERALDA. Oh, Mrs Higginbottom, you are a – you are a mother, are you not? This is a mother's cake. Baked by my poor mother and salted with her tears. Let him take it, while he's waiting for – for Mr –

MRS HIGGINBOTTOM. Hopkins –

ESMERALDA. His permission? Your permission. Just a cake. Made with eggs. Keep his strength up. You're a mother?

MRS HIGGINBOTTOM. Just a cake.

UNDER-CONSTABLE. Just a minute. Didn't I see you –

ESMERALDA. No. That was –

WILLIAM. My sister. With the actors.

UNDER-CONSTABLE. But this is your sister?

ESMERALDA. No. Not the same one. That was Chloe. I am Esmeralda. Chloe, dreadful girl, has not yet been forgiven. I am sorry to tell you that it was more than pawntickets in her case. Much more. Oh yes. *She* has been struck out.

WILLIAM. Struck out of what?

ESMERALDA. The family Bible, William, and so will you be too unless you do what I tell you and keep your mouth shut at once! There, can I give it him?

WILLIAM. Who made it?

ESMERALDA. Me.

WILLIAM. Ugh! Darling, ask me anything, but don't ask me to eat your cooking.

She passes the cake into the gaol and hurries out. WILLIAM *gives it scornfully to* LUKE. ESMERALDA *runs full tilt into the* CONSTABLE *who is returning.*

CONSTABLE. Ho ho, what have we here? Illicit visiting – contraband consignments – sneaking in and snooping round! Come into the light, young lady, explain yourself directly. Tears, tears, tears, she's half-hysterical. Higginbottom, what *have* you been permitting, the minute my back was turned?

UNDER-CONSTABLE. Compassionate reasons, Mr Hopkins, I can't really see there was any real objection –

MRS HIGGINBOTTOM. No real objection, poor soul, and all the pawntickets –

CONSTABLE. And what did she hand in to him, hey?

UNDER-CONSTABLE. Cake.

CONSTABLE. A what?

MRS HIGGINBOTTOM. Cake.

CONSTABLE. A what's that?

ESMERALDA. Cake!

CONSTABLE. Shut up, you'll blow me ears out. Cake, indeed . . . It's not allowed. At least it's not, without a proper payment. Half a crown or six fat kisses. Which?

ESMERALDA. I – I haven't any money . . . please, sir, please . . .

CONSTABLE. You haven't? . . .

(*He starts to kiss her.*)

Ooh, theatricals, how the blood boils over – a fair disgrace to the morals of the nation – ye-es . . .

Enter CROKE.

CROKE. Sir, unhand that lady! This is no office for an officer, restrain yourself for shame!

CONSTABLE. I thought I ordered you to remove yourself from this vicinity.

CROKE. Why, yes, you did. And so I was in process of so doing. But lo, a messenger, spurring his foundered horse along the highroad, rears to a halt and cries – 'Are you the actors?' 'Certainly we are.' 'Then here, 'says he. 'A letter, from the King!'

CONSTABLE. A letter from the King?

CROKE. The King.

UNDER-CONSTABLE. The King?

MRS HIGGINBOTTOM. The King?

CONSTABLE. For you?

CROKE. For me, Marcus Antonius Croke, tragedian – also comedian, and acrobat, and irregular entertainer. Read it – if you can.

He hands the CONSTABLE *a scroll of parchment.*

CONSTABLE. His Majesty's Privy Council . . . why, it's a Royal Pardon . . . all actors, players, buffoons, jesters, minstrels, tumblers and mountebanks . . . to be permitted, despite all offences committed against whomsoever . . . to be permitted, requested and required to go to London directly . . . in order, in order, to present plays before the King. . .! Have you just confected this—you and your confederates?

CROKE. Do I possess the Great Seal of the Realm?

CONSTABLE. H'm – and what am I supposed to do?

CROKE. Release him from his durance vile! William, my child, we are commanded, by His Majesty – our company entire – fame at last, success, high privilege – step forth, and come to London!

CONSTABLE. His Majesty, in my opinion, is most sadly deluded. But the Great Seal is the Great Seal and certainly outweighs such local applications of the Law as may be vested in my humble self. Higginbottom, let him out – in silence, if you please. I have a difficulty in finding words to fit this most deplorable contingency.

MRS HIGGINBOTTOM. Deplorable.
CONSTABLE. Be quiet.

The UNDER-CONSTABLE *opens the gaol and lets* WILLIAM
out.

ESMERALDA *(embracing him)*. Dear William –
CROKE. Come to my arms – not yours, you're not the Manager!

LUKE *has also walked out.*

UNDER-CONSTABLE. Where are you going – ?
LUKE. To stretch my legs. I thought maybe . . .

He returns as the CONSTABLE *appears about to charge at him.
The cell is locked again.* CROKE *beckons* ESMERALDA *and*
WILLIAM *impatiently.*

CROKE. William, we are off to act before the King! Buck up,
girl, for heaven's sake. Come.

He stalks out, arm in arm with WILLIAM.

ESMERALDA *(to* LUKE).
      You look hungry.
      Eat the cake.
      Don't be angry
      If you break
      A tooth or two
      Upon the crust.
      A starving man
      Eats what he must –
      Who knows,
      It may be good for you?

She goes out.

LUKE *(calling after her)*.
      This kindness I will not forget.
      Behind hard iron they hold me yet:

        A hand can open what a hand can shut
        And that stays true of every gate.
        I will repay you soon or late.

CONSTABLE. Let us not, Mr Higginbottom, consider that our work has been rendered, by this injudicious interference from a higher authority, entirely null and void. We still have one prisoner in custody, and by the time I have organized my evidence against him, he is going to catch it hot. I intend to create for myself in this district a reputation as a scourge of evil-doers which will resound beyond our boundaries. I tell you in confidence that I have ambitions extending far in advance of rural misdemeanours. Have you ever considered the possibilities open to a talented man like me if once my zeal and initiative can be satisfactorily noised abroad? London, Mrs Higginbottom, is the goal of my aspirings – and not merely a job there pounding the pavements and keeping a check on the drunks and disorderlies – no. I want to be a regular thief-taker – undercover, incognito – a Detector is the word they use. You'll have heard of them, I dare well say –

        They creep and creep in dark disguise
        And track down crime by secret ways
        With a great big hat pulled over their eyes –
        All is concealed till the end of the story
        And then, at the end – ha ha, the surprise:
        For the rogue, the knotted rope –
        For him that catches him, the glory!

    What's the time?

UNDER-CONSTABLE. Quarter past.

MRS HIGGINBOTTOM. To.

UNDER-CONSTABLE. It's a quarter summat, anyway. Does that tally with yours?

CONSTABLE. It tallies with my stomach. My dinner will be smouldering. So you keep guard while I get off – I'll be back in fifty minutes.

Exit CONSTABLE.
LUKE *has been eating the cake. In it he has found a file.*

UNDER-CONSTABLE. His dinner will be smouldering. What about mine?

MRS HIGGINBOTTOM. Cold meat pie, so there's no bother.

UNDER-CONSTABLE. Go and get it then, I'll eat here.

MRS HIGGINBOTTOM. Get it yourself, can't you, and leave me on the watch. You know I always like to keep an interest in your work. Besides, you'll want a beer and I don't like going into the public if I can possibly avoid it – there's all them rakish fellers there what look at me conspicuous.

UNDER-CONSTABLE. I suppose it's all right – Mr Hopkins did say –

MRS HIGGINBOTTOM. Mr Hopkins won't be back till he's eat his roast and Yorkshire. Fifty minutes was his word – a slice of pie takes five. Get on.

Exit UNDER-CONSTABLE.
LUKE *grins at* MRS HIGGINBOTTOM *through the bars.*

LUKE. Cold enough for you, mum?

MRS HIGGINBOTTOM. You eat your cake.

LUKE. Draughty, though. I'm perished.

MRS HIGGINBOTTOM. On account of the bars. Mr Hopkins had them put in with gaps in between them, for to see what was going on inside, do you see? He said it's for security.

LUKE. Good of you to tell me so, mum, I appreciate a bit of information, when provided free of charge and outside of the routine minimum.

MRS HIGGINBOTTOM. Oh yes, there's no objection to a bit of a chat, I suppose.

LUKE. But it rattles, don't you see? It's not what I'm used to. I mean, I've had a hard life, as you'll appreciate, in the army, but this locality is peaceable, thanks to you and Mr Hopkins, and we don't need a noise going on all the night

from a rattling doorlatch – twice as loud as musket volleys –
I tell you no falsehood, mum.

MRS HIGGINBOTTOM. I don't know there's anything *I* can do
– you'd best wait until –

LUKE. Here though, I've got a notion. I thought – if you'd
assist me, being a good strong woman with a generous pair
of hands – I could just smooth the surface of this bolt where
it fastens, then it fits a little easier and it makes a sight less
clatter. If you took the other end of this file I've got here, you
could pull and I'll push and we'd do the job in half the time.

MRS HIGGINBOTTOM. Oh, I see now – you want it this way?
(*She helps him file the latch.*)
Quite a practical lad, aren't you? I don't suppose Higginbottom would have thought of a dodge like this. Nasty noisy
door, it's quite a shame to put you next it, I couldn't bear it
meself if I had to sleep there.

LUKE (*as the latch gives way*). Oh darn it, it's broke.

MRS HIGGINBOTTOM. Oh, now you've done it. Now you've
wrecked it. You'll be in trouble over this, you know. You'll
have to pay for this, you will, when *Mr* Hopkins gets back.

LUKE. Put a bit too much pressure on. I never thought it
wouldn't take an ordinary expenditure of muscular force –
isn't that what you're up against every day with these iron-
mongers – shoddy careless workmanship – here, you pop
inside, mum, and just see if you can't fix it from in there
while I have a look at the outside of these hinges . . .

*They change places. While she is fiddling with the latch he
creeps away.*

MRS HIGGINBOTTOM. Oh no, you've done it now. You've
gone and spoiled this lock completely. It's Government
property, you know, and there'll be forms to be filled in and I
don't know at all who's going to have to sort it out – oh
where on earth is Higginbottom, why don't he come and
help with it?

Enter HIGGINBOTTOM *with a pie, and a bottle of beer.*

UNDER-CONSTABLE. What's the matter, Mabel, I thought I heard you shouting . . . ? Good evening.

LUKE. Good evening, Constable, it's cold.

UNDER-CONSTABLE. Fair perishing, I'll take my oath.
(*He sees what has happened.*)
Hey wait a minute, come back here –

He runs after LUKE, *who finds no exit the way he is going and doubles back – only to run into the* CONSTABLE *coming in the other side. General confusion and dodging about the stage. In the course of this,* LUKE *seizes the pie and bottle from the* UNDER-CONSTABLE *and tackled by the* CONSTABLE, *fells him with a blow from the bottle and makes his escape.*

UNDER-CONSTABLE. Oh my lord, he's hit the Constable!

MRS HIGGINBOTTOM. Who has? Broken off short and the screw lost as well, it's going to need a blacksmith.

UNDER-CONSTABLE. A blacksmith – more like an undertaker – I think he's killed him, woman!

MRS HIGGINBOTTOM. Oh! It's Mr Hopkins! It's Mr Hopkins – he's been bashed!

CONSTABLE (*recovering*).
Felonious assault would be the correct description
For a blow of this nature, of deliberate infliction.
Indeed, I would go further –
See, I write it down as a case of attempted murder.
The murder of a badged and buttoned Constable
Is of all crimes of violence by far the most considerable.
The man who would commit it is a danger to the State.
The Law has rightly provided him an inexorable fate.
Nought shall prevent him being tracked down and found
Whether upon English ground
Or upon the soil of France or Spain.
I shall not turn again

Till I have caught him and brought him
To the foot of the gallows.
Wherever he may go, remorseless vengeance follows,
In disguise, close behind him,
Till with chains and ropes I bind him.
I shall not give over
Till he lies beneath the clover.

(*He takes off his badge and gives it to the* UNDER-CONSTABLE.)
Here, you take this: you'll want it. Clue Number One: he
grabbed your meat pie. It's a good thing your good lady
here makes her pastry so very flaky. There's bits of it dropped
all over the stage. Couldn't be easier if it was a regular paper-
chase. Here's a crumb and there's a crumb: and here's a
crumb and there's a crumb: and here's a crumb, and another
crumb, and another crumb, and another crumb here, and
another, and another here . . .

He goes out, sleuthing.

MRS HIGGINBOTTOM. Did he take the beer and all?
UNDER-CONSTABLE. He did.
MRS HIGGINBOTTOM. Eh dear . . . we might as well dis-
mantle. It's not much use keeping up a gaol if there's nobody
to put in it and the lock being broke and everything, did he
leave you his badge?
UNDER-CONSTABLE. He did. So I'm Chief Constable. I
suppose we'd best go home – we don't want to look for
trouble, do we?

*They go off, dismantling the gaol and taking the bars with them.
Enter* LUKE. *He is carrying the pie – half-eaten already.*

LUKE. Being a man of some initiative and considerable self-
respect, I find my situation particularly irksome. In Flanders,
you'd expect it. But this is old warm-hearted England that
sent me forth to fight and welcomes me now home again with
iron bars and truncheons and the sort of coarse contempt for

years of service that you'd scarcely look to find in – in the deserts of Siberia. At least in such deserts, there are, as I have been told, bands of wandering Tartars who would extend the hospitality of their tents to the homeless hunted fugitive. Hello, there's someone coming . . .

(*He turns his red coat inside out.*)

> No time now for foolish pride;
> Let the glory lurk inside.
> Here's a useful place to hide –
> Open eye and open ear –
> Oh oh, I've seen this lot before.
> Gipsies or beggars or a tribe of Tartar horse,
> I think if I went much further
> I might do a great deal worse.

He conceals himself as the ACTORS *enter, to rehearse (with refreshments.).*

CROKE. The tragedy of *King Arthur*. Certainly it merits a revival, does it not?

MRS CROKE. In the days when we played regularly before the nobility and gentry, *King Arthur* was by far the most popular piece in our repertoire. It is really so wonderful to have the opportunity once more of putting on these fine old classics. Antonius, do you think His Majesty would prefer –

CROKE. I am quite sure, my dearest love, that His Majesty would prefer us all to be word-perfect. So let us run it through, here in this convenient meadow, and waste no more time. You can play the King, my boy.

WILLIAM. The lead, Mr Croke?

CROKE. It is the title-part, dear William, yes.

ESMERALDA. Sir Lancelot's part is longer and a good deal more sympathetic.

CROKE. Of course it is, my dear – of course it is, dear William, but really you can't complain if the manager decides for once to stand upon his rights and eat a bit of the fat of the ham. I mean, frankly there are two magnificent male parts in this play and any actor worth his salt should be only too happy to attempt either one of them. You *are* happy, aren't you? Have a sandwich. My dear, what have you here – can I believe my eyes – it is, it is –

MRS CROKE. A bottle of wine. I thought that some small celebration of our great good fortune might not be out of order. It is such a beautiful morning, with the birds and the daisies and the cows in the pasture – are there cows?

CLOWN. There have been.

MRS CROKE. Oh Charles, you might have mentioned it before – now you've quite spoiled the rehearsal – I wonder if we shouldn't move –

CROKE. Certainly not, we're very well as we are. Shall we start work? I'd like to run through that very lovely scene where Sir Lancelot first declares his forbidden love for Queen Guinevere. You remember it – my dear – in the garden, under the rose-trellis.

MRS CROKE. Indeed I do remember it – also do I remember the very first time you and I played that touching scene together, Antonius – it was at a special gala performance – my dears – in the courtyard of the Duke of Grosvenor's castle upon the occasion of the seventy-seventh birthday of the dear Duchess of Grosvenor. The Duke of course had his own private company of actors – alas long since disbanded by his unappreciative successors – and Antonius and I had been called in for this particular production, very specially, upon the recommendation of Lord and Lady de Brack – I remember oh so clearly how Lady de Brack said to her daughter – 'Clarissa, my darling, do you not agree with me that when one sees Mrs Croke as Guinevere one really knows at last what it is to be a woman?' Ah, those days are gone, and the water that has run beneath the bridges since has been by no means fresh and clear – but perhaps at long last we are coming once again into our own?

LUKE (*aside*). I wish they would come once again into the play. At this rate they'll have nothing to put on before the King but the litter of a picnic. Very agreeable picnic – I wouldn't dispute that – ah, there's worse work in the world than being an actor, it appears.

CROKE (*jumping up decisively*). Yes, well, now then, to work! Scripts, Esmeralda darling, scripts, properties, we need the rose-trellis, where is it? Set it up, my dear, no delays now – we rehearse!

(ESMERALDA *hands out scripts and brings in the trellis, which is rather shaky and she finds it difficult to erect it.*)

Guinevere, sitting down. Lancelot beside her, thus, the palm of his hand upon the back of her hand, thus – I think that's how we used to play it. We'll start from 'a double passion'. Don't bother with the trellis, child, it's only making difficulties, we'll carry on without. Ha ha, let me see –

A double passion wars within my breast.
Now that my love for thee has been confessed
My duty to King Arthur must needs fly.
He is my Lord, for whom I once would die.
Alas, he is thy husband too. 'Tis plain
If I am not his enemy, he is mine.

MRS CROKE.

Nay, should he find us here, his angry blade
Must pierce thy heart and thou on turf be laid.
Sweet knight, there is such peril in thy devotion.
I sorely fear it will destroy this nation.

CROKE.

Yet am I not still loyal to the crown?
I swear it, by this rose that I pluck down!

No, no, it's altogether too difficult to do it without props. I must have the rose – I have to smell it and kiss it, and put it in your bosom and so forth – trellis, Esmeralda, trellis, if if you please. The imagery of the rose is of prime importance to this scene – William, are you watching? You may find yourself playing Lancelot one of these days; learn, me boy, learn – there's a tradition in this part, you know, as in all the great classic parts – we ignore it at our peril.

(ESMERALDA *has set up the trellis.*)

Good, good, try again –

I swear it, by this rose that I pluck down –!

(*In endeavouring to pluck the rose from the trellis, he finds it is too firmly fastened on. The whole trellis sways dangerously.*)

Oh, for heaven's sake – when was this last used? Who's been looking after the props? Esmeralda, really, this is frankly quite ridiculous! I cannot possibly continue with this scene until the whole thing's been overhauled. Not just now, dear, not just now – we'll carry on from somewhere else. We'll get on to the discovery. Mordred, the villain, brings in King Arthur to observe the guilty couple. William, are you ready? I'll give you your cue:

But hark, I hear a footstep on the sward.

No matter, I have my weapon, I am on guard.

William, I am on guard. But against whom, might I ask?

WILLIAM. It's not quite King Arthur yet. Mordred comes on first.

CROKE. Well, where is he? Where is Mordred?

ESMERALDA. You haven't cast him yet, Mr Croke.

CROKE. Oh. Charles. Leave those sandwiches alone for a moment, and pick up a script.

CLOWN. What, me, to play the villain?

MRS CROKE. Impossible. Do have some sense, Antonius. This isn't a comic villain, you know. I don't see how Charles can conceivably –

CROKE. Then who do you suggest, my love? We are but a small company.

ESMERALDA. I'll have a go. I've played breeches parts before. And he is meant to be a young man. Is that all right? Shall I enter? Mr Croke?

CROKE. Can you fight ? There is a battle in the last act. Otherwise I don't –

MRS CROKE. Let her try it, at any rate. You'd better take your
skirt off.

(ESMERALDA *takes off her skirt – she has tights on under it.*)
She'll have to double with the lady-in-waiting in Act Two –
I must have the lady-in-waiting or my entire hysterical scene
will go for nothing. Remember I have to slap her, it's my
best moment in the whole play. So carry on, my dear, roll
your eyes and don't forget to swagger. You'll be wearing a
sword-belt, of course.

CROKE. Just one moment. If Esmeralda is going to play the
villain, and really, you know, there is no reason why she
shouldn't because apart from the battle it's not a very large
part – who is going to be Merlin ?

MRS CROKE. Can we not cut Merlin, my love ?

CROKE. I don't think so – he's most important – he has to
warn Lancelot about the – no no, we can't cut him. It would
be better to cut the lady-in-waiting if we have to . . . I
have it. I can double Merlin with Lancelot, play it myself.
A white beard, sky-blue mantle, throw it over my armour –
the character is attractive – sophisticated, whimsical, rather
terrifying when he prophesies. I've never played him. It's
a challenge.

ESMERALDA. They have a conversation.

CROKE. Who has a conversation ?

ESMERALDA. Merlin and Lancelot. They have a conversation.

MRS CROKE. So you can't play them both.

CROKE. Esmeralda, this is a classical poetical tragedy. The
Dramatis Personae do not have 'conversations'. Their dialogue is couched in a splendour of language, which –

MRS CROKE. Which leaves us with Charles, who is the only
member of the company not yet provided with a part.

WILLIAM. It is possible, of course, we have chosen the wrong
play.

MRS CROKE. I had set my heart on playing Guinevere before the King and all his Court.

CLOWN. Tell you what, I'll send him up a bit. You know, make him a kind of absent-minded professor type – his magic spells always going wrong and losing his spectacles, that kind of thing. Supposing he should have got muddled with one of his enchantments and every time he comes in he has to roll in upside down – like this – you see, he's lost his centre of gravity – hilarious really – besides, we need a bit of comic relief if we're on in front of royalty – they can't stand the heavy stuff, get far too much of that in their ordinary life. Look, I'll do it again, just to show you, what do you think of it – ?

CROKE. No. This is classical poetical tragedy. We cannot possibly –

MRS CROKE. Indeed we cannot. So what is the solution?

LUKE *comes forward.*

LUKE. Me. I'm not precisely whimsical, and certainly not sophisticated. But the terrific prophecy bit ought not to be too difficult. My voice is well trained, having had experience of half the parade grounds in England, let alone three-quarters of the battle-fields of Europe, and my physique is well adapted to any running, jumping, stamping or strutting that may be in request. I don't expect you to take me straight away without an opportunity to shew what I can do: but give me a script and half a moment to study it and I'll let you have an earful . . . By the way, if there's any sword-fighting in the part, you've got the very man. Luke is the name – or the first part of it anyway – I'd better not tell you the rest of it: for personal reasons, which I dare say *you* (*To* ESMERALDA.) can guess at, I prefer to remain anonymous. Right then, what about it?

CROKE. We are not conducting auditions, my dear sir. This

company is already complete. Thank you very much – good
morning.

LUKE. I am sorry I intruded.

He retires but does not actually go away.

CROKE. Admittedly an extra man would be very useful but
I have no intention of lowering our standards by taking on
non-professionals. Particularly in view of this most important engagement. Charles: you will play Merlin and you will
play it with dignity. Give him a script. First entrance in the
garden once again. Lancelot and the King have quarrelled,
Lancelot has fled, Queen Guinevere sits weeping – sit
weeping, my dear – that's right – and Arthur is talking with
Sir Mordred about – ah –

ESMERALDA.

> The need to kill your most unfaithful wife,
> Whose crime has brought upon this land cruel strife.
> The blood of one will save the blood of all.
> Condemn her: let the sword of justice fall!

CROKE. Not at all bad, my dear. But roll your eyes a bit more.
You're not entirely sincere, you know – you *want* a civil
war – you are *dissembling* with the King. Carry on, William.

WILLIAM.

> I have loved this wicked woman since I was but a boy.
> If I kill her I kill my pride and joy.
> Why is not Merlin here? He would advise
> Some deed to do both merciful and wise.

CROKE. Now then, Charles, let's see what you *can* do.

CLOWN. Alas! The great Round Table is no more.

CROKE. You sound like a broken-down pensioner at the gate of
the alms-houses. Never mind pretending to be a doddery old
man. You're supposed to be a genius, an intellectual – a sage!
I know it is not easy for you, Charles, but it ought not to be
entirely impossible. Try it again.

CLOWN.

     Alas! The great Round Table is no more.

     Those knights so bold who numbered fifty score

     Scattered, confused, their loyalties divided,

     Some stand on one side, some on the other, some

     stand astride it –

CROKE. What!

CLOWN. One party thus, another party thus, and another in
     middle,

     And now I've split me breeches and I've fallen in a
     puddle!

MRS CROKE. I don't know how that got into the script, but it is
out from this moment!

CLOWN. I'm sorry, Mr Croke – but –

CROKE. Carry on!

CLOWN.

     My magic arts may yet put all things right.

     Observe these roses blooming, red and white –

     See, I will –

I can't do it without the rose-trellis, Mr Croke.
Esmeralda, be a darling – just hold it up for me –

     See I will strike them with my enchanted wand,

     And as their petals fall upon the grateful ground

     So shall forgetfulness flood into your sad mind.

     But one is plucked already. That is bad.

     By whom?

No it isn't – it's still there. Lancelot should have plucked it. I
have to find it on the grass, don't I? Here, this one will do –
Half a mo, Mrs Croke, I won't inconvenience you more than
I have to –

*Tugging at a rose he brings down the whole trellis again, this
time on top of* MRS CROKE.

CROKE (*giving way to despair*). And this. And this, ladies and
gentlemen, is the show we propose to put on – by Royal

Command – in London! I have never felt so disgraced in all my life by so incompetent a collection of pier-end pierrots! I think I shall disband the company. I shall do a one-man act instead. I shall recite Homer's *Odyssey*, from end to end, with no assistance, in the original Greek! At least I shall know then whom to blame if things go wrong.

LUKE (*coming forward again*). Who's that then – yourself?

CROKE. No sir. Homer! . . . I would be very glad to know what you think you are laughing at?

LUKE. Carpentry. Now, what you need is a good, stout pair of battens, say four-by-two by two feet each, fixed here and properly strutted. Hammer? Nails? Haven't you got any? (ESMERALDA *goes and looks for them vaguely*.) Don't you know? Give 'em to me then – let me handle it. Practically nothing at all that I can't handle in the way of tangible work and swift action in emergency. God knows, I've had experience. All right, so it's turned me sour. My manners as you might put it are a little bit abrupt. (*To* ESMERALDA.) But I think that you think that that might not perhaps be altogether to my discredit. Am I right then? What do you say?

ESMERALDA (*sings*).

    'I stand alone against the world
      On two extended feet:
    I need no help from anyone
      To save me from defeat,
    Except a hammer, and a nail,
      And timber all complete:
    Oh please dear, could you find for me
      A piece of cake to eat –
    Oh please dear, could you find for me –'

LUKE. Cake? Oh no – I'm eating pie. *And* I went down upon no knees to obtain it, I can tell you.

ESMERALDA. It's a question of ingredients. Sometimes one can find in cake what you'd never discover outside of it.

LUKE. Oh yes, that's very true – by chance, one might so find. Now according to *my* philosophy, what one picks up by chance is there to be made use of: but it doesn't necessarily commit a man to a dependence upon anyone. Hold it firm for just a minute, that's right, and I'll jam the nail in this way – no point in elaborating the workmanship more than we have to . . .

WILLIAM. You seem to be elaborating it a fair amount already. We *were* in the middle of a rehearsal. How much longer do you think it's going to take?

LUKE. Now look here: your holiness: do you want this done or don't you? You've got yourselves landed with a pergola that won't stand up: as it so happens there's a man here that can mend it. Now which of the two are you going to stand fast by? It's all equal to me: I can take me pie and be off: you've only to say the word –

CROKE. There's no need to be offensive . . . I'm sure we all appreciate . . . I'd be very much obliged if . . . What do you think, my dear?

MRS CROKE. Perhaps if we were to continue the rehearsal at a little distance – over there – then we could safely leave this good man –

LUKE. Luke is the name, madam. As I told you. Recollect it?

MRS CROKE. Just so. As I was saying, we could safely leave Mr Luke to continue his good work, which I am sure we are very grateful for. Esmeralda, perhaps you would stay to give him a hand and fetch him anything he needs. We don't require you at the moment, my dear – we do, however, require *you*, Charles. And I will thank you to forget your usual vulgarity and pay proper attention to the text, if you please.

CLOWN. You can't teach an old dog new tricks, Mrs Croke –

MRS CROKE. Yes we can, and we mean to. Antonius, come.

Exeunt the CROKES, WILLIAM *and the* CLOWN.

ESMERALDA. I don't think they liked that.

LUKE. Liked what?

ESMERALDA. Well, the way you said it. You're too sharp with them. Good God, they're going to London to act before the King! They expect a deal more obsequiousness from an unemployed handyman.

LUKE. A handyman? On the tramp.

ESMERALDA. On the scrounge.

LUKE. Just like them, so where's the difference? Besides, I'm not, am I? I'm doing a job.

ESMERALDA. You don't expect to get paid?

LUKE. Why not? It's measurable. Time spent and skill laid out. They do pay *you*, I suppose?

ESMERALDA. Now and then.

LUKE. But you stay with them?

ESMERALDA. I've no choice. I was born into the business. And I don't know any other.

LUKE. None at all?

ESMERALDA. None at all. Well . . . none I care to follow. What about you?

LUKE. Ah, but I'm a soldier. That's exceedingly flexible. Soldier in a uniform once: soldier of fortune now. Which means I can be an actor as easily as anybody. So I am.

ESMERALDA. No you aren't.

LUKE. Stage-carpenter. It's the first step. I'm stuck in here and I'm staying. Have you any objections?

ESMERALDA. No. But I'm surprised. Did you desert from the army?

LUKE. It deserted from me. That'll do. No more questions. Now lend a hand with the work, can't you?

ESMERALDA. You don't give much away.

LUKE. I don't. I've learnt better. Just yesterday, my little love, I was taught a thorough lesson. I can still feel the marks of it – two inches below my belt!

ESMERALDA. Are you married, by any chance?

LUKE. I said: no more questions.

ESMERALDA. I did give you that cake.

LUKE. Ah yes. To let me free. Surely not to grip me tighter . . . Yes, I am married. Twice. One of them's in Ireland: one in Flanders. The one in Flanders was a stratagem. Being on the run, you see, and short of cash. In both cases they had no business believing a word they heard me say. Because when all is said and done, a scrounging beggarman is not reliable. And that means *you're* not. So I don't rely. But, being dressed against my will in a dirty stinking cow-skin, I find it best to walk upon four legs and not be too conspicuous. So I am taking the risk and I'm joining your company. That is – supposing old Sir Lancelot there – what's his real name?

ESMERALDA. Croke.

LUKE. Yes. Supposing croaking Lancelot should confirm me in my new job – obsequious and degrading though it very well may be – I intend to stay with it, until – until what? You're on your road to London, right? To àct before the King, right? Under precisely what circumstances – I mean, Royal Pardons, and all that – surely it's not usual?

ESMERALDA. The son of the King of England is going to be married to the daughter of the King of France, to celebrate the end of the war.

LUKE. Ho, they call it a war, do they?

ESMERALDA. And what do you call it?

LUKE. A muck-up. I was part of it. Never mind, carry on.

ESMERALDA. And the wedding is going to be held in Paris. And the King of France has offered a prize of one hundred golden guineas to the best company of actors, either English or French, to perform a play before him as a part of the festivities. So our King, having, as you might imagine, no proper actors of his own, has ordered all the companies in England to come straightaway to London, and the ones that do best in London will be sent across to France. It won't be us, of course.

LUKE. Not unless you smarten your visual effects up, it won't.

You'll have gathered, I daresay, I have a pretty strong contempt for the standards of your profession.

ESMERALDA. Not a very flattering opinion. It's an honest one. You take my advice and keep quiet about it here; if you keep quiet we will. Even the Crokes will. They don't like the the police any more than you. I suppose that is what you're after?

LUKE. Keeping quiet?

ESMERALDA. Oh, about cake and all sorts of other things.

LUKE. Yes, you could put it that way.

You see, your Royal Pardon doesn't cover what I've done.
I am as you know a man on the run:
I must hide from my pursuers in whatever way I can.
I must construct for my own self my own dark secret place
Which might be on the stage with a mask upon my face,
Or it might be with the hammer and nails behind the scene.
But either way I cannot, I dare not, take part
In a gaudy public celebration of the beauties of art.
The best I can do is contribute in private
To the success of your troupe. If ever you arrive at
The King's Court in Paris, no doubt I could advance
And appear before the world as the equal of you all.
I cannot imagine they'll be seeking me in France:
But my danger is yet urgent. With your little file
I cracked the bar and broke the gaol:
I hit the Constable on the head:
If they catch me I'm as good as dead!

ESMERALDA. Go on, it's not true. It's like something out of one of our plays.

LUKE. Ah, that's just the way I tell it – I'm getting caught up with the atmosphere. General degeneration, you see, blurs the realities of life.

      I hit the Constable on the head:
      If they catch me I'm as good as dead!
      Oh oh, look who's here!
ESMERALDA. Hide yourself – quick – behind the bushes or –
somewhere –
LUKE. No no, this'll do . . .

He bends over a box of properties with his back turned as the
CONSTABLE *enters, backwards, tracing bits of pastry.*

CONSTABLE. Here's a crumb, and there's a crumb and another
crumb and another and a crumb here. (*He bumps his bottom
into* LUKE'S *bottom. They both turn round.* LUKE *has put on
the* CLOWN'S *mask.*) Hello hello hello – what's all this?
LUKE (*mimicking the* CLOWN). Hello hello hello – we don't
require any milk this morning, thank you very much!
CONSTABLE. And what do you think you mean by milk?
LUKE. Ow I've split me – no no, no no, no no no, perfectly all
right, Officer, not a stitch out of place! I thought for one
terrible moment – oh, I still do – oh dear – let me see –
(*He rolls over trying to see the seat of his pants.*)
      Heel and toe go over head
      To test the work of needle and thread.
In any case, we're out of your district now, you can't arrest
us here. So take yourself off, my good man, double-quick
time, poppity-pop!
CONSTABLE. That is perfectly correct as far as your trousers
are in question. And talking of trousers – (*He is looking at
Esmeralda's tights.*) Are you aware that it is not allowed to
impersonate the opposite sex in public? If *I* can't arrest you,
there'll be others that can. On a point of attempted murder,
however, my jurisdiction is infinite. Where is the man with
the meat pie? I've been a-following of his crumbs. All night.
LUKE. Crumbs. Was that the soldier?
CONSTABLE. So he described himself.
LUKE. Oh yes. Well, he ate his pie.

CONSTABLE. Here?

ESMERALDA. Here.

CONSTABLE. Here. Yes. That seems borne out by the circumstantial evidence.

LUKE (*surreptitiously wiping crumbs off his clothes*). And then he moved on.

CONSTABLE. Whither?

ESMERALDA. Thither.

CONSTABLE. To drown himself, no doubt? That road leads nowhere but the edge of the –

LUKE (*covering up by pointing in a different direction*). Thither.

CONSTABLE. I didn't say thither. I was about to say river.

LUKE and ESMERALDA (*together*). Ah yes, the river. Yes, to drown himself, no doubt.

CONSTABLE. He appeared to have something on his mind?

LUKE. On his mind? Oh Officer, he was –

ESMERALDA. Distracted with distress.

CONSTABLE. Remorse, of course, he would be. The bed of the river must forthwith be dragged. I shall go and find a boatman and we shall see what we shall see.

Exit CONSTABLE.
As soon as he goes the ACTORS *re-enter.*

CLOWN. Hey, you, take my face off.

CROKE. Never mind your face. Is the document safe?

LUKE *gives the mask to the* CLOWN *who puts it away, offended.*

ESMERALDA. The document, Mr Croke?

CROKE. The Royal Pardon, nitwit! You know who that man is who has just gone away. Why, he would like nothing better than to purloin that piece of parchment and then he would be able to arrest us once again. Without the Pardon we are nothing –

(ESMERALDA *finds it in the basket and gives it to him.*)

But with it in our safe possession, we are –

ALL. The King of England's Players!

They strike attitudes.

CROKE. Is the scenery ready, Mr Luke?

LUKE. If it is, sir, can I count myself engaged?

CROKE. As what?

LUKE. Stage carpenter, stage manager, property manager, scenic artist, wardrobe superintendent – whatever you like! Name it, sir, I'll do it!

CROKE. Then do it, Mr Luke – for we are to act before the King: we must present ourselves without a blemish.

Musical interlude, during which the scenery is set up – largely by LUKE – *and the* ACTORS *all put on their costumes and masks for the 'King Arthur' play. At the end of the music, they advance and bow, acknowledging applause. The* KING *and the* PRINCE *have entered behind the audience and they stand and bow graciously to the* ACTORS, *clapping with discretion.* LUKE *quietly withdraws. The* ACTORS *remove their masks.*

CROKE (*with emotion*). Your Majesty, Your Royal Highness, we are Your Majesty's most honoured and most faithful servitors, and for this opportunity which we have had tonight to act before Your Majesty in Your Majesty's own palace, we offer to Your Majesty our most unfeigned and humble gratitude.

The LORD CHAMBERLAIN *bustles through the audience and addresses the house.*

LORD CHAMBERLAIN. Ladies and gentlemen, the King has now seen examples of the work of all the English actors whom he has called into his presence. He is about to announce which of these many companies have pleased him the most, and which shall be the one to travel to France for the wedding of His Royal Highness. Are you all properly dressed to receive the King's decision? Are all your company present?

CROKE. All. Save of course the Stage Manager.

MRS CROKE. Surely, my love, we need not bother about him –
he is not –

LORD CHAMBERLAIN. Oh yes, indeed, madam, the King
desires to see everyone.

ESMERALDA. But he can't see the Stage Manager – *he* has to
stay behind scenes – he mustn't –

CROKE. Esmeralda, be silent. You are in the Royal Presence.
Of course the Stage Manager comes forward to be presented
to the King. He is part of our company, he must take his
proper place. It is insulting to His Majesty to put on such
false modesty. Mr Luke, forward!

While this has been going on, the KING *and the* PRINCE *have
come on to the stage. They talk in whispers to the* LORD
CHAMBERLAIN *with their backs turned to the* ACTORS.
The CONSTABLE *appears – dressed as a beefeater – in an
unexpected corner and speaks to the audience.*

CONSTABLE. I have been patrolling thus disguised through
the back corridors of the Palace. There was nobody at all at
the bottom of that river. Clearly the man I want has travelled
with these actors. Did not his very crumbs stop short beside
their resting place?

    I am now a true Detector:
    Oh, what glory I shall win
    If I track down my murderer
    In the presence of the King!

(LUKE *comes sheepishly forward in obedience to* CROKE, *sees the*
CONSTABLE *and abruptly retires.*)

    Goodness gracious, was that him –?
    I didn't have time to see.
    Never mind, I'm on the watch –
    It takes a clever lad to diddle *me*!
    Somewhere behind
    They have got him confined.

On my tiptoes prowl around,
Lurk with lug-hole to the ground,
His doom already is bespoken
His dirty neck already broken!

Exit CONSTABLE.
As soon as he goes out LUKE *re-enters with a false nose on.*

CROKE. Mr Luke, what on earth have you got there! Take it off at once!

LUKE. No no, if you'll excuse me, I have a very nasty boil upon my nose. His Majesty surely would not want to be confronted –

LORD CHAMBERLAIN. Ssh ssh – it's too late now. Stand very still and quiet and pray heaven the King won't notice.

KING (*to the* ACTORS). We have seen a great many plays in a great many days. We didn't like any of them at all, Mr – er –

CROKE. Croke, Your Majesty. Marcus Antonius Croke.

KING. Yes. None of them were funny and there were very few beautiful actresses – which is the only sort of thing I enjoy in the theatre. And the scenery in general was exceedingly shoddy. In fact yours was the only company whose scenery didn't quiver in the wind, let alone fall down, which happened to that deplorable lot we saw yesterday. Didn't it? Didn't it? Ridiculous. I don't know much about plays, but I do know a decent piece of construction when I see it. Pretty sound, this, really – what d'you think, me boy, hey? Who is your Stage Manager – he deserves congratulation?

CROKE. Stage Manager, Your Majesty . . . Here is the Stage Manager – he has a – has a boil upon his –

KING. Gad, you know – how droll! Some comedy at last! So you are an actor too, are you, are you, hey! But you did not perform? How's that – how is it?

LUKE. No, Your Majesty – not exactly perform – I – er I was to have –

ESMERALDA. He was to have spoken an epilogue, or speech

at the end, Your Majesty, but we didn't have time for it.

KING. No time? But your scenery proves you to be a real old-fashioned craftsman, we must certainly hear an epilogue from such an excellent and conscientious fellow – I think you have here a valuable member of your troupe, Mr Croke, am I right? First-class professional standards and no mistake about it. Carry on then, carry on.

CLOWN. He's not, of course, Your Majesty, the regular comic. Oh no, oh no, oh no. I should say not indeed. But let's have some equality, let's have some fair treatment. If you want some hilarity –

CROKE. If you want some hilarity, yes indeed, Your Majesty, we have here the very man. He does his little dance very deftly. Charles, do your little dance. Very deftly indeed, sir . . .

The CLOWN *dances with abandon: but he receives nothing but a cold glare from the* KING *and relapses into an embarrassed silence.*

PRINCE. Well. We are waiting. We are waiting for the epilogue.

KING. Do you not intend to deliver it at all?

LUKE. Er – very well, Your Majesty – yes.

CROKE. Oh good lord, this is the end. Our fortunes are all ruined.

MRS CROKE. How could you, Esmeralda!

LUKE. It's in the nature of a – do you see – of a tribute to the gallant soldiers who fought so well for Your Majesty in the recent wars in Flanders, now so happily concluded.

PRINCE. Very appropriate.

KING. Carry on.

LUKE.

> Starving though we were and tired and ill
> We never did forget our soldier's skill:
> We kept our boots clean and our bayonets bright,
> We waved our banners and we marched upright,
> We dared the French to meet us and to fight.

And when we met we fought till none could stand.
Our bodies now lie in a foreign land,
Defeated, they have said. But we know better:
We obeyed our general's orders to the letter.
If blame there is to be – indeed we did not win –
Blame not your loyal soldiers, gracious King,
But blame those ministers, who sitting warm at home
Sent us across the seas, unfed, unclothed, alone,
To do our duty the best way that we could.
We did it, sir, by pouring out our blood.
There is no more to say.

LORD CHAMBERLAIN. Indeed there is no more to say. I have never in all my life heard such insolence before His Majesty. Do you desire me, my lord, to throw him into prison?

KING. Prison? What do you think, me boy? Shall we throw him into prison? Or shall we send him to Paris?

PRINCE. I think we would do better if we invited him to become a member of the Government, father. At least he appears to have some common sense and humanity, which is more than your ministers generally can boast.

KING. We won't go into that now. But Gad it was a good speech, most courageously delivered. Shall you speak so plain at the Court of the King of France? Shall you, shall you, hey? I do hope so. We must remind them, must we not, that though we may be forced to seek for peace, we rule over a people who are bold, free, independent, and downright devilish awkward. Let those fellows over there forget that at their peril. What? At their peril! Go to Paris, Mr Croke, with your magnificent company, you will do credit to us all! Very well, you may disperse.

(*The* KING *with the* PRINCE *and the* LORD CHAMBERLAIN *remove themselves a little way from the* ACTORS, *who all gather round* LUKE *and shake him by the hand.*)

Lord Chamberlain, how will the actors travel? In the same ship as the Prince?

LORD CHAMBERLAIN. Their scenery and baggage will travel in the same ship as the Prince. There won't be room for the actors themselves. They will have to be provided with a vessel of their own.

The CONSTABLE *creeps in.*

KING. Well, see that it's a good one. The prestige of these fine artists is the prestige of the whole of England. Remember that.

CONSTABLE. Psst psst – Your Majesty – one moment – if you please.

LORD CHAMBERLAIN. Ssh ssh – go away – go away –

KING. And of course they will need passports. How many of them are there – six ?

LORD CHAMBERLAIN. So it appears, my lord –

KING. Then issue six passports –

LORD CHAMBERLAIN (*handing the documents out of his satchel to the* ACTORS). There you are, six passports.

KING. And – er – enough money, of course, to cover the costs of the journey.

LORD CHAMBERLAIN (*handing them money*). Three and four-pence each, for travelling expenses.

CLOWN. Only three and fourpence and all the way to France ? Quite fantastic. Are you sure that those are your instructions, my good man ? Oh make it six and eightpence, there's a darling – do.

LORD CHAMBERLAIN. I take my orders from His Majesty and from nobody else. There, sir, are your expenses.

CLOWN. Ho, we'll see about that.

(*As the* KING *takes the* PRINCE *aside for a private word, the* CLOWN *sneaks up behind him, takes off the crown and puts it on his own head. He then addresses the* LORD CHAMBERLAIN [KING'S *voice*].*)

Lord Chamberlain, three and fourpence is most damnably stingy. Give them six-and-eight!

General sensation. The KING *turns to see himself confronted by what is apparently another monarch, and is completely at a loss for a moment.*

KING. What's that? Who are you? Good God, you've got my . . .

CLOWN. I'm sorry, I didn't really . . . A bit de-tropp really . . . It was just a . . .

KING. Off, sir.

CLOWN. Just a little . . .

PRINCE. Take it off, sir.

CLOWN. Gag . . .

LORD CHAMBERLAIN. Take it off at once!

KING. Mr Croke, is this usual?

CROKE. Your Majesty . . . he is instantly discharged from my employment. Charles, you are discharged.

MRS CROKE. Do you hear, Charles, you are discharged!

CLOWN. But you can't sack me. Who's going to play Merlin?

CROKE. *I* shall play Merlin.

KING. Give your passport back at once to the Lord Chamberlain and take yourself off. Or I'll clap you in irons.

The CLOWN *returns his passport and then kneels, pathetic, before the* KING *to ask for pardon. Suddenly he straightens up again.*

CLOWN. I've split me breeches!

He cartwheels off the stage.

KING. Good heavens, such behaviour! And now, if you will permit me, I desire to speak to my son.
(*The* ACTORS *bow, and disperse.*
The KING'S *eye falls on the* CONSTABLE.)
Who is this person? Lord Chamberlain, will you please ask him to wait.
(*The* LORD CHAMBERLAIN *moves the* CONSTABLE *away,*

*but finds himself held by the buttonhole and forced to listen to an
elaborate whisper. The* KING *addresses the* PRINCE.)

Now, the Princess of France is a very beautiful woman. You
are not to fall in love with her. You are only getting married,
do you understand, in order to provide a year or two of peace
between the two countries. When my army has had time to
pull itself together after its unfortunate defeat, we shall once
again go to war.

PRINCE. With the French?

KING. Of course with the French. Who else then, who else,
hey? And this time, we shall win. When we go to war, you
and your new wife obviously will not be able to live together:
so you see, don't fall in love.

PRINCE. I shall take care to do whatever you say, father.

KING. Splendid, splendid! Of course you will. So: off you go.
You have my blessing. Your retinue awaits. And don't let the
King of France go taking advantage of you. Sound the
trumpets, beat the drums, the Prince departs for Paris!

Exit the PRINCE, *to the sound of music.*
The KING *turns to the* CONSTABLE.

Now sir, what do you want?

LORD CHAMBERLAIN. It might be very important, my lord.
This gentleman is a police officer, a thief-taker, he is at
present in disguise. He says he is on the track of a murder.

KING. Gad, you don't tell me! What, in the Palace, in the
Palace – where?

CONSTABLE. He is somewhere among those actors. I followed
him across country and I am positive that he travelled here
with them. Er – that is to say – milord.

KING. Which one of them is he?

CONSTABLE. Ah, there's the problem. You see, they *will*
disguise their faces. It makes it very difficult. But the original
Royal Pardon that got them out of trouble listed five persons
and no more. Now your Lord Chamberlain here has just

given away six passports and no less. So, making an allowance for that clown-chap that didn't give satisfaction and, very rightly, had to go – we discover, by deduction, that there is still an Extra Man.

KING. Oh, most acute of you. But it can't be helped, can it? They are extremely good actors and they're all going to France. I can't possibly hold them back. Who else am I going to send? All the other theatrical companies were absolutely terrible. Scenery tottering all over the shop. England would be disgraced if such hobbledehoys appeared in Paris. Croke's men have had their passports, and that's enough of that. They have received our Royal Approval. Have they not, Lord Chamberlain?

LORD CHAMBERLAIN. If you say so, sire. But who did he kill?

CONSTABLE. Me, milord. That is –

KING. You? Come come, sir – you're no spectre. Here is my fist – does it go through you? No.

CONSTABLE. Attempted was the word I was endeavouring to articulate.

KING. Oho, so that is different. Indeed, it's very different. Altogether, hey?

LORD CHAMBERLAIN. Altogether, yes. Murdering is one thing, but attempted murder of an Officer –

KING. Good God, we can't have that! What are you waiting for? Get after him, man. They've all gone to the harbour. You must catch 'em before they sail. If they're on board ship already, you'll have to hire a boat and follow them. Lord Chamberlain, give him a passport: and give him fifty guineas, for his travelling expenses.

(*The* LORD CHAMBERLAIN *does so. Prompted by a whisper from the* CONSTABLE, *he makes a special note in the passport.*)
And another fifty guineas, if he finally gets his man!

Our stern protective justice shall extend
Into the very realm of France and thence

Haul back by force the villain who would dare
Lift hand against an Officer of mine!
Go forward, sir, be bold, you need not fear –
Your King defends the defenders of his power.

(*The* CONSTABLE *is hurrying out when the* KING *calls him back.*)

But wait a moment, just come back – you must not arrest him until the wedding is over, you know – we can't postpone the wedding – international politics – very delicate – very fragile, so you just watch it, do you hear ? Find out who he is, wait till the festivities are finished, and strike home at that moment with all the Majesty of the Law. Very good – carry on . . . no, look here, come back here – don't let anybody in France know what you are there for. Bad for prestige . . . isn't it, isn't it, what ? . . . Well: what are you waiting for . . ?

Exeunt.

Act Two

The ACTORS *are rowing across the sea to France in a boat.* LUKE
is not with them. ESMERALDA *stands in the stern at the tiller and
acts as shantyman.*

ESMERALDA (*sings; the others join in on the chorus-lines*).
      'For travelling expenses three and fourpence per head
       (Rowing over the sea to France)
      They'd pay more to the gravediggers when we are
        dead
       (If it blows up a gale we haven't a chance).
       The King's great Lord Chamberlain found us a boat
       (Rowing over the sea to France)
       But he couldn't be bothered to see if it would float
       (If it blows up a gale we haven't a chance).'
CROKE. We must be about in the middle by now. Can you see
   the lighthouse at Calais?
ESMERALDA. Not a sign of it, Mr Croke.
WILLIAM. I can't see the Dover lighthouse any longer, that's
   something anyway.
ESMERALDA. We must be in the middle by now.
MRS CROKE. Very comforting to hear that, I'm sure, it's the
   deepest part just here.
CROKE. Come on, sing up, can't you. We've got to keep going.
MRS CROKE. Oh dear, I feel so sick.
ESMERALDA (*sings*).
      'Right down underneath us the horrible monsters
       (Rowing over the sea to France)
      Are waiting for the water to crash in amongst us
       (If it blows up a gale we haven't a chance).'
WILLIAM. It's begun to crash in already – hasn't anyone got

a tin can or something – we shall have to bail the boat out.

CROKE. Use your hat, you blockhead, and save your breath for your work.

MRS CROKE. Oh Antonius, do stop shouting so – my poor head will split in three! Oh dear, I feel so sick.

WILLIAM. Use your hat, you blockhead, and save your breath for the work.

MRS CROKE. What did you say, William? I will not permit impertinence!

CROKE. Just you mind your manners when you are addressing Mrs Croke! If you want to keep your job with this company, my man –

ESMERALDA. Oh row, everybody, row – for heaven's sake, row – do you want us all to be drowned?
(*Sings*).
    'Indeed I am sure we do not want to drown
        (Rowing over the sea to France) –'
I can't think of anything to rhyme with drown. Just carry on singing the chorus until we get there . . .

They do so.

WILLIAM. Oh where the devil is Luke? Why isn't he with us? Travelling with the Prince. On a great galleon. It's not fair!

ESMERALDA. Don't be jealous. You know perfectly well that somebody has to look after the scenery.

WILLIAM (*getting up in his agitation*). But he's only been with us a week!

MRS CROKE. Oh do sit down, everybody, please sit down – please –

ESMERALDA. Hey – whoops – breakers ahead – rocks and reefs and terrible cliffs – turn the boat round – out to – sea quick –

MRS CROKE. Too late – we're going over –

They all give a great cry as they are spilt out into the surf.

After an interval of disastrous confusion they all struggle ashore.

CROKE. Where are we?

WILLIAM. We're on shore.

ESMERALDA. It must be the coast of France.

MRS CROKE. It can't be the coast of France, there ought to be a lighthouse.

WILLIAM. It's a Channel Island – it's Guernsey, it's Jersey – could it possibly be Sark?

MRS CROKE. But there ought to be a lighthouse.

Enter a FRENCH OFFICER.

FRENCH OFFICER. A thousand pardons, *Madame*, but the lighthouse is out of order. We have so recently been at war and it is – how you say – a shortage of oil for the lamp. I am Chief Customs Officer in the service of the King of France – I must ask you all, at once, please – to come up with me to my office and to bring your baggage if you have any and your keys to open it up. Your boat, I much regret, is destroyed to smithereens.

CROKE. But it can't be – it's not ours. It belongs to the King of England.

FRENCH OFFICER. Indeed? How most interesting. Shall we discuss it in the office? Follow me – if you please.

They go off.
The CONSTABLE *then comes on rowing after them. He is wearing oilskins and sou-wester.*

CONSTABLE (*sings*).
  'Fifty guineas is the prize he gave me
   Fifty guineas is the prize I seek
   This wretched tub warn't worth that money
   But I'll get to France if it takes me a week.'
  Never would I have agreed to this job if I'd known what

was involved. Where's the British Navy, I'd like to know, lounging and boozing in the saloon bars of Portsmouth, idle, ignorant bell-bottomed layabouts – they ought to send *them* out when it's a question of overseas duty – over seas is the word an' all – over seas over, and into my boat – I've never seen such waves – wow, there's a whopper – watch it, watch it, wait a minute, can't you, I've lost me starboard oar – ow, help, murder, I'm drowning, catastrophe, help – police!

He too is wrecked and scrambles ashore exhausted. The FRENCH OFFICER *re-enters.*

FRENCH OFFICER. French Police and Customs. Will you come up to the office at once, please, and bring your baggage with you.

CONSTABLE. Hey, what about my boat? It cost me fifty guineas.

FRENCH OFFICER. *Vraiment?* And who gave it you? The King of England, *hein?*

CONSTABLE. Gave me what? The boat? The money? What?

FRENCH OFFICER. We'll find out. So come along then – *vite, vite, venez!*

They go off.

The FRENCH OFFICER *re-enters and arranges the stage to establish an office divided into two sections. The* CONSTABLE *is led into one room, the* ACTORS *into the other. The* FRENCH OFFICER *joins the latter. The* ACTORS, *like the* CONSTABLE, *are all wearing sou-westers, and from where he is he cannot see their faces.*

FRENCH OFFICER. I am sorry, *Messieurs, Mesdames,* but I cannot accept your account. You tell to me first, your ship belongs to the King of England, you tell to me after, you have lost all your passports. With the King of England we have just had a most serious war. We do not therefore regard the King of England as a trustworthy person. It is in my opinion you are spies, if not assassins.

CONSTABLE (*peering at them*). One two three four – something's gone wrong. There ought to be five. At least I've caught up with 'em. I must make sure I don't lose touch.

CROKE. I thought I had made it clear, sir, that we are a company of actors. Do we look like assassins?

FRENCH OFFICER. You would be very poor assassins indeed if you did. How do I know but that the King of England does not wish to murder the Princess of France? Then there would be no marriage. Then the war will start again. And this time, so he hopes, the English will win. You are under arrest, until you prove your identity. Actors indeed . . . *Nom d'un nom d'un nom d'un cochon !* . . .

(*He goes through into the next room.*)

As for you, you also have no passport, is it not?

CONSTABLE. No it's not! It so happens that I have . . . sh-ssh, this is private . . . do you see what's been wrote in it?

FRENCH OFFICER. Agent of Police? You are the King of England's police? And you intend to do – what? In the King of France's boundaries?

CONSTABLE. Yes, well, now – that's a question. International delicacies, fragilities, andcetera – what on earth am I to say? I've got it. Security Duties.

FRENCH OFFICER. Security Duties? To protect the Prince of England in case that some French man should desire to assassinate and thereby begin the war again?

CONSTABLE. Very forcibly put. That's precisely the –

FRENCH OFFICER. It is an insult to France to suggest that she does not know how to protect her own guests. *Monsieur Jacques?*

A VOICE (*offstage*). *Monsieur François?*

FRENCH OFFICER (*calling*). This gentleman is here to look after the security of the Prince of England. Will you please ensure that his own security is properly taken care of. *En prison, s'il vous plaît !*

VOICE. *Bien sûr, Monsieur François.*

FRENCH OFFICER. So go with the Officer who is awaiting you in there. Go quickly – he will attend to you. *Allez, allez – vite!*
(*The* CONSTABLE, *puzzled, goes out.*)
And that will do very well for *him* until the wedding is properly finished. *Allo allo* – what noise is this?

The FRENCH OFFICER *returns to the* ACTORS. *Enter* LUKE *with the* FRENCH ACTOR *and* ACTRESS.

FRENCH ACTRESS. *C'est absolument ridicule.*

FRENCH ACTOR. *Je vous assure, monsieur, que tous les artistes français détestent l'orgueil épouvantable de ces fonctionnaires. Eh bien, Monsieur le Capitaine, où sont les comédiens anglais?*

ACTORS. Luke! Thank heavens you are here – (*etc.*)

LUKE. Is everyone all right – they've not been mistreating you – are you all right, Esmeralda – Mrs Croke?

FRENCH OFFICER. *Les comédiens? O là là*, then they are really indeed comedians? But they have no passports, *Monsieur*, what else was I to do? *Eh bien*, you are now vouched for by two of the most celebrated members of the Royal Theatre in Paris – if indeed, you know them personally, *Monsieur?*

FRENCH ACTOR. They are identified, *Monsieur le Capitaine*, by this other English actor who has travelled with the Prince.

FRENCH OFFICER. Then it is with great pleasure, *Messieurs, Mesdames*, that I bid you welcome to France, to our beautiful France, and may you all enjoy your visit. You accompany them to Paris, *chère Madame?*

FRENCH ACTRESS. There are coaches prepared at the hotel in Calais. If you will all walk with me. Ah, how delightful it is for brother and sister artists to meet together in such amity after so cruel and so prolonged a period of war! Is it not that the only true temple of peace and goodwill amongst mankind is nothing but the theatre . . .?

She leads them all out.

The FRENCH OFFICER *remains and readjusts the stage. He addresses the audience:*

FRENCH OFFICER.

> We officers who serve the resplendent King of France
> In our so efficient loyalty we leave not a thing to chance.
> Therefore it is most necessary that, fast as they travel,
> To be with His Majesty when they come and to guard
>   his royal safety
> Is the act of a wise man, neither rash, my lords, nor
>   hasty.
> But, at a time of delectable festivity,
> It is not well to put on any front of hostility.
> As a decorous and subservient gentleman of the Court
> I attend my gracious master and I make my report.

(*The* KING OF FRANCE *enters, with great solemnity, with the* PRINCESS *on his arm.*)
Monseigneur!

The OFFICER *presents a chair for the* KING, *who very slowly sits down and extends his leg. The* OFFICER *places a footstool under this.*
The OFFICER *then places a cushion on the floor beside the footstool. The* KING *raps on the floor with his long cane, and the* PRINCESS *sits demurely upon the cushion. The* OFFICER *backs away a little and waits for the* KING *to speak.*

KING OF FRANCE. In fifteen minutes, *Monsieur*, we shall receive the Prince of England. He has arrived? He is correctly attended?

FRENCH OFFICER. *Monseigneur*, with the utmost respect and attention to protocol.

KING OF FRANCE. *Bien*. Before we have the happiness to receive this young man who is to be greatly honoured by the hand of our beloved daughter, we wish to be assured that all is prepared for the entertainments tonight. Tomorrow morning in the cathedral the marriage will be solemnized and immediately afterwards we must bid our child *adieu*. Therefore it is most necessary that her last night in France should be an occasion of artistry and joy. Does the Prince bring with him his troupe of English actors? Shall they contest with our own favourites of the stage for the prize of one hundred guineas?

FRENCH OFFICER. *Oui, Monseigneur* – the actors are in Paris. They have been escorted hither according to instruction by *Monsieur* Hercule and *Madame* Zénobie of the Royal French Theatre.

KING OF FRANCE. Ah, the ravishing *Madame* Zénobie! We have ever a tenderness for *Madame* Zénobie. We shall be pleased to speak with the actors at once.

FRENCH OFFICER. At once, *Monseigneur*. Admit the actors to His Majesty!

The ACTORS, *English and French, all enter and make their bows.*

KING OF FRANCE. *Madame* Zénobie, we are enchanted yet once more by the rare renewed pleasure of kissing your delicate hand.

(*The* KING *has actually risen to receive the* FRENCH ACTRESS *and he prevents her curtsy with a more than courteous kiss.*)

Indeed, *Madame*, you will permit us to kiss your delicate lips . . . Indeed, *Madame* – but no – this is not the proper time – upon a later occasion –*sans doute?*

FRENCH ACTRESS. *Sans doute, cher Monseigneur.*

The KING *now holds out his own hand for the* FRENCH ACTOR *to kiss.*

KING OF FRANCE. *Monsieur* Hercule – you may make your presentations.

FRENCH ACTOR. *Monseigneur*, I am most privileged to present to you, first *Monsieur* Crock, leading tragedian to

His Majesty of England. (*Kiss his Majesty's hand, Monsieur* Crock.) *Madame* Crock, who shall play the leading female roles.

KING OF FRANCE. *Chère Madame*, permit *me*.

He kisses her hand, but without undue familiarity.

FRENCH ACTOR. *Monsieur* Villiaume, *le jeune premier: Mademoiselle* Esmeralda, *soubrette.*

ESMERALDA. Sub-what?

FRENCH OFFICER. Ssh-sh-sh . . .

KING OF FRANCE. *Mademoiselle:* such beauty we had not believed out of England was to be possible.

(*He kisses her hand and rolls his eyes at her. She rolls hers back, which is clearly not the right thing to do. The* KING *freezes a little.*)

Enchanté, Mademoiselle. Now, *Monsieur* Hercule, *Monsieur* Crock, do you have the playbills for your entertainments tonight? May we be privileged to be informed what masterpieces are in store?

CROKE *and the* FRENCH ACTOR *hand playbills to the* OFFICER, *who reads out the titles.*

FRENCH OFFICER. *King Arthur.*

KING OF FRANCE. Very good. A story of chivalry. We shall expect it with keen delight.

FRENCH OFFICER. But what is this, *Monsieur* Hercule? *The tragedy of King Saul and David the Shepherd Boy?*

KING OF FRANCE. How an anointed King went mad and was succeeded by a young man of no account whatever?

FRENCH ACTOR. *Monseigneur*, it is a story from Holy Scripture.

KING OF FRANCE. There are many things in Holy Scripture unsuitable for public performance. You must alter the plot.

FRENCH ACTRESS. But how, *Monseigneur?* The poet who wrote the play is dead.

FRENCH OFFICER. Then you are to find another poet.

KING OF FRANCE. And what part is assigned to you, *chère Madame*?

FRENCH ACTRESS. I am to play the Witch of Endor, *Monseigneur*.

KING OF FRANCE. Oh no, you are to play a beautiful queen. Our favourite actress cannot possibly appear as an old and hideous witch, if she expects to earn for her company the hundred guineas we have promised.

FRENCH OFFICER. Have you the script of the play?

FRENCH ACTOR. It is here, *Monseigneur*.

KING OF FRANCE (*taking the manuscript*). We will rewrite it ourselves. Directly. You need then have no doubts of the correctitude of your portrayal of royalty. And the talents of *Madame* Zénobie will receive their best expression.

LUKE. That sounds remarkably like sharp practice to me.

KING OF FRANCE. Did somebody speak? There is a man in this room whom we have not yet observed. Who is he, and why is he here?

FRENCH ACTOR. Oh but yes, *Monseigneur* – a thousand pardons, *Monseigneur* –

CROKE. It is a terrible error, milord, yes – it appears –

LUKE. It appears I was forgotten. I was lining up at the back of the queue: but by some strange mischance I was totally invisible. Notwithstanding: I'm still here.

FRENCH ACTOR. This – gentleman, *Monseigneur*, is the English – Stage Manager.

KING OF FRANCE. Oh. But he is not an actor. He is a mechanical – a workman – he should not be here at all.

CROKE. Oh, Your Majesty, I do apologize, it is altogether my fault –

ESMERALDA. Well, I'm not apologizing. He's a perfect right to be here. If it hadn't been for him we'd never have got to Paris in the first place.

KING OF FRANCE. *Mademoiselle* – are you by chance a Democrat?

ESMERALDA. No I'm not, I'm a perfectly respectable professional. We've brought our own play with us and we're
going to do it as it's written – if you don't like it, you must
lump it. The King of England liked it and what's good
enough for him – well, I suppose *he* could have written a
better part for me if he'd wanted to – *I* wouldn't have
objected – but it never occurred to him. He led us to believe
it was a fair competition and so it ought to be – if it's not,
we'll go home, and I don't give a –

(*She is surrounded by everyone in a furious panic, compelling her
to be quiet. Her voice tails away, indignantly protesting to the*
CROKES.)

Well, I saw him kissing that French biddy over there all the
way up her arm, even if you didn't and you needn't tell
me . . .

KING OF FRANCE. No matter, she is English. Her ignorance is
excused. But as for this man, we do not like his tone of
voice.

He looks at LUKE.

LUKE. If you're expecting an apology, you're welcome, I am
sure. I don't want to be the man as fouls up the whole issue.
It's *my* bread and butter, you know, as well as these others.

KING OF FRANCE. This is altogether too extra-ordinary. We
do not understand it – we should prefer to forget it. *Monsieur*
Hercule, perhaps you will be so good as to conduct the
English actors out of our presence and – ah – shew to them
the beautiful pictures to our art-gallery or something, until
it is time to prepare for the entertainments. I suppose they
are aware of what an art-gallery is for ? They will not smoke
cigars, or write their names upon the paintings ? *Alors*, we
are happy to make your acquaintance, *Messieurs, Mesdames.*

(*The* FRENCH ACTORS *take the* ENGLISH ACTORS *out.*)

And now, my dear child, we must receive your fiancé:
must we not, my poor fledgling ? Before he makes his entry

there are one or two small things it were as well that I should tell you. *Monsieur le Capitaine* – you may bring hither the Prince to our presence.

FRENCH OFFICERS. *Tout à l'heure, Monseigneur.*

Exit the FRENCH OFFICER.

KING OF FRANCE. First then, you must not permit yourself to fall in love with this young man. This marriage is a marriage of politics, not affection. It is not at all impossible that a divorce or separation, within two years or three years, may have to take place. Once England and France recommence their war together, there will be no place for tender senti-ment. Do I make myself clear ?

PRINCESS. But only too clear, *mon père, hélas, hélas* . . .

KING OF FRANCE. *Hélas, ma chérie* . . . but such is this cruel world . . . However, you will treat the young Prince with all the courtesy and gentle deference with which you have been embued. He is not, I am informed, altogether un-pleasant. Had he been, I would never have given my consent to this wedding. Aha. I hear him come!

(*The* PRINCE *enters, attended by the* FRENCH OFFICER. *Advancing to embrace him*). Aha, my dear son, for so I must call you now. You take from our arms the sweetest treasure of our kingdom. Behold her. She is there. Do not make your reverences to me, my good young man – but make them to your wife.

(*He stands back and admires the* PRINCE *and* PRINCESS. *She rises from her cushion and he bows to kiss her hand. All very grave and tender. The* KING *dismisses the* FRENCH OFFICER *with a gesture of his stick.*)

Speak to her, my son. Give praise to her for her beauty. Our ladies of France expect their gentlemen to excel in poetic devotion. No doubt in England also this will be the custom – no ?

PRINCE.

It is a custom that we have learnt from your excellent
example.

Mademoiselle, if I were to offer to compare the white-
ness of your temple

As it shews beneath the dark curl of your hair, above
the ear,

To the gleaming egg-shells of the Bird of Paradise as
they lie in their nest,

Half-concealed by the soft feathers of their mother's
trembling breast –

Would you then condemn me for impertinence? I do
fear

That my tongue is too forward for true courtesy:

And yet it is compelled by the unprecedented mystery

That lies within your eyes. Your deep eyes, and your
smile,

Are they both an expression of the profundity of
your soul?

If they are, then I am happy and for all my livelong
days

My voice shall continue to proclaim my love and your
praise.

KING OF FRANCE. Quite exquisite. You are well instructed.
Now daughter – your reply?

PRINCESS.

Sir, the beauty that you claim to see in me

If it exists at all, is but the surface of my nature.

What lies beneath it must be revealed in the future:

I am certain that by reason of your love I shall find
myself so free

As to shew you myself utterly without any concealment:

And I trust that you will then find no cause for disappointment.

KING OF FRANCE. Perfect – upon both sides. So, my dear children, it is appropriate, is it not, that I leave you both together. You will have so much to say to one another, in private, as is only fitting, after all, when one is young, and in love.

He takes his departure.
The PRINCE *and* PRINCESS *look at one another.*

PRINCE.
>Because of England I must marry you.
>Because of the instructions of my father.

PRINCESS.
>Indeed indeed I would far rather
>That I should marry you because of what you are
>Than marry you because of France.
>Your hands are thick and red
>They would cut meat as well as bread
>You have upon your shoulders a strong round head
>Would thrust itself into a wall and break the bricks
>   and mortar down:
>Your body is the body of a hod-carrying clown
>And yet you speak in sweet words like the son of a
>   true king.
>This is to combine the earth and the fire
>In a way that we in France do not look for – nor
>   desire –
>Unless, like myself, we are lovers of all things strange.
>Englishman, rude, wild and strange, range
>Your arms round me. We wed for no affection
>But for politics only. Such is the instruction.
>Yet why should we not enjoy it while we can?

PRINCE (*a little embarrassed but touched by the fervour of her embrace*).
>*Mademoiselle*, I am a careful and obedient young man.
>When my father says 'Remember

The fate of nations is in danger'
It behoves me to mark his words and write them in
　　my heart.
I intend to continue as I swore that I would start:
I must not fall in love. Neither must you.
Nevertheless one flesh must be made out of our two
(By the blessing of the Church): and by the blessing
　　of good luck
Yours and no-one else's is the fruit that I must pluck.
Therefore, as I cram its fragrant pulp between my teeth
Let me not pause for a moment's heedful breath –
Let me tell myself rather 'Between this instant and my
　　death
There can be no pleasure equal to what I now feel.
Let me not scatter peel nor pip nor core
Upon the ground to remind me that I could have
　　eaten yet more.'
I shall swallow you whole
If only for a while:
Let us both tell our children
That we ate and we were full.

He picks her up in his arms and runs out with her.
Enter the FRENCH OFFICER *and the* FRENCH ACTORS.

FRENCH OFFICER. The order for the entertainments this
evening is as follows. His Majesty and Their Royal High-
nesses are to dine at six o'clock. As soon as the tables have
been cleared away, you, *Monsieur* Hercule, will present the
French play upon the floorboards of the dining hall. You
have acted there many times, you will be familiar with the
arrangements. Have your scenery in the kitchen passages
ready to be set up. There are no problems, no ? *Eh bien* – we
continue –

He makes as though to lead them out, but they do not follow.

FRENCH ACTOR. Problems, *Monsieur le Capitaine* – *sacré nom de Dieu*, but we have multitudes of problems!

FRENCH OFFICER. *Eh, quoi, par exemple?*

FRENCH ACTOR. *Eh, quoi?* Consider this. We have rehearsed at great trouble and with enormous expenditure of money and of time and of our vital resources – we have made it without question a matter of certainty that the work we present before the King and his daughter and her husband shall be of the most excellent quality that it is possible for us to shew. And at the last moment – the last conceivable moment, *Monsieur* – we are told it will not do! His Majesty, if you please, must find in our poor text some sentiments of subversion, republicanism, revolution, I know not what – indeed we are honoured he must rewrite it himself – but how long will it take, and how is it possible that we can learn the lines by heart? And as for *Madame* –

FRENCH ACTRESS. As for *Madame* – *bonté de bon Dieu!* – a completely new role, *Monsieur le Capitaine*, not even yet written, and my costumes already found and my make-up prepared – *oh là là là, c'est terrible, épouvantable* – *oh rage, oh désespoir!*

FRENCH OFFICER. I fancy, *Madame*, that it were better you should reserve these emotional transports for the occasion of the play. To console you, I will remind you that His Majesty has a great dislike for prolonged entertainment. Therefore such portions of your play that you cannot remember you can easily omit – provided that you do not omit any lines that the King himself has written. Will that make it more easy?

FRENCH ACTOR. *Mais non, Monsieur*, it will not! For it is only the lines of the King that we are likely to forget.

FRENCH ACTOR ⎱ *Entrailles du Pape*, but our reputation
FRENCH ACTRESS ⎰ from this day is entirely destroyed!

FRENCH OFFICER. No no, you are extreme. I cannot talk to you when you behave in this manner. I must go and see the

English actors and apprise them of their arrangements. Where are they – in the gallery ?

FRENCH ACTOR. *Je ne sais pas*. I last saw them looking for a cup of tea in the Privy Council ante-chamber – ridiculous, barbarous . . .

(*The* OFFICER *goes out*.)

Their own reputation is already more destroyed than ours. That is at any rate one thing we can be glad about.

FRENCH ACTRESS. But is it, *mon cher* ? Such ruffians, such rude peasants as are these English – is it not possible that the King will take such pleasure in their uncouth foreign ways, at the same time that he is *dis*pleased because we have forgot our parts, that in the end he will give to them the hundred guineas and we shall be for ever disgraced before all France ? Do you not realize it is necessary for the King to flatter the English, by reason of the peace treaty ?

FRENCH ACTOR. If only we could know how good they were going to be. Surely they cannot be any good at all, when their manners are so gross ? But yet perhaps they can – is there not a way we can find to make them so utterly ridiculous upon the stage that the King cannot for very shame award to them the prize ? Could we not, for example, contrive to make them drunk ?

FRENCH ACTRESS. It is not probable. They are, after all, professionals. I do not believe they will let themselves get drunk.

FRENCH ACTOR. I am afraid that that is true. What, then, do you suggest ?

FRENCH ACTRESS. A cup of tea. They cried for tea. They are hungry, *n'est-ce pas* ? For the English, remember, tea is more than a drink, it is a great plate of bread and butter, with bacon and egg, and – now, supposing they were to be given their great plate – and in with the egg and the bacon and the beefsteak and the rest of it, there were to be a little something, a *soupçon*, that is all, which would make them feel so

queer that when they come to act, they – *oh là, là* – do you not
see it – *mon Dieu*, it would be catastrophe!

FRENCH ACTOR. Be silent – here they come . . .

They both retire to the back of the stage as the FRENCH
OFFICER *brings in the* ENGLISH ACTORS.

FRENCH OFFICER. At seven o'clock, *Monsieur* Crock, the
French play will commence in the dining hall – it will
conclude, I suppose, at about a quarter past eight – the King
does not wish to endure delay between the pieces, so it has
been decided that you will act in this room here. While your
French colleagues are performing, you will have time to
make yourselves ready: His Majesty and their Royal High-
nesses will move from one room to the other and you will
start directly they take their seats in here – twenty minutes
past eight. You understand? Are there any questions? No?
Then I will leave you.

ESMERALDA. Wait a minute – grub?

FRENCH OFFICER. *Pardon?*

ESMERALDA. I said grub – nosh – din-dins – you know – eggo,
soupo – fisho –

CROKE. The fact is, sir, we *are* hungry, and we wondered if any
arrangement –

FRENCH OFFICER. That, *Monsieur*, I regret, is not part of my
function.

The FRENCH OFFICER *goes out.*

WILLIAM (*reading a piece of paper over to himself*). We, the
undersigned, being members of His Britannic Majesty's
Company of Players, at present on tour in France, desire to
protest against –

CROKE. What on earth do you think you're doing? We must
get ready for the play. Come along now, Luke – where are
you, Luke, set the stage up at once, we have very little time.

WILLIAM. I am composing a formal protest, Mr Croke. The

French King himself is writing the play for his own actors to appear in. Clearly the prize has been awarded in advance. It is absolutely monstrous.

LUKE *and* ESMERALDA *start to erect the stage.*

CROKE. You are quite right. It *is* monstrous. But really, William, you should know better than to make a public quarrel about it. We must endure these political intrigues for I am sure it is political – with professional equanimity. Let us all make certain – all of us, my dears – that our own work, at any rate, should be beyond reproach – and keep these disruptive protests for a later date. When we get home to London would be the best time to make complaints. It is most unprofessional to start off with such ill-feeling.

MRS CROKE. But a protest in London, Antonius, will not bring back the hundred guineas.

CROKE. Nor will a protest in Paris, my dear – I can assure you of that.

MRS CROKE. At least they might have offered us something to eat. I saw the French actors quite distinctly sitting down to bowls of soup and glasses of wine – when I attempted to join them some sort of butler informed me that all the tables were reserved. We are very definitely being treated – from the beginning – as inferiors – and I feel it very deeply.

The FRENCH ACTOR *comes forward.*

FRENCH ACTOR. *Madame,* you do mistake. There was no intention whatever to deprive you of your tea. The servant was under an unfortunate misapprehension. I myself shall take order that a meal be brought in to you. You may eat while you prepare your play.

MRS CROKE. Oh well, that is *quite* different – we are really most grateful – thank you so much, Mister.

FRENCH ACTRESS. *Madame,* it is an honour to render service to fellow-artists. *Bon appétit!*

FRENCH ACTOR. *Bon appétit !*

The FRENCH ACTORS *go out.*

MRS CROKE. How very charming the French can be – can they not, my dears ?

LUKE. When they set themselves out to it. You haven't seen 'em dealing with their prisoners of war.

CROKE. Luke, that will do. The war is now over: and nobody here desires to be reminded of it. Most tactless, my dear fellow – please recollect yourself.

LUKE. Whatever you say, Mr Croke – you're the gaffer – we're just the workmen and mechanicals – aren't we, Esmeralda– we don't exist – we're disgusting, we have a bad smell – we should never have been brought!

CROKE. That is quite enough of that. You have caused sufficient trouble already today. Please remember your place and do the work that you are paid for.

LUKE. I am doing it. Very briskly. I am neither clamouring for food nor composing impotent protests. Esmeralda is assisting me. With her usual incompetent charm: but at least she's stuck into it. I observe nobody else is. Right then: Act One. You want the rose-trellis up.

WILLIAM. It's not needed until much later.

LUKE. But you want it in position. Anything else! What about the big box ? For Merlin's magic. Do we have it in the first act, or don't we ? There was some dispute in London.

CROKE. We decided to have it. So bring it on, please – don't waste time. I would like to run through again just the first few lines of the very first scene. Remember the situation.

Mordred has sent the King a poisoned apple with a letter pretending that it has come from Sir Lancelot. William, you enter, eating the apple – you are feeling exceedingly ill, you complain about it to the Queen. So do it, will you – carry on.

WILLIAM. 'I feel a strange disturbance in my bowels . . .'

CROKE. Exactly! I thought that was the line. 'Bowels' will have to come out.

WILLIAM. Why?

CROKE. You ought to know why. It should have become evident to you today that one thing the French cannot abide is vulgarity. 'Bowels' will have to come out.

WILLIAM. Then what am I to say?

CROKE. What about heart?

WILLIAM. But a poisoned piece of apple wouldn't lodge in my heart.

ESMERALDA. It goes past it on the way down – it might have stopped there for a bit of a kickback, mightn't it?

She gives a belch.

MRS CROKE. No, it might not – that, Esmeralda, is – if any-thing – an even more vulgar idea.

CROKE. Quiet, quiet, I am turning it over in my mind – here we are – 'I feel a strange disturbance – I am ill!'

MRS CROKE. One moment, Antonius, I think they are bringing us our tea.

CROKE. Ah, tea, tea – tea – splendid, we shall all feel much better and be able in a few moments to return to our work refreshed . . .

Enter a COOK (*if possible, a procession of* COOKS) *bearing silver dishes with great dish-covers.*

COOK. *Monsieur,* it is the order of His Majesty that these few trifling refreshments should be provided for your company.

The FRENCH ACTOR *and* ACTRESS *have come in behind the* COOK.

CROKE. This is really too good – shall we assemble ourselves here – if you will put the dishes down upon this box –
(*While the* ACTORS *are getting into position, the* FRENCH ACTRESS *distracts the* COOK'S *attention for a moment by*

flashing her great fan across his face. She apologizes charmingly, and while he is smiling an acknowledgement to her, the FRENCH ACTOR *whips away the dish-cover and sprinkles poison in the food.*)

We are most grateful to the King – I mean, my compliments to His Majesty – I mean – er – yes, well, most kind of him to think of us. And thank *you*.

COOK (*accepting a tip with disdain*). Zut, alors, Messieurs, Mesdames . . .

The COOK *and* FRENCH ACTORS *withdraw again with bows.*

CROKE. Now: we're not holding up the rehearsal just to sit here and guzzle – here's a plate for each of you – and we'll get on with the work while we eat. Hello – he's only sent four.

LUKE. That's right. I'm not here.

MRS CROKE. Oh but Mr Luke, I'm sure there's some mistake –

LUKE. Oh no there's not. But I'm not daft, I took precautions.

LUKE *takes out a packet of sandwiches and starts to eat as he works.*

WILLIAM. Where did you get those?

LUKE. While you lot were in the picture-gallery, I went out and found a café. They have them, you know, in Paris – they've got tables, on the pavement.

ESMERALDA. But it's not fair that he shouldn't have any of this – it smells beautiful – what is it? Garlic or something – I'm not going to eat if Luke's not going to eat.

LUKE. I am eating. For God's sake carry on and stop trying to be compassionate.

ESMERALDA. No no, you must have mine. I don't want it – take it away.

MRS CROKE. There is no need to sulk, Esmeralda – if you do not want your portion there are others here who would be glad of it.

She picks up ESMERALDA'S *dish.*

ESMERALDA. Oh, but I didn't mean –

MRS CROKE.

Didn't mean but had to say it

Took the bill and couldn't pay it.

You'll know better in future, my dear, to make boasts you can't fulfil.

She begins to eat from ESMERALDA'S *dish.* ESMERALDA – *angry – gets round behind her, touches her on the left shoulder, when she turns her head to the left,* ESMERALDA *snatches some food from the right of the dish.* MRS CROKE *catches her at it and gives her a slap, but she is too late to prevent her swallowing a mouthful, in triumph.*

LUKE. Oh, leave it alone then, and fill up with these.

He gives ESMERALDA *a sandwich.*

CROKE. Our behaviour is deteriorating. You do not appear to realize – *any* of you – that in a very short while we shall be in front of an audience. And a great deal depends upon it. We haven't even sorted out that first line of yours, William! Get upon the stage at once and we will begin from where we left off.

'I feel a strange disturbance – I am ill.'

And then will you give me the rest of the speech – I seem to remember there are other intestinal references that may have to be altered. Carry on, please – and no more foolery.

WILLIAM.

I feel a strange disturbance – I am ill.

Can I have eaten something I should not?

Can I have –

CROKE. No no no – where is the dignity and the royalty of this part? You seem to have forgotten everything we have rehearsed! What's the matter? Are you ill?

WILLIAM. Of course I'm ill – I've just said so, haven't I?

CROKE. I don't mean in the play. I mean in fact. Are you ill, boy, or what's wrong with you?

WILLIAM. I don't exactly know. What about you?

CROKE. What about me? I am always ill. It is idiots like you that make me ill. Good lord, boy, I remember playing Alexander the Great before an audience of drunken coal-heavers when I had a temperature of a hundred and six! And they gave me the longest round of applause at the end of it that I ever remember in the whole of my career! I spent six weeks in bed after that experience and the doctors all said they had seen nothing like it – didn't they, my dear?

MRS CROKE. Oh, don't talk about it, Antonius, the very thought of it brings me out in – in – oh dear, what *is* the matter with me? I shall faint if I have to stand here any longer.

There is a sound of trumpets offstage – and applause.

CROKE. Oh good lord, it must be later than we thought. There is the French play starting already . . . Are any of us fit enough to go on tonight – at all? Whatever is the matter with this company?

LUKE. There's nothing the matter with me.

CROKE. I think we are all suffering from exhaustion after the hardships of the journey, or something – perhaps we should all go and rest for an hour. Yes, yes, a good rest, get our feet up, lie down . . . Luke, if you are sure you are feeling fit, you had better hold the fort here – see that everything is quite ready . . . and – er – don't forget to give us a call in plenty of time to begin . . . oh dear me, I am so giddy . . .

He staggers off, followed by MRS CROKE *and* WILLIAM, *all more or less incapacitated.*

LUKE. You know what's wrong with them, don't you – ?

ESMERALDA. No. What is wrong with them? They're not used to eating snails, I suppose, but neither am I and I did have quite a mouthful –

LUKE. Yes, I know you did, and you'd best watch out, dear –
or you will be going the same way. Why, it's obvious what's
happened. Those Froggy so-and-sos have hocussed the grub.

ESMERALDA. Hocussed it ?

LUKE. Alright, then, poisoned it – though I doubt if they'd have
the guts to run so far as murder. More likely just enough to
make everyone sick. It's a real old French trick – you know –
we had a half-a-company of pikemen laid out flat on their
backs once with galloping diarrhoea after eating their breakfasts in a little village alehouse just short of the Belgian
border. If they'd stoop to it in wartime, when there's supposed
to be international rules of conduct, they aren't very likely to
have any scruples with artistic prestige in question. It's a pity,
really, isn't it, that *we* didn't think of it first ?

ESMERALDA. So what are we going to do ?

LUKE. Ah, it may be a false alarm. It could be just they're
over-tired like the old fellow says. We'd better carry on and
make sure it's all ready, and then if they're still incapable,
we'll have to call the whole show off.

ESMERALDA. But we can't do that, Luke – what about the
hundred guineas ?

LUKE. You weren't counting on that – were you ? Not here –
not in Paris, with the leading lady of the Frog actors being
the sweetheart of the King ? Why, we never had the chance
of a pig-in-the-shambles of winning that there prize, so don't
deceive yourself. Now look here, are you certain that you
aren't feeling off it ? I don't give a damn over the state of old
Croke's stomach but I'd hate to see *you* going down in a
convulsion.

ESMERALDA. I have no intention whatever of going down in a
convulsion, so stop trying to be compassionate.

LUKE. Who's trying to be compassionate ? What I said, I said
on purpose. I said –

ESMERALDA. Luke, we've got to *do* something! Find a doctor,
find an antidote –

LUKE. No no no, use your sense, girl – Frog doctors – Frog poisons? Ah, not at all, nobody's dead. And they're not going to be neither. Let nature take her course: and serve 'em right for being so greedy. But you, you weren't greedy. Yet you did eat something. So how are you? Tell the truth then. I'm asking *you*.

ESMERALDA. I'm all right. At the moment . . . Well, more or less . . . Yes. Now *I'm* asking *you*. I'm not bothered about Flanders. But what about Ireland?

LUKE. Ireland? I'm not with you.

ESMERALDA. You're not with her either. But are you inclined to go back?

LUKE. Ah, ah – the penny drops! Ireland. You mean that wife?

ESMERALDA. She still *is* your wife?

LUKE. Oh God – the truth to tell you, she never was, she never was . . .

> The product of a rainy day
> Upon the shores of Galway Bay –
> A little cottage with a smoky fire,
> The old man gone, to sell his piglets at the fair,
> His daughter left behind, so agreeable and kind
> To the drunken trooper knocking rat-tat-tat upon the
> door –
> Half an hour of bright desire
> In the middle of a war.

I don't know why I bothered to remember it, even. There's nothing about *you* to remind me of it at all.

They kiss. Then ESMERALDA *breaks away.*

ESMERALDA. Except the half hour.

LUKE. Eh, what? I'm not with you . . .?

ESMERALDA. No, I know you're not. You're a vagrant. You've no loyalty nor anything. The whole company's in trouble, and the play's ruined and you don't care! Where are you going?

LUKE.

>My travelling expenses are not yet all spent.
>I am going back to the café
>Where I am perfectly happy
>To sit down in content
>On my own, all alone,
>And drink a bottle of wine.
>Nothing that you have
>Has anything to do,
>As far as I can see,
>With anything of mine.

Good-bye . . .

He makes to leave.

ESMERALDA. Oh, wait a minute, you silly man – I didn't mean –

LUKE.

>Didn't mean but had to say it
>Took the bill and couldn't pay it.

Heard that before somewhere, haven't we, this afternoon ?

He goes out.

ESMERALDA. And now he's gone. Well, I'm not going to let him sit all alone in the café – he's quite ridiculous to be so touchy.

>I shall go after him and follow him
>And if necessary I shall marry him:
>A single man of his age and attainments
>Has no right to lay claim to such proud independence.

She goes out after him.
She immediately returns.

But I can't go – and neither can he – we can't leave the stage and all our props like this – oh why not, anyway? – there isn't going to be a play and even if there is who on earth will want to steal any of this old lumber . . . wait a minute, here's an Officer – I'll ask him to keep an eye on it.

(*Enter the* CONSTABLE *disguised as a* FRENCH OFFICER.)

Excuse me – I wonder if you would mind looking after our stage until we come back?

CONSTABLE (*recognizing her with alarm, and concealing his face*). Not to speako Anglish – *polly-voo franzey, silver-plate.*

ESMERALDA. Oh dear – *noo: tootersweet: retoorn: sivoo-play: regarday apray no stahge? Sivoo-play?*

CONSTABLE (*anxious to be rid of her*). *We – wee-wee – wee.*

ESMERALDA. Thank you very much – er – *mercy bocoo. Bong swarr.*

CONSTABLE. *We – we-wee . . .*

(*She goes out.*)

Eh, that was a close one. For I am not what I seem. Not bad, though? With the accent and all? *Commong voo portey voo mounseer? Quelle* terrible weather *noos avongs ohjoort-wee!* Of course this disguising business would be a darn sight more pleasurable if it was done with the direct aim of catching the murderer. Instead of which I am forced to conceal myself from my own alleged colleagues – I mean, the French police, who locked me up, no less, in some sort of a fortress. By an intrepid manoeuvre, I managed to knock one of them over the nut and put on his change of raiment. Boldly I set forth, saluting to left and right, until I attained the open country. A discreet use of the lingo, picked ûp during my confinement, enabled me to get to Paris, and by means of quite remarkable effrontery and cheek I obtained entrance into the Royal Palace. So: here I am, and here's the traces of the one I'm after. I don't know where *she's* gone off to – but she didn't recognize me, which is good – and apparently the play has not yet taken place.

(*A burst of laughter and slow handclapping from offstage.*)

Ah – there is already entertainment now proceeding in some other room.

(*Boos and whistles.*)

And not, by the sound of it, particularly successful. Now, when they come to perform in here, I shall – by virtue of my uniform – take a discreet place in the wings and observe what's going on. I shall count the members of the cast, both on and off the stage, and when I have succeeded in making the numbers up to five, I shall then be enabled to eliminate the innocent parties, and in the end identify the miscreant in their midst. Which is good routine police work and just what I'm cut out for.

(*The sounds of audience disapproval offstage reach a crescendo. The* PRINCESS *runs in, smothering hysterical laughter – she flops down on the box and gives way to it in private.*)

Hey-up, here comes one of them. No she's not though – she's a stranger – there was but two women actors with the company and neither of 'em was her – you don't suppose that she could be a *he*? I mean, he has been in the habit of concealing himself very cleverly – I wouldn't put it past him to try to pass off as a woman – it's just what you'd expect when you're dealing with theatricals – no sense of morality or public decency whatever. I'll keep well into the background and observe his behaviour while he thinks he is alone. That is always most indicative.

PRINCESS. *Oh, par ma foi – quelle drôlerie fantastique!* It was necessary for me to go away otherwise I should have burst – and for a Princess of France to give way to helpless laughter in the middle of a play would have been so disgraceful – my father would never have forgiven me – never –

(*She laughs again.*)

They forgot – *oh mon Dieu* – they forgot every line my father had written for them, and *Madame* Zénobie whom I cannot abide, she burst into tears in the middle of the stage and she turns to the audience and my father in the middle of it and she curses and swears at us all like a fishwife in the market – and she strikes *Monsieur* Hercule across the face with her fist and he kicks her in the bottom – *oh, mon Dieu*, I should not say that word – it is not a good word for a Princess of France – but he kicks her at any rate where I have wanted for so many years for to kick her myself – and she falls upon the stage and all the audience whistle and shout – and there is my father with a face like the public executioner – he cannot speak, he is so angry – he will never again, never, speak to *Madame* Zénobie – she must earn her living from this day forth in the cheap workmen's cabarets and the little theatres of the streets and for that I am so happy – she was an avaricious wicked woman and now thank God is she punished!

CONSTABLE. His demeanour – if it *is* his – is clearly uncontrolled, see, he rolls about and gnaws the backs of his hands as though in the torments of most justified remorse. Now what I think I'd better do is to creep up behind him and give him – at what we call the psychological moment – a little reminder of his crime. Watch me – this is crafty . . .

(*He creeps up behind the* PRINCESS, *sits down with his back to her, pulls his hat down over his eyes, and speaks in an unexpected high strained voice.*)

Blood on a bottle and a hole in his head
But strange to say he was not dead.

PRINCESS (*whipping round*). Eh, bon Dieu – quoi?

CONSTABLE.

You'd better have buried him where he lay
Lest he walk and talk on a latter day.

(*He whips round too and seizes her.*)

Right, you're frightened. Pale as death, you give away your very soul! Take off that wig.

PRINCESS. *Qu'est-ce que c'est que ça? Un gendarme de mon père? Vous m'avez suivi, n'est-ce pas, parce-que le roi mon père croit que j'aime le prince et je veux qu'il me baise dans une chambre particulière – mais ce n'est pas vrai – je ne suis pas fausse et je vous assure, Monsieur –*

CONSTABLE. Jabber jabber jabber – ? You can't deceive me,

you're as English as I am. I said take it off. And we'll have off
that gown and all – I want to see the soldier's coat you wear
beneath it –

Enter PRINCE.

PRINCE. Good God, sir, take your hands off!

He grabs the CONSTABLE *and throws him across the stage.*

CONSTABLE. Ah – an accomplice. So I'll take you in as well.
At least you haven't got the gall to try and talk in French –
why, I could tell this lad's accent a mile away – get on with
yer. Now just wait there while I get my truncheon found –

His disguise hampers him in this operation.

PRINCE. By heaven, you are English.
CONSTABLE. Of course I'm English. And proud of it – with
reason. I'm more than just mere English – upon this soil of
France I am the King of England.
PRINCE. What!
CONSTABLE. Because I am his Law and Order, and in his
unavoidable absence I stand here in his place. It is my duty
to warn you that anything you say –
PRINCE. So you're the King of England. Then who am I?
What's this – upon my head?

He indicates his coronet.

CONSTABLE. Cardboard. You can't fool me. I know a theatri-
cal property when I see one
(*The* PRINCE *has drawn his sword.*)
And don't you threaten me with your old wooden sword.
I've not reached my term of years and experience without
learning summat about masqueraders' ways and means.
(*The* PRINCE *pricks him with the sword.*)
Ow-hey-up, that's sharp! You've got no right to use a real

blade like that upon the stage – it's dangerous, you could hurt someone – ow-ow . . .!

In struggling with the PRINCE *he knocks the latter's coronet off.*

CONSTABLE. Wait a moment, that was a funny noise to be made by just a bit of cardboard . . .

PRINCE. Pick it up.

CONSTABLE. Wait a moment –

PRINCE. Pick it up!

CONSTABLE (*picking it up and weighing it apprehensively in his hands*). Where did you get this? I mean, please tell me that you stole it – or something like that – I mean – I mean, like, looking at your face, now that I have the opportunity to see you right close-up – I mean, in London, you were –

PRINCE. Yes?

CONSTABLE. Oh no – you're not the –

PRINCE. Yes.

CONSTABLE. The Prince . . .? I did, I saw you – just a minute, like, in London . . . oh my lord, what have I done?

PRINCE. You have insulted the lady who is about to be my wife.

CONSTABLE. Oh no – it's all a mistake – like, mistaken identity – it could have happened to anyone –

PRINCE. Yes it could – could it not? Of course you were not to know the lady's exalted rank. But nevertheless, she is a lady. Perhaps we should inquire of her what ought to be done to you? *Mademoiselle?*

PRINCESS. This man has laid his hands upon the daughter of a King – according to the laws of France he should be torn to pieces with red-hot pincers.

PRINCE. Very true, my love, but there's a problem. The laws of France are one thing but the laws of England are another. And according to the laws of England – why, this man *is* the laws of England. In fact, I would go further – I have half a notion that he is supposed to be my bodyguard. If we tear him to pieces, we tear the peace treaty to pieces. We're not supposed to do that – at least, not for a year or two. Therefore I suggest that for the moment we forget about the laws of either country and we forget about being the daughter and the son of a pair of Kings, and we knock him down and beat him up and throw him down the stairs and say no more about him. He, I guarantee, will say no more about us.

PRINCESS. I think that is a very good idea – I will help you to carry it out.

She does so. The CONSTABLE *makes his exit upon all fours, crying for mercy.*

CONSTABLE. Oh mercy, mercy, I didn't mean it – how was I to know that your crown was real gold – Oh! My lord, it looked like cardboard – cardboard, cardboard. . .

The PRINCE *and* PRINCESS *embrace.*
Enter the FRENCH OFFICER.

FRENCH OFFICER. Ah milord, His Majesty in a few moments will expect the English actors to begin. Where are the English actors? Gentlemen – *Monsieur* Crock! You are to start a little earlier! *Monsieur* Crock!

Enter CROKE. *He looks pretty ill.*

CROKE. Hello – oh yes, the Captain – yes . . . What, is it, Captain – please . . . ?
FRENCH OFFICER. Are you ready to begin?
CROKE. Oh – oh – oh yes, we are quite ready – yes indeed, we must perform. Oh – oh – oh – William, my dear wife – are you ready – we must perform, my dears.

CROKE *goes out.*

FRENCH OFFICER. But what is wrong with him, milord? Such lethargy, such apathy –

PRINCE. Oh, I expect it's just stage fright. Even the best ones have it, you know. But these chaps are very good, I've seen them in London – they won't let you down.

FRENCH OFFICER. *Eh bien*, I tell His Majesty . . .

The FRENCH OFFICER *goes out.*

PRINCESS. Just one or two more moments we have yet to ourselves.

They embrace again.
Enter LUKE *and* ESMERALDA, *their arms round one another singing.*

LUKE *and* ESMERALDA: (*sing*).
'When cares and troubles throng about
Just take a glass of wine
I've got my arm around your waist
And you've got yours round mine – '

ESMERALDA *stumbles.*

LUKE. Watch it now – that vinn-rooge is stronger than what it seems –

ESMERALDA. It's nothing to do with the wine, love – I think it's the hocussing starting to work –

LUKE. Oh no! Oh dear – I thought you said you were immune – hello though – we've got company.

PRINCE. I am sorry to disturb your – your carousal, Mr Stage Manager – but I imagine you are wanted backstage. The King will be here directly and the play must begin on time. Now the French actors, I am glad to say, made a very poor impression indeed, we're expecting a great deal from you and for God's sake don't let us down. You have a very good chance of winning the prize.

LUKE. That's all you think. Are they conscious, back in there?

PRINCE. What's the matter? They've not got drunk!

LUKE. Not drunk. They're all ill.

PRINCE. Impossible!

LUKE. I don't tell stories.

PRINCE. All of them? Not all of them? But you two are all right – both of you –

LUKE. One of us.

ESMERALDA. Both of us.

PRINCE. Well, you'll have to act the play yourselves. You'll have to get on there and do *something*.

LUKE. But *I* am not an actor. I'm a proletarian mechanical and I'm strictly non-professional.

PRINCE. But think of England, Mr –

LUKE. Luke.

PRINCE. Mr Luke – think of the national prestige. You have been a soldier, have you not – you have confronted the French upon the field of honour, Mr Luke – then here is your Creçy, your Poitiers, your Agincourt, today – pluck up your spirits, man, remember your country, remember your King!

PRINCESS. Remember, *Monsieur* Luke, the one hundred guineas.

LUKE. Now that's a better argument.

PRINCESS. I would so love to see you win it. You are a strong English roastbeef, just like my dear *fiancé* – I too am now English – go on, and win the prize.

LUKE (*as* PRINCESS *kisses him*). A much better argument – it has a great deal of force.

ESMERALDA. Not as far as I go, madam: but I am a professional and I fully intend to act.

PRINCE (*to* ESMERALDA). Now you're not to be jealous – it is but once in a lifetime he can kiss a real princess. And once in a lifetime that you can kiss a prince.

He starts to kiss ESMERALDA, *but is interrupted by a trumpet.*

PRINCESS. No, no, the King will enter.

PRINCE. If they can act at all back in there, they must do

whatever they can. If not, you must do it for them. Good
luck then, and good hunting.

LUKE *and* ESMERALDA *go backstage. The* KING *of* FRANCE
makes his entry, the FRENCH OFFICER *in attendance.*

KING OF FRANCE. We trust that the misfortunes of the earlier
part of the evening will be fully redeemed by what we are
about to see. *Monsieur le Capitaine,* we are ready, I think. Let
the actors commence.

FRENCH OFFICER. *Mais oui, Monseigneur.* The play may now
commence! Do you hear me, there? Begin.

Enter WILLIAM *as King Arthur,* MRS CROKE *as Guinevere.*

PRINCE (*to the* PRINCESS). Well, thank God, at least there's
two of them can walk upon their feet.

PRINCESS. But for how long – ? That is the question . . .

WILLIAM. I feel.

A horrid silence.

KING OF FRANCE. Do not let yourself be embarrassed by the importance of your audience. We lend a gracious ear. Continue.

WILLIAM. I feel . . . I feel – a strange disturbance in my
bowels!

KING OF FRANCE (*to the* PRINCE). Bowels? What is the meaning of this – this crudity, *Monsieur* – ?

MRS CROKE. And so do I – Your Majesty, excuse us – if you
can –

MRS CROKE *subsides into* WILLIAM'S *arms. He supports her
for a moment and then collapses also. They both stagger feebly
out.*

KING OF FRANCE (*rising*). This – is – not – what – we expected!

LUKE (*behind the scene – very loud and frantic*).
　　　Of course it's not.
　　　We've changed the plot.

>The King is dead before the play's begun.
>
>(*He enters – he has not changed his clothes, and is wearing Lancelot's mask.*)
>
>Who is to continue?
>
>I alone survive:
>
>King Arthur's eldest son!

KING OF FRANCE. *Oh* . . . pardon our interruption. For one moment, I quite thought –

LUKE.

>So did they all.
>
>Poisoners, assassins,
>
>Traitors who to secure their wicked ends
>
>Murdered their sovereign
>
>And his wife
>
>And all his friends.

KING OF FRANCE. But – surely your King Arthur lost his life in a great battle?

PRINCE. Oh yes . . . This isn't him. It's King Arthur the Second. (*Prompting* LUKE.) King Arthur the Second.

KING OF FRANCE. King Arthur the Second? This is most interesting. Well, well, we shall be educated as well as entertained. Continue, continue . . .

LUKE.

>So: I am left to rule the land
>
>Alone. The sword is for my hand –
>
>The crown is for my head. I wear –
>
>(*He turns his coat red side out again. He picks up William's sword, and crown.*)
>
>– The blood-red garb of royalty and I swear
>
>To seek those villains out to the world's end who
>>would dare
>
>Destroy my father and my mother –
>
>What's more they've gone and killed my brother –
>
>(*He turns and looks backstage and calls.*)
>
>What? . . . I thought they had.

I swear to fall upon them all
And – what's that then?
(He peers in backstage again.)
Did I hear someone call?

ESMERALDA *(off)*. My lord, my lord –

LUKE.

Aha, it is the voice of one I love.
I hear her through this rosy grove,
The lady whom I should have married.
Now they must know their plot's miscarried –
For she and I as man and wife
We shall pursue them all our mortal life
And never cease to –

(ESMERALDA enters wearing MERLIN'S gown with the hood pulled over her head.)

What is this –
Where is the face I used to kiss?

(She holds her face well away from him, revealing to the audience that she is wearing a monstrous mask.)

Your aspect is most sorely changed –
Tell me, my love, are you deranged?

ESMERALDA.

Not deranged – enchanted.
Alone in my chamber I was confronted
By so horrible an apparition
That I am scarcely in condition
To explain in simple syllables what took place:
But certain he did something dreadful to my face –
Do not look upon me! Or flesh, blood and bone,
Arms, legs and head, you will be turned to stone!
I know it past all question to be true
I tried it out just now on one or two
Old aunts and uncles in the garden
Who met my gaze and straight began to harden.
My face is all black magic and my hair

Has turned to serpents – oh true love – beware –

Each eye of mine is now a murderous organ:

I was your love but now I am a gorgon!

Kill me – kill me – Hocuss – hocus-pocus – I'm
finished, carry on . . .

KING OF FRANCE. This English tragedy is almost too terrifying
to be endured. Such monstrosities upon the stage are scarcely
decent – but no matter – we will endeavour to accustom
ourselves to the horror of the scene. It is certainly well acted.

LUKE.

No. I will not kill you.

Such an idea is a counsel of despair.

It would be better to lock you up in this box lined
with lead

And from the world conceal your dreadful head.

While you remain hid

We can drop your food and water through a slot in
the lid.

In the meantime I will set afoot a thorough investigation

Find out this false enchanter who has wrought this
transformation –

Find out the other murderers (or perhaps are they
the same ?)

Through whose poisonous plots my whole family has
been slain,

And when I have discovered them –

When I have discovered them –

And when I have discovered them –

Oh, my God, I'm at a loss . . .

He has by now got ESMERALDA *shut in the box, and he ranges
the stage apparently in a frenzy but in fact searching for inspiration. The* CONSTABLE *enters at the back of the audience – he is
suffering from delayed concussion, and carries a huge sword.*

CONSTABLE. Discovered them? Them? Discovered them, did you say?

LUKE (*trying to bring him into the play*). Discovered, yes, discovered.

CONSTABLE. I once believed that I could discover. Detect was the word that we used to employ.

LUKE. Detect – very good, that's exactly what I want.

CONSTABLE. Ah yes, but what? I mean, that's the question – what? (*Advancing on to the stage.*) I thought it was no more than a crown made of cardboard. The son of the King and I would have struck him with my truncheon! His father is the huge King and his crown is on his head and his head is made of cardboard and there is no doubt whatever that he will kill me when he sees me . . .

(*He suddenly fixes his eyes on the crown that* LUKE *is wearing.*)
Look, look he does see me – his wide glaring eyes cry out for revenge upon his son the injured Prince and his horn upon his forehead like the horn of a rhinoceros –

> Rhino rhino in your fury and your pride
> I will strike off your hard head
> With my great sword and wide –

LUKE (*holding him off with his player's sword*). Hey-up, no you don't –

CONSTABLE (*fighting* LUKE).

> He ducks below and I strike too high –
> Next time goes the point of it
> Right into his red eye.

LUKE. He swings too short and he swings too wide
> My death runs past on the left-hand side.

CONSTABLE.

> Down at his legs and cut them off
> By God and he jumps right over the top.
> Once again –

LUKE.

> And in vain –

CONSTABLE.
    I was under his chin.

LUKE. But he's gone and he's dodged –

LUKE runs backstage.

CONSTABLE.
    And he's run away in.

He follows after LUKE, *whirling his sword.* LUKE *reappears and addresses the audience.*

LUKE. I knew his ugly face as soon as he walked on. The question is – does he know mine? I doubt it. Is he drunk? Or is he running lunatic? That sword of his is real, which is more than can be said for mine – dear goodness, I never thought I'd be in for the like of this when I agreed to be an actor.
(*The* CONSTABLE *enters once again, sees* LUKE *and roars.*)
He's caught sight of me once again – I've got no alternative but to carry it through to the end – the show, as they say – has got to go on!
(*A great chase supervenes – at intervals, when he can,* LUKE *throws off a few remarks as though part of the play.*)
Thus my unfortunate kingdom, imperilled by lunatic conspirators – because there is no doubt in my mind that this is the very villain – he has destroyed all my family – thus my kingdom must await – in trepidation and helplessness – the inevitable duel to the death that you see enacted before you –

PRINCE (*to* LUKE). Keep going, keep going, you have him bewildered – confuse him – outwit him –
(*To the* PRINCESS.)
Of course it's the same man that we had our little trouble with. Very convenient – really – to have him dealt with in all the fury of a melodrama.

PRINCESS (*as* LUKE *and the* CONSTABLE *scramble all over the hall*). So elegant, so delightful, so athletic – the grace of these

English actors! Their virility – *Monseigneur*, is it not en-
chantment?

KING OF FRANCE. We are not at all clear as to precisely what is
going on. But the performance, in all truth, is of a most
singular dexterity.

The CONSTABLE *has now chased* LUKE *out of the hall altogether. He is left alone, very out of breath. He sits down upon
the box.*

CONSTABLE.
A breathing space.
Here upon this box
Take breath, wipe from my clotted locks
The blood and sweat. Take stock. Shock?
Being, as you see, terrible, in state of suspended shock . . .
I chased him and I lost him
And I found him again and chased him.
And now at last has he gone?
He was wearing a crown. Let me see. I do see.
One, I see, two, no I don't, I see three –
They weren't there before. Or were they? Don't remember.
Can he have split himself up like an earthworm and so hoped
to evade me? He is given away though, by his glittering
top-hamper. We will see then if these three will split them-
selves likewise . . .

He advances with his sword upon the PRINCESS, *who screams.
There is real panic among the royalty.*

PRINCE. No, by George, this goes too far – you will offend the
King, sir – oh, what's the good of talking to him – he's as mad
as a hatter – where on earth is that man Luke?

LUKE (*entering from behind the audience*). It's all right. It's all
off. It's all under control. The crown's off –
(*He has taken his own crown off.*)
I've put it down. Cardboard. It's all cardboard. They're all

three of them cardboard – so put them all down.

(*In some bewilderment, the royalty obey him. The* CONSTABLE *looks at him in a dazed manner.*)

All that you can see is cut out of cardboard and paper with nothing more dangerous than a little pair of scissors. Look, here they are . . .

(*He stands in front of the* CONSTABLE *and snips in the air with a pair of scissors, hypnotizing him. When the* CONSTABLE *appears to be fixed by the movement of the scissors,* LUKE *begins to sing.*)

> 'Cardboard and paper and patches and glue
> Pleated and crumpled and folded in two
> With a pair of white fingers and a little bit of skill
> We make a whole world for the children to kill.
> Prop them up on the table and set them in a row
> And from the far corner lean your face out and blow
> They'll all tumble down, both the sword and the
>   crown
> And the glittering gold weathercocks on the towers of
>   the town.
> After they've fallen the clouds will grow dark
> And the children will creep home from the cold
>   empty park
> The raindrops will soak the wet cardboard into mud
> Will soak the dark hair on your hot little head
> Will soak the hard crust on your butterless bread
> And the clothes on your back and the shoes where
>   you tread –
> Then the sheets on the bed
> Then the leaves on the trees
> Wetter than the warm wet westerly breeze –
> So lie down, lie, lie and grow dry
> Wrapped in a blanket and drowsy your eye.
> Tomorrow you'll cry and tomorrow you can weep
> All you need now is to fall fast asleep . . .'

There you are now, he's fixed, he's in a trance. And now:
the opportunity to get him to undo all the mischief he has
caused. Are you receiving me? Are you receiving me?

ESMERALDA *(in the box)*. I am receiving you.

LUKE. Thank God for that . . . Loud and clear?

ESMERALDA. Loud and clear.

LUKE *(to* CONSTABLE*)*. You are the false magician who turned
my love into a gorgon.

CONSTABLE. Gorgon. Gorgon. Yes that's right. So I did.
What's a gorgon?

LUKE. Those who behold the gorgon turn straightaway to
stone.

CONSTABLE. Stone? Stone . . . ah, stone.

LUKE. You know it. Don't prevaricate. You are now willing,
are you not, to remove the spell from her forthwith?

CONSTABLE. Forthwith.

LUKE. Then say it, after me. Arise, poor lady, from out your
living tomb.

CONSTABLE. Arise, poor lady, from out your living tomb!

LUKE.

    She does arise – she does –
(He gives the box a kick and ESMERALDA *slowly and painfully
climbs out.)*
    I hide my face for safety – woe alas.

CONSTABLE. Eh eh eh eh eh eh eh eh – gorgon – !

LUKE. Speak to her – release her –

CONSTABLE. She's turning me to stone!

LUKE. Oh no no, she can't be – you're not liable – you're the
magician! Look sharp, now – can't you? She's not yet
petrified your vocal chords – speak to her – tell her – 'you
are once more a woman, free and beautiful'.

CONSTABLE. You are once more a woman, free – and – and –

ESMERALDA *(taking off the gorgon mask)*. Well, free, at any
rate.

LUKE. And beautiful.

ESMERALDA. Not very – I'm still suffering the after effects of the –
LUKE. Hocus-pocus, of course. You can't be expected to recover
all at once. But in time, my love, you shall, my dearest love,
you shall . . .

> Now at long last we join our married hands,
> A King and Queen in twin magnificence:
> While the false miscreant for ever stands
> A stone memorial to his own malevolence.
> Let all the little children run and leap
> And throw their eggs at him and throw their rotten
> tripe
> And caper round his base in mockery –
> We have concluded all his trickery.
> And so we kiss – and so we here embrace –
> And so our land is once again at peace!

(*The* PRINCE *gets up and joins them.*)

PRINCE.

> England at peace with France and all the world!
> How happy a resolution this to ancient sour discord.
> The gods will smile on you, and on you too,
> And on your marriage and your policy.
> We all congratulate you on your artistry –

And on your improvisation too – but what on earth has *he* to
do with it?

This last remark, in an undertone, refers to the CONSTABLE
*who is standing like a statue, tragic and rigid. There is general
applause.*

LUKE. Oh, him – you might well ask.
KING OF FRANCE. Is it – is it finished?
PRINCE. I think so, *Monseigneur* . . . It is?
LUKE. It is.

The royal personages resume their crowns.

KING OF FRANCE. Indeed it was a play full of many sur-
prises . . .

FRENCH OFFICER. There is, however, one question. Why, when the play is presented in the Court of the King of France, have you found it to be necessary to clothe your assassin in the uniform of one of our own officers?

LUKE. Yes, of course. Yes, that's right. In England, as it were, we're all anxious for peace. Right. But of course there's always those that claim that peace with the French can never be relied on. Warmongers is the word. Like, they apply it to the French. But we know, as you know, that this is not the case. Right?

FRENCH OFFICER. It is most certainly not the case.

LUKE. So: the man that makes the French out to be the biggest villains in the world is himself the biggest villain, and therefore we dress him up as a Frenchman so we pay him back in his own coin. Poetic justice, right – ? Very clever satire really – right – ? Do you see what I am driving at?

KING OF FRANCE. Oh, I think so. It is – intellectual! Yes. We are very pleased indeed by the enormous vigour of your work. *Monsieur* Crock, you have astonished us, you have enlightened us, you have most thoroughly entertained us! We are graciously delighted to award to you at once the one hundred guineas that we promised for this evening!
Monsieur le Capitaine, hand *Monsieur* Crock the purse.

LUKE *has taken off his mask.*

FRENCH OFFICER (*gives him the purse, then does a double-take*). But, *Monseigneur*, this is not *Monsieur* Crock.

KING OF FRANCE. Why no, no more it is! So Mr Crock himself did not play the leading part? Forgive me – who are *you*? I have seen your face before somewhere – but where – I do not know? You were not presented to me with the others of your actors?

LUKE. No sir; I was not.

KING OF FRANCE. But why not? This is – peculiar. There is but one, two, three – and only the young lady have I ever met before. *Explication, explication, s'il vous plaît, une explication . . .?*

PRINCESS. *Monseigneur*, does it matter? You have seen their performance, you have awarded them the prize –

Enter the CROKES *and* WILLIAM, *recovered.*

CROKE. Awarded us the prize: Oh Your Majesty, this is too much!

FRENCH OFFICER. You will pardon us for thinking, sir, it is a great deal too much. Why did you not perform your play with the full strength of your company, for which reason His Majesty has brought you here?

PRINCE. I think, in fairness to all, we should tell the King the truth. Your Majesty, Mr Croke and his good lady and these two other gentlemen, by very great ill-luck, at the very last moment, were taken seriously ill. What you saw tonight was not a rehearsed play, but an absolute improvisation, presented, I may safely say, with complete success, by the intrepid Mr Luke, normally the Stage Manager, and the equally intrepid Miss Esmeralda, actress.

KING OF FRANCE. But this is remarkable! You deserve to have two prizes for such courage and resource. *Monsieur le Capitaine* – another purse of gold at once for these brave actors!

FRENCH OFFICER. Alas, *Monseigneur*, the Exchequer is a little bit depleted by reason of the war – it is not possible, I fear, to expend more money this season upon the arts.

KING OF FRANCE. But gentlemen, we would indeed have given it if we could . . .

The CROKES *and* WILLIAM *kiss the* KING'S *gracious hand, kiss each other and generally rejoice.*

LUKE (*suddenly*). I'm going to tell him.

ESMERALDA. No, no, you can't do that – !

LUKE. Yes I am, I'm going to tell him. Sir!

KING OF FRANCE. *Monsieur.* Are we addressed?

LUKE. You are. Old Croke and his missus and the funny little Willy there – nay and Esmeralda, too, but she only had a mouthful – were deliberately poisoned!

KING OF FRANCE. *Mon Dieu!* But by whom? In our Palace! Our English guests! Poisoned? Is this true?

ESMERALDA. Perfectly true.

KING OF FRANCE. Then the honour of France has been called into question – and the honour of France must immediately be redeemed. *Monsieur le Capitaine* – an investigation – instantly – you will set it afoot this very moment, now, you will spare no-one – you will –

LUKE. You don't need to investigate very far. We know well who did it! Your own French actors did it.

KING OF FRANCE. *Madame* Zénobie? – you accuse *Madame* Zénobie? But this – is not possible . . .

LUKE. Isn't it just . . .?

KING OF FRANCE. No . . . no . . . there has been here a very great mistake . . . *Madame* Zénobie, in any case, has been disgraced and will appear no more upon the Royal Stage of Paris. It will not be necessary to persecute the poor woman further. We do not wish to cause pain and suffering to any artist . . . My dear Prince, just one moment . . .

(*He takes the* PRINCE *aside.*)

For the future of our international relations, this unfortunate business must not be noised abroad, *comprenez-vous?* I would not for the world have the peace treaty made invalidate. So how then can we best prevent these actors from talking about it?

PRINCE. Not difficult at all. Let me handle it. I think I know the way . . . Now, Mr Croke, you do appreciate that even if true, these allegations are unable to be proved and may in fact be complete fantasy?

CROKE. It is possible, of course – but I really do think – sir – that something should be done. My poor wife has been taken exceedingly ill – and – er –

MRS CROKE. Never in all my life have I experienced so much
   pain. And before an audience too – the humiliation – the
   indignity –
PRINCE. I am sure we all sympathize very deeply, Mrs Croke.
   But let us not – er – let us not look solely upon the dark side
   of the affair. Suppose now that my father – and I am sure
   that he will – were to offer you – all of you – a permanent
   contract as players to the Royal Household? We have no
   company of actors at present in receipt of regular salaries
   from the Crown, and I for one, have, regretted this, for a
   long time. The King of France has his own theatre – why
   should not the King of England? What do you say to that –
   well, what do you say to it, Mrs Croke?
MRS CROKE. Oh, Your Royal Highness –
CROKE. I am overwhelmed –
PRINCE. Exactly so. So – no more trouble? And of course you
   have the hundred guineas?
LUKE. Oh no sir – pardon me. *I* have the hundred guineas.
   It was no chance that I did not consume
   Your poisoned dinner in this very room.
   I was regarded as being by far too rough:
   I had to buckle-to and work while you sat down to
      stuff.
   But she stood up and she walked forth,
   This very day, you saved their play:
   And now you share the prize.
   Therefore if you're willing, we will say our fond
      good-byes.
   Take yourselves off to London, act before the King:
   We two will attempt together a far more dangerous
      thing.
   We will travel, hand in hand,
   Across water and dry land –
   We will entertain the people
   Under castle-wall and proud church steeple

> Throughout Switzerland and Germany
> And the arid plains of Spain –
> You're going to get a nice fat subsidy –
> You can leave with us your scenery,
> You'll not need that again.
> In any case, by my workmanship it came to its present
> state,
> So I fancy if I claim it there can be no just dispute.

He and ESMERALDA *fold up the scenery and begin to carry it off.*

WILLIAM. Wait one moment – no – you cannot possibly –

PRINCE. Oh I think they can, sir – yes – I really think it's better this way. Don't you think so, Mr Croke? Mrs Croke? No?

MRS CROKE. I have no intention whatever of expending words upon such unprofessional ingratitude.

CROKE. Oh never mind them, never mind them, my dear –
> (*He sings.*)
> 'We're all going to London
> And our bonnets are a-cock
> Dirty grouchy grumblers
> Need not share in our good luck –
> The King is now our patron
> And the Prince will wish us well
> And those who do not like it
> They can rapidly run to hell!'

The CROKES *and* WILLIAM *go out singing and dancing.*

PRINCESS. Permit me for one moment to wish *you* well, *Monsieur* Luke – and Esmeralda – perhaps, before too long, we shall see you act again – in England?

KING OF FRANCE. But certainly not in France. You are to leave this country at once, sir: and never never never return to it again. *Monsieur le Capitaine* – you will make certain that he takes his immediate departure.

The royalty are about to go out when the KING *suddenly becomes aware of the* CONSTABLE – *still standing like a statue.*

Oh yes – I was intending to ask. In God's name – who is this?

LUKE. Oh, he's all right. He's a statue. He'll decorate your Palace for you. And if he don't – he'll wander home again. Nobody's worried about *him* any more. Are we right then? Let's get moving.

He and ESMERALDA *go out one side.*
The ROYALS *go out the other.*
After a pause the CONSTABLE *slowly comes to life and starts to sing.*

CONSTABLE (*sings*).

    'I do not know what has been happening
    I do not know where I am now
    I wish I had a little farmyard
    With a pair of chickens and a cow.
    It is no use to be a policeman
    The force of anarchy wins all the time:
    I did not like what I saw around me
    I did not like it so I called it crime.
    With a truncheon and a brace of handcuffs
    I did my best for Order and Law:
    I was overwhelmed by such loose behaviour
    Such goings-on I never saw.
    And now the Kings have stuck their foot in
    And made it legal what was not allowed.
    There's nothing more for me to do – sirs –
    But to hide away from the madding crowd.
    I will become a hairy hermit
    And live alone in a scruffy old cell:
    I never felt such a fool before – sirs –
    I suppose you'll say: it's just as well.'

He staggers stiffly out.

The Little Gray Home in the West

An Anglo-Irish Melodrama

1972

Margaretta D'Arcy

and

John Arden

We would like to express our gratitude to Gerry O'Neill, who made his theatre (The Sugawn, off Balls Pond Road, Highbury, North London) available for the first reading of *The Little Gray Home in the West* on 1 May 1978.

And also to the following people, who took part in the reading:

John Blanchard
Terry Dougherty
Don Foley
John Joyce
Michael Loughnan
Anne O'Connor
Timothy O'Grady
Treasa Ní Fhátharta
John Quinn
Stephen Rea
Roger Sloman

(John Joyce, Stephen Rea and Roger Sloman were in the original 7:84 production of *The Ballygombeen Bequest* which was taken off because of a libel action in 1972.)

They all gave their services free and the greatest appreciation is due to them for their act of solidarity and trust in the play.

M. D'A. & J.A.

Characters

BAKER-FORTESCUE   a business man
CROTCHET   a solicitor
SEAMUS O'LEARY   a smallholder
TERESA   his wife
PADRAIC   his son
SIOBHAN   his daughter
HAGAN   a contractor
LIMEGRAVE   an agent of British Military Intelligence
BUTLER McREEK   an agent of Irish Political Police
MULHOLLAND   of the Republican Movement in the West of Ireland

AN INTELLIGENCE OFFICER
A CORPORAL   } of the British Army
A PRIVATE

The action of the play takes place in Britain and Ireland between nineteen forty-five and nineteen seventy-one.

Airs to songs: The titles of the traditional ballad-airs are given only as a rough guide. Other tunes of the same type may be found more suitable for particular performers or particular circumstances of production. Also it may be necessary to adapt the airs slightly here and there to give the words of the songs the fullest emphasis. This should always be done in preference to adapting the words to the music.

Act One

Scene One

Enter PADRAIC *as a dead man.*

PADRAIC.
Between England and Ireland to this day is so great quarrel,
To introduce it in a play I know well is to keel the barrel
Of old dried blood and new wet blood
And steaming pitch and shit and rancorous deep complaint
And altogether such a poisonous flood
As sure would make a cannibal cyclops faint
For very stink of it: and yet I have no choice.
This is my only voice.
For I am dead and murdered. Out of my grave
I cannot walk alive
Except in an actor's mask. My tongue in another's throat
Explaining, arguing, persuading fruitlessly how it should all
   come about
That I am dead and cannot walk alive upon my own
And yet for nothing that I myself had done
For only that which I myself had been
In life before my life, before I was even born . . .

Padraic O'Leary: died under stress of inhuman and degrading treatment – but in no sense *torture* – nineteen seventy-one. At the age of twenty-six. Having returned home to the west of Ireland after ten years in the north of England, where I worked on the buildings and learned about class-struggle, where I joined a trade union and learned about solidarity, where I adhered to a socialist party and learned that colonialism in my own country, resistance to it, armed struggle, the republican movement, were symptoms of nineteenth century political atavism and that no-one opened their mouths about 'em but a crowd of backward paddies . . . I was then to discover that my journey home again from Liverpool had been anticipated the year of my birth by another man's doomed travelling. He went for the same reason – as the result of a death, for a testament, a bequest. Here he is.

THE LAST LEGATEE OF THE OLD DISPENSATION
RECEIVES HIS INHERITANCE: NINETEEN FORTY-
FIVE.

Enter BAKER-FORTESCUE, *wearing dark glasses.*

BAKER-FORTESCUE. Good day to you. Baker-Fortescue at
your service. Roderick Baker-Fortescue – the Honourable
Roderick Baker-Fortescue, for what such a handle is worth –
financially not too much – but . . . Ha h'm: released, very
recently released – five minutes ago, in fact, from patriotic
wartime service, in a department of government which must
alas remain nameless – security, the nod-and-the-wink . . .

*He takes off his dark glasses and replaces them with a business-
executive's horn-rims.*

Observe my glasses, no longer dark but clear and bright.
The war is over. Democracy has won the long long fight.

PADRAIC.
Nineteen hundred and forty-five:
Not only the backroom boys are glad to be alive.

BAKER-FORTESCUE. Mind you, a most productive and
advantageous back room for some of us. Oh, not exactly
military intelligence . . . not military at all, as a matter of fact
. . . departmentally very very closely connected. Germany,
Italy, rehabilitation of responsible government under the
guidance of the allied occupying powers – you will readily
understand commodities of all sorts in very very short supply.
Currency, coupons, immeasurable bumph: moreover some
most remunerative sidelines in relation to the investigation of
war-crimes, the political past of public figures, wrap it up, keep
it smooth, united front against the *Reds*, and above all re-
establish regular commercial communications. Co-ordinating
thus our national defence with my personal advantage, I have
returned home highly confident that my own business in
Harrogate – export-import cost-price intimate novelties – will
not have suffered in my absence: my partner tells me my new
European contacts will add enormously to future activities.
None the less I must break myself in slowly to the diminuendo

of British life as infected by socialism, though Comrade
Attlee's new government is not yet, perhaps, *red*: sub-fusc
would be a better word. I'll go to my club and look out for
some refreshment.

PADRAIC *as a club-servant, hands him a bundle of letters.*

Aha, as I thought, no end of letters awaiting me. The world of
legitimate business resumes its cohesive flow . . . From a
solicitor – ho ho . . . ?

I am not rich, but I have always found
That where a lawyer creeps upon the ground
Profits accrue, emoluments abound.
Whatever news he sends me by this post
I have no fear but I shall soon acquire
Some crafty carving-knife with which to rule the roast!
I am, you see, a business-man:
I look to the main chance where I can.

Reading the letter:

Good God: I have inherited property! My distant relative the
Marquess of Ballydehob deceased. Bricks and mortar, fertile
acreage, productive land – a sight more appropriate to the name
of Baker-Fortescue than a scruffy little office in Harrogate: ha, a
stake in the country! *Which* country? Ireland. God help us . . .
A castle in the boglands of Munster. Rotten purlins in the roof,
nettles and thistles in the cracks of the stonework, hired
assassins I suppose, taking cover in the park? No, no, a dead
loss, I'll not accept, I'll sell. Wait a moment, not even a castle
. . . My spectacles, typing error . . . ? God-dammit, the word
is *chalet*. The Chalet, Kil – Kilna – something – Kilnasleeveen
indeed. And fifteen acres. You can't call fifteen acres a park. A
paddock perhaps. And what's this about a small-holding? 'The
small-holding locally known as the Tintawndub, at present
believed occupied by Seamus O'Leary Esq . . .' You know I
very much doubt whether a character called Seamus could
possibly have any right to style himself Esquire. Be that as it
may, it appears he is to be my tenant. Oh-oh though, what's
this? 'The validity of Mr O'Leary's title to the Tintawndub is

open to variant interpretation . . .' 'Counsel's opinion . . .' No
no no: indeed by God, no: I have inherited or not! I must see
this attorney at once. What does he call himself? Croup,
Croup, Crotchet, and Croup. The man I am to deal with will
be Crotchet, I hope. At least, if he is, I shall not be
outnumbered, ha!

Enter CROTCHET.

Mr Crotchet? Good morning, Baker-Fortescue.

CROTCHET. Delighted to make your acquaintance, Mr
Fortescue.

BAKER-FORTESCUE. Baker-Fortescue.

CROTCHET. Please do sit down. Cold wind.

BAKER-FORTESCUE. Very cold.

CROTCHET. Blows from the left, I suppose. Not at all what we
fought and died for. Coal, railways, steel, the Bank of England.
Nationalise the lot. Even women, so they tell me.

BAKER-FORTESCUE. Good God, you don't say so.

CROTCHET. Oh yes, it's coming. *Levelling-down* is the accepted
phrase, I believe. Hand over your lady-wife to –

BAKER-FORTESCUE. I am a bachelor.

CROTCHET. You'll do well to remain one. Because otherwise,
hand her over to some sweaty-socked trade unionist and in
return you'll be permitted on the first Friday of every month to
avail yourself of the shared services of his slag-heap of a
daughter . . . Import-export, I believe? Unless you're on
permanent sub-contract to the State Authority for Public
Misery, you'll have the lot commandeered by the Chancellor of
the Exchequer – the Commissar for Loot, I suppose they call
him now. So this little legacy in Ireland will come in very
useful. It's their Ireland, you know, not ours – I mean the
neutral bit – *Eera* . . . ? You a Catholic?

BAKER-FORTESCUE. Good God no.

CROTCHET. Much better not to be – over there you couldn't
even offer your lady-wife a kiss without a certificate from the
priest. If you had a lady-wife. And if you're going to live there.
Are you going to live there?

BAKER-FORTESCUE. I hadn't really thought about it.

CROTCHET. You might have to in the end. I mean, there's no
possibility of a Labour Government over there. The Bishops sit
on *that* pot: oh, very firm posteriors the Bishops have, over
there. But if *you* don't want to live there, there'll be very many
who do. Delightful part of the country, they tell me. Fishing,
rough shooting, horses, all that – no rationing over there. You
should let the place to visitors – far from the madding crowd,
the slow Boeotian charm of the vanishing peasantry – oh they
touch their caps over there, pull the forelock, incredible, they
still do it . . . never see anything like it in England again.
People of your own class will pay twenty pound a week, for
nothing at all really, except a bit of the old respect. I do
recommend you to take the hint from my typing error, Castle
instead of Chalet . . .

BAKER-FORTESCUE. That would hardly be the proper
thing . . . ?

CROTCHET. No no, the third Marquess did indeed have a
fortified wall of some sort on the site . . . but it isn't
architecture after all that your visitors will be looking for.

BAKER-FORTESCUE. What about this 'Tintawndub'?

CROTCHET. You mean the O'Learys? They seem to be a
fixture. Perennial problem with inheritance through these Irish
peerages. The Ballydehobs could never get rid of them. They
add to the charm of the place. 'Faith and your honour's
welcome to a day on the lake with the boat and 'tis meself will
be after pointing out to you the locality of the big fish and the
contrivances for catching them . . .'

BAKER-FORTESCUE. Begorrah . . .

CROTCHET. Oh yes . . . they don't pay rent.

BAKER-FORTESCUE. Then what *do* they pay? I mean they *are* on the property?

CROTCHET. Lord Ballydehob used to describe it as matter of good will. You want an old retainer – at least I'm sure your visitors could use one – so there you are – gratis. Pay them the odd half-crown, you see, in the way of baksheesh – not too much, mind, you could spoil them – make certain their cows don't wander into the Chalet – ask Mrs O'Leary to keep the place clean for you – and remind your visitors now and again to give them the odd half-crown. They'll do more good for your business than an illustrated article in the pages of *The Tatler*. But don't mention any question of rent. It's rather a sore point in Kilnasleeveen.

BAKER-FORTESCUE. I don't understand.

CROTCHET. Lord Ballydehob's grandfather, on a visit to collect his rents, had his throat cut by the tenants – eighteen eighty-one.

BAKER-FORTESCUE. Good God.

CROTCHET. It's a long time ago. But you see, they don't forget.

BAKER-FORTESCUE. If that is the case, Mr Crotchet, it hardly seems to me a very secure investment, I mean, I am English, and a landowner, and a Protestant – I mean –

CROTCHET.
I don't think you'll find
That anyone will mind.
They need today the high-class tourist trade,
You bring them that and you are made.
With a shotgun and a fishing-rod
You will be worshipped like a god.
So long as you do not insist upon your legal right
You may live there in peace and never have to fight.
Consider yourself a guest of the country.
They will treat you as though you were one of the gentry.

BAKER-FORTESCUE. I *am* one of the gentry.

CROTCHET.
It does not do to say so.
But be yourself and they will know.

BAKER-FORTESCUE.
Were they not neutral in our great war against dictatorship?

CROTCHET.
Not the kind of remark I advise you to let slip.

BAKER-FORTESCUE.
Is not the hand of De Valera stained red with British blood?

CROTCHET.
It has done him little good.
Not blood but British gold is what he needs today.
He will put that red hand in your hand
If you can but show him the way
To make rich his ramshackle kingdom
While you yourself are made rich.
Do you know O'Leary's great-grandfather
Had to lie down and die in a ditch?

BAKER-FORTESCUE. Good God, did he really?

CROTCHET. Oh yes, upon what is now *your* property – he always maintained it was *his*. Ballydehob's agent had tried to have him evicted – since then, however, the family adopted a quite different policy – a matter of good will –

Never again what had been done
In the year of eighteen eighty-one.

I'll put my little bill in the post. I'm very glad you looked in. I'll just drop a line to the O'Learys to let them know you're on the way. You want to look over the place, I suppose. Travel by Liverpool – more comfortable than Holyhead, though it takes a few hours longer. Good morning.

Exit CROTCHET.

BAKER-FORTESCUE.
   It is with some trepidation
   I embark on this expedition.
   It seems there are both bogs and pitfalls
   I must put my feet across.
   I must keep tight hold of the old kitbag
   If I am not to suffer some loss.

Exit BAKER-FORTESCUE.

Enter TERESA *and* SEAMUS *(*TERESA *is pregnant and nursing a baby).*

TERESA. You came home in good time from the fair?

SEAMUS. I did.

TERESA. I had thought you would be drinking.

SEAMUS. I would too, for the news that's in it. But it's best you should hear it yourself. Lord Ballydehob is dead.

TERESA. Don't we know that already – sure wasn't it in the *Advertiser*?

SEAMUS. Oh it was, but I've confirmed it. I had it quite definite from Tim Hagan at the petrol pump. He died a month since in the London hospitals, there's no doubt about it at all. Now will you listen to me, woman, it's what Tim Hagan's after telling me – it's important, says Hagan. They have not been able to discover the direct heir to the property.

TERESA. Lord Ballydehob had a son, surely?

SEAMUS. Ah the title, now, you see, went always with that parcel of land in County Wexford. The bit that's in it here was never entailed. I don't know what that means, but Hagan tells me 'tis a legal loophole for us.

TERESA. What d'you mean, a loophole?

SEAMUS. Do you know what I'm after thinking? I think that the lot of it could belong to none other than us.

TERESA. Sure it always belonged to us.

SEAMUS. Were there not O'Learys set firm on this ground six hundred years ago when there wasn't an English landlord west of the Shannon?

TERESA. You will never get a lawyer to establish you that. Every corner of every paragraph of every law in this country was ravelled up by some Englishman. Our old Irish lawyers and their old Irish books all drowned in the ocean by order of Cromwell, or Queen Elizabeth, or one of 'em – it's all finished, we can't go back to it.

SEAMUS. Oh can we not? We are a Free State, and very shortly, by all the rumours, about to declare ourselves a Republic. Jasus the minute your man Dev puts that name to his constitution, not a saucer of English law will be left for the cat in the kitchen . . .

TERESA. I hear the postman – he has a letter.

PADRAIC, *as a postman, knocks, and hands her a letter.*

SEAMUS. . . . to say nothing of the rats that creep under the back door or the birdeens in their nest in the thick of the thatch – begod, that's not a letter? Who the divel writes a letter to me?

TERESA. Crotchet.

SEAMUS. Crotchet – what Crotchet?

TERESA. 'Tis Crotchet the lawyer. The ferret.

SEAMUS. From London?

TERESA. The ferret that lived ever in the long pocket of Lord Ballydehob's shooting-coat. He has teeth.

SEAMUS. And he says – ?

TERESA. He says that the land has passed to a relative.

SEAMUS. To an Englishman, begod.

TERESA. To an Honourable, a Baker-Fortescue, lives in
Yorkshire . . .

SEAMUS. Aha, now, that'll be Roderick! Didn't they name him
after the bastard evicted my great-grandfather – ho ho boys,
we've heard of *him*! A class of a pawnbroker in the streets of
Harrogate and a disgrace to a noble house, I remember Hagan
telling me –

TERESA. That Hagan'd tell you anything. Doesn't he dilute the
very petrol from his pump with a pint of paraffin to every
gallon?

SEAMUS. If he does so, good luck to him. Thanks be to God I
can't afford a motor-car. Nor ever like to, the way things go.

TERESA. So where are we, for all the fine words?

SEAMUS. He says nothing about the Tintawndub. Except he
hopes that we will make the Honourable gentleman welcome
when he comes. Very likely he's a decent man and will give us
no disturbance. Look at that now – here he comes!

Enter BAKER-FORTESCUE, *diffidently, carrying a small
suitcase. He walks about quietly, as though sizing up the property.*

TERESA. It would be best to offer up a small prayer, I do think.

SEAMUS. I am thinking 'twould be better to take hold of a small
drink.

He gets a whiskey-bottle and pours himself a glass. BAKER-
FORTESCUE *approaches them. They go into a stylised routine of
old retainers offering a formal welcome.*

TERESA. Ah sure and we're proud to deliver a great welcome to
your honour etcetera etcetera . . .

Aside:

He has teeth the size of gravestones, grin you to powder in a
minute and a half.

SEAMUS. We are honoured and proud, sir, to have your foot
   upon our threshold etcetera etcetera . . .

Aside:

Jasus Mary and Joseph I declare he was expecting it!

Aloud:

Woman, will you pull up a chair. Sure the Honourable
gentleman will take a small drink.

BAKER-FORTESCUE. Baker-Fortescue.

SEAMUS. Etcetera.

TERESA. Etcetera.

BAKER-FORTESCUE.
   I had really no idea they were going to be so polite.
   Mr Crotchet was quite right.
   Can they not be aware of the commercial possibility
   Inherent in this traditional antique hospitality?
   If they are not, I am: I will turn to account
   Their archaic deportment and their Seltic servility:
   I will turn it to account and amass a large amount.
   I am beginning to think well
   Of my neo-colonial estate.
   I will keep it. I will not sell.

All the above, to the audience as he walks about. Now he turns to the
O'LEARYS:

Good God, it's half-past eight.
I had not thought it was so late.
Very gloomy, is it not, in the bottom of this green valley?
Tell me, how long has my concrete-block Chalet
Remained uninhabited? I was led to believe it was new.
There are hens in its kitchen. I presume they belong to you.
The state of the floor would make my visitors want to spew.

SEAMUS.
  The late Lord Ballydehob, sir, always stayed in the hotel.
  The convenience of the chickens was a matter of good will.

TERESA.
  Sir, his lordship had in mind
  The Chalet was a mistake and should come down.
  Leaving the Tintawndub to stand
  As it always stood, upon its own.
  You did say – visitors . . . ?

BAKER-FORTESCUE. Did I not explain my intentions? Oh I
  do beg your pardon. I was virtually certain I had made myself
  clear – I hope I am not already seduced by the mist that does be
  on the bog –

SEAMUS. The what, sir?

BAKER-FORTESCUE. I am absolutely charmed by this little
  corner of the world, the blue lake, the green glen – much as I
  should like to, I can't live here all the time. I have a business to
  attend to in England. But such a well-suited Chalet left vacant
  for years on end –

TERESA. Oh indeed a terrible pity, sir, to have it go to rack and
  ruin. 'Tis a very strong-built little house.

SEAMUS (*aside to* TERESA). Does he know that the water from
  the bank above runs down on a wet day and floods out the
  front hall?

TERESA (*aside to* SEAMUS). He'd be blind if he hadn't noticed
  it. But we mention it when he does and not before – keep your
  wits awake, Seamus – *visitors* – and keep away from that bottle.

SEAMUS (*aside to* TERESA). Ah sure, just a noggeen – what
  th'hell d'you mean, *visitors*?

BAKER-FORTESCUE. So suitable, do you see, for a quiet
  untroubled holiday? Say a week or a fortnight at a time, a
  family-party . . . You could look after them, could you not?

SEAMUS. A family? Look after who . . . ?

TERESA (*gesturing at him*). Ss-ssh . . . Indeed of course we could, sir, and happy to do so, sure the bed-and-breakfast is all the rage these days, why Tim Hagan himself –

SEAMUS. Oh that's it, the tourists – ? Indeed, herself will do the cooking and any gentleman for a day on the lake or a stretch of shooting over the bog –

BAKER-FORTESCUE. I can put him safely in your hands.

TERESA. There's not a man in Kilnasleeveen with a better notion of the trout and how to attract them –

SEAMUS. Begod, sir, let me give you another glass in your hand. There's a raindrop the size of an egg just fallen smack into that.

BAKER-FORTESCUE. I did notice the Chalet has a problem with the wet weather –

TERESA. Oh yes sir, indeed it has, Tim Hagan says the porosity of the concrete –

SEAMUS. The porosity of the thatched roof in the Tintawndub, as you see, sir.

BAKER-FORTESCUE. Ah, thatch! So little of it left in our English villages, alas, we can't get the craftsmen, you see –

SEAMUS. There's a man above in Kilnasleeveen very good at repairing thatch.

BAKER-FORTESCUE. Splendid.

TERESA. 'Tis best to renew a thatch every five years –

SEAMUS. Or else with the birds and their nests and the rats and mice that's in it and the strong wind – Lord Ballydehob had this one attended to in nineteen thirty-five.

TERESA. His lordship was always most considerate.

BAKER-FORTESCUE (*at last looking upwards*).
  Five years? The chappie who repaired your thatch
  He must indeed have been the best of all good men.
  What should have lasted five years he has made endure for ten.
  It needs no more than a patch above the door
  To extend its rainproof life for at least a score.
  What else d'you need to make your home complete?
  Do I hear the patter of tiny feet?
  A mouse, a rat . . . ?

SEAMUS.
  Five hundred if there's one.

BAKER-FORTESCUE.
  So get a cat
  And then they are dead and gone.
  I am putting you in a great way to make money, don't you
    see –
  All you have to do is treat my visitors as you treat me –
  For every summer visitor that will bite upon my hook
  Five shillings I will give you for your Post Office Savings
    Book!
  And that does not take account of any gratuity
  Each visitor will give you of his own generosity –
  You have hens, you have cows grazing upon your land,
  Your eggs, milk and butter will be in constant demand:
  You have heard that in England we have the Era of Austerity –
  Enormous sums paid out for the most commonplace
    commodity:
  Eggs and milk and home-made bread
  And jam and country butter thickly spread –
  Imagine a pound of butter is now worth a pound of gold –

SEAMUS.
  We have been told –

BAKER-FORTESCUE (*sings*) [Air: *The Parting Glass*].
  'I am the man that brings to you
  The secret in the stony ground
  Of how the crock of gold beneath
  The blackthorn tree is sought and found!'

SEAMUS (*sings*).
   'We'll follow you with shovel and spade
   And dig and delve in bog and rock
   And drive the little green man away
   And wrap our arms around his crock.'

TERESA (*sings*).
   'We shall not fear his grin of rage
   And all his roars will be in vain –
   We have long deserved what we shall get
   When we come into our own again –'

SEAMUS and TERESA (*sing*).
   'When we come in, when we come in,
   When we come into our own again:
   O'Leary's house shall not fall down
   We shall have no more of grief and pain . . .'

*The refrain is repeated faster and faster; all three have joined hands
and spin round in a rapid dance.* BAKER-FORTESCUE *breaks it
off.*

BAKER-FORTESCUE.
   You will excuse me if I leave:
   My taxi to Limerick Junction and the Dublin train to catch.

The O'LEARYS *continue dancing.* BAKER-FORTESCUE
addresses the audience:

It would be better if my Chalet were built of stone with a clean
      thatch.
For my visitors more picturesque and I could charge a higher
      rent.
I could even call it a castle, people would take it as it was
      meant . . .
But I do not want to risk the O'Learys' discontent:
If I thought of swopping them from here to over there
I do not think they'd think I was playing them fair.
My advertisements in the newspapers within two or three
      days –

Mr O'Leary, the top of the evening – do I have the correct
   phrase . . . ?

The O'LEARYS *bid him a formalised farewell.*

O'LEARYS. So etcetera, your honour, etcetera etcetera, so . . .

BAKER-FORTESCUE (*moving away from them*).
   But here is a matter that fills me with gloom:
   You saw the baby at her bosom
   The other within her womb –

PADRAIC.
   The other within her womb
   Being Padraic O'Leary – me –
   In preparation for the tomb.
   According to Karl Marx, not one of us can see
   What we look at, except
   As our class-role may direct.
   My eyes at the time being as blind
   As the Honourable Fortescue's mind
   How could either of us foretell
   I was the one he must kill?

THE LAST LEGATEE UNDERSTANDS HIS
INHERITANCE TO BE OF LIMITED ADVANTAGE TO
HIM: BUT DETERMINES TO MAKE THE BEST OF IT.

BAKER-FORTESCUE.
   The value of my land is not enhanced, I am afraid.
   I had not thought this family would be a family that would
      breed.
   But what can be done?
   O'Leary has had his fun
   And I must suffer in my pocket for what he did in his damp
      bed.
   In the Irish Free State contraceptives are forbid:
   And even if they were not I would still be too late –
   I must at any rate dissuade her from conceiving any more:
   For if she does by God my property will burst open at wall and
      floor.

O'Leary gets drunk and his eyes are deeply sunk:
I have reason to speculate his blood will be degenerate.
However, just yet, I need not worry about that.
My advertisement for the papers must at once be written out:
I have a pile of prospective profits to assess and calculate.

Exit BAKER-FORTESCUE.

TERESA.
It does not seem to me he intends to renew the roof.

SEAMUS.
And as for his bloody visitors:
When we see them arrive, we will then see the proof.

Exeunt TERESA *and* SEAMUS.

Scene Two

PADRAIC.
The length of time that is past and gone
I shall sum in a little song.

NINETEEN FIFTY-EIGHT.

He sings, or rather chants, as the metre is irregular:

'So many years for good or ill
The Age of Austerity over the hill
The Tories are in and Labour out —
Private Enterprise runs about
On all four feet like a wolf in the night,
He chops with his teeth at all in sight
The foam runs out at the corner of his jaw
He gulps what he can and howls for more —
Give give give! Let him devour:
He'll burst his belly in half-an-hour . . .'

Enter BAKER-FORTESCUE.

BAKER-FORTESCUE. Oh no he won't, you know – the
market is expanding with the resilience of elastic but the margin
of safety is both catholic and commodious. The bookings of
my Chalet are constant – and at home the old restrictions upon
currency exchange, etcetera, have been lifted left and right –
such advantage in such matters, such augmentation of export-
import – Zurich Zurich Zurich . . . oh yes, I am alive to it,
duplicating, triplicating my Irish prosperity.

PADRAIC (*sings*).
'Labour is out and the Tories in –
The Suez war we did not win.
High time high time, Macmillan said,
To knock such nonsense on the head.'

BAKER-FORTESCUE. Only because they insisted on
chickening-out at the last moment. Nasser is a crocodile.
Trample him into the mud! Wog!

PADRAIC (*sings*).
'Pull in our horns, pull in our feet,
Withdraw the cruisers of the Fleet.'

BAKER-FORTESCUE. I judged it very wisely at the end of the
war when I decided not to remain in government service.

PADRAIC (*sings*).
'The Americans have a prodigious huge bomb
That can bring the whole world to an end
If we do not do what they tell us to do
We cannot be their little small friend.
They will leave us alone to cry and to groan
Like Anthony Eden with his face to the wall
Who weeps and weeps for the Suez Canal.'

BAKER-FORTESCUE. Serve him right. Yellow-belly. Doesn't
know where his bread's buttered. Personally I find the Yankees
exceedingly civil: provided one remembers their idiosyncrasies.
Here is a letter I have just received from one of them – a typical
satisfied client . . . !

He reads the letters:

'Kilnasleeveen,' she says, 'was the village of our dreams –'

PADRAIC (*sings*).
'But if we obey and we do as they say
They will feed us with ice-cream and steak every day
They will tuck us up tight in the dark of the night
In an air-conditioned bed with the blankets round your head
And whiter than the white of the White Cliffs of Dover
A pretty little lady to lie under and roll over
So warm and bare and flattering, she whispers in your ear,
'If you don't look out of the window, love,
You have nothing at all to fear . . .'

BAKER-FORTESCUE. 'Animal excrement all over the doorstep, huge tangles of hay filling up the back bedroom – the night of the big wind . . .' Odours, she says, noxious odours, fleas and lice from the farmyard . . . what in God's name has Teresa O'Leary been up to! Mr Crotchet, do you hear me . . . ?

Enter CROTCHET.

CROTCHET. Oh yes, I can hear . . .

BAKER-FORTESCUE. Just because Lord Ballydehob let them keep hens in the Chalet when there was nobody there . . . To whom do they think the property belongs?

CROTCHET (*looking through the letter*). They weren't *keeping* the hay in the Chalet, the wind blew it in, it appears . . .

BAKER-FORTESCUE. But Mr Crotchet – *cow-dung*! These people are Americans – from New York! They are terrified of the countryside. She refers further on to 'wild animals' loose in the lane.

CROTCHET. Dogs?

BAKER-FORTESCUE. Bullocks. O'Leary's bullocks. I shall write to his wife.

CROTCHET. Now be very careful there –

BAKER-FORTESCUE (*taking out pad and preparing to write*). I look to you to advise me if I make a mistake. So: 'My dear Teresa –' Okay?

CROTCHET. There is after all no *Mrs* Baker-Fortescue to take umbrage.

BAKER-FORTESCUE. Crotchet, I am serious. To continue: 'The letter I have received from Mrs Macnamara is extremely disturbing. If what she says about the fleas and the hay and the cow-dung is true –'

CROTCHET. No! Give her the benefit of the doubt *before* you put the boot in. A question of psychology.

BAKER-FORTESCUE. I see what you mean . . . 'If what she says about the fleas etcetera is *not* true, then I must know what happened to make her so upset. But, if it *is* true, I can only conclude that for some reason the fence between the Tintawndub and my Chalet is no longer fulfilling its function: I ask myself, how? Can Seamus have possibly taken some of it down to make himself an irregular short-cut? That fence is the legal limit of your tenancy –'

CROTCHET. 'Tenancy' – the word is perhaps prejudicial. 'Tenure' might be safer.

BAKER-FORTESCUE. Whatever you say. 'In any case it is clear that Mrs Macnamara feels herself subjected to the worst kind of rural nuisance. Until I am assured that all steps have been taken to prevent its recurrence, I am unable to forward you your usual gratuity. This will perhaps teach you –'

CROTCHET. No no no; no sir, no! You are *unable* to forward it. Do not put down on paper you are *penalising* them, for heaven's sake! Let them draw their own conclusions. Now, at once: a change of tone. Revert to your usual agreeable self.

BAKER-FORTESCUE. 'Oh, by the way, don't forget, our first guests for the coming year will be Major and Mrs Dreadnought Pole-Hatchet. The Major is a Member of the Belfast Parliament, and a close friend of the Prime Minister of

Northern Ireland. They will be arriving for three weeks shortly
before Easter. Most important you protect their privacy against
any offensive local demonstrations in relation to the anniversary
of 1916.'

CROTCHET. You don't think an Ulster Unionist something of
a provocation?

BAKER-FORTESCUE.
It is not like that these days in the West.
The bitter glue of Irish politics
In that soft climate now no longer sticks.
A Unionist, an Orangeman indeed,
Is seen there as the kind of man they need.
The curdled thunder of his furious drum
He modifies into the industrious hum
Of calculating-machines and clerks with ballpoint pens,
Peers mildly at the world through his bi-focal lens,
And for his only rampart of defence
He finds the ornamental grillwork of his bank
A stronger fortress than the strongest tank.

PADRAIC. He always did.

BAKER-FORTESCUE.
In erstwhile hostile Dublin now he frequently may be seen
Taking his lunch-time stroll in Stephen's Green:
Then back to the office, export, import, cash and credit,
The roaring hope of bomb and burst and blood at last is
    muted –
King Billy and the Pope now both inhabit
The yielding mattress of your Wall Street whore –
A patriotic man like me may well regret
That such is as it is, but we must not forget
Our gore and glory now is doused in an old piss-pot:
The British Empire terrifies no more
With Black-and-Tans and murderous threats of war.

PADRAIC (*sings*).
'The figures of unemployment
Throughout Ireland increase and increase:
The emigrant ships across the Irish Sea
Heave seasick onwards and do not cease . . .'

Oh I was to be on one of them: so I know.

CROTCHET.
You think the North and South are reconciled?

BAKER-FORTESCUE.
I know the Irish are no longer wild.

It's obvious, my dear Crotchet, they cannot afford it. Didn't
you tell me so yourself?

*A distant concussion, striking them rigid for a moment of absolute
silence.*

CROTCHET.
What was that sound
Far over the Northern Irish ground
Was it a bomb? Was it a gun?
Who is that man? I see him run –
An ancient ragged bleeding man
Across the green mountain fast as he can –
He cried aloud from a great wound in his head:

PADRAIC (*motionless at the back of the stage*)
'Who dares to say the IRA is dead . . . !'

CROTCHET *and* BAKER-FORTESCUE *look at one another
aghast.*

BAKER-FORTESCUE
I do not understand what this should mean . . .

PADRAIC
Lie quiet, my love, it was a dreadful dream.
We have them all locked up in a dark box.
It was no man, it was a hunted fox.
Cut off his tail and nail it to your door:

Smear his red blood from ear to ear.
Did I not swear you have no more to fear . . . ?

BAKER-FORTESCUE. Exactly so. Preventive detention both
north and south of the Border is most efficiently in force. Mr
Crotchet, here is an axiom:

Whether he walk abroad open
Or lie close concealed,
The boldest terrorist in the world
Is not able to thrive
Without the people conspire together
To preserve him alive.

And they certainly don't do that in the Barony of
Kilnasleeveen. Decent deferential folk, every one of them, I
assure you. So: I'll put this in the post.

*While talking he has finished his letter, put it into an envelope, and
stamped it. Now he hands it to* PADRAIC.

Now: to my luncheon-appointment. Stocks-and-shares,
Zurich, the dollar, the drachma, the yen . . . !

PADRAIC (*looking at envelope*). This should get to Kilnasleeveen
the day after tomorrow.

Exeunt BAKER-FORTESCUE *and* CROTCHET.

Enter TERESA (*pregnant again*) *and* SEAMUS. PADRAIC
hands TERESA *the letter. She shows it to* SEAMUS *and opens it.*

SEAMUS. Does he send a postal order?

TERESA. He does not. And why would he? The American
woman wrote to him a whole scroll of complaints. Didn't I tell
you she would?

SEAMUS (*taking the letter from her*). Fleas, he says, hay, cow-dung
– and begod what's all this about his fence? Sure the night of
the big wind six yards of that same fence were transported half
over the lake and every switch of hay in my stacks distributed
between here and Macroom! What the hell will we feed the

cattle on till the end of winter, does he say that? Ho ho, 'tis all
his fence and the repair and conservation of it, when Tim
Hagan dug his posts no more than three inches into the ground
for him, sure a field-mouse could thrust it over. Since he sub-
let the old petrol-pump and moved into the contracting, that
Hagan's truly proved himself a sharp feller for the main chance.
I wouldn't care to have the employment of him in the
Tintawndub.

TERESA. In my opinion, 'tis time we had the employment of
somebody.

SEAMUS. Falling down about our ears. But how can we repair
our own house, will you tell me that, when the operation of the
entire farm has developed into a status of economic disaster?

TERESA. And what d'you intend should be done about it, so?

SEAMUS. Ah sure, the old place will last our lifetime. God
knows but we're modest people, we have no great
requirement. Though, mind you, if we built a small silo for the
cattle-feed . . .

TERESA. The young doctor at the dispensary said it was
dangerous for the baby to live any longer here with the cold
and the damp that's in it.

SEAMUS. Baby? What baby? Oh Jasus, that's not for another six
months.

TERESA. Four.

SEAMUS. Jasus, is it four, already? You made a slip in your
calculations there, woman, I'm telling you –

TERESA. I wonder you're not ashamed.

SEAMUS. Who says I am not ashamed?

TERESA. Is it you or myself then that will stand up to the
Honourable Baker?

SEAMUS. Stand up to him and do what?

TERESA.
Stand up to him and demand
That in our farm upon this land
He shall pay money and he shall take pain
To protect our lives and produce
From the wind and the rain.
Did you say a small silo? He could well afford the cost.
And send him that hospital X-ray of your chest.

SEAMUS.
It would be as well first to get hold of a lawyer.
Let the lawyer then write to him a letter that would be strong:
He writes in his own letters every line of a lawyer –
Why should not a lawyer as well do right as do wrong?
Upon a matter of right this farm is our own.

TERESA.
He claims it for himself.

SEAMUS.
Then it is himself that should pay.

TERESA.
So let you go to town for a lawyer:
And let you go there today.

SEAMUS.
Tomorrow will be time enough.
Bedamn I would go this minute only for this fierce cough.
Is it catch the bus in this weather? You know well I am not
    well:
Besides, I am detecting a weakness in my left heel.

TERESA.
You have a weakness in your head.

SEAMUS.
I have indeed. 'Tis well-known.

TERESA.
Oh 'tis easy to see that nothing will be done.

SEAMUS.

Bedamn I often wonder I don't take to my bed . . .

And where the hell d'you think you're going?

TERESA. I am going into town. Upon your business.

SEAMUS. You have no right to do that. You are the woman of
   the house and your name is good for nothing at the bottom of a
   document. A terrible thing when a man can't have obedience
   beneath his roof . . . ! I'll tell you what we'll do. I'll go and talk
   to Tim Hagan. He can put the word out for some of them
   precast concrete blocks, have a silo begun as soon as the
   weather lifts up. Sure the Honourable won't know about it till
   the work is commenced, and by then it'll be too late.

TERESA. You're not expecting him to pay?

SEAMUS. If he don't, we put in our ferret, our own lawyer,
   directly! Or better still, let Hagan do it. If you dropped your
   man Hagan from a very great height, wouldn't he land with his
   claws in the neck of the best advocate in Munster?

TERESA. But – but – Seamus –

SEAMUS. That's enough. I have me plan, and we stick to it.
   I'm away to meet Hagan. He'll be in Driscoll's bar, above. Did
   you ever hear of an American that never complained about
   anything . . . ?

TERESA. I did not.

   Exeunt TERESA *and* SEAMUS, *severally*.

Scene Three

Enter BAKER-FORTESCUE, *reading a letter*.

BAKER-FORTESCUE. A most appreciative letter from Major
Dreadnought Pole-Hatchet.

PADRAIC
EXPOSURE OF THE CONTRADICTIONS OF
PARTITION: WHO GIVES THE ORDERS FOR WHAT,
IN WHICH HALF? NINETEEN FIFTY-NINE.

BAKER-FORTESCUE. Mr Crotchet, are you there? 'The
fishing was first-rate, and the people very civil – although of
course in Kilnasleeveen they would be Catholics to a man.
How absurd,' he writes, 'to imagine every Irishman is a furnace
of political rage. Except of course where outside-agitators have
made their impact.' Exactly so. Mr Crotchet – ?

Enter CROTCHET.

CROTCHET. Oh yes, I can hear . . .

BAKER-FORTESCUE. Major Dreadnought Pole-Hatchet had
an excellent holiday.

CROTCHET. Very gratifying, I'm sure.

BAKER-FORTESCUE. Or did he? Good God, but just listen to
this. 'Only marred,' he says, 'marred, by the strange odour
from the new silo and the demolition of the gable wall that
would have stood between the Chalet and the prevailing west
wind: for this one must thank the egregious Mr Hagan, who
cannot, it appears, put a new roof on a barn without first
removing every wall and fence for two hundred yards . . . !'

CROTCHET. I'm afraid I don't quite understand . . .

BAKER-FORTESCUE. By heaven, sir, but *I* do! 'Mr Hagan,' he
continues, and expects me to receive it as a *joke*! 'Mr Hagan
ought to be transferred bone-by-bone into the National
Museum as a prime example of "*Contractor Hibernicus Vulgaris
Tyrannus* – mid twentieth-century."' Does that make it any
clearer?

CROTCHET. "Contractor Hibernicus . . ." aha, now I follow.
Oh dear, my dear sir, you should never have begun work upon
improving that small-holding without asking my advice.

BAKER-FORTESCUE. I have *not* begun work.

CROTCHET. The consequences, I assure you, are unforeseeable,
and infinite . . .

BAKER-FORTESCUE. I tell you, Mr Crotchet, I have not
begun work!

CROTCHET. But you authorised O'Leary –

BAKER-FORTESCUE. Oh no sir, I did not!

CROTCHET. Are you perfectly certain? There is no letter that
could be quoted against you, no hint, no intimation? You had
better let me see copies of all your correspondence, just in case.
But if what you say is true, you are in quite a strong position.

BAKER-FORTESCUE. Position to do what? To pay Hagan a
bill for some thousands of pounds? Do you know how much
he charged me for putting up that useless fence? And that was
work I *did* order – I superintended it in person!

CROTCHET. But the fence was for the Chalet, not the
farmyard? You yourself have made no improvements to the
Tintawndub, is that not so?

BAKER-FORTESCUE. I myself have charged them no *rent* for
the Tintawndub! As you told me, the position of the O'Learys
is so very – non-committal – extra-constitutional – ah, outside
the established framework.

CROTCHET. Rather like the Irish Free State, as it then was. I
mean, within the British Empire, and yet –

BAKER-FORTESCUE. A very good friend of mine in Bomber
Command, 1943, had to make a forced landing in County
Kildare. D'you know, the bloody buggers tried to have him
interned! In a camp full of Oberleutnants out of U-boats, if you
please. But as I understand it, the Irish Free State was the result

of a treaty worked out with Lloyd George when I was no more
than a schoolboy. It imposed upon the Irish a number of
responsibilities they have signally failed to live up to. This has
not been the case with my property, Mr Crotchet. There can be
absolutely no doubt that the Tintawndub belongs to *me*. You
have the deed, have you not? If the O'Learys misconduct
themselves, I can turn them out: and I shall.

CROTCHET. But you don't want them out.

BAKER-FORTESCUE. Not at present, certainly not. They are
essential to the proper administration of my holiday-chalet. But
in due course, if I can discover a more – a more *loyal* set of
dependants, the law, even the Irish law, I am confident, will be
on my side.

CROTCHET. I am not altogether so sure.

BAKER-FORTESCUE. But the deeds, documents, papers – I
have the *papers*, Mr Crotchet!

CROTCHET. Which do not define O'Leary. You need at least
one more document, to *confirm* him in his place.

BAKER-FORTESCUE. I don't *want* to confirm him! I want it to
be possible to –

CROTCHET. If need be, to turn the family out. You can't have
that until you know exactly upon what terms he is there. He
won't live very much longer, but –

An old man of the sea
With his legs around your throat
And after him his weeping widow
And his children, and no doubt
His children's children also and their wives –
Have you not thought
How long and how far this inordinate rout
Of uncontrollable hunger will chase
And outface and disgrace
You to the rim of your grave . . . ?

You may wish to develop the property at some future date –
for example, an hotel. You may wish yourself to get married:
you will need to leave an unencumbered inheritance to your
son.

BAKER-FORTESCUE.
Yes yes, but do not forget
Any document for O'Leary
Must be agreed by O'Leary:
The Irish Free State
Was agreed by solemn treaty –
And repudiated at a late date.
They pronounced themselves cheated
And formed a Republic.

CROTCHET.
And yet in the end they were measurably defeated.

They laid claim to a Republic of 32 Counties; they are
compelled to make do with no more than 26.

BAKER-FORTESCUE. Mr Crotchet, you are confusing me . . .

CROTCHET. Oh no, I'm not: I am drawing a significant
analogy, which I'm quite sure you can grasp – *if* you have a
mind that is jumping and leaping like mine.

BAKER-FORTESCUE. But I haven't, and I don't pretend to
have. I am a simple business man, not a ballet-dancer. I leave
the slyboot bits to you: and I expect you to explain 'em to me,
damn your eyes, in black and white.

CROTCHET. Yes, yes, indeed you do, yes. You are in fact
becoming rather stupid, are you not, when confronted by my
dialectical agility?

BAKER-FORTESCUE. There's no need to be insolent. You first
of all intimidate me by telling me that generations of these
damned O'Learys will be squatting on my land forever if
something is not done: and then when I ask you to –

CROTCHET. Intimidated . . . confused . . . stupid . . . and yet you began with straightforward righteous anger and a most justified grievance. Don't you see – there is a pattern? And if I were your antagonist instead of your friend, what could I not now do to embroil you to your own ruin? Psychology, my dear sir. You can do just the same yourself.

BAKER-FORTESCUE. Ah . . . ?

CROTCHET. Ah . . . you take the point? You need to get O'Leary to agree to a document that will not be to the ultimate advantage of his family. He is filled with righteous anger: he is a simple farmer, just as you are a simple business man: you must therefore be his ballet-dancer. To return to my analogy: Lloyd George made a treaty with Michael Collins which to be sure Michael Collins would never have agreed to had he understood the implications. In black and white: the Irish leader was intimidated, and confused, and in the end made thoroughly stupid. He brought back to Dublin for his pains the ruin of his Republican ideal.

BAKER-FORTESCUE. But, if you are asking me to trick O'Leary out of his rights –

CROTCHET. Alleged rights –

BAKER-FORTESCUE. Of course, of course – alleged – goes without saying –

CROTCHET. No it don't.

BAKER-FORTESCUE. Surely, Mr Crotchet, this would be very far from the proper thing?

CROTCHET. I think you are confounding morality with legality.

He sings: [Air: *Pretty Polly Perkins*]

'Intelligent application of the process of Law
Is available to all without favour or fear:
Is available to all who can meet the small bill
Of a first-rate solicitor with hearty good will!'

PADRAIC (*sings*).
　'Toodle-oo toodle-oo toodle-oodle oo doo
　If the Law plays its tricks, let it play them for *you*!'

CROTCHET (*sings*).
　'The process of Law is Doe versus Roe
　If one of them will stay than the other must go:
　If one of them will fall then the other must stand
　All you need is the right bit of paper in hand.'

PADRAIC (*sings*).
　'Toodle-oo toodle-oo toodle-oodle oo doo
　If the Law plays its tricks, let it play them for *you*!'

BAKER-FORTESCUE (*sings*).
　'The process of Law can be long or be short
　But a claim more established in broad open court
　Is established for ever and any attempt
　To impugn its morality is denounced as contempt.'

PADRAIC (*sings*).
　'Toodle-oo toodle-oo toodle-oodle oo doo
　If the Law plays its tricks, let it play them for *you*!'

BAKER-FORTESCUE (*sings*).
　'The concept of *trickery* is quite out of place –'

CROTCHET (*sings*).
　'The word you should use, sir, is *Legal Device*:
　The opposite party being equally aware –'

BAKER-FORTESCUE (*sings*).
　'If he don't get in first, he will not get his share!'

PADRAIC (*sings*).
　'Toodle-oo toodle-oo toodle-oodle oo *dee*
　If a man is not blind, it's assumed he can see –'

CROTCHET (*sings*).
　'If a man is not deaf, it's assumed he can hear –'

BAKER-FORTESCUE (*sings*).
　'If a man is not barmy, it's assumed he has wit –'

Exeunt CROCHET *and* BAKER-FORTESCUE, *dancing*.

PADRAIC (*sings*).
   'O'Leary O'Leary the challenge is clear:
   Come up to the struggle and prove yourself fit!'

   Because already your proud contender is once more launched
   upon the tide!

   BAKER-FORTESCUE *enters with a small suitcase, and stands
   around helplessly*.

BAKER-FORTESCUE (*calling*). Mrs O'Leary! O'Leary! . . .
   Seamus! . . . Teresa! Where are you? You, boy, I see you, yes
   you, over there, don't try to hide from me – who are you?
   Patrick, is it? Pad–ray–ic? Pat! Pat O'Leary, come here, boy,
   you know me – Paddy, damn you – here!

PADRAIC (*off the edge of the stage, as a small boy*). Oh Mr Baker,
   Mr Fortescue, 'tis yourself . . . !

BAKER-FORTESCUE. Of course it is myself.

PADRAIC (*at side of stage, to audience*). 'Twas himself. What
   would I know of the situation with my father, only for the
   telegram that had come to put the heart across him and drove
   him to Driscoll's like a mad dog.

BAKER-FORTESCUE. Did he not get my telegram – your
   father – where is he?

PADRAIC (*as a small boy*). I think, sir, he will be beyond . . .

   He disappears, and then reappears unnoticed.

BAKER-FORTESCUE. The Chalet's locked up, the farmhouse
   is locked up. And good God, look at my gooseberry bushes!

   Enter HAGAN.

HAGAN. I'm sorry, sir, about them bushes – we had no choice
   in the matter –

BAKER-FORTESCUE. Eh? What . . . ? Oh, Hagan. I fancy you
   have some explaining to do, Mr Hagan, have you not?

HAGAN. Oh indeed, sir, a question of attaining the top of the cowshed roof. I had to put me ladder somewhere. The gooseberry patch was the only place where –

BAKER-FORTESCUE. And in my Chalet? The broken windows?

HAGAN. Ah: 'twas the same ladder: to manoeuvre it, d'you see, between the pigsty and the Chalet, where the wall of the one is adjacent to the –

BAKER-FORTESCUE. Mr Hagan, from whom, might I ask, do you receive payment?

HAGAN. The job was authorised, sir, by Seamus O'Leary himself.

BAKER-FORTESCUE. And who is Seamus O'Leary to authorise –

HAGAN. In his capacity as your agent for the property and the up-keep.

BAKER-FORTESCUE. Who told you he was my agent?

HAGAN. Why, you yourself did. You have always referred to him so.

BAKER-FORTESCUE. Now look here, Hagan: do you have my signature for this work or do you not?

HAGAN. It has always been the custom in this part of the world, sir, when the landlord is an absentee, that the agent should be delegated to –

BAKER-FORTESCUE. I assure you, Mr Hagan, you will not make that stand up in court before a Judge.

HAGAN. Oh I wouldn't be so sure: local custom in these parts is a very powerful word.

BAKER-FORTESCUE. All work upon this site will cease forthwith, Mr Hagan.

HAGAN. Whatever you say, sir. Good night to you, so.

BAKER-FORTESCUE. One moment. Where's O'Leary?

HAGAN (*hands him a paper*). I think he will be beyond. Just the invoice for the building blocks and timber . . .

BAKER-FORTESCUE *crumples the document furiously and throws it back.*

HAGAN (*sings*) [Air: *Chevy Chase*].
'Your honour dear, this was not wise.
Tim Hagan's a crafty lad:
And an enemy of great venom
If you choose to fight him at all . . .'

PADRAIC (*sings*).
'Remember his business interests
By politics are reinforced –
He's a climbing lad and a grasping lad
And a power in the Fianna Fail!'

BAKER-FORTESCUE. In the what?

HAGAN. Ah wouldn't you know, like an Englishman always, he pretends he doesn't know.

Exit HAGAN.

PADRAIC.
THE LAST OF THE IMPERIALISTS CONFRONTS FACE-TO-FACE THE LAST OF THE SONS OF THE SOIL.

The O'LEARYS *enter.* SEAMUS *nervously tries to hide behind* TERESA *when he sees* BAKER-FORTESCUE. TERESA *is pregnant again.*

BAKER-FORTESCUE. Ah, Mrs O'Leary, an unexpected pleasure!

TERESA. Oh your honour, why didn't you give the notice you were coming?

BAKER-FORTESCUE. I suppose the Post Office does not deliver telegrams?

Aside to audience:

Good God I declare the woman
Is about to litter again!

To TERESA, *taking her aside:*

Mrs O'Leary, I do warn you: this is not wise.
Do you want a child born that cannot open its eyes,
With a red hole instead of a backbone
And one-third of a living brain?

TERESA.
Oh God help us what kind of a devil
Would put words in your mouth like that!

BAKER-FORTESCUE.
Mrs O'Leary, I do warn you:
Your husband is not fit.
Unanimous medical opinion has consistently laid down
That a man of your husband's habits
And his weaknesses – all well-known –
Cannot without danger be permitted to procreate.
I find it most unfortunate it should happen on my estate.

TERESA. I cannot believe I have heard what you have said.

SEAMUS *comes over to them.*

Seamus – he said to me –

SEAMUS. Between meself and the Honourable there is an issue
of principle. I would ask you to leave us alone.

TERESA. Are you sure that you know what you're doing?
Perhaps tomorrow – ?

SEAMUS. Today.

TERESA. I know *I* am in no condition to speak reasonably to
that man.

Exit TERESA.

SEAMUS. Now sir: to transact business. An explanation, if you please?

BAKER-FORTESCUE. I came here, Mr O'Leary, to obtain an explanation from *you*! By what right have you given orders –

SEAMUS. – for the improvement of the Tintawndub? I will answer you that when you answer me this. Whose is it, yours or mine?

BAKER-FORTESCUE. You live in it, certainly. I am the owner.

SEAMUS. If you are, you have the obligation to see it is kept in repair. If you refuse then 'tis clear you concede that the rights of the property appertain to meself.

BAKER-FORTESCUE. Now look here, O'Leary, I have not hitherto charged you one penny of rent for this small-holding, but –

SEAMUS. You have not. And why not?

BAKER-FORTESCUE. Because –

SEAMUS. Because you knew you did not dare, the foul condition it was in! But the minute you see improvements – ho ho how the man's brain turns round in avarice at the escalation of the value! 'Tis the same tale we have been told in Munster for three hundred years – the poor man's roof is worth nothing till he makes it worth something: and every particle of that worth is directly diverted to the strong-box of the landlord. And what benefit has the landlord put into the land – by construction, by muscular toil, by the hump of his shoulders or the blistering of his skin? Bedamn you do not even *live* here – if you look over the place for one week in twelve months we are to consider ourselves honoured! Oh you pass with some diligence your fragments of paper from the head-office of one bank to the head-office of the other: and by the time you draw them out again, by the same token they are converted into the fat goose upon your table and the cabbage and roast potatoes and the gravy poured over it. I tell you truth, me bold and

honourable: all that I have said to you, I have writ down upon
this paper.

He takes a document from his pocket.

O'Leary is not deceived: nor will he be intimidated.

BAKER-FORTESCUE. My dear sir, I have no intention of
deceiving you, or intimidating you. There has clearly been a
most unfortunate failure of communication here. Will you not
sit down quietly like a reasonable man, and help me sort it all
out?

PADRAIC.
I was not there when Seamus took the sword
And dagger of his own unaided word
Aloft in trembling fingers holding true
Our ancient right of life in face of Fortescue.
I was not there: but I bear in mind the tale
Of how another Irish champion, brave and afraid
At the one same time, just like my father, made
His own defiance. They said afterwards, that he too failed . . .
Nineteen hundred and twenty-one, years upon years of hate –
Michael Collins with the bold Lloyd George
Sat down to sort it out.
Said Michael Collins to the bold Lloyd George –

SEAMUS (*as Collins*).
We have you beat both black and blue.

PADRAIC.
Said the bold Lloyd George to Michael Collins –

BAKER-FORTESCUE (*as Lloyd George*).
The next move is up to you.
You have driven us demented with your murderous IRA
The whole map is besmothered with blood.
We can fight and fight, and fight for ever –
But to whom will be the good?
You have been an enemy: you can be a friend:
Dear sir, let us make an end.

Lay down your terms and we shall meet them
With a free and generous hand.

SEAMUS *passes him the paper.*

But first of all we must not neglect
The hospitality of London town,
Whole-hearted admiration
Of the entire British nation
For your courage and determination
Such honour and respect –

He pockets the paper.

I'll look this over, let my ministers decide
Just how much we can give you and how soon.

BAKER-FORTESCUE *retires.*

PADRAIC.
It has been said
Brave Collins got most beastly drunk.
This was not true.
It has been said
Brave Collins found his head
So turned by adulation
That he knew not what to do . . .

SEAMUS (*as Collins*).
Responsibility, not liquor, compels my brain
Like a wild insane electric train
Around around around – around –
Where will it *stop* . . . !

BAKER-FORTESCUE *comes in again behind him.*

BAKER-FORTESCUE. Now, Mr O'Leary, shall we get down
to brass-tacks? You see, Mr O'Leary, the situation is this: as
you told Timothy Hagan, you are my agent in Kilnasleeveen:
the protection of my property depends upon you. You do
realise, by the way, that you yourself have no protection . . .? I
mean, security in your work, in the powers vested in you as

my accredited representative here. It's a heavy responsibility when I am so often away.

SEAMUS. An onerous bloody burden, so it is, so it is.

BAKER–FORTESCUE. It has been pointed out to me, that in fairness to yourself and family, your position in the Tintawndub here, your security of tenure, your right to the responsibility you so ably carry out, should be regularised and correctly registered . . .

He passes SEAMUS *a paper.*

PADRAIC.
Said Michael Collins to the bold Lloyd George –

SEAMUS (*as Collins, examining the paper*).
This is not the same document as the one I gave you.

PADRAIC.
Said the bold Lloyd George to Michael Collins –

BAKER–FORTESCUE (*as Lloyd George*)
Certain amendments for your own security:
Here and there . . . one or two . . .

PADRAIC.
Said Collins with the red fire on his cheek –

SEAMUS (*as Collins*)
You think that you are strong and I am weak –

BAKER–FORTESCUE (*as Lloyd George*).
So strong, my friend, that if you do not agree,
Immediate terrible war will be set free
Across the whole of Ireland, nothing you've known so far
From torturing Tans or hangmen shall compare
With that huge avalanche of horror I can rear
Above the mountain-slopes of your deceitful nation
Now, even now, before the sunset of this very day . . . !

SEAMUS (*as himself, suddenly broken*). Oh Mr Baker, sir, all I want, sir, is to enjoy for the rest of my life the rightful roof

above my house, sir, my own house, sir, my wife and family,
my bit of land –

Yet you tell me you'd turn me out to beg my way
Lie down in a ditch to starve and die
The same as my great-grandfather . . . My God I never
    thought
A decent English gentleman would do me such great hurt.

BAKER-FORTESCUE. Oh dear, my dear Seamus, you have
most totally misunderstood. I mean, supposing, my dear
fellow, I were to be killed in a motor-accident, someone else
would inherit the property, and that someone else, as things
stand, could indeed evict you: and without redress! You must
not be put at risk.

SEAMUS. Risk – ? Begod – no – ! Evict me, is it? Let any man
try that and I swear I'll have his blood!

BAKER-FORTESCUE. No no sir, not his blood. His legal
power, that is sufficient. And there is the defensive weapon by
which it can be achieved.

He indicates the paper. SEAMUS *studies it.*

PADRAIC. They called in a couple of the neighbours to be the
witnesses. And he read the paper, right through. And it was
explained to him.

BAKER-FORTESCUE. You do understand, don't you – this
gives you exactly what you told me you want – your rightful
roof, yours, for the rest of your life . . .

SEAMUS *signs the document.*

PADRAIC. This is a Life-Tenancy Agreement between the
Honourable Roderick Baker-Fortescue and Seamus O'Leary
Esquire. According to its terms the said Seamus O'Leary
receives absolute entitlement to reside for the term of his
natural life in the small-holding known as 'The Tintawndub'
appertaining to the property known as 'The Chalet,

Kilnasleeveen', said small-holding being absolutely the freehold property of the said Baker-Fortescue. Rent to be paid: nil. County-rate, and water-rate, where applicable, to be paid by the freeholder. The freeholder undertakes to keep said Tintawndub and all appertenances and messuages in good and sufficient repair at all times. Upon decease of said O'Leary, tenure of said Tintawndub reverts at will to the freeholder. That's it.

And that is that
And that is all.
If John Doe is to stand
Then Richard Roe must fall.

During the above speech, BAKER-FORTESCUE *has turned his back on* SEAMUS *and the audience.* SEAMUS *slowly subsides to the ground.*

BAKER-FORTESCUE. Before I return to Harrogate, a brief letter to the man Hagan – leave it in at the local Post Office – I don't want to have words with him personally.

Writing a postcard.

'Resume work upon *cowshed* alone: complete it as soon as possible.' He won't like it, but I am reducing the scale of his operations. He is only to do about half what he had hoped to do.

Exit BAKER-FORTESCUE.

Enter TERESA.

TERESA. What has he done to him? And what has he made him do?

PADRIAC *shows her the signed document.*

He has put his name to *that*?

She sings: [Air: *The Red-haired Man's Wife*]

'Oh shame upon Seamus O'Leary,
What have you agreed?

You've handed over your land and your house
Without any need:
Your wife and your children,
Your life you have given away
For a portion of paper
Like the pay that's the wage of a slave.

You are weak, you are sick,
A mere wreck of a man on the ground:
Alive you will never rise up
If you cannot stand now.
The children who loved you
Must break and forsake you and go
Far over the ocean
From the home that their father has sold.

It is not as though
The police and the bailiffs arrived
With bludgeons and rifles
To drive us all out in the night –
We'd have then had our pride
We could fight them and maybe we'd win:
What pride in a man
With one smile and one threat he gives in?'

SEAMUS (*struggling to his knees*). Oh God forgive me, Teresa, dear God, what should we do? For a start, we do this . . .

He strikes a match and burns the document.

It never happened, so. It is forgot.

TERESA. It is remembered: and by himself: at the time when we least shall want it.

She leads him away.

PADRAIC. And that is the end of the first half of the story – the first half of *my* story. But because, as you have seen, it was outside of my control, I daresay you'd do best to think of it as the Prologue. That was it.

Exit.

Act Two

Scene One

Enter PADRAIC, *as a living man.*

PADRAIC.
  NINETEEN SIXTY-EIGHT.

He sings: [Air: *The Wearing of the Green*]

'From the year of nineteen fifty-nine
To nineteen sixty-eight
The fat guts of the fat half-world
Had food on every plate.

The starvelings of the naked world
Grew leaner every day
And if they put their faces up
Their teeth were kicked away:

And if they dared to link their arms
Or set their shoulders wide
Such furious dogs were flung on them
They bled both back and side.

And if in narrow holes they crouched
Defences to contrive,
They were smeared with flaming jelly
Till not one was left alive.

For the fat guts at their dinner-board
Could never bear to think
That creeping fingers from below
Might steal their meal and drink.'

Seamus O'Leary my father so suddenly dead in the Regional
Hospital, for nine years now he was bent and bowed over like
the limb of a mountain thorn: alternate breath he coughed up
blood: Monday and Tuesday he would have died upon the
spot: Wednesday and Thursday he put his boots among the turf
and would dig for his living and cough: Friday and Saturday he

would crouch by the fire in Driscoll's Bar and his glass would never be empty: Sunday he would obey his duty, he'd uncover his head just inside the churchdoor: and Monday once again he would have died upon the spot. Who the hell could dance attendance on a man that went from us as slow and as tiresome as that? Me mother's telegram came to Manchester where I worked as a bricklayer: God knows she could not tell I had travelled that week to Dunfermline. He had but the one son: and three days late for the funeral. Already fallen down on my first responsibility . . . But begod I'll make up for it.

Enter HAGAN, PADRAIC *stands apart, his back turned, meditating.*

HAGAN. So he comes home, the son and heir, three days late. Fat men thin men, is it? Would you call *me* fat? Because if I am, then he's thin, and I don't care for the sound of such comparisons in Kilnasleeveen. Ah, Padraic – there ye are: I'm sorry for your trouble, son. Oh indeed, that's the grave. As you see there's no stone ordered yet. But you'll be wanting to sort out the debit and credit before you'd think of that.

PADRAIC. I haven't had a sight of the will. But the Tintawndub –

HAGAN. Will be left to you of course. Would you think it worth the working, that bit o'land now, I very much doubt it. In the heel of the hunt you'd be advised to look out for a class of job, that is if you mean to stay here. I could always use a bricklayer, part-time. Think it over.

PADRAIC. I haven't decided whether to stay or go back.

HAGAN. Maybe after all you'd do best to go back, take the old lady with you and your sister Siobhan, why not?

PADRAIC. What would happen to the Tintawndub?

HAGAN. Sure you'd always find a purchaser. Would you care for a jar at Driscoll's?

PADRAIC. Ah no, I must get home. I promised I wouldn't be long.

HAGAN. Good luck to you, so . . .

Exit PADRAIC.

HAGAN. 'What would happen to the Tintawndub . . . ?'
They've told him nothing of the state of affairs. Life–Tenancy
Agreement – ha! When he finds out, there'll be ructions: and
Tim Hagan is now established as the sympathetic friend and
compassionate counsellor.

I am, you see, a business man
I look for the main chance where I can.
Creeping fingers from below?
I smudge 'em out like flakes of snow . . . !

Exit HAGAN.

Enter SIOBHAN.

PADRAIC. Here's Siobhan, my youngest sister, the only one not
yet married or gone into a convent: something's to be done for
her directly, but what? You're still determined, are you, to
carry on through the college till you qualify as a physiotherapist
or whatever? But to support you out of three fields and a leaky
old half-rebuilt farmhouse, and all my work and contacts away
over in England, it's not good sense. Why don't you and
mammy come over with me as soon as we can get the
Tintawndub sold? There's not only colleges in England, there's
the welfare state, government grants – together with the money
we get out of the sale – and on my own account I'm doing well
enough there to organise a permanent home for you both.

SIOBHAN. Money out of the sale? You're not trying to tell me
Hagan has made you an offer?

PADRAIC. He seemed to be edging towards it.

SIOBHAN. Nonsense, Paudeen, how can he have been? He
knows as well as we do that you can't sell the farm so long as
the ownership is in dispute.

PADRAIC. Dispute? Who disputes it?

SIOBHAN. Harrogate, the Honourable Baker, who do you think?

PADRAIC. Ah no, he owns the Chalet, the Tintawndub was always ours. Baker-Fortescue never had a leg to stand on in that matter – sure, if he owned it, wouldn't we always have paid him rent?

SIOBHAN. I don't know: but I do know he claims it, all fifteen acres. So we can't sell. And what's more, we can't leave. As long as we stay put we are asserting our own claim, and there's nothing he can do except what he's always done – let us live here and work the farm. There's no reason at all why I shouldn't learn to follow my professional career in my own country these days: the time is long past an educated woman had to look towards England for a living. But if need be I'd give up the college for a year to set things on a sound footing. But I certainly won't quit just to please some British businessman who thinks that no-one in Ireland has a right to their own life. Anyway, mammy won't leave under any circumstances, I may tell you: so that's that.

PADRAIC. Sentimental idealism confounded with short-sighted economic confusion. High time we were rid of it.

SIOBHAN. High time we were rid of your Manchester fashion of talk. Denouncing everyone left and right out of a pocket-full of English pamphlets, and you've only been home a few hours.

PADRAIC. That's right, I'm a stranger in this bloody place. I've been away since I was seventeen, I'm no sooner back than everything you say to me makes me want to get out again as quick as I can –

Enter TERESA.

TERESA. Get out, did you say? Isn't that exactly what the man wants! But we're not going to give it to him, oh no . . . unless of course you were to sell under his feet so quiet and quick he would never know a thing about it till after it was done. Do you think that could be possible – perhaps a quiet word with Tim Hagan . . . ?

PADRAIC. It's not likely, it's a legal question – we'd have to have some sort of document about the ownership –

TERESA. Ah – document – is it papers? No, Paudeen, oh no, no more o' them! Thank you very much indeed –

PADRAIC. What d'you mean, no *more* of 'em?

TERESA. Never mind, he'll do nothing, so long as we're here, it's *ours* –

Enter HAGAN.

HAGAN.
SENTIMENTAL IDEALISM CONFOUNDED WITH SHORT-SIGHTED ECONOMIC CONFUSION.

Through the post comes a letter with an evil report.
Her hand takes the letter, the trap springs, the mice are caught.

He gives a letter to TERESA *and exit.*

TERESA. Paudeen, I can't read it. It is from him: there is poison, deadly poison in his words. The last child of all I should have brought forth into the world was born dead, for no other reason than the curse of this – this gentleman he spoke over me while I was carrying her. Paudeen, read the letter.

PADRAIC (*having taken the letter*). He says, he is sorry to hear of the death. He says, 'You do realise that the Life-Tenancy I afforded Seamus must necessarily expire at – at the same time that he did . . .'! If this means what I think it means we have not even got the right to stay put on the land and make any sort of claim on that basis. All the generations we have been here and none of it worth anything! What else does he say? He might have allowed you to stay on here, he says – except that he had heard you had 'entertained offers from certain business interests to dispose of what was not yours . . .'?

TERESA. Sure Hagan and some others of them were speaking about our selling the farm, but –

PADRAIC. 'Reluctantly therefore . . . left with no alternative
. . . reluctantly put the Life-Tenancy Agreement in the hands
of my solicitor . . . instructions to terminate forthwith. Rod.
Baker-Fortescue, H.O.N. in brackets.'

SIOBHAN. He wants us all off the land this minute: and no
recompense at all?

PADRAIC. If we don't go, he'll go to court and get the court to
put the sheriff in, and evict us – oh he has that power. Oh God
what the devil was in this Agreement? Do we not have a copy
of it?

SIOBHAN (*taking letter and looking at it*).
And this is the letter that he writes to be read
By the side of the death-bed
Of the man who did aid his interest year in and year out
Like an ass between the shafts of an over-loaded cart.

TERESA. Lord Ballydehob always said the historical right, the
moral right, he always put it, was our own, and he never
insisted we –

PADRAIC. Moral . . . historical . . . there is no right in Ireland
but the right of the English Law carried over from the old days.
Yet dammit we do have a Constitution in this country,
maintains as a basic principle the integrity of the Irish family
and all the children of the nation. It must surely prevent a man
signing over every right of his own children to some capitalist
across the water –

SIOBHAN. Then if that's so we meet him head on in the courts
and fight the case right down to the end.

TERESA. That's it: we're not budging.

SIOBHAN. We're not budging.

TERESA. Oh now that it's too late I see the whole thing so very
clear – the straddle of his great boots and the mud and blood
that stains them –

PADRAIC. Boots, mud . . . ?

TERESA.
    Oh 'tis apparent.
    'Tis the man with the long purse
    Spreads his feet across this land
    His boots that leave no room for the tread of anyone else:
    He opens his purse and dips in his hand,
    Pulls it out again tight-clenched
    Being full to the bend of his thumb:
    And those few for whom he opens it
    Are the same few every time.

SIOBHAN. Tim Hagan for one.

TERESA.
    Oh well indeed for himself
    Tim Hagan has done.
    And yet nothing more
    Than what was begun
    When the Harrogate Honourable
    Came to us out of the war
    And bought your father like a slave
    Body and soul and all alive.
    And now in the end he has killed him dead
    And he hangs his great red blade
    Hard over your mother's head.

PADRAIC.
    You shall not go.
    This home is your own
    And you are to remain.
    There is nothing I shall not dare
    To make sure that you do.

TERESA.
    Padraic, you are young.
    But you are my one son
    I put my trust in you.

    Exit TERESA.

PADRAIC. Ah for God's sake a bit of courage comes easy to anyone – the bloody practicality'll finish *me* before I'm started. Have we no legal papers whatever? Do we know any lawyers?

SIOBHAN. Do you think if he takes us to court and we don't have the papers we will lose?

PADRAIC. I don't know, but a court-case would stir up the politics –

SIOBHAN. You mean, barricade the Tintawndub like the days of Parnell? Put the posters up all over the country – 'No Brit Evictions in Kilnasleeveen!' – you mean that?

PADRAIC. Not quite. I mean Mass Support and the Solidarity of the Working Class –

SIOBHAN. Oh Manchester talk – fairy-tales – your English trade unions –

PADRAIC.
The very opposite to Parnell.
Parnell is not the name
I would summon for this game:
Trade unions to Parnell
Were very devils out of hell.
Trade unions would have fallen under condemnation and black ban
Had the government ever passed into the power of that proud man.

To put it bluntly, Siobhan, he would have sold out the Revolution.

SIOBHAN. Look, Paudeen, we have had the Revolution in Ireland.

PADRAIC. 1916 I suppose . . . ?

Ah Jesus in that glorious year
What did they do at all?
Shot to death James Connolly
Propped up against a wall.

> And those greedy men whom all his life
> He had fought till he could not stand
> Had the whole of the Irish nation
> Delivered into their hand.

SIOBHAN. Let you talk about your Socialism, you'll be denounced by the priest. But if, on the other hand, we had the priest on our side –

PADRAIC. Did you talk to him?

SIOBHAN. I think mammy did. 'The Law must take its course,' he said. Where do the clergy live but at the bottom of the long purse?

PADRAIC.
> There must be *something* in this land –
> Not to find it out, pick it up,
> Just like that, out of hand –
> But never will I credit
> That the people's dreams of power
> Justice, dignity, at last
> Are rising up on every shore
> Except the one that *we* inhabit – !
> Parnell, and the delusive past –
> Manchester-talk, oh yes, like withered winter grass:
> You laugh at the one and I sneer at the other.
> But sister and sister, brother and brother –
> We are the people and the land belongs to *us*!

Enter HAGAN.

HAGAN (*to audience*).
> They are standing all alone
> And their words are blown away:
> How *can* the land belong to them – ?
> They can talk they can talk
> But we know they cannot pay . . .

SIOBHAN *and* PADRAIC *are going out.* HAGAN *catches* PADRAIC's *eye and makes a covert sign. Mistrustfully* PADRAIC *lets his sister go on alone and joins* HAGAN.

HAGAN. Now I heard something at Driscoll's about your Harrogate man and his pretensions. Wouldn't you know the cute bugger'd be after holding the closest card up his sleeve the whole time? Does your mother intend to fight it in the courts?

PADRAIC. She does.

HAGAN. Ah . . . she won't win. Not a chance. But it's bound to take a long time and it's bound to arouse a deal of popular feeling. Now you want to be building on that. And you want to make friends with a few certain people – name no names but you take my meaning – they'll be able to look after you if and when things come to the worst.

Enter MULHOLLAND. *He has a poster reading: 'Land League and Small Farmers' Civil Rights. Public Meeting Sunday 12.30'. He also carries a paste-pot and brush.*

Ah – Terry Mulholland!

MULHOLLAND. Tim Hagan, the very man. You'll put a couple of these up for us on your building-yard gateposts, sure you will –

He hands HAGAN *one or two posters.*

HAGAN. This is Padraic O'Leary, you'll have heard about his trouble – the Tintawndub, you know what I mean. I'll leave you with him, so.

MULHOLLAND *greets* PADRAIC *and gets into earnest talk with him.* HAGAN, *downstage, looks at the posters with distaste.*

HAGAN (*to audience*). Public meeting – a sight *too* public, that's not the way at all – there's no need at all to disseminate this class of nonsense. I thought they were supposed to be an *illegal* organisation . . . ? People should stay where they belong, or we're all of us disordered.

He crumples the posters and goes out.

MULHOLLAND (*continuing his remarks to Padraic*). Keep clear of that Hagan – calls himself a Republican, but that's only for show. He's no more interested in civil rights or democracy than any other gombeen business character – it's men like him helped De Valera send the genuine Republicans into gaol as soon as the Brits put the screws on. I was interned myself for seven years, so I know what I'm talking about. I'm a qualified school-teacher, but damn the jobs I've been able to find since the day they let me out. I get expenses from the Republican Movement for organising things for them in these parts, and otherwise I live on the dole. So you see, when I tell you that Civil Rights is the one struggle worth fighting for in all Ireland north and south, you'll understand I speak from experience.

PADRAIC. And how does that affect me in regard to this eviction?

MULHOLLAND. If you join the movement, come to the meetings, make a few speeches for us, you'd find that this apparently minor affair of a ratty little Brit landlord, with a single bit of paper to force an Irish family out of their home onto the road, is a straight indication of all that's wrong with this country – the ownership of the Six Counties, the subjection of the Fianna Fail government to multi-national industrial syndicates, the Offences Against The State Act, internment for Republicans, the lot.

PADRAIC. You want to use me for your party advantage?

MULHOLLAND. Aren't you an Irishman? The Republican Movement is for the advantage of all oppressed people in Ireland: and you don't need me to tell you that the greater the agitation, the greater the pressures on the courts when your case comes to trial. It could even be that your mother's predicament becomes so notorious that they won't dare give a verdict in favour of the Harrogate man. None of the other political outfits in the country could do that for you, bet your boots. Ah . . . is it the physical-force secret-society side of the thing makes you twist your face at me? Oh it does, you've been mixing with your left-wing crowd in England who'd make out that all nationalism is directly opposed to socialism. But that's only because they have no experience of the colonial situation, except for all the benefits it's brought them over the years. But the bombing and shooting's a virtual dead letter these days – though the likes of Tim Hagan still hope to make use of it. What we're concerned about now is solid organisation to expose the economic contradictions.

PADRAIC. That makes sense.

MULHOLLAND. I thought you'd think so.

PADRAIC. My sister would even call it Manchester talk.

MULHOLLAND. Only because she's forgotten what Wolfe Tone had to say in 1798 – 'the people of no property' – his link with the French Revolution – remember, our republican roots are far deeper grounded in the true hunger of the people than any of your British chauvinist marxism. Come to Driscoll's and we'll talk about it . . .

Exeunt. (As he speaks, he has been pasting up one of his posters at the back of the stage.)

Re-enter HAGAN. He multilates the poster.

HAGAN.
SENTIMENTAL IDEALISM CONFOUNDED WITH BLOODY SUBVERSION.

And not only in Kilnasleeveen.

Scene Two

HAGAN.
NINETEEN SIXTY-EIGHT: OCTOBER

Exit HAGAN.

Enter CROTCHET, followed by BAKER-FORTESCUE.

CROTCHET. What the devil is going on in Londonderry these days? Just caught it on the television. Battering and bloodshed.

It could have repercussions! I must take immediate steps . . . my stockbroker . . .

He goes over to the telephone and dials a number.

Mr Giltedge? Good morning. Crotchet here. Now listen, my shares in Harland and Wolff of Belfast. I want you to get rid of them, sell them . . . that's right, and put the money in – ah – South African Mining stock, got that? . . . Oh, Giltedge, you still there? My friend Mr Baker-Fortescue would like you to do the same for him . . . Yes yes, very good, good-bye, my dear fellow.

He rings off.

He says he will do it for you. One must act in good time.

PADRAIC *and* MULHOLLAND *appear at the rear as a chorus.*

PADRAIC *and* MULHOLLAND (*sing*) [Air: *The Boys of Wexford*].
'Beneath the walls of Derry town
They marched with banners high
"One man one vote" and "civil rights"
United was the cry.'

BAKER-FORTESCUE. Thank you, thank you . . .

CROTCHET. Barbarous, isn't it?

BAKER-FORTESCUE. The police there, of course, are allowed very free rein, most necessary, I believe.

PADRAIC *and* MULHOLLAND (*sing*).
'They bore no arms, they threatened none
As they marched beneath that wall:
But the RUC with bloody glee
On the people were let fall.

They did not care whom they struck down
In their rage so blind and wild:
Old men's gray hair they did not spare
Nor the mother with her child.'

BAKER-FORTESCUE. Disgracefully exaggerated: but even
were it true I would thoroughly approve. We have had quiet
and good order in that part of the United Kingdom for nearly
fifty years. If anyone wants to dispute the fact he most certainly
should not do so by assembling large crowds and indulging in
emotional oratory.

CROTCHET. That sort of thing can only lead to violence: and it
is very good to see that the police are determined that no
violence shall take place.

PADRAIC and MULHOLLAND (*sing*).
'Let the men of Stormont tremble now
At the work they have begun
For by the blow that they have struck
Their power is all undone.

The blood they shed in Derry town
On the pavement let it lie.
Till Ireland's free from north to south
Those pools will not be dry.'

PADRAIC and MULLHOLLAND *withdraw*.

CROTCHET. Yes . . . from north, to south, yes? Do I detect a
faint suggestion that *no* part of Ireland is free? You know what
that means, don't you? Those agitators over there are not green
any longer, but –

BAKER-FORTESCUE. Not green?

CROTCHET. Red.

BAKER-FORTESCUE. But – but – surely not in Kilnasleeveen
. . . ?

CROTCHET. Yes . . . Concerning Kilnasleeveen: I am one
hundred per cent certain that the Irish court will give us the
possession order we are asking for. But, what d'you propose to
do with the Tintawndub once she's out of it?

BAKER-FORTESCUE. I think I shall probably sell it. Hagan is
interested, you know. There have been other enquiries as well.

My partner has a contact in Blackpool with a notion of developing the entire site – continental holiday-village, yachting, you know, girls in bikinis – I suppose the O'Leary woman has asked for compensation?

CROTCHET. Her solicitors have put forward the figure of £5,000.

BAKER-FORTESCUE. Good God, whatever for?

CROTCHET. For the improvements that they paid for themselves. I offered seven hundred and fifty. It might keep us out of a contested court-case, you see. Ticklish.

BAKER-FORTESCUE. Rubbish: and five hundred would have been more than enough!

Exit BAKER-FORTESCUE.

CROTCHET. I do beg your pardon, I'm sure . . .

Re-enter BAKER-FORTESCUE.

BAKER-FORTESCUE. No – Crotchet – one moment – you said '*red*'? Civil rights for Catholics is a *communist* demand . . . ? What religion is Teresa O'Leary? I have just had a letter from Timothy Hagan: he writes –

HAGAN *appears at the back as* BAKER-FORTESCUE *shows* CROTCHET *the letter.*

HAGAN. 'I have kept him as I told you under my eye in my own employ: but only that they know I will tolerate no trade-unions, he'd make more trouble with my other men than his presence is worth. All his talk about Manchester and some powerful great building-site strike he helped organise there last year.'

BAKER-FORTESCUE. D'you see what I mean – red, Crotchet – *red*!

HAGAN. 'He's also been involved in certain secret political meetings, d'you know what I mean. Most distasteful in the view of the large Dutch and German interests in the tourist

business in these parts. In regard to which my offer for the
Tintawndub still stands . . .'

HAGAN *withdraws*.

BAKER-FORTESCUE. Appalling how fast this perversion can
spread! In 1967 it was students in Berlin, earlier this year it was
students and just about everyone else in Paris – today it is
Londonderry – tomorrow . . . telephone!

He goes to telephone, looking up a number in his pocketbook: he dials.

Ministry of Defence? Extension 8967000. Hello . . . hello: I
wish to speak to Wing-Commander Black, if he is with
you . . .

To CROTCHET:

I suppose we are secure? This line is not equipped with a
scrambler, I notice.

Into phone:

Ah: Wing-Commander Black? I am right to call you 'Black'?
Same code-name as of old? . . . Yes, yes, of course, we're not
scrambled, must be careful, security . . . You do know who
this is, I take it? . . . Not? Then suppose I remind you of
another and less official sobriquet by which you were once
known? Ha ha – 'Dogsballock!' You remember – in a jeep
outside the burgomaster's office in Wuppertal, just after the
Hun had surrendered, with the wife of the Untergruppenführer
under arrest in the back seat . . . Yes, yes, indeed it is, it is
Roddy Baker-F! . . .

To CROTCHET.

Of course he remembers, he's an incredibly well-trained man.

Into phone:

Now, Dogsballock, look here – the current situation in the
Province of Ulster . . . Yes yes I know that at the moment it is
only the concern of the civil police. But let us not deceive

ourselves: no more than a matter of months before the armed forces of the Crown are involved there up to the hilt! Before they involve *them*, they are bound to involve *you*, can't bring in the troops without help from the Old Firm, eh! . . . There is no need to be discourteous, I am only endeavouring to help! I will continue, if you permit. A representative of the Stormont Government has already identified the so-called civil rights campaign as nothing more than a front for the IRA. And the IRA he has identified as a front for international C-O-M-M-U-N-I-S-M and we all know what *that* is. At least, *I* do: I hope *you* do: I mean, that's what you're paid for. Now: I have no doubt that you will already have considered the probability of IRA bases of support and supply being established south of the border to maintain the subversion in the north. The question is, where? . . . Dogsballock, I am this very moment giving you the answer! Kilnasleeveen – four syllables, and crammed to the brim with a priest-ridden malignant mob of – of damnable defaulters, evaders of rent, and squatters upon property to which they have absolutely not a shadow of title! I just thought I'd let you know . . . I also thought an officer as highly placed as you are in the occult milieu of military intelligence would be a little more forthcoming when an old – as you might say – associate condescends to volunteer some information. You always were an unwholesome little tick: and I am bitterly sorry I remembered your telephone number. You behaved like a perfect cad that evening in Wuppertal: and Penelope thought so too.

He rings off.

Yet he is, as I said, a highly-trained man – he'll not forget what I've told him.

CROTCHET. Who's Penelope?

BAKER-FORTESCUE. I do not propose to bandy a lady's name with you. You have your instructions, Mr Attorney – carry on!

Exeunt severally.

Scene Three

Enter PADRAIC, *dressed as a building worker, with appropriate gear which he carries across the stage as though engaged on a job.* HAGAN *is with him giving various instructions in dumb-show. They pass across the stage, then* HAGAN *leaves.* PADRAIC *hurriedly pastes up a poster reading 'No Brit Evictions: Mass Meeting! Saturday'. He goes out again.* HAGAN *re-enters and tears part of the poster down.*

HAGAN.
NINETEEN SEVENTY: MINORITY AGITATION
BECOMES A MAJORITY THREAT.

Exit HAGAN.

Enter LIMEGRAVE *festooned with cameras.*

During this scene PADRAIC *moves about at the back, at work and oblivious. At one point he replaces the torn poster.*

LIMEGRAVE.
Old Wingco Black, my chief, is said
To be already failing in his head.
The Secret Service falls on evil days –
He is too old, although he once was wise:
Against the Hun, the Red, the Chinaman, the Wog,
He did good service once: but what a fog
Comes down upon his mind from this Hibernian bog . . . !
Because the streets of Derry run with blood,
To Munster I am sent: and for what good?

He takes a rice-paper document from a false heel in his shoe.

He says: 'Kilnasleeveen: take a cottage, make use of an
appropriate cover.' No problem, my normal work, genuine
and unbreakable: I make documentary films for BBC2.
Ecology and conservation. The best-known perhaps would be
The Sloblands of Shannon, with soundtrack composed by a
traditional tinker from Antrim who plays the tin whistle.
Enough of that – *business*. 'Prepare a report upon subject
already known to Special Branch, Manchester: O'Leary,
Padraic: we have the files, trouble-making trade-union militant,

political overtones. Suggest examine links with Republican
Movement.' I have. Deeply implicated. Small Farmers' Land
League, Civil Rights for Offshore Fishermen, demonstrations
against pollution outside multinational chemical-works,
Limerick. So much trouble in the North: *West* of Ireland at all
costs must be kept quiet. 'Subject may well form nucleus of an
undesirable element.' Thank you, Wingco Black! O'Leary's
little sister is very far from undesirable. According to routine
procedure I have begun my surveillance there: nearest approach
to subject himself, so far, long-distance photography. Oh! I
was supposed to have got rid of this upon arrival. So easy to
forget, when women are confusing the trail . . .

He begins to eat his orders.

SIOBHAN has entered behind him.

SIOBHAN. If that is chewing gum, can I have a piece?

LIMEGRAVE. My love, you are late. No, chewing-gum – no. A
local herb, I'd have thought you'd have known about it – St
Brigid's Eyelash, traditional remedy for arthritis – does your
mother not use it?

SIOBHAN. If she has a pain she takes an aspirin.

LIMEGRAVE. Oh no she must try this, let me pick you a
bunch . . .

He is trying to kiss her.

SIOBHAN. You won't find any round my neck. I thought you
would be filming the mosses and fern at the lakeside. Well, here
you are, amongst them. Get out your old light-meter.

LIMEGRAVE. Not even BBC2 wants the mosses and fern
uninhabited. Sit down and display yourself, and unwind three
or four layers of wool.

*He starts to pose her, and attempts to remove her scarf. She prevents
him unfastening anything further.*

SIOBHAN. Mr Limegrave, do you know my brother? He is
   working just above: the new bungalow this side of the
   bohereen.

LIMEGRAVE. Oh he is, is he? Crafty colleen, you are protected,
   dear oh dear . . .

   Aside to audience:

   Little does she know it was with full deliberation
   I persuaded her to meet me in this very secluded place.
   I want a good close-up of the militant brother's face:
   We do not have one in our file.

   To SIOBHAN:

   So: there you are: your back to the bushes – and smile!

PADRAIC, *in the midst of his work, stops and watches them for a
moment.* LIMEGRAVE *is taking movie-film, chiefly of Siobhan, but
includes a shot of Padraic.* PADRAIC, *unaware of this, goes away
again.* LIMEGRAVE *speaks to the audience:*

   Out-of-focus, imperfect, zoom-lens on the bloody blink:
   Draw him in that little bit closer – how to do it – let me
     think . . .

   To SIOBHAN:

   Dreadfully ugly bungalow, don't you agree? Environmental
   disaster if ever I saw one.

SIOBHAN. Let me tell you there is nothing more important than
   decent houses in Kilnasleeveen! That bungalow would be God's
   gift to my mother if only she could afford it.

LIMEGRAVE. Oh I know I know I know – evicted by the Brits
   – you will never be anything other than a terrible little Fenian –

SIOBHAN.
   Tourist oh tourist, you come and you go:
   You talk and you talk, there is nothing you do not know.
   Is there nothing you can talk about you really understand?
   What is that in your hand?

LIMEGRAVE (*who has been picking flowers*). Snowdrops for a necklace for the whitest neck in the Emerald Isle. One thing I would talk about, I do understand –

SIOBHAN. So what is it, Mr Limegrave?

LIMEGRAVE.
Dear God, my name is Julian, how often must it be said?
I just want to get the measurement
Of the circumference of your sweet head . . .
I just want to talk about you, and about me:
We met by chance on a lonely road
In a gap of the broken weather,
Do we continue our journey apart and alone:
Or do we travel together . . . ?

SIOBHAN. I don't think I want to commit myself to anything like that.

PADRAIC *has come nearer.* LIMEGRAVE *finds he has not enough flowers and goes aside to look for some more.* PADRAIC *comes down to his sister. During the next passage of dialogue* LIMEGRAVE *succeeds in getting his close-up shots.*

PADRAIC. For Christ's sake I've been watching you for half the afternoon. I don't know who the hell that bloody man is, but he's not one of us. You should leave him alone.

SIOBHAN. I have told you who he is. He is an Englishman and he's here to make films.

PADRAIC. Exactly the same class as that bastard Baker-Fortescue.

SIOBHAN. He is not: he is an artist!

PADRAIC. One quarter of him may be: the rest is export-import, an exploiter in two words. Get rid of him.

SIOBHAN. I will not.

PADRAIC. Or at least confront him with the situation we are in: put his wonderful artistry to some test of the truth.

LIMEGRAVE *rejoins them.*

LIMEGRAVE. Oh . . . Hello . . . You must be –

SIOBHAN. This is my brother. Paudeen, I want you to meet Mr Limegrave.

LIMEGRAVE. Julian, please. How d'you do? Your sister has told me a good deal about you.

PADRAIC. Did she tell you we are fighting an eviction from an absentee British landlord?

LIMEGRAVE. Yes, she did mention it, most unfortunate business.

PADRAIC. And have you any suggestions as to what we should do?

LIMEGRAVE. Ah – a good solicitor . . . ?

PADRAIC. Pointless. We have had one: the case drags on and on.

There is but the one way that I can see at all:
Why wouldn't the IRA put a bomb under his block–concrete wall?

LIMEGRAVE. Dear oh dear, do we need to bring *violence* into it?

PADRAIC. Eviction is bloody violence! Will you look at the Six Counties and what your British Army's doing up there!

LIMEGRAVE. Surely, to keep the peace, protect Catholics against the Protestants . . .

PADRAIC. My God, but he *believes* it! So: Mr Englishman, settle the eviction without violence.

LIMEGRAVE. Can I ask you a straight question? Are you in any way connected with any branch of the IRA?

PADRAIC. And if I were, d'you think I'd bloody tell you? If I thought that they could help us, I'd join 'em like a shot. As it is, I put my trust in the recipes of Lenin.

LIMEGRAVE. Lenin? Oh dear oh dear . . .

PADRAIC. 'Educate, Agitate, Organise', was the precept of your man. And that's what we are doing in Kilnasleeveen at this moment.

LIMEGRAVE. Have you had much response?

PADRAIC. Kilnasleeveen, Mr Englishman, is a suburb of the Falls Road!

Exit PADRAIC.

LIMEGRAVE. He talks in such slogans. You've a tendency that way yourself. It could get you into trouble.

PADRAIC *suddenly comes back again.*

PADRAIC. What the hell do you mean by that!

LIMEGRAVE. Oh look here, my dear chap, I didn't mean anything . . .

PADRAIC. Sure I know you upside-down. Siobhan, begod, I know him, and I know him upside-down. Anything that anyone says that is *meant*, is a subversion of the status-quo! Siobhan, he has failed the test!

LIMEGRAVE. Test . . . ?

PADRAIC. When all is said, I take one look at you: you're just bloody inconsiderable – I'd insult myself by regarding you as a factor in our business. Siobhan, you know the score: your consciousness of this man is determined by his class-role!

Exit PADRAIC.

LIMEGRAVE (*waiting carefully till he has gone*). You see, slogans: he's still at it . . . Too bourgeois perhaps if I put this round your neck?

He offers her the garland.

SIOBHAN. It would not: but I think it would be taking a bit too much for granted. I have to go up to the shops before they close.

LIMEGRAVE. Ah. I'll come with you.

SIOBHAN. I don't think that would be a very good idea.

Exit SIOBHAN.

LIMEGRAVE. Now I think of it, neither do I. Still, I shall see
her again.
And then we shall see . . .

I am looking for a dead body in a heap of rotten manure.

He detaches one flower from the garland and looks at it.

I find it: and I find a single snowdrop growing there.
Its roots have been put down into the dead man's breast
Deep-groping in the gangrened gash that was the cause of
    death:
I cannot move the corpse unless I break the flower:
To take it out and cherish it is not within my power.

*He presses the flower to a pulp between his fingers and drops it. He
then realises he is still holding the rest of the garland. He looks at it at
arm's length.* BUTLER McREEK *comes in and takes hold of the
end of it, so that they are holding it up between them. A pause.*

BUTLER McREEK. Mr Julian Limegrave?

LIMEGRAVE. Oh yes, good afternoon. How do you do?

BUTLER McREEK. Butler McReek. I had heard you were living
amongst us. So, a bit belatedly, welcome to Kilnasleeveen.
You're making a film they tell me. We have a great country
here for the creative contemplation. If you're walking in the
direction of Driscoll's . . . ?

LIMEGRAVE. That's very kind.

BUTLER McREEK. I don't in fact live here. A Dubliner, in
point of fact. A class of an architect, by way of a trade. I take
occasion now and again to put the odd notion of a speculation
into the briefcase of a good friend. The tourism, now.
Possibilities of a holiday village; now we're in the EEC a

scheme like that'd fill many a decent man's bucket. You wouldn't be considering a stake in such a thing yourself?

LIMEGRAVE. I don't think so.

BUTLER McREEK. Aha, you're the cautious man! Would I be wrong now to suppose your careful demeanour suggests you are a fisherman?

LIMEGRAVE. I hope to do a little while I am here.

BUTLER McREEK. Ah, you'll need a good ghillie – I mean someone to explain to you the relative value of each separate trout. There's many in this lake are scarcely worth the length of your line, especially if you're hoping to – ah – market your catch in London. Most of *my* clients, of course, are to be found, rather, in – ah –

LIMEGRAVE. Dublin . . .

Aside:

Dublin Castle, Special Branch. I knew it as soon as he spoke to me. Wingco Black thought they would very soon be in contact.

BUTLER McREEK. Where are you going?

LIMEGRAVE. You said something about a drink at Driscoll's.

BUTLER McREEK. So damn crowded in Driscoll's . . . one question before we get there. Do you have precise *instructions* to confabulate with the Ould McReek: and are you just a cowboy playing your own game and damn the locals?

LIMEGRAVE. Look here, old man, don't you think you're a little bit too direct?

BUTLER McREEK. Jesus Christ, I've made an abrasion on his self-protective English skin. If you want to be a tortoise, be a tortoise, goddammit. But I've had *my* instructions. They say, the full honours of our Irish hospitality . . . Driscoll's?

LIMEGRAVE. Driscoll's.

Exeunt.

Scene Four

Enter HAGAN.

HAGAN.
THE RASH REPUDIATION OF THE TRADITIONAL
GUARDIANS OF THE OPPRESSED REAPS ITS OWN
REWARD: NINETEEN SEVENTY-ONE.

Agitate, educate, let the people organise,
Open their eyes, take stock, get wise –
Won't they look upon me and my legitimate enterprise
From an altogether different view?
Kilnasleeveen, Tim Hagan, will have seen the last of *you*.

MULHOLLAND, *followed by* PADRAIC, *comes in. They have
their arms full of posters, which they start to paste up, advertising
'Small Farmers' Rally and March': 'Civil Rights on the Land':
'Nationalise the Land Now': 'March against Foreign Landlords': 'No
Evictions': 'Tillage or Tourism, the People's Choice', etc. HAGAN
gestures towards* MULHOLLAND:

Now that feller, passing through the place twice a year with his
begrudging pamphlets, is no danger to anyone, unless and until
he slaps his mildew into the groin of a young man with a
legitimate grievance who is determined to remain here and
bloody *root* himself – will you look at him, fouling the ground
between his feet with the effluvium of irrational protest. Ahoy
there, Terence, d'you mind now if I borrow your young
activist a moment?

MULHOLLAND (*humorously to Padraic*). I think the wage-slave
is wanted by the expropriator – I'll finish the work . . .

PADRAIC *comes over to* HAGAN.

HAGAN (*to* PADRAIC). Look, the owner of that damn
bungalow's behind in his payment, so from tomorrow you're
off the job and I'm putting you instead to the repair of Matty
Driscoll's roof . . .

He looks at one of the posters:

Yet another weekend on the street? 'Tis the burning ideal, I suppose, will carry you through. I wouldn't have the feet for it.

PADRAIC. The Land Commission is permitting sound arable to be taken over for a motel on the road to the coast. Here's the leaflet.

HAGAN. Fair enough, 'tis a good cause. And how much has that same motel to do with the Tintawndub?

PADRAIC. We must view it in the proper perspective. Domination of the land by extra-territorial financial-political interests –

HAGAN. Of course of course of course, and 'tis best solved in the one way. Direct action against bricks-and-mortar. Why the hell doesn't the Movement put a bomb under the motel once it's built? By the same token, Baker-Fortescue. It's three years since your mother began wasting time and good money in that eedjit of a court-case – adjournment upon adjournment, and appeals I wouldn't wonder to the throne of the Pope himself – would you want me to drop the hint for you – just a word in your man's ear . . . ?

He indicates MULHOLLAND.

You may be too nervous to mention it yourself, sure you don't have the tradition, being so long away in England . . .

PADRAIC. What's in it for you? I mean damnit, you're Fianna Fail, the personal manifestation in Kilnasleeveen of Jack Lynch himself. Wouldn't you say the IRA is a bit of a threat to *you*?

HAGAN.
You are not as discerning as I had expected.
Don't you know that Tim Hagan has a great care to be protected?

PADRAIC. As far as I am concerned we have an overt political programme and that's the only way to get anywhere.

He turns his back on HAGAN *and goes to help again with the posters.*

Exit HAGAN.

MULHOLLAND. Now that he's gone, I've a piece of news for you. I had a message from Dublin. They're expecting internment to be introduced any day now in the North. The Movement's badly up against it there, and the Provos splitting away from us hasn't helped at all. We look to be losing half our strength in one swoop unless we're careful: and even if we are careful we have nothing like the men on the ground that we need if we're to hold our own. They're sending me to Belfast – at least, off and on – more of a liaison job than a permanent posting, but I shan't be able to give much serious attention to affairs in these parts any more. Good God, and to think I told you physical force was a dead letter? Civil rights – overt politics – the enlightened British public gave a short answer to that notion.

PADRAIC. British Army, you mean.

MULHOLLAND. And who turned the Army onto the Nationalist people three days after the British public put Ted Heath into Downing Street? Do we say 'God forgive them for they know not what they do'? Or, equally, 'God look after them for *we* know what they'll get!' Mind you, I'm not so daft as to believe that that Labour Party of theirs would have done any different in the long run.

PADRAIC. Just sufficient of an eedjit to have *hoped* for it, that's all.

They laugh.

MULHOLLAND. Here, how did you come by that cut on your forehead?

PADRAIC. A drunk in Driscoll's yard – ran against me with a bottle when I'm after taking a leak. I think he was put up to it.

MULHOLLAND. I'd say he was paid to do it. There are times when intimidation can only be defeated by the same thing in reverse.

PADRAIC. Ah, sure, but intimidate *who*? If you're to go north, what's to happen down here?

MULHOLLAND. Ah: there's the difficulty. Affairs in Kilnasleeveen, from now on, are peripheral. And I am deputed to inform you, official from the Executive, that they are left in your charge.

PADRAIC. What – all of it? The bloody eviction – and – and – this?

MULHOLLAND. I shan't be away till we've had the march and rally. But you do realise the motel is a foregone conclusion: and so, I am sorry to say, is the result of your mother's lawsuit. What we call a one-off issue. Irrelevant to the main campaign in the west.

PADRAIC. I thought they *were* the main campaign.

MULHOLLAND. Not any more. Redefined by the Executive. Direct all future effort among rank-and-file trade-unionists in the new industrial development around the urban population centres. That ought to suit you – it's what you did in England, and begod it's what you're good at.

PADRAIC. I'm not leaving the eviction to take care of itself – damn it, Terry, it's my own home – I shall have to take action!

MULHOLLAND. Then you must take it unsupported by the Movement outside of this area.

PADRAIC. If I have to, I will. All right, a foregone conclusion. My mother loses her court-case and they come to force her out of the farm. I'll fill the bloody farm with trade-unionists from your urban centres – civil rights and sit-down protest and 'We-will-not-be-moved' – I know these factory-workers, they know me, I've more than enough contacts built up with 'em by now: if the Executive don't like it, they can lump it, that's all! I think before we're done they'll be having to send a few Ulstermen down here to do your liaison job in reverse, so they will! We don't need the British Army to show us where the enemy is. And by the same token, Terry, no more is the motel

a foregone conclusion either. I happen to know that the
planning permission has not yet been obtained!

Enter HAGAN.

HAGAN (*to audience*). Ah, no: he's wrong there. The County
Manager already put the word out in private. It won't be
official till next week when the contract is awarded. Guess who
to . . .

He takes MULHOLLAND *aside.*

D'you mind if I have a word. About this Chalet and the
Harrogate export-import. Incompetent placing of gelignite
produces nothing more than a broken window.

MULHOLLAND. Is that a fact?

HAGAN. When I see the British Army in the North let loose
upon the Catholic people like a horde of bloody Balubas, I bear
in mind that I am more than a contractor for putting up
buildings. I am frequently paid for demolishing them as well. I
demand a true Irishman's right to make myself useful.

MULHOLLAND. Don't tell me – tell him. He's in charge from
now on.

He indicates PADRAIC.

HAGAN (*most disconcerted*). What's that?

PADRAIC (*coming over to them*). Tell him what?

MULHOLLAND. Oh, just to let you know that if an agent
provocateur is what you need around the place, who better
than himself to supply it? Keep the faith.

Exit MULHOLLAND.

HAGAN (*grimly*). I don't think you need trouble yourself to turn
up on any of my contracts any more. Sure your smallholding
and its care and maintenance will take all of your time from
now on.

PADRAIC. It'll take all of the time of this complacent
community from now on, I'll tell you that! We're neither
leaving it, nor selling it, nor bloody blowing it down: so work
out where you stand, my friend, in relation to the wrath to
come!

Exit PADRAIC. HAGAN *commences to mutilate some of the*
posters.

HAGAN.
Oh begod but it will come:
Maybe not from just where you think.
A bare-faced beggar the like o'that
Telling Hagan to swim or to sink . . . !
Oh no, it is not his homestead
Needs now to be blown down,
But himself in short order.
By no-one from this town –

We don't want to create too much of a scandal. The best way's
to prepare the way with a small word to the Parish Priest –
denunciation from the pulpit for atheist agitation – and then –
the next developments . . .

Enter BUTLER McREEK *and* LIMEGRAVE.

Indicates BUTLER McREEK:

And here in the nick of time arrives the first of them, with his
broad portfolio. Mr Butler McReek, a short word . . .

To LIMEGRAVE:

Good evening, sir, fine day . . .

To BUTLER McREEK, *confidentially:*

That feller we're after talking about, you know what I mean –
Manchester . . . oh 'tis worse now than ever it was. I have it
absolutely certain he has infiltrated the IRA with a proposal for
explosive sabotage of all foreign-owned property between here
and the banks of Shannon, if the Honourable's possession order
is turned down by the court. Now you know there's a certain

Senator with his £20,000 holiday-villa below at the mouth of the waterfall – why, he rang me up this morning, oh fearful of disturbances – he says, 'Hagan, what the hell goes on . . . ?'

To himself, checking over some money.

I have a fiver for the Priest, he's collecting for a new confessional . . .

He is about to go out, but BUTLER McREEK *stops him.*

BUTLER McREEK. For God's sake get on to your man in Dublin – find out about the bloody court-case!

HAGAN *nods and goes over to the telephone.*

LIMEGRAVE. He said 'absolutely certain'?

BUTLER McREEK. Does it tie in or doesn't it with what O'Leary said to you about bombs under block-concrete walls? What time did you say you would be calling for Miss O'Leary?

LIMEGRAVE. Half-past six. The film begins at eight.

BUTLER McREEK (*looking at his watch*). Six o'clock on the dot. She's not home yet: the old woman's gone out: himself is in the Tintawndub alone. Let you knock upon the door then and we will see what there is to be seen.

LIMEGRAVE *knocks. Enter* PADRAIC.

LIMEGRAVE. Hello, Padraic, there you are. Is Siobhan at home yet?

PADRAIC (*grumpily, but accepting the Limegrave relationship*). Oh, you're to take her to the pictures of course. You'd best come in. Sit down and wait for her. Would you want a cup o'tea – or something . . . ?

LIMEGRAVE. That would be splendid.

BUTLER McREEK. The cup o'tea would do us fine . . . or maybe – *something* – if you have that . . .

PADRAIC *goes out.*

PADRAIC (*from off-stage*). Milk or sugar?

LIMEGRAVE. No milk – a slice of lemon.

PADRAIC (*off*). Slice of what?

BUTLER McREEK. When exactly is the date for your mother's appearance in court?

PADRAIC (*off*). Twenty-third of next month.

BUTLER McREEK (*aside*). If she wins it, she is safe in the ould homestead for ever and thank God there'll be no function left for me in Kilnasleeveen. Where the devil is Tim Hagan, he could ha' made that call ten times over . . . ?

HAGAN (*at telephone*). Godsake, girl, I said *Dublin*! You've put me through to Ballyjamesduff and me last fivepenny piece has got stuck in the sodding slot!

PADRAIC *comes in with cups of tea*.

BUTLER McREEK (*to* PADRAIC). I wonder now with your politics, you wouldn't have looked for political help in this case. Sure the whole set-up is neo-colonial, I'd ha' thought that you Socialists –

LIMEGRAVE. *International* Socialists, old man. Trade-union backing? The Labour Party even?

BUTLER McREEK. The *Irish* Labour Party – go out on a limb to help a capitalist peasant-proprietor? Or maybe you had in mind the British connection – TUC from over the sea? Ah no, we've to look at this as an anachronistic aspect of our unsolved insoluble national question, what?

PADRAIC (*in a sudden outburst*). Which outside of the Republican Movement is of no interest whatever to working-class organisations anywhere! Internationalism of the working-class – as far as we go, it means nothing but do as you're told by the Brits – because begod didn't they *invent* it! Tolpuddle and Peterloo . . . ! Good God, we want you *out* of here – we do *not* require advice as to how best to retain your influence in the most painless proletarian form!

LIMEGRAVE. That's very strong.

BUTLER McREEK. The heartfelt utterance of the authentic Republican Croppy: mark and learn it, Mr Englishman, there's a death-knell in every syllable.

LIMEGRAVE *chokes in his tea*.

PADRAIC (*apologetically*). Ah never mind, but I'm half-distracted trying to dig up the cash for these lawyers. I banked everything on a high price for our Connemara ponies: but no good.

BUTLER McREEK. Ponies . . . I wonder . . . Have you thought of Enniskillen?

PADRAIC. I have not.

BUTLER McREEK. There is a fair at Enniskillen on – let me see – the thirteenth. I heard tell of a man called Pole-Hatchet is searching high and low for the genuine western ponies – he has a notable stud up there – he exports to America.

PADRAIC. Is it Dreadnought Pole-Hatchet? Sure we know about him – he stayed in the Chalet one time.

BUTLER McREEK. He's the man you want to see. You'll get no better price in Ireland.

HAGAN (*at telephone*). Is the Minister not there? . . . In the House for a division, is he? Well, his Personal Private Secretary – ah, Mr Foley, good evening to you, sir. This is Hagan, from Kilnasleeveen. I was ringing to enquire, oh entirely confidentially, about this application by the Honourable Baker-Fortescue, his property here . . . Aha, yes. Jasus, 'tis just as I thought. Will ye pass on to the Minister I consider myself free to take whatever local action appears best. Good-night, sir, I'm more than grateful.

He rings off. BUTLER McREEK, *having noticed him talking, has crept up behind him.* HAGAN *draws him into a corner, and whispers.*

'Tis as I thought. A fixed job. They have a Fianna Fail judge put up to take the case and he's bound to decide in favour of the Honourable. They're aware there'll be local ructions: but the Minister is very keen on a Riviera-type holiday village to be built on the lakeshore, and he's confident that any subversion can be *contained*. D'ye see what I mean . . . ?

They both look at PADRAIC.

In regard to the holiday-village – how long will it take you to get the plans drawn up?

BUTLER McREEK (*taking papers out of his portfolio*). I have a rough class of a sketch-design already prepared for you. It will involve the demolition of both the farm-buildings and the Chalet . . . You know: I don't think we ought to be looking at this here. Fold it up into your pocket, man, have some sense!

HAGAN. Ah security, yes indeed: when the Minister himself has enough money in it to sink Noah's Ark.

BUTLER McREEK. At any rate, we go ahead, Julian: we go ahead.

HAGAN *withdraws*.

Enter SIOBHAN.

So I'll leave you to your motion-picture.

Exit BUTLER McREEK.

LIMEGRAVE. Oh . . . Siobhan. It's damned awkward, but I can't make it tonight, as a matter of fact I'm going back to England first thing tomorrow morning.

SIOBHAN. Tomorrow? Why so soon?

LIMEGRAVE. The truth is, I think I've done all I can do here.

Exit LIMEGRAVE.

SIOBHAN (*sings*) [Air: *The Streets of Laredo*].
'Oh why would I think that he might have stayed longer
Oh why would I think that he might have delayed?

Our trouble is our own and he cannot be sharing it:
And the dark of our evening is the dawn of his day.'

PADRAIC. To get the ponies to Enniskillen, I must acquire a
class of a van. I wonder would Tim Hagan let me have the use
of his?

HAGAN (*coming forward again*). He would, boy, he would. She's
a grand ould yoke for the road.

SIOBHAN. Enniskillen?

PADRAIC. The ponies.

SIOBHAN (*alarmed*). But you'll have to cross the Border.

PADRAIC. Thousands do it every week.

SIOBHAN. Paudeen, for God's sake, take care of yourself, so.

Exit SIOBHAN.

HAGAN *retires*.

PADRAIC.
Care of myself – what care?
What have I to do there
But make use of the Six Counties, accept Partition
For the sake, for God's sake, of the O'Leary family fortune?
Baker-Fortescue can in no wise be destroyed upon his own:
So where do I go, what do I join?
In the end do I take up the traditional Republican gun
Or pay heed to Mulholland and break every nerve in my brain
Attempting to organise unorganised ignorant women and
    men –
Impossible choice of two horns, unbridged since 1916:
So many so courageous have fallen down dead in between.

In the meanwhile, get rid of these ponies.

He sings [Air: *The Black Horse*].

'On the thirteenth day of August in nineteen seventy-one
I took a load of horseflesh up to Enniskillen town.

The sun was bright and the grass was green and the western
    wind did blow:
Not carelessly nor light-heartedly along that road I drove.'

Nonetheless in the wide quiet landscape all the turmoil in my
mind became ridiculous, out of proportion.

He sings:

'I did not think until too late of what had taken place –'

HAGAN (*coming forward, singing*).
    '– That on the ninth of August many men had met their fate:
    Internment was determined on, half Belfast was on fire.
    Throughout the North the torturers gave vent to their cruel
        desire.'

PADRAIC (*sings*).
    'In the middle of that bloody week three ponies I had sold
    To a certain Orange officer who filled my purse with gold:
    I turned my empty van around and for home I did set forth.
    May God destroy the day on which I entered in the North!'

Enter BUTLER McREEK *and goes to the telephone: he dials.*

BUTLER McREEK. Royal Ulster Constabulary, Enniskillen?
    Special Operations? Thank you . . . Inspector? Butler McReek,
    Kilnasleeveen. Mr Limegrave's young friend has gone to the
    fair. A large red horsebox, *Hagan and Son Contractor*, number
    NZM 432. You have that? . . . You'll pass it on.

He rings off and exit.

HAGAN (*sings*).
    'On the road towards the Border out of Enniskillen town
    You go five miles, you go six miles, the road goes up and
        down,
    There's a hump-back bridge and a twisted bend like the leg of a
        broken dog:
    They have blocked the road with a barb-wire coil that is nailed
        to a twelve-inch log.'

Exit HAGAN.

Sound of a van approaching at speed. Twin headlights illuminate the stage. Brakes screech and van heard to come to a stop. The CORPORAL *is picked out in the headlights. He carries a sub-machine gun.*

CORPORAL. Switch off them lights and get out of that truck! Come on, come on, move it!

The headlights go out. Another light is now cast on the stage from a powerful handlamp carried by the PRIVATE. PADRAIC *comes in from behind the source of the headlights.*

Right, let's be having you!

PRIVATE. Driving licence, insurance, customs clearance, come on –

CORPORAL. Come on, let's be having you!

PADRAIC *fumbles with the documents. The* CORPORAL *snatches them and riffles them through.*

Name?

PADRAIC. I – O'Leary – I – ah –

CORPORAL. Can't hear you!

PADRAIC. I said –

CORPORAL. Vehicle number – come on, your fucken number!

PADRAIC. Jesus, I can't tell you – it's gone out of my head –

PRIVATE (*over by the van*). NZM 432.

CORPORAL. That's it. We take him in.

PADRAIC. But I –

CORPORAL. Don't you *but* me, you bastard Fenian murderer!

PADRAIC. I'm here to sell my ponies and that's all –

CORPORAL. And I'm here to sell *myself* – I'm what you lot call a mercenary. To make my wife a fucken widow because the fucken Irish have all gone mad. An't you found his fucken gun yet?

PRIVATE (*who has been searching Padraic*). He ent got one.

CORPORAL. Ent he? He fucken will, by he gets to the barracks.
MOVE!

They run PADRAIC savagely off the stage.

Enter INTELLIGENCE OFFICER.

INTELLIGENCE OFFICER. Erroneous to believe that
interrogation-in-depth involves simply a process of
uncontrolled brutality. We recognise the violent terrorist is a
mentally-sick person. Our methods are therapeutic. If you like,
a branch of the Medical Services. I myself have been trained as
a doctor and am subject accordingly to the Hippocratic Oath.
We know already that this man is a member of the Official
IRA. In that capacity he becomes one of my patients.

*PADRAIC, stripped, with a bag over his head is brought in by the
CORPORAL and PRIVATE. His exposed body is foul and bloody.
The soldiers' manner is relaxed – they have cans of beer in their
hands.*

Over there, please.

*The soldiers stand PADRAIC against the wall, his hands above his
head. He sags and the PRIVATE beats him until he stands upright.*

INTELLIGENCE OFFICER. Serjeant!

VOICE OFF. Sir?

INTELLIGENCE OFFICER. Audio-augmentation, please.

A high-pitched whining/buzzing noise commences.

Carry on, Corporal Bones, let me know when you get
anything.

*The INTELLIGENCE OFFICER strolls aside, studying a 'Teach
Yourself Irish' handbook, reciting simple phrases aloud.*

CORPORAL. Your name's not sodding O'Leary, your name is
fucken Teague –

PRIVATE. You ran that fucken lorry over the Border on an unapproved road –

CORPORAL. You brought ten ton of gelignite into fucken Enniskillen –

PADRAIC. No – no – no – !

CORPORAL. Don't you speak to *me*, you fucken cuntstruck bastard – !

PRIVATE. You fucken answer the man when he asks you a fucken question! And keep your fucken feet still! Gord, how the bugger's trembling. Here, have a feel.

PADRAIC *collapses*.

CORPORAL. On your feet, Teague, your fucken *feet* –

PRIVATE. Hey, I think he's talking.

CORPORAL. Sir, he's begun to talk.

The INTELLIGENCE OFFICER *puts up his book and comes over, crouching down beside* PADRAIC, *who is talking very fast inside the bag.*

PADRAIC. Life-Tenancy Agreement never knew that that bastard meant *his* life always thought it meant *his* life, the Honourable's, his life till his death, his death his death not ours, when mammy went to Mass every week of *her* life so she did and only seven-fifty no class of compensation at all . . .

CORPORAL. His mother and the fucken Church, it's all they ever talk of.

INTELLIGENCE OFFICER. No good. Wait!

PADRAIC (*still in the same stream*). In every generation the Irish people asserted asserted their right national freedom sovereignty six times during three hundred years asserted it in arms in arms their national right in arms their national right in arms their national right to bear arms . . .

INTELLIGENCE OFFICER. Ah, that's more like it. Come on,
son, I'm afraid you've had rather a bad time but it's all over
now. I want you to tell me quietly just what you – oh God,
we've overdone it. Jesus Christ, the man's dead! Get him out of
it, and keep quiet. Serjeant – will you switch off that blasted
machine!

The mechanical noise stops.

Dear goodness, what a mess. Think of something, quick. Aha,
yes: I have it . . .

The SOLDIERS *carry out* PADRAIC's *body.*

INTELLIGENCE OFFICER (*sings*) [Air: *The Gray Cock*].
'Upon a dark and murky midnight
South of the Border but a little short way
They bring him out and there they leave him:
Let those who find him do what they may.'

The two SOLDIERS *re-enter from the side opposite to the one where
they went out: they carry the body – or rather a dummy resembling it.
The bag has gone from the head. The body is covered with tar and
feathers. A large piece of paper stuck on the chest reads 'IRA
VENGEANCE: INFORMERS BEWARE!' They tie the body
upright to a post, the arms above the head.*

CORPORAL. That's it, then. Back to Enniskillen and not one
word to no-one. Open your mouth and we're in the fucken
glasshouse!

Exeunt.

Enter, after a pause, TERESA *and* SIOBHAN *in mourning.*

*During the following speech they cut down the body and carry it
away.*

INTELLIGENCE OFFICER (*in tones of a TV newscaster*). A
spokesman for the Department of Justice in Dublin has stated
that Padraic O'Leary of Kilnasleeveen, whose body was found
by local people beside a road in County Cavan, is known to
have had connections with a subversive organisation and it is

assumed that his death was the result of internal disputes within the organisation. The Taoiseach Mr Lynch has repeated his condemnation of all such organisations, which, he said, are not only illegal, but a deterrent to investors of foreign capital in the national economy . . .

Exit INTELLIGENCE OFFICER. *A drum taps a slow march.* MULHOLLAND *and a* VOLUNTEER *(in black berets and paramilitary gear) enter carrying* PADRAIC *(the real actor) laid out on a bier under the tricolour flag. They set the bier down.* TERESA *and* SIOBHAN *re-enter. They silently lay out a funeral meal on a shelf or table, over which they have draped a black cloth.*

MULHOLLAND (*giving formal funeral oration*). We indignantly repudiate the insolent slander that Padraic O'Leary was done to death by members of the Official Republican Movement. Rather do we accuse the criminal aggression of the so-called security-forces that occupy the Six Counties. We are proud to accord a soldier's salute to this brave martyr who has gone from us.

MULHOLLAND *fires revolver shots in salute.*

SIOBHAN, *who has stood well back in silence, now suddenly comes forward and sings, with an angry emphasis.*

SIOBHAN (*sings*) [Air: *The Sash My Father Wore*].
'He has *not* gone from you – he was dragged
And torn away to die:
They murdered him in darkness
With a blindfold round his eye:
They butchered him like Connolly
Or Emmet or Wolfe Tone
Or a thousand thousand other ones
Who likewise are all gone!

The martyrs that you shout about
Roll over in their graves
But those alive you do not know
Bewildered work like slaves –
They cannot tell for whom they work

Or why they draw their pay:
All that they have is martyred bones
And glorious names to praise.

I will not praise my brother's name
I will not weep one tear
I will not name the nation
That betrayed and laid him here.
He came back home from Manchester
With a new word in his mouth:
They stopped that word and murdered him
Before he let it out.'

MULHOLLAND *and the* VOLUNTEER *bow to* TERESA *and go out. A pause.* SIOBHAN *and* TERESA *stand in silence of grief.* PADRAIC, *as a dead man, sits up on the bier.*

PADRAIC (*sings softly*) [Air: *The One-eyed Reilly*].
'They have killed me dead and laid me down
They have covered me up and buried me under
The men of power and pride confide
I can never arise and blow them asunder.
    Giddy-i-ay giddy-i-ay
    Giddy-i-ay I am dead for certain
    Giddy-i-ay tiddle-iddle-oo
    How many more like me?'

Enter BAKER-FORTESCUE *with a letter.*

BAKER-FORTESCUE. A most horrifying letter from Timothy Hagan – the Tintawndub has been blown up – my Chalet has been blown up! And he has the nerve to offer me what he calls a fair price for the site!

Enter HAGAN *with a roll of banknotes which he holds out to* BAKER-FORTESCUE.

No sir, it is not!

HAGAN. Sure it's more than ye'd get from anyone else with the political implications that are in it. Will you not sit down quietly like a sensible man now and –

He sees TERESA. *He holds out some money to her.*

Oh, Mrs O'Leary, ma'am, some of the neighbours got together and deputed me to give you this – 'tis the price of the fare to England. You have a sister in Wolverhampton . . . ? Sure ye do.

BAKER-FORTESCUE. You must double your offer, sir!

HAGAN. Begod I will not.

PADRAIC *has slipped in behind them: he gives a covert blow to* HAGAN, *who thinks it is* BAKER-FORTESCUE.

If you dare to lay hand on me I'll reduce it be forty percent!

PADRAIC *repeats the same business to* BAKER-FORTESCUE.

BAKER-FORTESCUE. So you add to your extortion, sir, a physical assault!

He pushes HAGAN.

HAGAN. Bedad I've flattened a better man than yourself with me left fist tied behind me – come on come on – !

He snatches a custard pie from the refreshment table and throws it at BAKER-FORTESCUE.

Not one more penny outa me, I'll take hold of your bloody paddock and squat in it meself – ho ho will ye evict *Hagan*?

He throws another pie.

BAKER-FORTESCUE. No sir, oh no – you are not to get away with it!

He throws a pie at HAGAN.

Ha, you have not the advantage of having de-nazified the whole of Germany!

More pies. HAGAN *tries to dodge, slips in a fallen pie, and hurts his leg. He rolls in agony.* BAKER-FORTESCUE *lands on top of him and secures the banknotes.*

BAKER-FORTESCUE.
Take yourself off, sir, and think yourself glad

I have let you get away with what you have had.

HAGAN (*to audience*).
Had he chosen to behave with some common respect
God knows the height of the price he would have been able to
    collect.

HAGAN *hobbles out.*

BAKER-FORTESCUE. Considering I got the property for
nothing, I suppose I've not done too badly.

Meanwhile I will continue and continue to look out
Ever and about for what I can obtain:
The main chance is now in Europe, not in Ireland –
Not any more in Ireland – never in Ireland – no never again!

As he is about to leave, PADRAIC *slips another pie under his feet,
and he makes his exit in a grotesque tumble.* PADRAIC *begins to
sing and dance, arm in arm with* TERESA *and* SIOBHAN, *who
join in the refrain.*

PADRAIC (*sings*).
    'Let him go to Germany, France or Spain
    Or anywhere else in the whole of Europe
    He'll find no rest from the likes of me
    Crowding around him the whole of his journey.
        Giddy-i-ay we'll crowd him round
        Giddy-i-ay he can not withstand us
        Giddy-i-ay tiddle-iddle-oo
        We'll finish him before he's done!
    When you act in a play it is easy to say
    That we shall win and never be defeated
    When you go from here it is not so clear
    That power for the people is predestined.
        Giddy-i-ay but don't forget
        Giddy-i-ay you must remember
        Giddy-i-ay tiddle-iddle-oo
        There are more of us than them!'

Exeunt.

Vandaleur's Folly

An Anglo-Irish Melodrama
The Hazard of Experiment in an Irish
Co-operative, Ralahine, 1831
1978

Margaretta D'Arcy
and
John Arden

Characters

SINGER

PRESENTER

WILLIAM THOMPSON } *revolutionary*
ANNA WHEELER } *philosophers*

PEASANT GUERRILLAS *'Lady Clare Boys'*

MICHEAL *a small-farmer/fisherman*

ROISIN *Micheal's sister, a servant-girl*

SOLDIERS *of the British Army*

WILBERFORCE *an American slave-trade agent*

HASTINGS *an estate-steward*

VANDALEUR *a country gentleman*

EMILY *Vandaleur's wife*

ROXANA *an American lady*

SERJEANT *of the British Army*

RECEPTIONIST *at the Shelbourne Hotel*

DOWAGER

MAJOR BAKER-FORTESCUE *an absentee landlord*

LORD MAYOR *of Dublin*

ARCHBISHOP *of Dublin (Church of Ireland)*

ROBERT OWEN *philosopher*

LADIES

GENTLEMEN

WAITER *at the Hell Fire Club*

CRAIG *a socialist co-operator*

PEASANTS

HAGAN *a publican*

CATHOLIC PRIEST } *at Ralahine,*
CHURCH OF IRELAND PARSON } *County Clare*

KITTY *Baker-Fortescue's kitchen-maid*

HIGH SHERIFF *of County Clare*

LAWYER

SURGEON

RELATIVES *of William Thompson*

FLANAGAN *a builder*

CHURCH OF IRELAND PARSON *of*
   Thompson's parish, County Cork

CROUPIER *at the Hell Fire Club*

The action of the play takes place in Ireland (County Clare, Dublin and County Cork) between 1831 and 1833. The precise dates of the various events are not closely defined.

Vandaleur's Folly was first performed on tour in 1978 by the 7:84 Theatre Company, with a company of nine actors.

Prologue

A ship at sea. Storm and stress. THOMPSON *and* ANNA *are on the deck, muffled up against the weather, leaning on the rail and bracing themselves as the vessel heaves.*

To one side of the stage: the PRESENTER. *To the other: a (female)* SINGER.

SINGER (*air: 'Long Lankin'*).
    'It's an old song and a true song as cold as a bone
    That I cannot stop singing till I come into my own.'

PRESENTER (*speaks*):
    Gray storm upon the sea from the rocks of France
    To the roaring tide-race of the Cove of Cork —
    Foul wind tonight for those who strive toward Ireland . . .

SINGER.
    'Till I come to my own in my own Irish land
    An old song and a true song and where is the end?'

THOMPSON. There can be no end before death's end and death comes too soon. I, William Thompson, Revolutionist, Irishman, Socialist, hereditary landowner and therefore a born thief —

ANNA. I, Anna Wheeler, daughter of an Archbishop, acclaimed the Goddess of Reason in the salons of revolutionary France, and a notorious social outcast . . .

ANNA *and* THOMPSON. We return home to our own land —

ANNA. From our wanderings in France we return, among the disappointed voices of the revolutionaries of Europe —

THOMPSON. Desperate seasick from the wanderings of my life, already condemned to the death of my body — the irreversible black cap of judgement stuffed into the blood of my lungs, making black every breath of my polemic — (*He breaks off in a fit of coughing.*)

PRESENTER. What came you into this wilderness to see. . . ?

> An old man broken coming home to his home to die
> Who yet has wealth enough to make his death
> In comfort with his woman like a pasha
> Amid quilts and silks and sensual warm baths,
> And yet can find no comfort because he is
> An Irishman and Revolutionist . . . ?
> What hope to solve the furious contradictions — ?

THOMPSON. The furious contradiction of Ireland is this: the alleged revolutionaries all over Europe believe that the Age of Revolution has given way to the Age of Reform.

ANNA. Call it the age of defeated revolution — like the Americans we rose up against Great Britain for independence from colonialism, like the French we rose up against our cormorant ruling-classes. The British Army broke our back.

THOMPSON. We broke our own back. We had a Parliament, oh a Protestant landlord Parliament, but by God, woman, it was our own: and we sold it to the pimps of London! And once again they all bend and are bent by the bribery of Reform. . .

ANNA. Five million of the dispossessed: there is nobody can bend them.

THOMPSON.
> They were not bent, they were not even broken
> When bold Wolfe Tone in 'ninety-eight was taken,
> Huddled to prison, badgered to his death. Forsaken
> Only, for the time, this multitude, that's all.

ANNA.
> They seem to sleep, turn hungry faces to the wall:
> And yet they dream most dangerously. When they awaken —

VOICES (*all around*). END BRITISH RULE, GET OUT OF IRELAND NOW, TROOPS OUT, BRITS OUT. . . !

PRESENTER.
> Were Marx and Engels crazy when they said:
> No freedom for the English working-class
> Until at last exerted to reverse
> Its base acceptance of Imperial chains
> Wrapped spike and hook and padlock round the flesh,

Divided bloody human meat of Ireland —
Marx, Engels, Connolly — the words of —

The storm noises drown his speech, with the slogan-voices again.

SINGER.
'The cold rain of Ireland blows over the water
To furrow the face of fair England's proud daughter.

How long will it fall, O as sharp as a knife?
Till the dogteeth of England let go of our life.

Let go of our heart and the voice in our throat:
Till the day of that good-morning, no end to the fight. . .'

The storm rises to a climax. They go.

Act One

Scene One

The Irish Coast. A foggy night. SOLDIERS with muskets slouch across the stage, patrolling. When they have gone, a few whistling calls: then a group of PEASANT-GUERRILLAS, disguised in women's shawls, gather swiftly and silently together. One of them is MICHEAL. Another whistling call, offstage.

MICHEAL. Who's there?

GUERRILLA-LEADER (*off*). Lady Clare.

1ST GUERRILLA. Lady Clare and who else?

GUERRILLA-LEADER (*off*). Lady Clare and her Brave Boys.

> *The LEADER (disguised like the others) slips in. He holds a bunch of small sticks, one of them shorter than the others. He distributes these, keeping one for himself.*
>
> One, two, three, four, five — six.
>
> *They all check their sticks. MICHEAL has drawn the short one. He stands a little apart from the others.*

(*To MICHEAL*:)
> We do not know who you are.
> But Lady Clare is well aware
> You are her Brave Boy and you will dare.

> *He gives MICHEAL a double-barrelled pistol, a powder horn and shot.*

You will wait here till word comes of where he is.

> *He clasps hands with MICHEAL: so do the others, and they go, leaving MICHEAL alone. He begins to load his pistol: whistles 'The Wearing of the Green' softly to himself. Quick footsteps, off. He starts.*

ROISIN (*off*). Who's there?

MICHEAL. Lady Clare.

ROISIN (*off*). Lady Clare and who else?

MICHEAL. Lady Clare and her Brave Boys.

   ROISIN, *a hunchback, scurries in — he recognizes her with
   surprise. MICHEAL is about to speak but she stops him.*

ROISIN. Ssh. . . I do not know you. If you know who *I* am, you
are to keep it to yourself.

MICHEAL. He will be at his house?

ROISIN. He will not. He is on the road. He is on the road to this
place. But be careful: there is another man, a stranger, tonight
upon the strand. Take care he does not see you — and patrols —

   Heavy footsteps, off.

MICHEAL. Patrols — *now* — get out of it — hide — !

   *Some confusion as he scrambles with his pistol-loading
   business, dropping things.*

ROISIN. No: *you* hide, you damfool — I'm not the one with the
gun — !

   *She manages to hustle MICHEAL into hiding with his weapon
   as the SOLDIERS enter. They hear the sound and stop,
   suspicious.*

1ST SOLDIER. Hello there — who's that!

   ROISIN *makes a dash for it, coming out of hiding in a different
   place from where she thrust MICHEAL in.*

2ND SOLDIER. Don't move — stay where you are or I shoot!

1ST SOLDIER. Catch im — !

2ND SOLDIER. Get im that way — !

   *They chase ROISIN around the stage, corner her, and pull
   her shawl off. When they see who she is —*

1ST SOLDIER. Fuckin roll on, look at this.

2ND SOLDIER. D'you call it a bint or a bloody baboon?

They toss her back and forward between the two of them, and laugh at her.

The SOLDIERS *go out. The sound of their footsteps recedes. When they are completely away,* MICHEAL *comes out of his hiding-place. His shawl has slipped off, revealing his face.* ROISIN *recognizes him, and clasps him in her arms.*

MICHEAL (*putting her off*). Are they gone? Name o' God, *you* go! You are not to be here when —

ROISIN. Put the bullet deep into him. So deep into his cruel womb they will never be able to dig for it.

She runs out. MICHEAL *finishes his pistol-loading, whistling as before. He is suddenly aware of another whistling — 'Dixie' — from offstage. He slips into hiding again.* WILBERFORCE *enters, strolls around edgily, lights a cigar, strolls, whistles, looks at his watch.*

WILBERFORCE. Punctilio of the Irish: three-quarters of an hour late. . . where to tarnation is he? (*He calls softly:*) Hastings. . . ? Are you there. . . ? Hastings?

HASTINGS (*offstage, calling softly*). Over here, sir, over here.

WILBERFORCE. Where? Where, I can't see you?

HASTINGS (*offstage*). To the north. Walk to the north.

WILBERFORCE. What kinda location is north in this wilderness? This way?

HASTINGS (*offstage*). No no sir — this way. And don't make so much noise. There are soldiers' patrols on the strand. (*A shot offstage, followed by a scream from* HASTINGS.) Oh God I am killed! Mr Wilberforce, sir, Mr Wilberforce — please — !

A second shot, offstage. HASTINGS' *cries become a sickening gobble.* WILBERFORCE *moves away in horror, backwards.* MICHEAL *runs out from his hiding-place, and bumps into the back of* WILBERFORCE, *tangles with him briefly, losing his shawl as he does so, and runs off.* WILBERFORCE *holds the shawl, but does not seem to notice it.*

WILBERFORCE. That's it. That's it. Finished. (*He runs out.*)

Scene Two

Ralahine House in County Clare. Enter VANDALEUR *fussing with his botany, and* EMILY.

VANDALEUR. All the portions of seed-potato, different heights, different temperatures — a variety of parts of the house, let them germinate. Mrs Vandaleur, would you be so good as to hold this thermometer, *here.* Put a hook in the wall, later. Already a hook for this one, *here.*

EMILY (*holding a thermometer at the height he indicates*). How long, Mr Vandaleur, do you desire me to stand —

VANDALEUR.(*not listening to her*). My correspondent in Wiltshire suggests three or four weeks, but I fancy —

EMILY. What?

VANDALEUR. Hastings, of course, once I can stir him from his natural indolence, will have prepared a manure-bed at the corner of the orchard — where *is* Hastings. . . ? What's that noise. . . ?

ROXANA (*off*). Hi, hello there — anyone at home — ?

VANDALEUR (*as* EMILY *makes a move to see who it is*). No don't move, pray do not open the door, the drop in the temperature —

Enter ROXANA *struggling with a great travelling-trunk.* EMILY *goes to embrace her.*

EMILY. Roxana!

VANDALEUR. No no the thermometer — !

He takes the thermometer and holds it as EMILY *greets* ROXANA.

EMILY. Why, Roxana, here already, what kind of a journey — Mr Vandaleur, my cousin Roxana, from America, you must have remembered her visit? My dear, how did you carry that gargantuan box all the way from the coach? Why didn't you ask for a servant?

VANDALEUR *abstractedly greets* ROXANA *and wanders out*

again, after putting the thermometer back into EMILY's *hand.* ROXANA *sits down on the box, and gives an agonised jerk.*

ROXANA. My dearest Emily, do you *have* servants, the whole estate seems entirely deserted — oh! My back, I must have twisted it —

EMILY. Oh dear what are we going to do — I can't move with this — Roisin, Hannah, Padraic, where are you — ! Roisin!

Enter ROISIN.

Linament, girl, quick!

ROISIN. We were all of us held up, ma'am, with the crowds in the town after the election.

EMILY. I don't want to hear another word about that dreadful election. Linament!

ROISIN *goes off to get linament.*

All my family, you know, and Mr Vandaleur's family, such *partisans* — on the losing side; and the supporters of O'Connell have been so fanatical — ssh. . .

ROISIN *comes back with linament and undoes* ROXANA's *clothing to rub her back.*

But oh my goodness, how long can you stay, one month at least, two. . . ? Such excitement, there'll be all the parties, the balls at the Limerick Assembly, but with the political trouble, I do wonder if —

ROXANA. I guess this is going to be a mighty disappointment, but I can't stay a week, let alone a whole month. I have to go right away to Dublin.

EMILY. Oh my dear. But we understood you would be in County Clare till the time came for your visit to London. Oh I'd love to go to Dublin with you, but my husband with his wretched experiments —

ROXANA. Just before I took ship from New York — in the hotel — there was this man, I saw him, thank God he didn't see me, he was booked on another ship, left a day or two earlier direct

for Dublin, Shelbourne Hotel, Dublin, I saw it on his baggage
— I have to follow him, find out what he's up to.

EMILY. But my darling — is this *romance* — you have incurred
an attraction to a mysterious stranger —

ROXANA. No stranger, no mystery neither. A notorious slave-
trader.

EMILY. But the slave-trade is illegal.

ROXANA. Not in America, not in Cuba, which is where this man
operates. And the ships in his illegal trade carry sugar back to
Europe, and that could be his business here: my father told
me, if I find him, follow him up. . . oh!

She has moved and hurt her back again. Business with ROISIN:

No, lower down, honey, rub it there, there, that's it, I'll try to
stay still. You've got to appreciate, cousin Emily, when my
father's plantation in Carolina went bankrupt, he began a new
business in the Northern States. You say — political
troubles. . . ? So you know what I mean. Columbia the land
of the free is tangled into nightmare by the one issue of negro
slavery. . .

Enter VANDALEUR, *rummaging.*

VANDALEUR. A crucial piece of potato left down in that corner,
did I put it by error back inside my laboratory — ?

EMILY (*getting between him and* ROXANA's *déshabillé*). Mr
Vandaleur, no — you can't come in now — out. . . ! Roisin,
the thermometer!

She thrusts the thermometer into ROISIN's *hand as she urges
him out of the room.*

A crucial piece of potato. . . ? Under the box! Roisin —

They forget the thermometer and lift first ROXANA, *then
the box. The potato is crushed, underneath it.*

ROISIN. Oh ma'am, pulverised — no good to the master at all. . .

EMILY. Get rid of it, hide it —

ROISIN gets rid of it. ROXANA, *displaced, finds she can walk
about more easily.* EMILY *starts to do up her dress for her.*

So your father expunges his guilt as a repentant slave-owner
by sending you all over the world to investigate like a Royal
Commission, I declare it's pure tyranny. Ah, the one we should
get you to meet is Mrs Wheeler, in County Cork, I say Mrs
advisedly, because of course she's not. . . but she can tell you
all about it, statistics, everything, absolute horrors out of all
the blue-books — she —

SERJEANT (*off*). You that way, you that way, round the back
there one man: move!

EMILY. Goodness gracious, what is that?

Enter SERJEANT *and* SOLDIERS.
ROISIN *goes out.*

SERJEANT. You'll excuse me, madam, ladies, I have my duty to
perform. You, through the front garden, two potting-sheds
and a summer-house, make sure they're clear!

1ST SOLDIER. Serjeant.

The SOLDIERS *crash across the stage and out the other side.*

SERJEANT. What happens through here?

Enter VANDALEUR, *confronting him.*

VANDALEUR. Through here, sir, is my laboratory. Might I ask
what you are —

SERJEANT. In accordance with the provisions of the Peace
Preservation Act as applicable to County Clare under the
military emergency imposed as of yesterday morning, we have
instructions to search your property for the perpetrators of
last night's outrage. There's the warrant.

He hands VANDALEUR *a document.*

VANDALEUR. Last night's — ?

SERJEANT. Last night's outrage. Of course there's no suggestion,
sir, you yourself might be implicated, but we believe the men
in question could have taken refuge in your servants' hall.
Would you think now that was likely?

Enter ROISIN.

ROISIN (*to* EMILY): Oh madam, madam, and the children so terrified, the poor little lambs. . . !

VANDALEUR (*having read the warrant, nearly collapses*). Oh my God, Emily, help. They have murdered my steward.

EMILY. Mr Hastings?

VANDALEUR. Upon the beach of the estuary. They blew his face away.

SERJEANT. And his belly, sir, his lower belly. Point-blank range. Revolting circumstance.

VANDALEUR. If the murderers are in this house, then of course they must be found. But I cannot believe —

SERJEANT. If we find 'em, you'll have no choice but to believe it, Mr Vandaleur.

EMILY. But Daniel Hastings — why why why? — such a respectable jovial man, and his wife, and his poor children —

SERJEANT. They left a message for his wife, nailed it up to his cottage door. (*He gives* VANDALEUR *a second, dirty, piece of paper.*) Written in blood by the look of it.

(*He calls to the* SOLDIERS *offstage:*) Hey Dobson, Wilkins, if there's nobody in the summer-house, check out them clumps of evergreen, they could hide a whole half-company! Move!

VANDALEUR. Serjeant, you said — emergency. You said — military emergency. What the devil did you mean?

SERJEANT. No more nor what I said, sir. On account of the recent prevalence of agrarian crime, martial law in a manner of speaking has been imposed upon the county by order of the proper authorities. I had assumed you'd have been informed.

(*To the* SOLDIERS *again:*) All right if there's no-one there we'll pack it in and move on down the road. Get fell in on the gravel avenue!

(*He puts his hand out for the dirty paper:*) I'll take that back if you don't mind. Requisite evidence, need to keep it.

VANDALEUR (*dazed*). I — I can't read it, what does it say. . . ?

EMILY. I don't want to look at it. Oh my God that poor woman.

ROXANA (*taking the paper*). May I see? (*She reads:*)
'Daniel Hastings Number One
Walked to the strand and never came home
Who will be next now the work is begun?
All slave-drivers and informers beware
Of the vengeance of Lady Clare. . . '

SERJEANT (*taking the paper back*). My advice to you, sir, you
should leave home, leave today, don't waste no time. Look
after the ladies, that's your duty.

The SERJEANT *goes out.*

VANDALEUR. I believed that my duty was the reform of the
rural economy, I believed that a landlord who was absent from
his estates was the worst landlord in the whole world. . . Yes:
we must go to Dublin. Bring the children. Bring the nursemaid.
For the time being, abandon Ralahine. Oh yes: we shall go
today.

They go out.

Scene Three

*The Shelbourne Hotel, Dublin. A RECEPTIONIST (male) trying
to keep order amongst a throng of excited people struggling with
luggage and great cloaks, hats etc. It is clearly foul weather
outside. The babel of voices augmented, if there are not enough
actors, by taped soundtrack. Among the guests are VANDALEUR
with EMILY and ROXANA, and — a little later — a DOWAGER.*

VOICES (*overlapping and sometimes concurrent*). Absolute
nonsense you can't let me have a room — would you rather I
went home to the west and was murdered in my bed?
I did write a week ago to bespeak accommodation — is the
postal service utterly disrupted by the emergency? —
Good God, man, the chaos in Dublin, playing right into the
hands of O'Connell and the Catholics, dammit they *want* us
disorganised — But we must have a room, our lives are in
danger — we must have a room — we must have a room, we
must have a room we must have a room — !

RECEPTIONIST. Ladies and gentlemen, would yous all of yous listen please! Be *quiet!* (*A sudden hush.*) The Shelbourne Hotel is well aware of the terrible conditions of disaffection, revolution, peril to life in the western counties: let me assure yous all that Dan O'Connell and his crew of hooligans, ladies and gentlemen, will not be permitted to disrupt the routine of the Shelbourne Hotel.

Now, sir, you said three bedrooms and a sitting-room for an entire family, 'tis out of the question. O'Halloran, the Vandaleur baggage into number thirty-four sharing with another family, look sharp or they'll have your head off —

VANDALEUR (*to* EMILY): Good heavens, is that all right?

EMILY (*exhausted*). Just take it and be thankful.

The DOWAGER, *forging through, bounces off the reception-desk and changes course towards* EMILY, *whom she carries into a corner.*

DOWAGER. Did you say *Vandaleur. . .* ? Good heavens, Emily, that's not you! Emily *Molony* of County Clare, and what were you doing, Vandaleur, to protect her from all the violence? Nothing at all, I suppose, as usual except grafting your damned gooseberries, impractical as always, improvements improvements and just look where it has led!

VANDALEUR. Ma'am, you will excuse us, my wife is —

DOWAGER. Shattered, of course, *bouleversée,* what else do you expect —

VANDALEUR carries EMILY *off with him, while the* DOWAGER *retains* ROXANA.

You don't suppose now he's in Dublin, he's going to start his old habits all over again? More fool her, she should never have married him, such a spirited girl once —

BAKER-FORTESCUE *has entered and received a letter from the* RECEPTIONIST. *Before he opens it the* DOWAGER *is onto him.*

Oh ho ho, Major Baker-Fortescue, ho ho ho my raucous ravisher — I don't suppose *you're* tempted to resume residence

in County Clare, with every Catholic in the district in arms
like an army of cockroaches — poor Vandaleur, you know,
quite *shattered* by the murderous outrage!

ROXANA *goes out.*

BAKER-FORTESCUE. And why not? Are not all of us? Did you
say he was here? Where is he, I can't see him?

The DOWAGER *surges out:* VANDALEUR *re-enters:* BAKER-
FORTESCUE *confronts him.*

Aha indeed yes, Vandaleur, hello there, come here, sir,
appalling news!

VANDALEUR. Baker-Fortescue, the very man I want to see. This
military emergency —

BAKER-FORTESCUE. The only possible solution. As soon as I
heard of the victory of O'Connell in the County Clare election,
I went straightway to the authorities to demand law and order!
Damme, my dear fellow, I took post upon the doorstep of
Viceregal Lodge like a bully in a brothel-house till that cow's
udder of a Lord Lieutenant was compelled for very shame to
comply. (*He looks around at the noisy throng.*) Five thousand
people if there's twenty — not a man of them dare sleep in
their own beds for months! (*He has unfolded his letter and
finds a printed leaflet.*)

Good God look at this! Rotunda Auditorium, a public lecture
by some bastard called the 'Distinguished Mr Robert Owen',
from England wouldn't you know, upon the 'Advantages
Economic and Social of the Co-operative System of
Agriculture!' Do you go to it?

VANDALEUR. It is tonight?

BAKER-FORTESCUE. It is indeed. Under the patronage of the
Protestant Archbishop and the Lord Mayor of Dublin! Do you
go to it?

VANDALEUR. Long had greatest interest in Mr Owen's most
lucid philosophy, but just now, I don't know, I —

BAKER-FORTESCUE. Oh you must go, you shall, we must all
of us go. It's an obvious Papish trick to soften the gentry in

the face of O'Connellite political obduracy. By the same token, as soon as it's over, I'm making up a small party of a few of our old friends, hearts of oak, bucks and bruisers of the right sort, don't you know, to play the tables at the Hell Fire Club. Do you come?

VANDALEUR. As you know, I do not gamble: and I abhor all games of chance. Our Divine Creator, Fortescue, provided us free will and a reasoning brain that by rational effort alone we might augment opportunity and enlarge our accomplishment.

EMILY *and* ROXANA *re-enter.*

BAKER-FORTESCUE. Oh He did? Perhaps He did. . . At all events, the Rotunda, eight o'clock don't forget!

BAKER-FORTESCUE *suddenly sees* WILBERFORCE, *looking around as though in search of someone. He breaks away from* VANDALEUR *and takes* WILBERFORCE *abruptly into a corner.* EMILY *has come up behind her husband.*

EMILY. The Rotunda? You are going out? Dear me, with the Rapist Fortescue?

VANDALEUR. A learned lecture, Mrs Vandaleur, for economic self-improvement. Do you wish to come too?

EMILY. The children are ill, poor Roisin is unable to cope — my economic self-improvement for this evening will remain domestic. (*She looks at his watch.*) Seven forty-five, you will be late.

VANDALEUR. I shall be late.

VANDALEUR *goes out, calling 'A cab, a cab. . . !'*

EMILY. He surely doesn't hope to catch a cab in this weather — Roxana, what are you staring at?

ROXANA (*who is hiding behind* EMILY, *and watching* WILBERFORCE). Who's that?

EMILY. Major Oliver Baker-Fortescue of His Majesty's Sixth Dragoons — a rural neighbour, when he's at home, which he hardly ever is — we would not call him a friend.

ROXANA. You referred to him as the *rapist*?

EMILY. My dear, he refers to himself so: as a boast: and with truth. In the service of the Crown, but oh yes with truth. Why the interest?

ROXANA. Because the one he is with is my man from New York, that's why. Now what has your military rapist got to do with the Cuban slave-trade?

BAKER-FORTESCUE (*to* WILBERFORCE). What do you mean, County Clare, you were supposed to come *here* to report to *me* first! County Clare is in political turmoil, I will not have you blundering about there all on your own messing everything up!

WILBERFORCE. Major Fortescue —

BAKER-FORTESCUE. *Baker*-Fortescue to you, Wilberforce: I do not relish familiarity.

WILBERFORCE. *Judge* Wilberforce to you, Major. I tell you sir, the political turmoil has already produced enough mess to make you and me reconsider every arrangement we've already made, and the sooner we get it fixed, the safer for both of us.

BAKER-FORTESCUE. Oh very well. But not here. Ten to eight, I'm going to be late. The Hell Fire Club, Mr. Wilberforce — *Judge* Wilberforce, dammit — upon midnight — make sure that you're there. At the card tables as though by accident, don't let them know we know each other. . .

BAKER-FORTESCUE *goes out.* ROXANA *and* EMILY *have crept close enough to hear these last remarks unnoticed.*

WILBERFORCE (*aside as he goes out*). Hail Columbia: and God's own country be the death and doom of decadent aristocrats. . .

WILBERFORCE *goes out.*

ROXANA. I wondered what he'd call himself when he got over this side of the ocean — Wilberforce, sure is appropriate — and *Judge,* too — my God, what a civic conscience. You say this Major Fortescue owns property on the western seaboard of Ireland? They could put slave-ships into the shore there?

EMILY. Slave-ships? All full of black men?

ROXANA. No don't be silly — trade-cargo for Africa for the purchase of black men — they've to fill up their ships somewhere with a clutter of Birmingham rubbish, they can't load them in a regular spot because the revenue men have it embargoed. We have got to find out more!

EMILY. Now you aren't going to try to go to the —

ROXANA. To the Hell Fire Club? Where the hell else? How do we get there — ?

EMILY. But we don't. It's for gentlemen only. They would never let us in without —

ROXANA. Without some sort of reason to believe that we were gentlemen? All the scrimmage of this hotel, we don't know where they've put our baggage — so —

She looks quickly around, sees that no-one is looking at them, and grabs up a couple of large caped men's over-coats that are lying about nearby. The two women are already wearing travelling boots under their skirts — they hitch up the skirts under the long over-coats —

Now here, my dear, an adventure, you'd never have dreamed the like in Ralahine, next time that you meet your outrageous Mrs Wheeler of Cork, you can make her quite blue with jealousy, I'll bet *she* never dared, anyway. . .

They clap on a couple of top hats with their hair crammed underneath — rearrange their scarves to look like men's cravats — EMILY pins hers in place with her brooch.

EMILY. Roxana, I cannot believe this — we are the heroine and her confidante from a nautical melodrama —

She sings (air: 'Polly Perkins of Paddington Green'):
  'Attired in man's raiment
  She bravely set sail
  To fight for sweet liberty
  'Mid gunshot and gale — '

ROXANA (*readjusting EMILY's brooch*). No, no, your neck — let me see — so —

They are now dressed and find themselves face to face with the RECEPTIONIST.

Shall we go out into the street and take the air, like two gentlemen?

RECEPTIONIST. Call ye a cab, gentlemen — at the steps of the door directly — O'Halloran, a cab for these gentlemen — where to, sir?

ROXANA. The — ah — the Hell Fire Club!

RECEPTIONIST. May ye be favoured at the tables, sir, by the luck of St Patrick!

ROXANA (*gives him a tip*). And may St Patrick favour you to — ah — drown the shamrock with this — isn't that right?

The RECEPTIONIST *performs his gratitude ritual and they go.*

Scene Four

The Rotunda Auditorium, Dublin. A large notice announcing ROBERT OWEN's *lecture, and a Union Jack at the back of the stage. The* ARCHBISHOP *and the* LORD MAYOR *take their places with* OWEN *in between them.* VANDALEUR, BAKER-FORTESCUE *and some* LADIES *are in the audience.*

LORD MAYOR. Mr Owen, the economic philosopher, well-known to you all, what more appropriate than a few short words from His Grace the Archbishop. . .

ARCHBISHOP. My Lord Mayor, such terrible times, the Irish nation torn in sunder — political sectarian strife. Indication of our communal will to contest these manifestations, shall we all of us please rise for the National Anthem. . .

'God Save the King' is played. All rise. THOMPSON *and* ANNA *enter through the audience. He has a French tri-colour at the end of his walking-stick, she has a red cap of liberty with a tri-colour cockade and a tri-colour sash. They sit down pointedly facing the audience below the platform. The anthem ends, everyone else sits: the* ARCHBISHOP *rises again.*

ARCHBISHOP. My lords, ladies, and gentlemen, desperate violence, assassinations, one hundred and ninety-six motiveless murders within the space of twelve months. For the social amelioration to be propounded by Mr Owen, enormous hopes of all persons of good will in the community —

ANNA. As the daughter of an Archbishop, may I point out to the Archbishop that the motiveless murders are largely provoked by the system of tithes, whereby the Roman Catholics are compelled by law to contribute to the coffers of an alien church, the Archbishop's own Protestant Church — ?

THOMPSON. You not only cause terrorism by your annual income, Archbishop, but when terrorism is extirpated, you must do without your port-wine.

Cries of anger from BAKER-FORTESCUE *and the* LADIES.

If the Lord Mayor will take into account the blatant failure of the London Government to give Catholics the legal ability to hold seats in the House of Commons, this meeting could prove constructive.

ANNA. No payment of tithes without representation!

LORD MAYOR (*rising*). Myself a whole-hearted advocate of Parliamentary reform —

BAKER-FORTESCUE (*from the floor*). Let the Papists into Parliament, they will crush the Protestant community — but the Loyal Orange Order will never —

LORD MAYOR. The brilliant Mr O'Connell, I happen to know, is totally loyal to the British Crown —

BAKER-FORTESCUE. The loyalty of O'Connell, sir, directed solely to his bank-balance —

ANNA. Are we talking about the stock exchange or pitch-and-toss at Donnybrook Fair?

BAKER-FORTESCUE. I will not bandy arguments with a female dressed-up as poll-parrot! Can lead only to a repetition of the Jacobin rebellion of 1798.

LORD MAYOR. Mr O'Connell the staunchest opponent of the egalitarians of '98 —

BAKER-FORTESCUE. A mere cloak to cover over his subversive intent to break the link with Great Britain!

THOMPSON. But what harm, sir, to the British, if we did break the link?

BAKER-FORTESCUE. Good God, you do not *advocate* republican separatism! A separated Ireland is a permanent military threat to the integrity of British democracy, and I speak as a professional soldier.

THOMPSON. I don't think the Americans —

BAKER-FORTESCUE. I don't want to hear about America — the Americans are like the French, they stretch out for Empire everywhere, the West Indies alone —

ANNA. You have an interest in the West Indies?

BAKER-FORTESCUE. Madam, never you mind where I have an interest —

THOMPSON. International financial manipulation, is that it, ho? How many bribes were paid to Protestants in shape of Empire Free Trade to secure the Act of Union? How much are you paid to beat your sectarian drum by the likes of the Duke of Cumberland and the rest of the English Tories?

BAKER-FORTESCUE. The English Tories at least will preserve our Protestant liberty!

THOMPSON. Did not your Protestants in the seventeenth century chop off the King's head? Dear sir, if you're a logical Protestant, you will also be a Jacobin —

ANNA. Once you start dispossessing the mighty of their seats, Major Charlotte Corday Fortescue, who can tell you where it will stop!

BAKER-FORTESCUE (*in a baffled frenzy*). Ho ho the female revolution, hen treading cock arsey-versey — cock-a-doodle-doo, cock-a-doodle-doo, papa papa I have laid an egg. . . !

LADIES (*joining in at the same time*). Bitch — virago — go back to your husband, (*etc., etc. . .*)

BAKER-FORTESCUE. They should fuck the likes of her upon

all fours like the animal she is — cock-a-doodle-doo —

He seizes the Union Jack and flaps it in THOMPSON's *face.*

THOMPSON (*stands on his chair and holds up his tri-colour*).
England observe: when the Irishmen run mad,
Now is your chance to take from them all they had.

ANNA (*on her chair too*).
England beware: when the Irish are quiet and cool,
If you do not stir them up, they will take back from you all
you stole.

Comparative quiet is restored by the LORD MAYOR *and his
gavel.*

LORD MAYOR. Mr Owen, Mr Owen, Mr Owen has not yet been
heard. . . !

OWEN (*rising, as the meeting subsides*). Your political national
problems amount to no more than wrangling over great bags
of bandits' booty. The intransigeant attitude of each partisan
in these disputes is the product of the environment in which
he or she willy-nilly has grown up toward stunted maturity.
Instead of competition, the ravening hunger of the deepsea
shark, I offer you the benefits of Socialist co-operation —
whereby every individual should endeavour to put forth the
same active exertions to make each other happy and
comfortable as they have hitherto done to make each other
miserable. Allow your work-people to receive full-fold the
fruits of their joint labour, let their elected representatives
confer with yourselves upon boards of management, assist
actively to determine all projects of self-improvement — and
above all let them share equally in the profits of all your
enterprise. You will say — "But where do we start. . . ?" —

VANDALEUR (*starting up in the audience*). Mr Owen, sir,
excuse me. In County Clare already a start has been made.
Immediately before the recent outbreak of terrorism, a large
number of our resident gentlemen got together and agreed
that the selfishness of the landowners was largely to blame for
the disaffection of the rural poor.

OWEN. Very good, sir, excellent, indeed — may I suggest: one

small estate, only one out of the whole country, to be at once
and without reservation, developed by its enlightened
proprietor under form of a co-operative — it would infallibly
succeed, and be seen to succeed: and another would immediately
follow, and another — till within five years the whole of
Ireland could be operating, nay, flourishing, as a congenially-
supportive, fully-Socialist commercial structure! What need
then of terrorism, what need of these states of emergency, what
need of the Orange Order or even of Dan O'Connell within a
commonwealth so harmonious. . . !

ANNA. *Utopia redivivus sub manibus dominorum magistrorum
episcoporum* — behold a miracle. . . !

THOMPSON. Co-operation from above, extended to the people
by the idealism of their controllers — Owen, you're a good
fellow, but a fundamental blockhead: for what motive should
great men deprive themselves of their only reason for being
called great?

BAKER-FORTESCUE. Has every man in this room gone mad. . . ?
Co-operation, do you call it that this — this — *speaker* is
prating about? There's only one word for *your* word. . .
REVOLUTION: and my God, an Archbishop under your
armpit as you preach it to us, a Lord Mayor in his golden
chain. . . .

THOMPSON. Astonishing the rapidity with which Major
Fortescue agrees with me.

ANNA. Only one word for your word indeed and it's my word
too.

THOMPSON. I did hope, this evening, Owen, it might in truth
have become *yours,* but you speak as you always did, to the
wrong crowd and there's no remedy.

VANDALEUR (*running forward*). Ah no, my dear Thompson,
you think *that* — you are in error! Mr Owen, how many times
has the co-operative system been tried?

OWEN. In Scotland, America, Scotland again, at least according
to *my* principles. I have a pamphlet to indicate at some
length the lessons to be derived from the mistakes we might
be thought to have made —

VANDALEUR. Effectively, though, not yet a complete success?

OWEN. Ah, but I would emphasise —

VANDALEUR. No no, sir, no excuses — I am a scientific man
and I well understand the hazard of experiment. Mr Owen,
I am prepared to place my own fortune in such hazard. I
have endeavoured for many years to run my rural estate
upon the most enlightened and approved modern methods —
not so much with no success, I would say rather abysmal
failure. Culminating this month in the murder of my steward.
Philosophical agriculture applied only to the soil, to the livestock, the crops, is quite useless in this country. The social
patterns of the human being at work upon that soil are the
very first specimens we must transfer to our laboratory —
because I did not do that, because I observed my farm
prosperous with the high price of corn in England, and
omitted to examine the *non*-prosperity of my work-people,
I have reaped a most blighted harvest. No: I am decided —
Ralahine shall be co-operative!

Applause. THOMPSON *and* ANNA *shake him warmly by the
hand.*

As I say, my steward is dead: by my own culpable neglect,
short-sightedness, dead. I would be grateful if you could
recommend me some person to take his place,
well-experienced in your theoretical principles.

OWEN. My dear sir, I can most certainly. My most hearty
congratulations: our first convert in Ireland!

More applause. He shakes VANDALEUR's *hand.*

There is one name immediately comes to mind — Mr Edward
Craig at present in Manchester —

VANDALEUR. I will trouble you for his address, I must see him
at once, go to Manchester at once, oh yes yes yes, there is
no time to be lost. . . !

BAKER-FORTESCUE (*as* VANDALEUR, OWEN, THOMPSON
and others confer). When this news is heard in England, there
will be cotton-mills and coal-mines set on fire by Luddite mobs
from Newcastle to Stoke-on-Trent! God forgive you,

Archbishop, for you know not what you do! Whosoever in this room has felt the truth of my discourse in the thick of his entrail, you can meet me at the Hell Fire Club — I shall have a proposition for all right-minded Britons of good spirit and no womanish scruples. . . .

They go out, generally.

Scene Five

The Hell Fire Club, Dublin. ROXANA *and* EMILY, *dressed as men, enter and are conducted towards the card-tables by a* WAITER. *There are* GENTLEMEN *playing cards, drinking, singing; maybe later, dancing. The atmosphere is boozy and ribald but not yet really wild.* BAKER-FORTESCUE *and* 1ST GENTLEMAN *come confidentially to the front of the stage.* WILBERFORCE *is among the company at the back.*

1ST GENTLEMAN. Your information, I'm afraid, Oliver, was only too correct — the liberal faction in the Commons are determined to force through the Bill for Parliamentary Reform: moreover there is no hope whatever for renewed legislation against the trade-unions. . . By the end of next year, a guillotine in St James's Park! How long can the King live? His opposition to Reform is feeble enough, God knows, but at least it does signify. When he dies —

BAKER-FORTESCUE. The eventual heir to the throne a virgin schoolgirl straight from the cradle, under the tits of a liberal wetnurse, to control the British Empire. . . Did you speak to the Duke of Cumberland?

1ST GENTLEMAN. He wants you to be responsible for the activation of the Orange Lodges throughout all the regiments in Ireland.

BAKER-FORTESCUE. No difficulty there. He will himself be making sure of the troops in England.

1ST GENTLEMAN. But when, Oliver, when? We cannot let it hang fire for ever!

BAKER-FORTESCUE. If Princess Victoria is to be deprived of
the succession, and the patriot Duke to become King in her
place, and if we all do what's expected of us our military *coup
d'état* can be ready to be sprung by the end of next year. Go
to the tables, enjoy yourself, we've been in the corner long
enough. . . .

1ST GENTLEMAN *goes to the card-table.* BAKER-FORTESCUE
catches WILBERFORCE's *eye and moves across the stage as
though drunk. They engineer a collision.* EMILY *sees this and
draws it to the attention of* ROXANA. *The two women creep
up to hear the conversation, but the men move about and
they only hear those passages enclosed in square brackets.*

BAKER-FORTESCUE. Dammit, man, you're drunk, do you
propel yourself into me, sir?

WILBERFORCE. Make it appear we have a quarrel. . . ?

BAKER-FORTESCUE. Perhaps we have. [I instructed you to find
a way to make confidential secure arrangements for the loading
of my cargo at the most convenient secret place in or around
the Shannon Estuary: I did *not* want you doing anything
within ten miles of Fortescue Grange: you have been pouring
out my stinking bath-water on my own front-garden-path, you
bloody fool!

WILBERFORCE. Keep it courteous, between gentlemen, between
partners, I am *not* repeat not your hired man, Major Fortescue,
okay . . . ? My concern in this business is to oversee financial
arrangements, to hire and fire correct executives. As soon as
you wrote me that your brig 'Maria Edgeworth' was now
known as a suspected slaver — I came right away to the River
Shannon to sniff out the land. So my report, when I made
it to you, would have the advantage of precognition, okay. . .?
So what did I find? Tidal mudflats, you didn't tell me about.
A low-lying coast-line with precious few highways of access,
you didn't tell me about. So we got to have a man who
knows the tides and the shallows and the hiding-places
inshore like he knows the intimate pimples in the concavities
of his own wife. So I find me such a man: and he sets me up
a surefire deal, and –]

BAKER-FORTESCUE. And in the very middle of your surefire deal your 'correct executive' gets himself *shot*. . . . ! God in heaven, Daniel Hastings. . .

WILBERFORCE. Political complications of your Irish aristocracy and their naturally obnoxious lackeys ain't none o' my business. I'm a republican.

BAKER-FORTESCUE. [So we now have a stranded cargo, in and around the shores of Shannon —

WILBERFORCE. Cached away safe and sound, Major, in the ruins of an an-tique monastery.

BAKER-FORTESCUE. But the ship, the ship, where is the ship — ?

WILBERFORCE. Gone up the coast standing for orders on and off the port of Sligo.] Just as soon as we can locate a replace-ment for Hastings, we call her back and she loads up. Guess your West Indian investments can hold off their foreclosure another few weeks. . . ?

BAKER-FORTESCUE. That's what *you* think. . . But Goddammit, that monastery is on Ralahine land, don't you realise John Scott Vandaleur has given over all of Ralahine to the blood-enemies of Church and King!

WILBERFORCE. Economic and social complications of Ireland none o' my business. . . .

BAKER-FORTESCUE. And yet. . . why not Ralahine. . . ? By God, it will work two ways! Either my slave-venture, my investment will be secured by the transaction: or else it will be discovered, Vandaleur will get the blame, his thieves-kitchen co-operative discredited for ever. . . ! [Why, Judge, I'm a bloody genius — if Napoleon Bonaparte had known about me, he'd have shat in his cocked hat all the way home to Corsica!]

He has been drinking steadily and now becomes uproarious. The room in general is becoming uproarious, and the GENTLEMEN *are beginning a degree of brutal horseplay.* BAKER-FORTESCUE *suddenly finds himself confronting* ROXANA *and* EMILY.

Are there one of 'em or two? I'm too drunk to deal with two of 'em. But what a lovely little gentleman, how soft and sweet the curve of his neck. . . You are a stranger in this place, sir? To our Hibernian hospitality? And so are you? (*He sways from* ROXANA *towards* EMILY, *and fingers the brooch at her neck*.) Where d'you come from, that you wear soup-plates of silver-gilt at your Adam's apple? Hungarians, or what are you?

EMILY (*very nervous, but rising to the occasion*). Ce que je me demande c'est pourquoi la plume de ma tante se trouve dans les pantalons de Monsieur le Curé —

BAKER-FORTESCUE. Scrotum o' the Pope, no games to be played with no fucking Frenchmen.

ROXANA. I'm not French: and I do calculate, sir, from my accent you'll deduce my regular domicile? The name is Van Leyden, Jedediah Van Leyden Junior of —

WILBERFORCE (*staring hard at her*). Boston, Massachusetts.

ROXANA. No sir. Philadelphia.

BAKER-FORTESCUE. You are aware of this gentleman's name?

WILBERFORCE. No, Major, not his name.

BAKER-FORTESCUE. Well, I am: he's just told it me. We have Hibernian hospitality — the grand tour of Europe for the young pups of Harvard College, am I right, boy, that's what you're doing here? So leave him alone, he's mine. Your place is the mudflats of the Estuary of Shannon: you go there. . . .

WILBERFORCE *grins ominously and moves away, trying in vain to get close to* EMILY. BAKER-FORTESCUE *pours* ROXANA *a drink and puts his arm round her*. GENTLEMEN *are now firing pistols and smashing things*.

Philadelphia: brotherly love: what they call it pacificism — ?

ROXANA (*letting herself go in a sort of frontier fantasy*). Sir, I had instruction in marksmanship from the younger brother of Daniel Boone. Put a bullet in the right eye of a grizzly-bear at five hundred paces, there ain't nobody can whup me Jedediah Van Leyden Junior between Pittsburgh and Vicksburgh and the mountain-lions o' Newark New Jersey. . . !

She borrows his pistols and indulges in a variety of extravagant feats, to the roaring delight of the company.

BAKER-FORTESCUE. God, a strong horse-pistol in first the left hand then the right, can stand fire and give fire like a true-hearted young buck! And we should all of us take example. . .

They all calm down and gather round him. His tone becomes low, ominous.

You don't need me to tell you civil war like a dead dog is buzzing with flies at every road's-end just the same as ninety-eight. Gentlemen, this poor country is a rotten bog of seditious conspiracy, we are all about to sink.

2ND GENTLEMAN. The only cure for agrarian terrorism is —

BAKER-FORTESCUE. The only cure that the leaders of our Protestant community are apparently aware of is to deliver over everything into the hands of a dirty mendicant. Every morsel of prosperity that our forefathers erected here by their courage and endurance to be surrendered like a bowl of pigswill to all those who would have prevented us even setting foot on the shores of Ireland! Thirty years ago in the rebellion we stood up for our own and prevailed. And the reason we could do so, was, by God, that we acted first! In the autumn of '97 I took part in the Dragooning of Ulster. Armed horse-soldiers like reaping-hooks into every village, every townland, Catholic, Protestant; who cared? Sword, fire, the cat-o-nine-tails — we spread the women in the mud under us, had the men and the brats watch while we put ourselves through them by troop and platoon. When the rebellion did break, the following year, three-quarters of all Ulster lay as silent as — not quite silent. . . now and then they moaned and groaned. The French, when they landed, found very few friends. The Rapist Fortescue had done his work. Jesus Christ I want a vomit. . . We do the same thing in Clare. But this time, unofficial. The Lord Lieutenant, the High Sheriff, are men of a different kidney: they lie in their own crap in their own beds and they mean to die there. They have forgotten there are still some of us with the old Orange spirit — we'll go to Clare, we'll prove it, and we'll live! I will reopen Fortescue Grange, and from the

portals of my ancient home we will ride to defy and to utterly
ruin the O'Connellites, the midnight murderers, the — the —
vomit again — the co-co-operators and Jacobin socialists.
Order the horses: we leave tonight.

See the look of him there:
So childish-ignorant, so wise. . .

How would you, boy, like Ireland to throw truly wide open
   your eyes,
Dabble blood upon the curls of your soft smooth beautiful
   hair?
Hey, what, boy, do you dare
Make mincemeat out of murderers in the beautiful green
   soft county of Clare. . . ?

You've got a horse? Then we'll get you a horse. Gentlemen,
your last bottle, your last vomit, your last leak into the
fireplace — the sun has already risen, we are on the road in
twenty minutes!

He starts a song, which the GENTLEMEN *all join in. (Air:
'Lillibullero'):*
   'Out on the road in the wind and the rain
   We know what we want and we have it and hold
   Rake it and break it and take it again
   Let nobody tell you we're bought and we're sold!
   Slitter slaughter holy water
   Scatter the papishes every one
   Lillibullero lillibullero
   Finish it ever before it's begun. . . !'

EMILY (*aside to* ROXANA *while the song is being sung*). Roxana,
you're not going to —

ROXANA. The closer I stick to him the closer we will hold him
   when all the evidence is complete — no, you must keep out
   of it, stay with your family, keep alive for my messages, and
   for God's sake be there when you're needed for God's sake. . .

BAKER-FORTESCUE (*pulls* ROXANA *away, speaks to* EMILY
en passant): Wear your soup-plate over your bollocks, Frog,
you might want it to protect you from a good solid Hibernian
boot!

All the GENTLEMEN *go out with* ROXANA *and* BAKER-FORTESCUE *in their midst, the song still continuing.* WILBERFORCE *watches them off.*

WILBERFORCE (*sings — air: 'O Susanna'*):
   'Soho my pretty Yankee boy, does the wind set fair that way?
   He runs you off to County Clare to run and sport and play,
   To sport and run and fire his gun with his arm around your
      waist,
   Oh pretty Philadelphia boy, where have I seen that face. . . ?'

WILBERFORCE *goes out. As he goes out he sees* EMILY *and makes a move towards her — she sees him and dodges out of sight.*

Scene Six

The Shelbourne Hotel, Dublin. Enter VANDALEUR, *followed by* ROISIN.

VANDALEUR (*sings — air: 'The Boys of Wexford'*):
   'For Manchester with no delay
   To seek and find at last — '

Coat — shawl —

ROISIN *equips him for his journey.*

   'The gambler's throw turned upside down
   The whole of a lifetime past — '

Carpet-bag —

   'I never lived but what I could — '

Umbrella umbrella I want my umbrella —

   'This way and that change course:
   With no delay John Vandaleur
   For Manchester sets forth. . . !'

You give that to your mistress — where the deuce is she, she never disappears in Ralahine. . . (*He hands* ROISIN *a letter.*) And this — (*He gives her an abrupt kiss on the forehead.*) Good-bye.

VANDALEUR *goes. Enter* EMILY, *re-establishing her female clothes.*

EMILY. Doesn't she know that Baker-Fortescue is called what they call him because he *does*? Oh, cousin, you *do* know, you crafty colonial, oh that's why you have me out of it in the very heat of the apprehension. . .

ROISIN. Excuse me, ma'am, the master, he's gone, ma'am, he left this letter.

EMILY (*tearing open the letter*). Oh dear God, Manchester. By the night boat and I have missed him.
(*Sings — air: 'Laredo'*):
   'Oh why do I stand here unable to handle
   Irresponsible people now this way now that?
   I want and I need to take part in the drama:
   Each time I make an entrance they tell me 'not yet!'

Oh Roisin there's a child crying, go and see to him, go on, girl, irresponsible, hurry — !

They go out.

Scene Seven

The Ralahine Estate. Enter CRAIG.

CRAIG. As a young lad I crouched appalled beneath the horse-hoofs and swinging sabres upon the cobble-stones of Peterloo. . . The whole of my life in Manchester, violence, deprivation, immeasurable squalor: but when I came into County Clare it was as though I had travelled from the bright fields of Eden to the Slough of Despond. Clustered like lice into their rat-ridden cabins, enthralled with disease and the blank apathy of congenital vice — have you ever seen a faction-fight? Debased gentlemen of the countryside stand grinning between two mountains while their ignorant tenants will beat each other's brains out — and the gentlemen themselves from their stronghold of Fortescue Grange lay waste their own lands in an orgy of terrified revenge — and if they don't do it, the soldiers do it. To be frank, I have despaired.

Some PEASANTS *are hanging around. One of them throws a stone.*

My grandfather was a Gaelic Highlander, brandished his clay-more for Bonnie Prince Charlie: but all they can see of me, I'm an Englishman fetched over for the *improvement* of Ralahine — don't that tell you the dead depth of the whole cruel business? *Improvement* is the word here for nowt less than mortal hatred. Means eviction, risen rents, means forced export of miserable emigrants by the shipload to America — and that's me, that's my significance. . . (*He takes a scrawled paper out of his pocket.*) Not only stones. They laid this upon the doorstep of my cottage for me to find. Aye, it's a coffin: and no metaphor. 'Beware the vengeance of Lady Clare.' Of course there are now and then smiling faces to be met on the way — but the implications of those smiles. . . ?

1ST PEASANT *passes, raises his hat politely.*

1ST PEASANT (*in Irish*): *Go to the devil.* *

CRAIG (*pleasantly also — imitating the phrase in Irish as well as he can*): *Go to the devil* my good fellow.

Enter VANDALEUR.

VANDALEUR. Ah, Craig, good morning. A spot of trouble with Paddy Murphy?

CRAIG. Trouble? By no means. Why?

VANDALEUR. Heard you telling him to go to the devil — I presumed —

CRAIG. I said nothing of the sort, sir. He said to me good-morning, I said to him —

VANDALEUR. 'Go to the devil.' Your instruction in the Irish language from these people — a little mischievous, misleading, they will have their joke.

CRAIG. Oh, joke, Mr Vandaleur, yes: is this a joke?

He shows VANDALEUR *the picture of the coffin.*

VANDALEUR. Ah. On your doorstep? Ah yes. . .

---

* *Go to the devil*: Teigh don diabhal.
  Approximate pronounciation: 'Chay don jowel'.

CRAIG.
> Daniel Hastings Number One
> Neddy Craig Number Two now the work has begun. . . '

You let me think Mr Hastings died suddenly in the midst of his duty. But he didn't, I have been *told* how Mr Hastings came to his end. What I've not been told is why.

VANDALEUR. I am said by many to be a good landlord: the fact is proved by the fact that I went to Manchester to fetch you over to help me to become a good landlord. I will confess this is all nonsense. I've been a damnably bad landlord: and for one reason, cardinal, the very worst reason of all: I had no notion, Mr Craig, of what my steward Daniel Hastings was up to. I knew what rents he paid me on behalf of the tenants: I never sought to find out what rents they had paid him. I will confess, Mr Craig, that —

CRAIG. Nay don't confess, we're not Papists. Give me reasons instead why I should bide another minute on this God-forsaken turf! You've put me and my good wife into fearful danger, Mr Vandaleur, bringing me over here to replace that scoundrel! I am not going to get killed for the crooked tyranny of Daniel Hastings, nor for your weakness neither in allowing him to carry it on.

VANDALEUR. But Mr Craig, you have *not* replaced him! You are not here as my steward: but to organize a co-operative.

CRAIG. Aye but have you told that to the folk, and if you have, did they comprehend it? You and I, at length, in private, have discussed our plans for this co-operative: now or never make them public. Find out who is opposed to it: and for what reason they are opposed. Mr Vandaleur: it's the last chance: either we take it or I go home.

He heard me: and the bell was rung beside the stable wall.
Into the yard they crowded one and all —

A bell rings and the PEASANTS *assemble.*

He briefly told them what he had in mind
And who I was and why they would not find
That Daniel Hastings was alive once more.

VANDALEUR.
>   No stewards in the co-operative, no middle-men, but a power
>   From all the people, by election, to control and plan
>   The work, the wages, and the wealth of Ralahine.
>   Rules, we shall have, they have been written out,
>   A constitution, ratified by vote,
>   Committees, trustees, an universal voice
>   By which you all can prove the virtue of your choice.

MICHEAL. If you please, sir, the poor people, sir, who do not
have the English — will I put what you have said into Irish for
them before you go on?

CRAIG. What he said to them in Irish took twice as long as in
English, twice as long, three times as passionate, and the same
question flung out from the crowd over and over —

PEASANTS (*one after another abruptly, in Irish*): *What about
the Englishman, what is he doing here?* *

MICHEAL. There is a question, Mr Vandaleur, from some of the
rural people, d'you see what I mean, on the matter of the
guarantees. The new English gentleman, sir, are we guaranteed,
Mr Vandaleur: he will understand the misunderstanding some
of the lads is after having with Mr Hastings, when he was alive?

CRAIG.
>   I myself made it clear
>   I did not want to hear
>   Neither for good nor for bad
>   About Daniel Hastings finished and dead.
>   I myself made it clear
>   There was nothing they need fear —
>   My own name would be put forward to the hazard of the vote:
>   If they did not want me, then by God I should get out —
>   If they agreed that I should stay
>   I would work here every day
>   Upon equal terms the same as they —

* *What about the Englishman, what is he doing here?*: Céard faoi an
Sasanach, céard a ndéanaigh sé annseo?
Approximate pronounciation: 'Caird fwee on sashna, caird-a-nuneena
shay onsha?'

To advise but not command
The administration of the land
And the people and the livestock and the tillage
And the building of the new most salubrious model village
Mr Vandaleur and I had planned —
The sanitary cottages, the school, the public hall.
The public voice, the public vote, supreme above it all.

Once again put into Irish, they considered it in Irish, looked
at me, looked at each other, I looked hard at the strange
young man who had taken it upon him to interpret.

PEASANTS (*growling dubiously in Irish*): *What about the rent. . .?**

MICHEAL. They had a most hard question for the master: I
put it to him — if we are all in the co-operative, sir, and we all
vote together for ourselves, to whom and how much do we
pay rent?

VANDALEUR. The Ralahine Co-operative Association as a body,
that is yourselves, self-determined, will pay rent as a total
body, in form of produce. Of course, guarantees for your
security under the arrangement. In a sense I shall pay my own
rent from myself *ex-officio* President of the Association to
myself as Proprietor of the land. By the same token, no
individual liability for the iniquitous tithe. The whole of that
is taken care of, under guarantee, by me.

Nothing else I could have said
Would have hurled up their hats so high
So fast from every head. . . !

The PEASANTS *cheer.*

MICHEAL. And for the vote — I told them in Irish they had all
marched to support the vote for O'Connell, when not one of
them themselves was qualified for a vote, not being
freeholders nor even leaseholders but the poor slaves of
Ralahine — and yet now, within Ralahine, there was all of a
sudden a vote — what they call beyond in England the *universal
suffrage* which not even in England have they got! And here it

---

* *What about the rent. . . ?*: Céard faoi an ćios. . . ?
Approximate pronounciation: 'Caird fwee on shoss. . . ?'

was given to them: so I told them they should take it.

CRAIG. And they did. They elected me amongst them as a member of the co-operative. There was some question, wrangled over in Irish, that the proposed rent would be too great. I made it clear, through the interpreter, that control of the production in the hands of the Committee would ensure that once the rent, already fixed, had been paid, the remaining surplus, and indeed growth of surplus, would be entirely at their own disposal: and this contented them.

Mr Vandaleur, at this point, with his own hand had written down His own personal regulation, as a *sine-qua-non*. . .

VANDALEUR. Gambling, alcoholic drinking, opprobious nicknames will be totally forbidden in the Ralahine Co-operative. They are all of them symptomatic of the most corrosive degraded envy: the competitive envious spirit is the first thing to be banished from the bounds of our new community. Is that clear?

MICHEAL. Clear enough, it gave small pleasure: the worst to be hurt by it — Cornelius Hagan, who had the shop, the public house, the grip of the usurous gombeen upon everyone of us there — he made a point not to speak the Irish. . .

HAGAN (*pushing forward*). The only vote that we need is the *Catholic* vote in Parliament: O'Connell alone can provide it: O'Connell alone can secure the good word of the Pope for deliberations and associations so Holy Ireland once again can come truly into her own.

MICHEAL. They knew him for what he was. They voted him out.

HAGAN *goes*.

(*Sings — air: 'What would you do if you married a soldier?'*):
'Will we patch up our quarrels or will we be fighting
Or can it be worse than ever it was
We've never a hope if we do not try something
Ride on a cow if we can't find a horse.'

To the people, in Irish, I said one thing more: Lady Clare and her Brave Boys are neither dead nor departed from Ralahine. We have heard guarantees. Lady Clare will be walking wide-awake every night to make sure they are held to: so long as they are held to she will not be seen. The print of her feet nonetheless in the morning dew. . . So why not dance. . . ?

ROISIN (*sings, as they all dance*):
'I looked to me mother I looked to me father
I looked to the holy man high on the hill
And never a word from the one to the other
But "Do what ye have to do, then come and tell". . . '

CHORUS (*sung as they dance*).
'A rout the da dee, the dum diddly da dum
A rout the da, doubt the da, diddly da dum
Da da diddly da dum
Da dee da dum da diddly da dee da diddly da dum. . . '

The PRIEST *and the* PARSON *have entered and stand in an attitude of formal benediction.*

PRIEST.
God's blessing on the work, my friends —

PARSON.
Rebellion, and revolt, now ends
Forever on this day in Ralahine.

CRAIG.
And all at last that needed to be done was done:
The Papist and the Protestant had both joined in the fun.

They go, with cheers and more dancing.

Scene Eight

Fortescue Grange. Enter ROXANA, *dressed as a man.*

ROXANA. Month after month everywhere, even over the water to England, and then back again to Clare, thank God so much of the time I was free and clear from this Fortescue Grange, and its crew of debased gentlemen.

She sings: (Air: 'George Collins'):
'They ride out by day and they ride beneath the moon
The green fields bleed and groan —

> If a ragged slave of Ireland came crying to me for help
> I must show him a face of stone.
>
> Be free, be free, poor Christian, I would say,
> Be free by your own angry hand:
> For what have I to do with a white man's broken life
> When my mind is in the black man's land. . . ?'

At last, this afternoon, it has been there to some purpose. In the dense rhododendrons under the ever-shuttered windows of the dark house of Fortescue, I have found Wilberforce has fixed himself an exclusive secret meeting. Here he comes.

ROXANA *conceals herself as* WILBERFORCE *enters, lights a cigar, walks about whistling 'Dixie'. Enter* MICHEAL, *whistling 'The Wearing of the Green'. They wander about covertly for a while, then become aware of each other.*

MICHAEL. The man beyond is after telling me that the foreign gentleman, meaning you, sir, had been concerned to have the word out for a good man with the share of a boat and an acquaintance with the tides of the river. I could put the word out for one of the Ralahine boys meself, sir: with the new co-operative, there's great work to be done there at Mr Vandaleur's lobster-pots, would give grand opportunity for the feller that's accorded the charge of it. 'Tis the matter however of the right price for the work. The young feller I have in mind, sir —

WILBERFORCE. Accorded the organizing of the Vandaleur lobster-pots? Tarnation take it, man, my Havana ceegar is swirling smoke under his nostrils this minute. How much?

MICHEAL. When you blew that same ceegar into the long nose of Daniel Hastings, he had information well enough there was a crowd of coal-black niggers to cure and roll the baccy. To my mind that's more than the smuggling of brandy: the devil of a high price in it, 'twould be the gallows for the lad that goes wrong.

WILBERFORCE. Just you name it, we'll agree. . .

MICHEAL. And the month, sir, the day of the month? Dark nights and high enough water don't come all that often together.

WILBERFORCE. We'll let you know. Just name your price.

MICHEAL. I'll put the word out. I'll let you know.

    WILBERFORCE *and* MICHEAL *go out.*

ROXANA (*emerging*). My God, Ralahine, and a slave-dealer's
    garter-snake in the very middle of the new co-operative! I
    have got to warn Emily — no I can't get her involved yet —
    God I've got to warn somebody: find out who is that *villain*. . .
    Lobster-pots, he said lobster-pots. . . !

    She goes.

Scene Nine

The Ralahine Co-operative. Enter CRAIG, PEASANTS, ROISIN
and MICHEAL — *they are all very respectably dressed in new
white festive smocks, and they carry garlands which they put
up round the stage. A large banner reads 'Our First Harvest:
Each for All'. CRAIG fussily supervises the decorating-process.*

MICHEAL (*to the audience*):
    Ah the great celebration. . . sure wouldn't you know
    When you see us all dressed like eedjits as white as the snow
    That the Englishman Craig has at last put his mark
    On the Irish barbarians brutal and dark?
    He has brought over for this harvest a marvellous machine:
    If it works, or does not work, is yet to be seen.
    Nonetheless, what he has done,
    We ourselves can make our own.
    And with this in my mind I have composed a small poem.

    'Not Vulcan nor Daedalus
    Of the ould Grecian genius
    Had ever contrived
    Such an engine so various:
    Not crafty King Solomon
    Nor proud Archimedes
    Could have dreamed in their sleep
    Of such a phenomenon — '

1ST PEASANT (*improvising*).
    'With the spin of two wheels
    We will cut in three days
    All the corn we were scything
    At each others' heels
    If the weather held good —

3RD PEASANT (*improvising*).
    For a week or a month:
    In the blaze of the heat
    Like an axe on our head — '

    — Improvise how we like in the spirit of the co-operative, it
    takes a true poet to think up for us Archimedes and the pagan
    nymphs —

1ST PEASANT. There will *be* pagan nymphs in it, with their long
legs and their snow-white bosoms — ?

ROISIN. Oh there will, there will surely — Did ye ever know my
brother to ever leave any of that out?

General laughter. CRAIG *leads them all out. As they go, enter*
ROXANA *at one side, to attract* ROISIN's *attention. She is
still wearing her male clothes, but without a hat and her hair
is long and free.*

ROXANA. Ssst — Roisin — !

ROISIN *avoids the others as they all go out.*

ROISIN. Miss Roxana — ! But you're dressed like a — but we
thought you were in England — but we —

ROXANA. Ssh, don't let them see me — Roisin there are the
most terrible things going on inside Ralahine. I just don't
dare tell the Vandaleurs, because we've got to find out who is
implicated and who knows about it, if it gets out too soon
it could just *ruin* the co-operative, it would break Mr
Vandaleur's heart and his poor wife — Roisin who is the man
who's in charge of the lobster-fishery?

ROISIN. The lobsters, why sure it's —

ROXANA. What I have found out about that man I could send
him to the *gallows* —

ROISIN. Oh my God —

ROXANA. He is using his lobsterpots as a criminal concealment for aid and comfort to the slave-trade —

Enter MICHEAL *briskly, lilting a jig and clapping his hands.*

MICHEAL. Aha, Roisin, are ye there, girl, they have the new reaping yoke dismantled from its travelling-car, and Neddy Craig is assembling it this minute in the great paddock, come on, girl, the new machine — !

ROXANA *stares at* MICHEAL *transfixed*: ROISIN *gives a moan of fear*: MICHEAL *stares at* ROXANA *first in astonishment and then in admiration. He sweeps off his hat.* (*Declaims*:)

'Oh tell me in time if you are not divine
Or a god or a goddess the senses to confuse:
Sure would glorious Diana wear the Armour of Lysander
Not a hero on earth would such a maiden refuse. . . !'

ROXANA *glares at him in horror. Bewildered by her hostility, he turns to go.*

ROISIN. Micheal!

MICHEAL *halts, and stares at the two women.*

You said lobster-pots and that's the truth. The truth also he is my brother. About the slave-trade I have heard nothing. But if you know what you know, you will tell the magistrate and have him taken?

ROXANA. Oh my God, child, your own brother. . .

ROISIN. You will have him taken, you have the proof? There are those would kill you if they knew that, and I would not be the last of them, me! Because it can not be true, not the slave-trade — no not true. Or if it is true itself, then *he* does not know what it is he is after doing.

MICHEAL (*to* ROXANA): Where did you hear this?

ROXANA. Fortescue Grange.

ROISIN. Fortescue Grange, Micheal, the very house of the marauding Orangemen!

ROISIN *goes out.*

ROXANA. May I say —

MICHEAL. May I say, before you speak, that I have indeed been a party to the enslavement of the Ethiopian blackamoors — and I had reasons.

ROXANA. Oh the devil of a high price in it — I know all about that one.

MICHEAL. The height of the price, ma'am, alone, was to my mind coherent reason. This co-operative might well fail: and if it does, the Ralahine tenants will once again be in search of money for whatever defence and protection they can get.

ROXANA. Yes, but the protection, the defence of the black slaves —

MICHEAL. Ah. I take your meaning. Is it possible, do you ask me — and do you not think I have asked myself? — to raise up the oppressed people by the oppression of somebody else, children of Ham and accursèd though they may be. . . ?

ROXANA. Accursèd — ! Who told you that?

MICHEAL. I was one time on my way to becoming a priest at the seminary. It got no further because Daniel Hastings had my father evicted: so the fees for my schooling could not be assembled. But some instruction I did have. If, in your opinion, it was not complete — and I see now indeed it was not complete — I would be grateful for you to put that right. Indeed, ma'am, for you and for the hold you have over my spirit, I would do anything till my last day: you are an American republican, of such kind I have never met in my life. From an Irish republican, true service, as it were a marriage between our two ideals. (*He takes her hand with a gallant bow, kisses it, and turns to go.*) Believe it, within *my* devising, there will be no more of this dirty slave-trade.

ROXANA. No — wait — please. Maybe there should be.

He pauses, surprised.

We need to do more than find out about the slave-trade. We need to stop it, to destroy it, if we can, from *within*.

MICHEAL (*after a moment's thought*). I take your meaning.
I will continue. I will inform you. For you, everything.

Sounds of people offstage. ROXANA runs out hurriedly.
Enter VANDALEUR, EMILY, CRAIG and PEASANTS. Two
of the latter bring in an easel with a fancy cloth veiling a
picture.

VANDALEUR. My good friends, the golden grain is ripe for the
reaping-hook, and the reaping-hook, my good friends, being a
mechanical invention, the first time ever in this country, is the
crown on the brow of the Palladium of our success —

CRAIG. Don't we want to take a look at the official portrait of
the mechanical marvel? Mrs Vandaleur?

EMILY. Mr Craig, members of the commune — with pleasure — !

She unveils a brightly coloured representation of the reaping-
machine. Applause and a burst of music.

CRAIG. Mr Deputy Secretary, will you read the address?

1ST PEASANT (*reads*): 'To the agricultural labourers of County
Clare: this machine of ours is one of the first machines ever
given to the working classes to lighten their labour and at the
same time increase their comforts. Any kind of machinery
used for shortening labour — except used in a co-operative
society like ours — must tend to lessen wages, and to deprive
working men of employment: but, if the working-classes
would cordially and peacefully adopt our system, no power or
party could prevent their success. There would thus, under the
socialist and co-operative arrangement, be no more starvation
in the midst of abundance.' May I say, Mr Vandaleur, sir,
this address, sir, should be posted on every church-gate in the
Province of Munster.

Applause.

VANDALEUR. And sent furthermore to every landlord throughout Ireland. I have already taken steps. For tonight, my friends,
you will all enjoy yourselves, and tomorrow let the reaping
commence. But one thing before we all give ourselves up to
the revels — to our sober, indeed biblical, revels, affording
without indulgence praise to the Lord for our communal

energy as did Boaz the Patriarch in the Book of Ruth — one thing — our intended crop of scientifically-derived winter-wheat, if sown in the great paddock as soon as the present harvest is saved, will infallibly pay for the cost of the reaping-machine: and the present harvest, if sold in the earliest market by reason of the rapidity of the reaping-machine, will infallibly pay for the capital expended already in the first stages of our most hopeful development. Congratulations to every one of you — music — Mr Secretary, will you lead Mrs Vandaleur into the first figure of the English country dance you have been at such pains to teach the people?

CRAIG. I have always maintained that the English mode of dancing has a most admirable influence towards order, method, discipline, and courtesy. We will see with what diligence my pupils have profited therefrom. . .

He forms them up to perform a polite and solemn English dance. As they dance, to one side of the stage —

Scene Nine (A)

Thompson's Tower in County Cork.
This scene takes place on the opposite side while the dance continues. THOMPSON *and* ANNA WHEELER *enter, writing letters.*

ANNA. *Ma chère amie* . . . Tell our fellow-socialists in France that Ralahine has truly proved the value of the co-operative system as a means toward the emancipation of women!

THOMPSON. Dear Friend. . . Once again a list of complaints from Ireland to England. No mention in Owen's *Co-operative Magazine* of my new book *Practical Directions for the Establishment of Communities.* And also no help from the English branch of the movement for my own co-operative project here in Glandore.

ANNA. The change amongst the women and children of Ralahine! The new residential school — fresh milk, green vegetables — the mothers left as free as the men all working together in the fields and dairy. . . Alas the women do not yet receive equal pay, but their votes are equal to those of the men! Mrs Craig, who runs the school, has been most tactful in regard to her Protestant persuasion — thereby happily evading the scorn of my dear Thompson who sees the dead hand of the religious Brahmins in every aspect of Irish life.

THOMPSON. God in heaven, the co-operative movement should be blazing bonfires of pure joy at the success of Craig and Vandaleur — the very first complete commune totally integrated with the indigenous people to be commenced anywhere, I believe, in the whole world — and without external finance, without any need for the *kow-tow* to our Yahoo Hibernian gentry!

ANNA. The Owenite block in the movement so frustrates all the work of my Thompson — and this, with his worsening health, casts a shadow over my life. Nonetheless his physical energies continue always to astonish me. *Entre deux amies,* in the learned language, *coitus philosophicus interruptus non est. . .* Your devoted Anna.

THOMPSON. I knew it, I knew it, *vae victis,* Daniel O'Connell has sold out the Irish multitude — in return for Catholic seats in the Westminster Babel-brothel, he has agreed to the disfranchisement of the forty-shilling freeholders — the main body of his support! My dear friend, a political vacuum, but where is the co-operative movement? If only I could live for ever — in the love of my Anna — as it is, I must make the best of a short life. I remain, Thompson.

The PEASANTS, *impatient with the decorum of the country-dance, break into an enthusiastic Irish reel* — CRAIG *and the* VANDALEURS *are willy-nilly involved in it.*

They all go out.

Act Two

Scene One

Fortescue Grange. Enter BAKER-FORTESCUE *and* GENTLEMEN, *dressed for hunting, but with pistols. Hunting-calls on a horn.*

BAKER-FORTESCUE. Gentlemen! I have had this letter from the High Sheriff of County Clare! Our operations on behalf of the security forces are to cease forthwith. (*He holds out a letter which the* GENTLEMEN *angrily grab at.*) We are an offence to the leaking urine of the bloody liberal conscience. . .

1ST GENTLEMAN. The craven spirit of John Vandaleur has infected every gentleman in the county! Why cannot the Duke of Cumberland awake to the situation — he will never seize power if he delays any longer —

BAKER-FORTESCUE. It progresses — leave it alone. But today, I regret to tell you, we must content ourselves with hunting *foxes*.

The GENTLEMEN *groan, and put their pistols away.*

I thought best we should hunt Vandaleur's. That model farm of his *deserves* security from all manner of red-tailed predator.

2ND GENTLEMAN. From what I hear it has it already. Did you not know that his foxes were *shot*?

BAKER-FORTESCUE. So for Ralahine, no foxes. . . So, for Ralahine, we should follow a drag. Kitty! Have you not got that aniseed on your fetlocks yet — come here, girl! Gentlemen, you remember the traditional Fortescue drag-hunt. . . ?

Enter KITTY, *stripped to her shift, trembling. She gives a frightened curtsey.*

First one to catch her has her all to himself for the whole night!

So run for us, girl, twice as fast as the swoop of a hawk,
South for two miles, into Ralahine by the turn of the cross,
Through the home farm, and straight over the paddock —
Keep your hard young feet firm on the mire on the moss
On the stone on the rock on the corn and so after —
By God there's one bloody Teague will give thanks for the
    speed of his daughter. . . !

*He sets her off running with a crack of his whip — she speeds
off and out of sight.*

No-one's to catch her till she gets across Vandaleur's crop! Call
up the hounds, boys, whip, huntsman — we go — !

Whoops, cheers, horn, and they gallop off after her.

Scene Two

*The Ralahine Co-operative. Action continued from the previous
scene.* KITTY *re-enters, and runs about the hall, dodging and
doubling — the cries of the hunt are heard, off. A great cry of
'view hallo' as she runs clear through the middle: then she
disappears from sight by some rapid movements.* BAKER-
FORTESCUE *enters in the back of the audience amid a chorus
of baffled hunt noises, hounds yelping, desultory yells of the men
from different corners etc.*

BAKER-FORTESCUE. Gone to ground. . . ? Aha, not her! The
    paddock — we can't jump because bloody Vandaleur's staked
    his hedges!

GENTLEMEN (*off*). Oliver, Oliver — go round by the farm-yard
    — they have the gate open through to the paddock that way — !

More yells and blowings of the horn etc. Enter, on stage,
MICHEAL *and* PEASANTS.

MICHEAL. He has his hounds streaming over the great paddock
    and the winter-wheat — look sharp, boys, look sharp — or the
    horses'll be into the yard!

PEASANTS. All the work will be destroyed — for the clearing of the debt for the machinery — shut the gate, boys, shut the gate — !

With angry exclamations the PEASANTS *all join in a fierce dancing movement, to form a barrier across the stage, which* BAKER-FORTESCUE *confronts.*

BAKER-FORTESCUE. Open the gate. . . open the gate when you're told. . . God damn you, I'll cut off your — blow off your — Vandaleur — ! *Open the gate!*

PEASANTS. We will not.

Enter VANDALEUR *at a run, behind the* PEASANTS.

BAKER-FORTESCUE. Will you order your servants, John Vandaleur, to throw open this gate at once —

VANDALEUR. Major, they are not my servants, they are the members of the committee of the Ralahine Association. I am not in a position to —

BAKER-FORTESCUE *roars and points his pistol.*

If you threaten us with that weapon, sir, you will be liable to a most serious charge. Surely, your pursuit of the vulpine species does not entitle you —

BAKER-FORTESCUE *puts his pistol away.*
ROISIN *enters through the auditorium, with a basket of turf.*
BAKER-FORTESCUE *sees her and turns on her.*

BAKER-FORTESCUE. Vulpine, who the devil said *vulpine?* Every fox on this land has been shot and you know it; two legs and not four, you egregious eedjit, the greasy vixen we're after today! And begod if we've lost one there's always another —

He chases ROISIN *and tumbles her over. A yell from offstage:*

GENTLEMEN (*off*). View hallo view hallo – Oliver, look to the west, Kitty Mulroney is over the hill west — Oliver — after her — !

BAKER-FORTESCUE. View hallo — !

BAKER-FORTESCUE *goes off screaming. Hunt noises in crescendo, then they fade away. The* PEASANTS *relax their barricade delighted.*

VANDALEUR. I would have thought it would have been better to have opened, the normal courtesy of a country gentleman to his neighbours, what could I do, he called you my servants — Mr Craig! — did he say *shot*? There has been shooting of foxes on this land? Mr Craig, Mr Craig —

Enter CRAIG *at a run.*

Who gave the orders, sir, for the shooting of foxes! Utilitarian damned ignorance, is this what they call the Manchester school of economy — breaking all bonds of courtesy, comradeship through the whole district — ?

CRAIG. Excuse me, a serious problem, elimination of vermin, scientifically-co-ordinated agronomic procedures concomitant with the mechanization of — Mr Vandaleur, the continued complaints of the workpeople, as expressed within committee, outrageous depredations among the poultry, we could not tolerate —

ROISIN (*coming up on stage*). Death alive, did you not see who it was they were chasing! Did ye not see Kitty Mulroney out of Fortescue's kitchen, the creature, running her heart out up hill down dale to keep the teeth of the dogs from her back!

MICHEAL (*amid expressions of approval from the* PEASANTS). Did ye not see they would have chased my sister the same way for the same purpose, and begod she's not even one of Fortescue's own tenants!

ROISIN. Ye do not believe, surely, Mr Vandaleur, Mr Craig, 'twas the heat of the sport only brought these gentlemen into Ralahine today! Oh ho no sir, he knew well, did your purple Major, that the ploughing and sowing the great paddock was such dignity and pride to the small people of Ralahine, he had rather he'd run mad than endure it, so he would.

The PEASANTS *all acclaim this.*

MICHEAL. Mr Vandaleur, may we therefore be clear about one thing: this co-operative is organized, and well organized, by every one of its members together — and we are not the Lords and Gentlemen — we neither know, sir, nor care for the normal forms of the big-house courtesy. We do not want the fox-hunt, we have said so, and we have shown it.

ROISIN. We would be obliged for you to recognize such is now the position.

> VANDALEUR *stands awkwardly as* CRAIG *goes out with* ROISIN *and the* PEASANTS. MICHEAL *ignores him, and he goes out alone.* MICHEAL *remains behind and addresses the audience:*

MICHEAL.
> At last we are proud in the proof of our power.
> Let us see is it not time to do something more?
> Roxana is my heart's love: and tonight she and I
> Will leave the Orangeman and his damned slave-ship
> Totally stranded high and dry.
> Secret work: dangerous: why wouldn't we dare?
> Begod I have done worse things in the name of Lady Clare.

He remains on stage as the scene changes.

Scene Three

The Irish Coast. Enter ROXANA (*in female clothes*), *meeting* MICHEAL. *They embrace fervently.*

ROXANA. My darling, is there enough evidence still left at that monastery to clinch the case against Baker-Fortescue?

MICHEAL. There is. We've got him!

> *As they embrace again, they hear voices off.* MICHEAL *hastily slips out. Enter* EMILY *and* BAKER-FORTESCUE, *on opposite sides.* EMILY *embraces* ROXANA, *and stands beside her.* VANDALEUR, *agitated, hurries in and joins them. The* SERJEANT *enters with a portfolio of papers.*

SERJEANT. Be upstanding for the High Sheriff of County Clare!

> *Enter the* HIGH SHERIFF. *He takes a document from the* SERJEANT *and looks round at the company.*

HIGH SHERIFF. The lady from America, please. Madam, you pronounce yourself, here, the protagonist of an alleged adventure, last night, under cover of darkness, whereby a vessel — the — the —

ROXANA. The brig 'Maria Edgeworth'.

HIGH SHERIFF. Be silent, I have the name. You claim that this brig by complicity of an unidentified associate was induced to run aground upon the sandbank, as alleged, over *there*, thus defeating an attempt to have her loaded with illegal cargo in the furtherance of the abominable slave-trade. Serjeant! Do you see any ship on the sandbank?

SERJEANT. No sir.

ROXANA. She floated off at the ebb tide, the only place he dare take her was down-river and she's gone — it is in my affidavit!

HIGH SHERIFF. Not reported by the coastguard. Now, the cargo — where is it?

ROXANA. They had it hid in the ruined monastery. It was still there this morning at sun-up.

SERJEANT. Pursuant to your orders, sir, I checked the ruin of the monastery, the graveyard, the purlieus. No evidence of illegal storage.

ROXANA. Don't you see they will have moved them — they've had all morning to get rid of them — did you not look for hoof-prints, tracks of wheels — ?

SERJEANT. Adjacent surface of an unyielding nature, rocks and stones, dry, afforded no trace of surreptitious transport.

HIGH SHERIFF. Mr Vandaleur, *your* land, your monastery — any knowledge of such usage for the ruins?

VANDALEUR. Certainly not — but if Miss Roxana is so positive, then —

EMILY. Of course she's positive! Why I was with her myself when we heard Major Baker-Fortescue and his American agent, they were plotting, in secret —

BAKER-FORTESCUE. Oh indeed, madam, where?

EMILY. In Dublin, in the — I — I had rather not say where.

HIGH SHERIFF. This is nothing but hearsay. Most dubious hearsay. This person you allege acted as pilot to the 'Maria Edgeworth' caused her to strike upon the sandbank — where is he?

ROXANA. I gave him my word he would not be implicated.

HIGH SHERIFF. But of course he would be implicated if your story is true. An accomplice in a felony. Were he to turn King's Evidence, however —

BAKER-FORTESCUE. Draw your attention, High Sheriff, to the peril inherent in any offer of clemency to disaffected individuals of a certain religion, to incriminate a landlord, Protestant landlord, draw your attention to the unsolved murder of Daniel Hastings on this very property.

HIGH SHERIFF. Yes. . . You either produce him unconditionally, or not. But if not. . .

ROXANA. I gave my word —

The HIGH SHERIFF *ostentatiously tears up her deposition.*

BAKER-FORTESCUE. On the other hand, my *own* associate, I can and will produce, Mr Wilberforce!

Enter WILBERFORCE.

High Sheriff, Judge Ephraim Wilberforce, prominent American jurist, and my partner in my perfectly legal West Indian traffic, sugar, exotic fruits. And here are the papers to prove it.

WILBERFORCE. Well aware, sir, I have no mandate to practise the law within your jurisdiction, sir, but if this was Atlanta Georgia, and you-all had been duly sworn in the presence of *my* bench, I would proceed by — (*He registers the identity of* ROXANA *and suddenly becomes decisive instead of tentative.*) I would proceed by examination of the known character and antecedents of the principal complainant. He said Philadelphia — didn't I tell *her* Boston? Oho, *she* is well-known. Being the born bastard daughter of a high-yaller whore from her own father's slave-cabins!

BAKER-FORTESCUE (*choking with shock*). You mean — *she* — Jedediah — in *my* house — Jedediah Van Leyden Junior — (*He prevents himself with an effort from striking* ROXANA.) All forms of your god-damned treachery — every way, all of it, flesh, blood, spirit — be certain, *boy,* I won't forget. . . !

WILBERFORCE. She's an example, High Sheriff — you wouldn't maybe know the term — in Georgia we call it *philo-phallic race-envy* — I'd best not go into it on account of the lady's presence, but . . . (*He whispers in the* HIGH SHERIFF's *ear:*) . . . inflamed sexuality, glandular, some of 'em do it with hogs, on account, you understand, of their African heritage. . . and she has set herself these last few years to lay out false accusations and indecent scandal broadcast against no end of honourable white-folks all up and down the Atlantic seaboard!

EMILY. Roxana, your father — his wife was my own father's sister — she was —

ROXANA. His wife was not my mother. I'm sorry, what he says is quite true. At least, about that. Not the rest of it. Oh God, not the rest of it. Does it make any difference?

EMILY (*with an effort*). Difference. . . no of course not. . .

BAKER-FORTESCUE. Remarkable fine brooch, Vandaleur, like a soup-plate. . . your wife's taste. . . French?

HIGH SHERIFF (*scribbling hastily on a paper*). Under the provisions of the Peace Preservation Act, military emergency coercive draconian powers, am entitled by my office to present you, madam — (*Gives the paper to* ROXANA.) with this order for your immediate deportation from the Kingdom of Ireland. Serjeant, ensure the lady leaves for Limerick before sunset, put her personally aboard the first vessel sailing out of the port.

VANDALEUR. Upon what grounds, sir, my wife's relative — ?

HIGH SHERIFF. I have defined her as an undesirable. And she is *not* your wife's relative. . . Oliver, the black stallion, you know we discussed a price, now I have had another offer from Colonel O'Brien. . .

He and BAKER-FORTESCUE *withdraw, talking horses.* WILBERFORCE *tags along with them.*

ROXANA. Don't you realise they had the whole thing arranged before they got here — Emily, you must help me — that cargo can be no more than five miles away — make immediate inquiries, surely someone in the co-operative —

VANDALEUR. The co-operative. Don't *you* realise, the reputation of my co-operative has all but been destroyed before my face with your meddling and muddling!

EMILY. Don't you realise that the High Sheriff was trying to *save* the co-operative, Roxana! Don't you realise the Rapist Fortescue would do everything he could to put the blame for that cargo upon Mr Vandaleur, had it been found in the ruins — and my God what a relief that they had managed to get rid of it!

ROXANA. Do you mean to tell me that you all know that my story was quite true! And yet you allowed them to serve me with — (*She flourishes the deportation order.*)

EMILY. Roxana, my dear Roxana — it is not as though you were really my cousin any longer, but — Of course we all knew it was true. Mr Vandaleur indeed confronted that horrible Fortescue, with his guilt. Made him swear never again would he so much as *breathe* toward a slave-agent!

VANDALEUR. Or else, no stone unturned before absolute exposure! And moreover he must refrain from harassment of our co-operative —

EMILY. Roxana, do you hear, Mr Vandaleur made him swear, upon his honour as a gentleman.

VANDALEUR. I have lived in this country all my life, as a gentleman. Philosophically scientifically endeavoured to lift up the poor people toward a condition of humanity. Out of what? Out of slavery. *My* slaves, and I am responsible. My co-operative the sole token of the responsibility of my life, my status in society, I live *here*. It's a question of blood.

VANDALEUR *goes.*

ROXANA.
　　Such blood indeed as we all now comprehend

In my light body to be of such a kind
Stained in my very womb by the womb's blood of my mother

EMILY. Roxana, my darling, no stain in your spirit, your mind —

ROXANA.
Nonetheless, where I am one
And in this island all alone
You know yourselves to be the other.
There is no doubt your co-operative must be saved from its
    ruin:
For if it fail, the black slaves, who are not saved, will reap
    no gain. . .

ROXANA *goes with the* SERJEANT.

EMILY (*to the audience*).
I am made small by her fortitude
By the width of the wound
That this news has laid open in her side:
In my own heart.
From now there is but part
Of me beneath my husband in his bed
To furnish love
Toward him as a good wife should.
The rest must rove
With my heart's darling wherever she goes
Far over far over the gray Atlantic wave. . .

EMILY *goes.*

Re-enter BAKER-FORTESCUE *and* WILBERFORCE.

WILBERFORCE. Reckon you didn't appreciate, Major, old Judge
Ephraim and his intelligence service could operate so far and
so fast. . . ?

BAKER-FORTESCUE. Far enough. Shall we try for a change a
little bit nearer home? This turd of a Teague fisherman
brought my ship upon the sandbank — where's he gone? Find
him out — and find out how we can hang him! Anything,
anything, to incriminate the rabble of Ralahine!

They go.

Scene Four

Thompson's Tower in County Cork. Enter THOMPSON, *very ill, staggering about with his arms full of papers. Noise, off, people shouting, and* ANNA's *voice expostulating.*

THOMPSON. Keep them out, my rapacious relatives, I will not have them at my death-bed, Anna, keep them out — !

ANNA enters, the LAWYER *behind her. She disposes* THOMPSON *into an arm-chair, tucks a rug around him. There is a large black-draped jar on a small table at his side marked 'For the Head of Wm. Thompson.'*

Down, dog, to your basket — who's this — it is not that damned clergyman, the pundit, the brahmin, the rabbi, the mad mullah of Trinity College — ?

ANNA. Your attorney — you asked for him, you know who he is — (*She finds a paper and gives it to the lawyer.*) Here is the will, please look through it carefully and correct it before he signs it.

THOMPSON (*snatching it*). No, no, he will endeavour to dissuade me — only way, do it all yourself, so — so — (*He reads through the paper, making sweeping corrections to it.*) *Fait accompli*, you see — so! Where's the sawbones? He should be here. Dammit, Anna, do I have to take my own pulse to the very last?

ANNA. I don't want to know about that surgeon. He can't cure you, he can only —

THOMPSON. Collect my head for the phrenologist — Monsieur Pierre Baume of Paris, to whom it has been promised — and why not? For the philosophers the authenticated brain-box of a philosopher — the complexity of life, as I always say — infinite: through his head and his books, they will deduce the complex soul of Thompson, and by God they will be wrong! Anna, I *told* you, *your* head as well, mouth-to-mouth, nose-to-nose, cuddling up in the same jar. . . !

ANNA. Romantic — but impractical.

THOMPSON. You are about to say I am a hypocrite. We shared

our bed, we shared our book-writing, page between page, we
shared everything all these years – and yet we did not share.

ANNA. Hypocrisy, with men, it is a common condition.

THOMPSON. As we have abundantly proven within the argument
of our joint works. Our joint works with *my* name on them.
But common should be curable. I mean *this* man, Anna, *me*,
all of my life — have *I* not worked hard enough to rid myself
of it, Anna, of *some* of it. . . ? Anna?

ANNA. Your ideas have been presented. If they are true and
you are not, does it matter?

THOMPSON. It does if they are not in truth *my* ideas. I am
asking my betrayed collaborator, Anna, for God's sake to
tell me the truth!

ANNA. This world of competitive enterprise demands each new
idea be the jealously-guarded property of but one individual.

THOMPSON. I have called all property *theft!*

ANNA. So there you are, the new idea — and you, the landed
gent, necessarily the proprietor of it. . . What else is this will
but the chart of the buried treasure of an old pirate hanged
in his chains?

> You will not see before you die —
> And Thompson, Thompson, neither will I —
> The fad of the rich become the faith of the poor
> And your crushed heart like an underground dungeon
> At last able to fling open its door. . .

THOMPSON. And yet what has been happening at Ralahine,
Anna! Like a city set upon an hill for the world to wonder at!
I craved only that Glandore, down there, through the window,
do you observe the half-finished brickwork? — craved only to
redeem our own New Jerusalem, our own complete co-operative
from the obscurity of paper and watch it flourishing before I
died. And here, no not *there* — (*The* LAWYER *is looking at
the documents* –) not the paper – through the window –
here there would be no landlord — not the tittle of a title of
Proprietor nor *ex-officio* President throughout the whole

constitution! Self-electing, democratic, beholden to no High
Priest, no Owen, no John Scott Vandaleur, not even a Neddy
Craig! The people alone to control, through their communal
wisdom. I *must* have it all set down.

ANNA. Attorney, for God's sake help him. He must have his will
completed with the constitution of the co-operative truly
established in legal terms, so the trustees, to whom he leaves
everything —

THOMPSON. No no not everything: there is an annuity for my
dear Anna —

LAWYER. To whom, sir, you are not married, and she is not a
blood-relative. . . Oh dear oh dear, this testament, I foresee
vast complications. . . It will inevitably be contested by your
family, you realise that?

THOMPSON. They shall not get one penny — Yahoos, Orange
Junkers, the cormorants of the Irish common-weal — !

Enter the SURGEON. RELATIVES *attempt to follow him.*
ANNA *repulses them, and then turns to find the* SURGEON
taking out some medicine.

SURGEON. Dear lady, he must not excite himself —

ANNA. Why not, it is the last thing left for him. And he don't
want loblolly, he wants to talk, don't he?

THOMPSON. You came to measure it, so measure it. If you don't
they will infallibly attempt an exchange when I am dead.

The SURGEON *starts to measure his head and makes notes
of it.*

LAWYER. I do fear, Mr Thompson, so frequent in such cases,
the whole estate to be swallowed in costs. And I have grave
doubts the law will not recognise this — this fictional
commune —

ANNA. Fictional! It already exists, look there out of the window —

THOMPSON. Get Flanagan, get him quick — fictional — no no no
no no no no — !

As he cries out, ANNA *hurries off, shouting* 'Mr Flanagan!'

The RELATIVES *push past her and crowd in.* THOMPSON
lies back, eyes closed, exhausted.

1ST RELATIVE (*as* ANNA, *re-entering, tangles with them all*).
Where is the will?

2ND RELATIVE (*grabbing the will*). Here is the will!

3RD RELATIVE (*snatching it from the* 2ND RELATIVE).
Good Lord, it's not been signed!

ANNA. Give that to me —

1ST RELATIVE. Too late, madam, no signature — he is dead
and the will invalid!

There is a struggle over the document. FLANAGAN *enters.*

THOMPSON (*surprising them all*). Ah, Flanagan — you finished
that community-centre yet?

FLANAGAN. Have the roof on by the end of the week,
Mr Thompson.

1ST RELATIVE. His *building contractor...* ?

2ND and 3RD RELATIVES. Absolutely, he is out of his mind.

THOMPSON. Tonight, not next week, I should have lived to see
the roof — nonetheless, it is *not* fictional! Flanagan, you're a
witness — Sawbones, so are you! I put my name upon this
document.

He signs the will. FLANAGAN *and the* SURGEON *do so too,
as witnesses. The* PARSON *enters with a bible.*

God in Heaven — who is that!

PARSON. God in Heaven, Mr Thompson, indeed. I am informed
you are about to depart, a most dread and uncharted journey.
Behold, sir, I bring you the form of your itinerary —

ANNA. Cannot you see he has not finished his packing! Out
out out —

THOMPSON (*leaping up*). Out out out — !

They drive the PARSON *and the* RELATIVES *out. The*
LAWYER *and* SURGEON *follow.* THOMPSON *shakes hands
with* FLANAGAN *as the latter goes out.*

Yes, a journey — oh Anna, my dearest love, flesh of my flesh,
bone of my bone, dream of my deepest dream — why can you
not come with me. . . ?

They go out.

Scene Five

The Ralahine Co-operative. Enter CRAIG.

CRAIG. Fellow-members of the Ralahine Co-operative
Association: before we resume our wonted labours this
morning, I would ask you all to stand for a few moments to
pay tribute to the memory of Mr William Thompson. We must
never forget that our great co-operative movement owes almost
as much to the men of intellect as it does to those who pursue
its purposes, as it were, spade in hand. Be that as it may, by
his death we are all bereft.

*A short solemn silence. CRAIG puts on his hat and leaves the
stage — as he goes, he meets EMILY, and takes off his hat,
briefly and mournfully, to greet her.*

*Enter ROXANA, wearing a lady's travelling costume, quite
different from her previous outfit. EMILY runs towards her
with a joyous cry, but ROXANA puts her finger to her lips
with an urgent gesture.*

EMILY. Roxana — oh my love — but of course — you are
forbidden! You have broken the law to come back here — ?
But my darling, how? Where did you go, what did you do, for
what reason do you —

ROXANA (*cutting the torrent short*). Not a word to Mr Vandaleur —

EMILY. My dear heart, oh my sweet, I wouldn't dream, no not
one word —

ROXANA (*cutting it short again*). They put me out, I went to
England, I went to America, to Jamaica — I came back.
And I have found out at last how to prove everything about
Baker-Fortescue. But not here — I must go to Dublin. There

will be documents in the port of Dublin in possession of the master of the 'Maria Edgeworth', next month. She is due to dock there on a voyage between —

EMILY. But why do you come here?

ROXANA. In case anything goes wrong, someone in Ireland must know what I am doing.

Enter ROISIN *in a flurry, as the* HIGH SHERIFF, BAKER-FORTESCUE, VANDALEUR *and* HAGAN *enter noisily behind.*

ROISIN. There's the High Sheriff and the red soldiers, they're all over the home farm — they said something about Micheal — they have a warrant for arrest!*

ROXANA. My God, they're coming after him for what he did to the 'Maria Edgeworth'! My God, if that's true, they'll be —

EMILY. They'll be coming after *you!* Go with Roisin, get hold of Micheal, go down by the path through the woods — oh hurry hurry hurry — oh my love — !

She and ROXANA *exchange an embrace —* ROXANA *and* ROISIN *then flee.*

HIGH SHERIFF (*this dialogue to start at * above*). A question of harbouring fugitives, I am sorry, Vandaleur, the information is specific, we have the man's name and evidence against him on a sworn affidavit. I have had no choice but draw up a warrant.

VANDALEUR. I have absolutely no idea what it is you are talking about. Man, name, fugitive — ? Who? And why is the Major here — and who is this?

SERGEANT (*offstage*). You that way, you that way, round the back there one man — move! You, through the front garden, two potting-sheds and a summer-house, make sure that they're clear!

EMILY. Mr Vandaleur, pray, invite the gentlemen up to the house.

HIGH SHERIFF. Most unfortunate shadow upon the good work

of your co-operative — fear prevalent for some time such
idealistic institutions leave the way far too wide for subversive
manipulation. The man we want is Michael Sullivan, known to
his friends as Slippery Mick.

VANDALEUR. Micheál O Súilleabháin, supervisor of our
lobster-fisheries. A most responsible man. Slippery Mick?
Nonsense — never heard of it. We do not permit nicknames.

HIGH SHERIFF. But you *do* permit murder? If you are hiding
him here I must close down your co-operative.

VANDALEUR. This is surely not possible — he is —

BAKER-FORTESCUE. I will tell you what he is — the denounced
killer of your man Daniel Hastings, so what d'you think of that?
And you promote him to *supervise*! Hagan, say your piece.

HAGAN. Mr Vandaleur, you know me. In the days I was
permitted to sell a small measure of porter to the rural people
and they thirsty from the hard work, Slippery Mick and his
brave boys was constant customers at my bar. Upon the
night of Hastings' death, sir, they rose up and went out with
the womens' shawls about them, so. And this is the shawl that
he wore. I take oath to it.

BAKER-FORTESCUE. It was found the following morning beside
Hastings' dead body.

Upon a sign from BAKER-FORTESCUE, HAGAN *goes.*

VANDALEUR. Daniel Hastings died by *my* default, and therefore
I regard myself as the only murderer in this community. Arrest
me! I intend to hunt down no other man for it.

The noise of SOLDIERS *shouting to each other, offstage.*
A pause. The SERJEANT *enters.*

SERGEANT. Seems like the bugger's gone, sir, not a trace of him.

HIGH SHERIFF (*to* VANDALEUR): When we find him it is
probable that proceedings will lie against you.

The HIGH SHERIFF *and the* SERJEANT *go.*

BAKER-FORTESCUE. Probable. . . ? If *he* shirks his duty be
very certain *I* won't stand idle. I said from the start this dogs-

vomit co-operative was a stalking-horse for revolution — proved,
Vandaleur, proved — Lady Clare and her Brave Boys, hey — and
you knew that I knew this and because you knew I knew it,
you dredged up that abortion of a yarn about the slave-trade,
hey? Tried to fix the Rapist Fortescue before he could fix you?

EMILY. Major Fortescue, it was not Mr Vandaleur who —

BAKER-FORTESCUE (*acknowledging her presence for the first
time*). Oh indeed, we're in mixed company. . . Have you a
notion just *how* mixed? Did you notice, the last occasion,
abortive slave-trade day, did you notice then how your
gracious lady refused to say where she met the excellent
Wilberforce? Did you ask her afterwards to amplify? Bet you
didn't, you didn't dare. Put the question to her now, go on,
man, go on, where was she when she —

VANDALEUR. Do you attempt, sir, to compromise Mrs
Vandaleur in my presence! Implication that she conceals from
her husband certain —

EMILY. Mr Vandaleur, I do not conceal. You never pressed me,
I did not say — but I will. Roxana and myself went unescorted
to the Hell Fire Club, the night you left Dublin for Manches —

VANDALEUR. No you could not have done that — they do not
permit ladies within that club, I know perfectly well.

BAKER-FORTESCUE. These ladies were dressed as men.

VANDALEUR. You suggest that my wife's purposes in — in a
place where she could not have been — were salacious?

BAKER-FORTESCUE. They kissed and cuddled in a room full
of bucks like Mother and Father Baboon in a public zoo.

VANDALEUR *strikes him.*

Ha. My honour, as an officer and gentleman — I demand
satisfaction.

EMILY. My honour as the wife of a gentleman has been
compromised by these accusations. I demand the opportunity
to explain the whole story —

VANDALEUR. Have the goodness to keep out of this! Your
ignorant interruptions are reflecting upon my honour.

BAKER-FORTESCUE. Time and place? My friends will wait upon yours.

VANDALEUR. No they won't, we'll do it now.

BAKER-FORTESCUE. Without seconds?

VANDALEUR. Why not? Are you afraid, sir, to stand on your own? Emily, my pistols!

EMILY. You haven't got any pistols, and if you had, you wouldn't know how to use them — Mr Vandaleur, will you come to your senses!

BAKER-FORTESCUE. You have no pistols? As it happens, I have two. Both loaded, you take one.

(*He pulls a pair of pistols from his belt.*) Choose.

VANDALEUR *takes one of them. They turn back to back.*

VANDALEUR. Emily, you drop your handkerchief.

EMILY *is holding her handkerchief, helplessly.*

When she drops it, ten paces, turn and fire.

A pause while EMILY *dithers. Several* PEASANTS *come in all around.*

PEASANTS. Come on, boys, my God, the gentry are having a faction-fight — every man to support Vandaleur — *etcetera. . .*

EMILY *bursts into tears.*

VANDALEUR. Take that handkerchief from your eyes, woman, will you hold it out and *drop it!*

EMILY (*suddenly stops weeping*). John Vandaleur, I am ashamed. This is totally ridiculous. What I did in the Hell Fire Club from now on shall be *my* business. I shall tell neither you nor anyone else anything about it whatever. The wife of the President of the Ralahine Commune should be above suspicion. If she is not, then I am bound to question the very basis of this co-operative! — freedom of thought, mutual harmony, democratic discussion, enlightened intercourse between the sexes. John Vandaleur, I say fiddle-dee-dee, you are a hypocrite — and a bloody fool.

*She stalks out, unconsciously dropping the handkerchief as
she goes.* BAKER-FORTESCUE *and* VANDALEUR *have
been staring at the handkerchief like automata all through
her speech, they immediately start to walk, counting 'one two
three —' up to 'ten'. At 'ten' they both turn and level their
weapons.*

A PEASANT (*near* BAKER-FORTESCUE, *and very loud*).
Hooray for the Major!

FORTESCUE *fires, but has been startled by the shout. He
misses.*

BAKER-FORTESCUE. Dammit you raving eedjit, you caused
me to miss! (VANDALEUR's *pistol misses fire.*) Misfire!

VANDALEUR (*fumbling with the trigger*). Something wrong here
with the flintlock —

VANDALEUR's *pistol goes off, terrifying him. The bullet
hits* BAKER-FORTESCUE *across the midriff — his belt-
buckle flies off and his trousers fall down. The* PEASANTS
cheer exuberantly.

Good God, I never intended —

PEASANTS (*rushing at him and lifting him shoulder-high*). Sean
Vandaleur for King, the best shot in the whole of the west,
Sean Vandaleur the only man to fly the breeches-belt beyond
the skyline — *etc.*

BAKER-FORTESCUE.
    Some filthy Frenchman taught you that,
    You planned and tricked your way to it all through —
    One day, my friend, and not too long
    I too will have my laughing game with you.

BAKER-FORTESCUE *goes out furiously, amidst the jeers and
mockery of the* PEASANTS, *who then carry* VANDALEUR
*out the length of the audience. Before they complete their
movement,* CRAIG *enters on stage, a paper in his hand. He
motions to the* 1ST PEASANT, *who leaves his fellows, joins*
CRAIG, *and checks the list with him.*

CRAIG. Mr Deputy-Secretary! 'Total food and lodging eighty-
one persons: six pound seven and fourpence ha'penny —

averaging per week less than one shilling and sevenpence each . . .. Four hundred forty-six quarts of new milk at one penny per quart: one pound seventeen and two. Potatoes and other vegetables: two pound thirteen six. Butter, twelve and a penny; pork, nineteen sevenpence ha'penny: comes to one eleven eight and a half. Cottage rent four and three; turf for fuel, ninepence: five bob.'

They go, still checking the paper.

Scene Six

The Hill of Howth overlooking Dublin Bay. Moonlight. Sounds of a distant bell-buoy at intervals. Enter ROISIN *and* MICHEAL, *furtively.*

MICHEAL. Is this the place? It's very open, if anyone followed us — who's that?

ROISIN. A bush of gorse in the moonlight. Stay still, keep your face out to sea. Micheal, have you said anything yet to Roxana about —

MICHEAL. I have not.

ROISIN. But how do you expect you are going to go with her unless she is told —

ROXANA (*calling softly, offstage*). Roisin, oh Roisin — ?

MICHEAL. Here she comes.

ROISIN *answers with a cry like a seagull.*

Begod, if I do not tell her now, I will never be getting out of this country at all.

ROXANA *hurries in, softly — she whistles,* ROISIN *answers, they all come together.*

ROXANA (*breathless*). Fine, fine 'n'dandy, all in Dublin fixed like we wanted it. I saw the lawyer whose name was given me by the committee in Philadelphia, quite right he does have the ear of the First Secretary at Dublin Castle. We carry on just like I said —

MICHEAL. Madam —

> ROXANA *looks at him in surprise at the formality of his stance.*

I must inform you, you have let yourself believe what you should maybe not have believed. That I am with you on this affair only because I have loved you — and yet that is true. That I am with you only because I am concerned to give you help to prevent the slave-trade — and yet that is true too — God knows it is true. But the first reason, the chief reason: I have come all across Ireland with you in such secrecy because I need to escape, through your means, to America, but for nothing at all to do with that slave-ship.

> *A pause.* ROXANA *looks at him. He moves away, and starts again.*

'Twas a scorching hot day, we were reaping the harvest for the home-farm, we had a can of cool water, now and then the men took breath and a full swallow to keep going. Daniel Hastings came down to us, the length of the long field, his wife's good sweet tea brimming him up to the corners of his mouth. 'Too damn slow', he said, 'refractory buggers, ye have the can there for no reason but to cost Sean Vandaleur time and money — he pays me to bloody save it for him.' And he kicked over the water, trod it into the dry stubble till every drop of it was lost. Oh a small trick, but it was the latest of all his mean-minded tricks and therefore the worst. It brought upon him his death. Because he is dead, we have now the co-operative. And the police have the papers out upon *me*. It was me that put the bullet into Daniel Hastings — it was me wrote the poem that they found on his door, madam.

ROISIN. I was the one that had taken it there and nailed it, madam.

> *A pause. Suddenly* ROXANA *sees something out at sea.*

ROXANA. There he is, that's the signal, a white light three times. The 'Maria Edgeworth' has dropped anchor outside the harbour like they said. We give them three white flashes back, the captain puts off in his boat to the bottom of this cliff — (*She takes a dark lantern from inside her cloak and flashes it three times.*) When he gets to the shore he will whistle and we go down to him. . . . Ever since we left Ralahine, you have been calling me 'Roxana'. But just now, you said 'madam'. But I am not. I am one of the Children of Ham, and accursèd.

A pause. MICHEAL *looks at her. She moves away and starts again.*

Upon my twenty-first birthday, the City of Boston, a great meeting of the Anti-Slavery Association. My father, most popular speaker, upon the platform, a huge placard of a naked black man, kneeling, his chains broken, his hands uplifted to heaven and a white hand out of heaven holding the Bible above his head. My father's voice all of a sudden in the midst of his discourse broken with sobs — the huge audience astonished — not me. *My* astonishment already made for me in emotional privacy the previous evening. 'Brothers and sisters', he shouted, 'if this our movement is not totally open and candid before the Lord, we are as dust in the nostrils of enlightened mankind. Therefore it is meet that I make my confession: my fair daughter, whom you know and love, is not — as you have been led to believe, as indeed she until last night had been led to believe — she is not the child of my wife. But of the slave-woman who attended to the worldly surface of my wife, put on her clothes for her, dressed her hair. As you know, many years ago, I gave their freedom to all my slaves. Yet my young daughter I still held within the vile servitude of a cowardly lie. Today I make recompense to her and to all of you.' And they clapped and they cheered, they wept tears, they slobbered my cheeks. That very day all those young gentlemen from the most elegant evangelical abolitionist Boston families who were invited to my birthday party mysteriously fell ill of the ague or goddammit the *gout*, and the work I continue to do for the Association, by general agreement I have done most of it in *Europe*. I never thought of *not* doing it. Because once having known freedom, till I discovered that by inheritance in my birthplace I had no right to it — I cannot get out of my head, out of my bowels, all the

horror of those thousands who had to make my discovery
before they were even able to walk.

*A pause. She speaks now direct to the audience, moving from
speech into a song — (Air: 'The Red-Haired Man's Wife'):*

Whereas *my* walk, my work through this world
I had made up my mind
Must be always alone, without hope, without help
From any one of my own kind —

'For how could I find any kind of myself in this world —
And yet now I allow this young man to believe that the hold
Of true love in my soul for his beauty had at last been declared,
That the truth of his touch on my body was taken and
    shared. . . ?'

MICHEAL (*sings*):

'So nearer and nearer to the land of America we rove,
The silver and gold of freedom's stronghold to be proved:
Don't I know that the truth of her touch on my body will lie
To enkindle no longer than the sting of a quick summer fly.'

ROXANA (*sings*):

'And yet I can not and I will not refuse to proclaim
These days of green leaf and white flower on the spike of
    the thorn — '

MICHEAL (*singing now to* ROXANA).

'Let the branches of winter once more rear up dark in the air
Like the arms of a slave in his chains — '

MICHEAL *and* ROXANA (*singing*):

'— yet we do not despair. . .'

They hold hands for a moment.

ROISIN (*sings — air: 'Spanish Ladies'*):

'O where will we be when the voyage has ended
O where will we be when the ship comes to port?
Sure I think there's no reason to curse our creation
We will all of us live longer than ever we have thought.'

For this Ralahine Co-operative, who was I before it was made?
Roisin Wry-neck, that's the name they had for me, runs one-
two-three, *bump* two-three, one-two-three *bump*. But oh in

the end, what glory came out of it? I am Member of Committee,
Mistress Roisin in my own right — and all that I do is what they
all do — and we *all* decided. . . !

MICHEAL. Roisin, I never thought of it, you did not tell them at
Ralahine you were going away — when you get back to the
co-operative you must explain yourself or be expelled. If you do
explain, will you not be incriminated, giving aid to your
brother on the run?

ROISIN. Death alive, boy, you know better than that. Within the
co-operative we are all agreed, we do not bring the law, the
police into our affairs. Even the Englishman, Craig, by this
time understands how the people will feel about that. No no,
we are all safe as regards Ralahine.

A sharp whistle, as from a bosun's pipe, offstage.

MICHEAL. My God, there's your man come ashore to us already.

WILBERFORCE *crosses the back of the stage, watching them.*

ROXANA. Do we all know what we're doing? I have here the
document I brought with me from Philadelphia: he'll have
the other one, the extract from the ship's papers — with the
two put together and brought up before the authorities we
have the evidence to cook Fortescue like a mess of clam
chowder. Let's go!

They go.

Scene Seven

The Shelbourne Hotel, Dublin. Enter several GENTLEMEN, *with*
BAKER-FORTESCUE. *They lounge around, smoking.*
VANDALEUR *enters, with his overcoat and hat etc., and his
carpet-bag, which he deposits modestly in the corner. The*
GENTLEMEN *notice him.* BAKER-FORTESCUE *moves quietly
out of sight behind a potted plant.*

1ST GENTLEMAN. Good heavens, it's Vandaleur! Scarcely
expected to find you in Dublin, by Jove — we all believed you

were single-handedly abolishing poverty in County Clare!

They all crowd round him warmly and shake his hand.

2ND GENTLEMAN. But of course he's in Dublin, Jasper, haven't you seen the posters? John Scott Vandaleur Esquire to lecture at the Rotunda upon the success of his communal agriculture — and by George, sir, though I was the first to abuse you for it in the past, your success is indeed notorious!

1ST GENTLEMAN. Notorious and deserved. Not another man in Ireland could have kept his wages down, put his total rent up, and kept all the people happy, by God! And by God everyone else in the country is following his example! It's in the newspapers. By your achievement, crimes of violence in County Clare non-existent. Ah, this military emergency —

2ND GENTLEMAN. Isn't it time, John, for government to call the whole thing off?

VANDALEUR. Ah. Yes — my exact conclusion. I have an appointment tomorrow morning with the Lord Lieutenant, gentlemen, for no other purpose. I shall use all my best endeavours. In the meantime, tonight, my lecture—

1ST GENTLEMAN. Oh be certain we shall all be there — in support of the good cause —

GENTLEMEN. Oh by Jove, yes, certainly, by George, the good cause. . . ah, yes, yes, of course —

They indulge in a nodding and nudging business between the two of them.

2ND GENTLEMAN. John, to be frank, this little meeting, not exactly by chance.

1ST GENTLEMAN. The two of us, you see — we are commissioned to — as it were, waylay you.

2ND GENTLEMAN. Oliver Baker-Fortescue. The fact is, ever since you — ah — that unhappy affair —

1ST GENTLEMAN. The breeches-belt — no need for details —

2ND GENTLEMAN. Dammit, Vandaleur, the poor fellow took his humiliation devilish hard. He wants to apologise.

1ST GENTLEMAN. I thought more than apologise. I thought he was already thinking —

2ND GENTLEMAN. Not until he knows his apology is accepted, Jasper.

1ST GENTLEMAN. John Vandaleur with a loaded pistol has proved himself no man to trifle with!

2ND GENTLEMAN. Well, sir, what d'you say? He really is most frightful ashamed.

VANDALEUR. But of course if my neighbour apologises, I accept with the greatest goodwill. Baker-Fortescue and I have known each other for years and —

1ST GENTLEMAN. Then you'll be all the more delighted that he quite seriously intends to turn Fortescue Grange into a co-operative — on the Ralahine model and he requests —

2ND GENTLEMAN. — he requests, in all earnestness, that you loan him the services of that Manchester miracle-man of yours, what's his name — ?

VANDALEUR. Mr Craig? But of course of course — why gentlemen, this is marvellous —

1ST GENTLEMAN (*having been round the potted plant*). Ah, John, I don't know how you'll take this, but poor old Oliver — behind the shrubbery — too embarrassed, silly fellow, to come out and brave the thunderstorm —

GENTLEMEN. Come on, Oliver, come on, it's quite all right, he's as happy as a sandboy!

BAKER-FORTESCUE *emerges and sheepishly shakes hands with* VANDALEUR.

BAKER-FORTESCUE. No no, don't say a word, I heard it all. John, you are a white man, dammit as white as whitewash. Look here, we must have a bumper, celebrate the buried hatchet, pipe of peace —

VANDALEUR. I do have to be at the Rotunda in a couple of hours —

BAKER-FORTESCUE. I would ask you to come with us

beforehand, except I know you have your principles —

1ST GENTLEMAN. In fact, on our way, you see, to the temptations of the Hell Fire Club —

2ND GENTLEMAN. And we know you never gamble.

BAKER-FORTESCUE. Ah dammit, must postpone the pleasure, devilish pity — would very much liked to have had a long chat!

VANDALEUR. Now gentlemen, this is not fair, you make me labour under obligation to you —

1ST GENTLEMAN. If he does come, he need not play: absolutely no obligation to do *that*.

VANDALEUR. But in that case you would feel, perhaps, I was lacking in the proper spirit —

ALL except VANDALEUR. Not at all not at all not at all not at all. . . !

VANDALEUR. Ah, well then — perhaps — yes.

They group themselves into a stylized posture as the scene changes.

Scene Eight

The Hell Fire Club. A Faro table set up by a CROUPIER. *The game commences. The* GENTLEMEN *and* BAKER-FORTESCUE *play with a great deal of infectious laughter.* VANDALEUR *watches them, intently, his excitement growing all the time.*

CROUPIER. Gentlemen-sportsmen stake your wagers for the Imperial Game of Faro. . . Captain Prendergast wins, one hundred guineas. . . Mr Butler wins, seventy-five guineas. . . Captain Prendergast again, fifty guineas. . . Standoff, no bets paid. . . House wins, no bets paid. . . House wins again, no bets paid. . . *etcetera.*

   VANDALEUR *suddenly makes up his mind, and lays chips on the table.*

Four is the loser, six is the winner — Mr Vandaleur wins — twenty-five guineas.

VANDALEUR *moves away from the table with his winnings.*

Are you leaving the game, sir?

VANDALEUR. Ah, yes, apologies, I must, my lecture at the Rotunda.

CROUPIER. It is the custom at the Hell Fire Club for gentlemen in good fortune to allow their fellow-sportsmen to regain their losses before taking leave of the table. You'll not wish to rebuff tradition, Mr Vandaleur, I'm sure. . .

VANDALEUR. I — ah — my lecture — there should be a carriage at the door. . .

He freezes in the act of putting on his coat, and addresses the audience.

> I did not expect to win.
> I do not want to go on.
> I cannot endure to go out.
> Oh God, have they got me caught?
> I had not played this game
> Not felt erect in me this creeping lechery of shame
> This sacrificial avaricious tumult of self-exposure
> So to command me nerve and brain
> And quivering fragment of my frightened loin
> I had not felt — since I was twenty-one
> This need, this hunger, this desire today as then . . .
> Again. . . ? Again. . . ?
> Why gentlemen, my friends — I did not expect to win. . .

He takes off his coat and returns to the table.

I don't like these stakes — twenty-five guineas a chip not nearly sufficient, no room for them on the board — agreed, agreed, gentlemen, we raise it to fifty? The house will accommodate? Good. Play — we all play. . . !

CROUPIER. King loses, Queen wins. Major Baker-Fortescue the winner, five hundred guineas. . . Major Baker-Fortescue again, four hundred and fifty. . .

BAKER-FORTESCUE. Raise the stakes! One hundred a chip.

CROUPIER. Is that agreeable to the gentlemen? The house will accept it. . . The house wins, no bets paid. . . The house wins again, gentlemen, no bets paid. . .

VANDALEUR. Raise the stakes, raise 'em again — two hundred a chip — I insist!

CROUPIER. Discard ten, nine loses, seven wins, Major Baker-Fortescue two thousand. . . . Four cards only left in the deck, gentlemen, the house pays four-to-one if you guess their correct order — Mr Vandaleur?

VANDALEUR. Six-to-one, six-to-one — I know it, I have it — at this stage of the game only the scientific mind can correctly estimate the extent of hazard — !

CROUPIER. Four-to-one only the house odds, if you want a larger stake, make a side-bet with the Major. . . . With the stakes so very large, gentlemen, upon bets with the house we would be glad for some small class of guarantee. . .

VANDALEUR (*scribbling a bill*). Yes of course, yes, paper — I O U, J S V, good for anywhere in Ireland — Ralahine, you've heard of it, flourishing, flourishing, a co-operative estate, all of it — prosperity — !

BAKER-FORTESCUE. You're already acquainted, Colquhoun, with *my* guarantors.

CROUPIER (*getting a series of significant nods from the GENTLEMEN*). Of course, Major.

VANDALEUR. Oliver, Oliver — a side-bet — ten-to-one — do you dare, do you dare — ?

BAKER-FORTESCUE *glances round at the* GENTLEMEN.

1ST GENTLEMAN. Oliver, this is serious, you don't really intend to go on?

BAKER-FORTESCUE (*grim and implacable*). John Vandaleur from the beginning has been the victor upon every turn. I have not even begun to masticate my revenge.

(*To the audience*):
   I have so often heard them say
   That a moral man who will not play
   At cards at women at the buttock of a smooth young boy
   Knows far too well how far he would enjoy
   Such huge excess, were he just once to let his fear
   Be loosened just one button-hole. . . John Vandaleur
   Is such an one. I knew it. I have proved it — and I have
   Him now cascading maybe even to the grave.

2ND GENTLEMAN. Come on, Oliver, you're afraid of it, you're holding back your stakes!

1ST GENTLEMAN. Bear in mind, Oliver, he opposed the Act of Union.

2ND GENTLEMAN. Bear in mind, Oliver, he advocated Catholic Emancipation in Parliament.

1ST GENTLEMAN. Bear in mind he has ruined our farming with his new-fangled science, his machine-methods, his —

BAKER-FORTESCUE (*to* VANDALEUR): Done!

VANDALEUR. Eight hundred guineas — no, one thousand, Oliver — done? Five, Nine, Ten, Six!

BAKER-FORTESCUE. Five, Nine, Ten, *Five.*

VANDALEUR. No — Six — not two Fives, there is one Six left in the deck!

BAKER-FORTESCUE. Colquhoun?

CROUPIER (*turning out the last four cards*). Five, Nine, Ten —

VANDALEUR. No, wait, wait — Oliver — Fifty-to-one it's a Six not a Five!

BAKER-FORTESCUE. Done.

CROUPIER (*revealing the last card*). Five.

VANDALEUR. Another pack, another game, come on come on come on —

He grabs at the cards furiously, scatters chips all over the table.

CROUPIER. Any other gentlemen care to join? Very well,
gentlemen, a new pack, the second game —

VANDALEUR. Wait, I can't see the cards, my eyes are all clouded,
red red on the green table — what the hell is the matter —
Colquhoun — !

CROUPIER. Might suggest, sir, a pause for refreshment before
you continue. . . ?

VANDALEUR. No no no no no no no no —

CROUPIER. Ah — there is the matter of the gentleman's paper —
after that side-bet. It won't carry any more.

BAKER-FORTESCUE. I too bear in mind how he crammed his
damned Ralahine with Jacobin murderers — threw open the
whole of Ireland to republican French anarchy.

VANDALEUR. I — I — my paper — did you say 'no' . . . ?

CROUPIER. We had rather you came back, sir, some other
occasion, give us a chance to clear your arrangements with
the guarantors you have named. . . ?

VANDALEUR (*very stiff and dignified, standing back from the
table*). My estate, my co-operative, everything. . . gone. . . ?

*He starts to put on his coat again, and can't manage it,
fumbling with coat, hat, shawl, bag, umbrella, dropping them,
trembling. He speaks to the audience, while the others freeze.*

Emily. Emily Molony. Of the ferocious Molonys, of the ancient
clans of Munster, and they changed their religion. Turned her
back on me in bed — when I put my hand between her legs,
I would have thought she would have bitten it off. . . I am
the proprietor, but Craig said, no — president, Craig said —
but the people said, no — the committee, the committee
went so far as to close the gate. . . Recognize such is now the
position. Or else. . . My wife's cousin, not her cousin, she was
murder, to the committee, they were saved, the estate saved,
the state saved by Cicero, so sage a grave statesman. Let the
Consuls see to it that the Republic takes no harm — get her
out of it, deport her — nigger blood, you can always tell,
look at the blue under her finger-nails, the retrograde heels

of her feet, who else put the sharp teeth between the legs of
my wife. . . ?

*He drops his coat, bag, hat etc., kicks them away from him,
and stumbles around amongst them.*

 I am the proprietor. I am not. I am nothing.
 I have dropped it on the ground
 I have kicked it around:
 I have given it to all of *you*
 To you all and Fortescue. . .

*He kicks and throws his belongings fiercely from him, making
chaos on the stage. The Faro table is knocked over. He quietens
down.*

It was not to rule Ireland my Anglo-Saxon forebears came in
their black keels to the seacoast of England. . . We should have
kept our own maggots within the putrefying flesh of our own
privy members — not to scatter them broadcast upon the green
fields of the world like God's manna to the men of Israel,
bringing death to the red deer, the trout in the swift rivers, the
seed of the corn before even it springs — creeping heaps of
white poison for those who gather it in baskets. I make desolate.
I abandon.
 Where I go I shall have gone
 And none shall see me ever again. . .

He staggers out. A pause. As he goes, BAKER-FORTESCUE
and the GENTLEMEN *commence a jeering roar which rises
to a ferocious animal climax — then breaks off as* WILBERFORCE
enters, bringing BAKER-FORTESCUE *downstage for an urgent
conversation.*

WILBERFORCE. Tracked the whole thing all the way, Major,
 to the declivities of the Hill o' Howth. That goldarn renegade
 traitor of a sea-captain sold himself body and soul to your
 sweet little mulatto from Boston —

BAKER-FORTESCUE. He has given her the papers — ?

WILBERFORCE. Ah no, at the last minute, refused point-blank
 to turn King's Evidence on shore just in case he was double-
 crossed — he hands over the papers to no-one save a regular

peace-officer on the quarter-deck of his ship. They made a
rendezvous for midnight — ride like hell to the Hill o' Howth — !

BAKER-FORTESCUE. I have no weapons — a gun — a gun —
Colquhoun, have you got a gun!

CROUPIER. Nothing here but the old blunderbuss that we use to
deter drunks — take it, Major, and welcome — the Major's
horse to the door there!

He gives the gun to BAKER-FORTESCUE *from under the
table. They go out in a great commotion.*

Scene Nine

The Hill of Howth overlooking Dublin Bay. Moonlight. Enter
BAKER-FORTESCUE *with the blunderbuss and* WILBERFORCE
with a pistol.

BAKER-FORTESCUE. Jamaica — ? You said riots in Jamaica?
You said burning — the whole sugar-cane crop destroyed — ?
But how — how — ?

WILBERFORCE. We lay for 'em *here* as they come down the lane,
ain't no way those guys in the boat behind the breakwater
are gonna sus-pect our ambush till it's sprung, and by then
it'll be too late, so crouch, Major, crouch. . .

They take up their positions, concealed.

BAKER-FORTESCUE. Goddammit, you must tell me your news
from Jamaica!

WILBERFORCE (*whispering*). Ssh, do I hear footsteps. . . ? Not
yet. . . Seems like emancipation of all slaves in your British
colonies has been rumoured so strongly that the blacks in
Jamaica have rose. Your partner in Montego Bay is bankrupt
and fled to Mexico.

BAKER-FORTESCUE. What the hell are we doing here then?
The money from my sugar-cane was financing my slave-
ventures to Cuba — if it's gone who gives a damn for this
ship-captain and his King's Evidence?

WILBERFORCE. Way you told it to me it was the profits of
the slave-trade in Cuba was financing your run-down Jamaican
plantations — either way your whole fortune was dependent on
a parcel o' niggers — and by God, Major, the niggers these
days is dead dogs. All you've to look for now is to keep
yourself out of prison, and *that*, Major, is the damn we gotta
give for the King's Evidence. Are you ready, here they come. . .!

ROXANA *and* MICHEAL *enter, with a dark lantern.*

MICHEAL. If there's a Dublin Castle officer on that ship, I'm
not going on till he gets off, I remain in the boat, so, till all's
clear. Do your business with the papers, call me aboard.
You're quite certain this captain has agreed on our passage to
America?

ROXANA. He's a double-dealing rogue, but he knows if he plays
us dirty I can put his neck in a noose and I will. Don't you
worry, we are safe — Where the devil is that boat. . . ?

BAKER-FORTESCUE. Here.

He has come out with his gun behind them. WILBERFORCE
comes out in front, and they see they are trapped.

MICHEAL *opens his mouth to call out, but* WILBERFORCE
*chokes off his yell with his hand over his mouth, then stuffs
a gag in.*

BAKER-FORTESCUE (*to* ROXANA): Now don't *you* call,
Jedediah, because your bully here will hang if you do, and
you know it. Ephraim, your judicial function — secure the
enemies of the public peace.

WILBERFORCE *ties* MICHEAL's *hands, kicks him down and
stoops to tie his ankles.* MICHEAL *kicks.* WILBERFORCE
raises the butt of his pistol to hit him on the head.

No! If you hit him too hard he'll feel sleepy, he'll close his
eyes, we can't have that.

WILBERFORCE *ties* MICHEAL's *feet and feels his clothes.*

WILBERFORCE. He ain't got no papers — so they must be —

BAKER-FORTESCUE. So she has it, so she would have it, *she*

is the mainspring. Emancipation, liberalization, elimination of all authority — by her own blood she makes mongrels of the crown of the human race, like an eel climbing a tree, black and slimy, sticks to the fingers. Ugh. So where is it?

ROXANA. On board ship with the King's Officer, it has already been delivered, you are too late.

BAKER-FORTESCUE. Oho no, *boy*, I know better. . . Whatever persuaded you, Jedediah, my little love-pocket, to dress up as a stinking bitch?

He strokes ROXANA's *neck. She spits at him.*

So, tonight the Rapist Fortescue is going to show you what is meant by the name he has been given, male or female it's all one to him, there will be no end to it before death's end — and your long-tooled Popery bullcalf can glare his eyes out while I go into you, and then the bullet for *him* too.

He takes her bonnet off and perches it on his own hat, crowing like a cock. He then pulls off her shawl and drapes it around his shoulders. The document falls to the ground.

WILBERFORCE. Wait a minute, Major, that's it! So we got it — so we finish — so we don't do no more to 'em — okay — this is no place for fun and games!

BAKER-FORTESCUE (*draping himself in more of* ROXANA's *clothes*). You don't think I came here just to *save* myself, Wilberforce?

He rams his blunderbuss into ROXANA's *stomach, she falls on all fours, retching.*

But to *re-affirm* - to lay claim to the whole life they would have taken away from me — !

He makes to mount her from behind, crowing like a cock again. While this has been going on, ROISIN *has slipped in at the back, has freed* MICHEAL, *and has sneaked up behind* BAKER-FORTESCUE *to pick up the blunderbuss.* MICHEAL, *creeping forward, has taken* WILBERFORCE's *pistol.*

MICHEAL (*aiming the pistol*). Back, or you're both dead!

WILBERFORCE *and* BAKER-FORTESCUE *spring around to face him.* ROISIN *jams the blunderbuss into* BAKER-FORTESCUE's *back.*

Roisin, behind me, I'll cover you till you get to the boat —

ROXANA (*scrambles to her feet, grabs the document*). Come, Micheal, the boat — !

She runs out.

ROISIN. You to the boat, you damfool, I've no need for it, *my* place is Ralahine. Keep the pistol, I've got this. Go, go, boy — go! Roxana has the paper — *go*!

MICHEAL *runs after* ROXANA.

BAKER-FORTESCUE. No more than a snot-sucking hunchback — here — !

He flings himself at her, and aside as the blunderbuss fires. WILBERFORCE *falls dead. Cries and running feet from offstage — 'Hold them, halt, in the name of the law' etcetera.* BAKER-FORTESCUE *grabs* ROISIN. *Enter* 1ST *and* 2ND GENTLEMEN *in great haste.*

1ST GENTLEMAN. Oliver — where are you — good God, what has — ?

BAKER-FORTESCUE. Is he dead, yes he's dead, he was shot by this woman, known associate, I know her, agrarian terrorism — in the name of the King, for a capital crime, I give her in charge.

ROISIN. Roxana, Roxana, I am free — go to the ship — you are safe.

2ND GENTLEMAN *takes her out.*

1ST GENTLEMAN. Are you hurt?

BAKER-FORTESCUE. No.

1ST GENTLEMAN. Perhaps you should have been. Your whole affair, the Duke of Cumberland, the Orange Order, military *coup d'état* — finished. Exposed, Oliver, betrayed, went off before it was ready — they have the documents, everything.

BAKER-FORTESCUE. Everything, all of it, no. . . you said,

'*your* affair'. Your own part in it — not yet public knowledge?

1ST GENTLEMAN (*taking off his Orange sash*). Never will be. Have found it expedient to make my peace with the liberals — has been put to me, very persuasive, for the honour of the Service, preservation of good government, preservation of a gentleman's good name, need be none o' that nonsense about court-martial, any o' that. . . the Duke, most convenient, has inherited the Kingdom of Hanover. He goes over there, for ever. You, being less important — though more important than *me* — Oliver, alas *you* have inherited this. (*He hands* BAKER-FORTESCUE *a pistol*). Understand your financial difficulties in the West Indies have come to a head. Unable to face your creditors. Do the needful. . .

BAKER-FORTESCUE. No.

1ST GENTLEMAN. If you don't, public disgrace. Upon complaints of certain women. From your estates in County Clare. Would you really permit yourself to be drummed out of the regiment for the ravishing of milkmaids?

BAKER-FORTESCUE. No. I mean yes. I mean — oh Lord Christ we went share and share about, even in that, oh Lord Christ, why me and not you — why is it me, me, *me* — ! I won't do it — !

1ST GENTLEMAN. Violation, for the time being, is replaced by seduction. More appropriate for an age of reform. And in the end, even so, the consummation of the longed-for cunt will still be for *us*. Not for you, you're too old, too late, you can't cope, I'm very sorry. . . I made sure it was properly loaded.

BAKER-FORTESCUE. Me, why me, me, ought to be you, you, you —

1ST GENTLEMAN. Not gentlemanly, Oliver, to whimper over your gruel. The Duke said, before he left, that he hoped his friends would understand, but in fact he found most of them were worth no more than a bucket of shit.

He puts his arm round BAKER-FORTESCUE, *kisses him, and goes out.* BAKER-FORTESCUE, *left with the pistol, holds it for a moment in a shaking hand, and moves it shudderingly towards his jaw. The muzzle of the weapon lodges under the jawbone, and before he is ready for it, the trigger jerks and he dies.*

After a pause, BAKER-FORTESCUE *and* WILBERFORCE *rise abruptly from the stage and go off, to clear the scene for the Epilogue.*

Epilogue

The Irish Coast. Enter ROISIN, *as though hanged, her face whitened, and a noose around her neck.*

ROISIN (*sings — air: 'Long Lankin'*):
 'It's an old song and a true song as cold as a bone
 That I cannot stop singing though I am dead and gone.

 I swung from the gallows all tattered and torn:
 The high hope of Ralahine was left all forlorn.'

 Enter CRAIG.

CRAIG. John Scott Vandaleur had disappeared for ever. His wife's relatives, the Molonys, took over the bankrupt estate.

EMILY *enters, on the opposite side.*

The Anglo-Irish legal system did not recognize the co-operative. Our members were held to be common labourers and that's all, with no rights nor any claim for the improvements they had made to the property. It was legally correct — it was an act of outright robbery — social co-operation at an end, we were remorselessly evicted.

PEASANTS, *with their bundles, enter slowly, and walk past him. He puts money into their hands.*

I was able, from my own resources, to redeem all the labour-tokens we had issued to the members, in lieu of coin-of-the-realm, for their work on the commune.

EMILY (*deadpan, to the audience*):
 The estate was made safe for my children and their future.
 This could not have been done if my husband, John Vandaleur,
 Had not been regarded, by the Law, as sole proprietor.
 For the loss to these others, I have nothing but grief.
 What else could be done? The estate has been made safe.

She goes out ignoring, and ignored by, the others.

CRAIG (*to the* PEASANTS): My dear friends, before I leave
you — I would be most grateful if you would find it possible
to subscribe your names for the last time to a formal
declaration — I will issue it to the public press.

He hands a paper to the 1ST PEASANT.

1ST PEASANT (*reads*): 'We, the undersigned members of the
Ralahine Agricultural and Manufacturing Association, have
experienced for the last two years, contentment, peace and
happiness under the arrangements introduced by Mr Vandaleur
and Mr E. T. Craig.'

One by one they sign the paper, and CRAIG *shakes hands with
them.*

CRAIG. Thank you. . . thank you. . . my good friend. . . God
bless you. . . God bless you all.

(*To the audience*): Ralahine had been an Irish point of
interrogation erected amidst the wilderness of capitalist
thought and feudal practice, challenging both in vain for an
answer.

The PEASANTS *begin to file out, uttering a muted keen.*

PEASANTS. Sean Vandaleur, why did you go from us. . . ? Why
have you left your own Ralahine, Sean Vandaleur. . . ?

CRAIG *goes.*

ROISIN (*sings* — *air: 'The Red-Haired Man's Wife'*):
They hanged me up high and I swung on the tree:
My brother and his true-love went safe across the sea.

Enter MICHEAL.

MICHEAL (*sings* — *air: 'The Red-Haired Man's Wife'*):
'O nearer and nearer to the land of America we sailed
The silver and gold of freedom's stronghold did not fail —
If that's what you call such hard work and few dollars to
earn
And such news from the shores of Ireland as caused my whole
heart-root to burn. . . '

The great hunger, coercion, emigration, rebellion, and the penalties for rebellion — not only my sister — the dark gibbets all over the land. It was brought to me, in America, running out at the scuppers of every ship that dropped anchor. What good, at that time, at that place, to cry to the wind: 'Had Ralahine but been heeded, no famine, no dispersal, no need ever again for Lady Clare and her Brave Boys. . . !' As it was, from all four provinces, in exile we re-gathered, we were re-dedicated, the Fenian Brotherhood, made safe for the cause with great oaths — and we have never to this day given up in the work we put hand to. Let the red soldiers of the red-stained Crown pay heed to us yet.

ROISIN (*sings*):

    'It's an old song and a true song as hot as a fire
    That half-way is no way to attain your desire.

    You know what is needed, you will give it or deny:
    What good for a blind man to open one eye?

    Till we come to our own in our own Irish land
    An old song a true song, will it never have an end. . . ?'

MICHEAL. Our Brotherhood in due course became known as the Republican Brotherhood.

    They go.

Immediate Rough Theatre for Citizens' Involvement

(1974–1977)

The Devil and the Parish Pump
Corrandulla Arts & Entertainment (*summary of plot*)

Sean O'Scrudu
Galway Theatre Workshop (*abridged text*)

The Hunting of the Mongrel Fox
Galway Theatre Workshop

No Room at the Inn
Galway Theatre Workshop (*abridged text*)

Mary's Name
Galway Theatre Workshop (*brief note*)

A Pinprick of History (1977)
devised by Margaretta D'Arcy

We were looking up texts for this book, and we came across a file full of fragmentary scripts (and notes for scripts) which had been a series of quickly-improvised topical plays and playlets got together in the west of Ireland and put on in houses, pubs, streets, meetings and so forth to answer immediate needs of the day. Parts, or summaries, of them can still be read in the spirit with which one reads through a pile of old newspapers; and indeed it was the local and national newspapers of the period, council minutes, and government reports, that gave us a solid base for improvisation. Also, in the '70s, there was a very effective satirical programme on Irish television called *Frank Hall's Weekly*, which provided us and our audiences with a familiar vernacular style, a total irreverence toward all figures of authority, and a common point of reference.

In the early years of the decade we found ourselves (as playwrights) in a socially debilitating position as the result of three concurrent events:

1) A prolonged libel case over our play *The Ballygombeen Bequest*, (here reissued as *The Little Gray Home in the West*);
2) Our official strike (later becoming unofficial, and still continuing today) against the Royal Shakespeare Company over who controls the playwright's script;
3) The Stalinisation of an Irish socialist/republican party (to which we belonged), giving all power to the urban bureaucrats and to hell with the rest. As we were not bureaucrats, nor at that time urban, we were no longer relevant to the party and so no longer members.

All this left us in a state of creative isolation.

We had just moved from an island in Loch Corrib to Corrandulla ('the turning of the two swans'), a rural parish ten miles from Galway, controlled by an ancient conservative misogynist Greek-classic-loving priest who vetoed every suggestion that the community hall should be *used* by the community that had paid for it. The local postman, Johnny Keaney, indomitable and garrulous, had heard of films and plays which we had been making on the other side of the lake when we were members of the party; he came to us with tales of cultural deprivation; and, prompted by him, we opened our cottage in the spirit of what is traditionally known as the Ceilidh-house or Rambling-house, a place of informal festivity. We called it The Corrandulla Arts and Entertainment; we showed films, held play-readings and music-sessions, and made a long inconsequential super-8 movie of the life of the parish. This brought about a feeling of trust and participation which in turn began to reveal the inner tensions of the community.

The Devil and the Parish Pump

A pressing issue was the new piped-water scheme. Some of the people of one 'townland', or hamlet within the parish, felt that they should not pay as much money for the installation as those in the next townland, with the result that no water ran and everyone in both townlands (Drumgriffin and Tonagarraun) was still drawing water by bucket from the old hand-pumps. So, for one of the Entertainments, five of us decided to make a play. We ourselves were not involved in the dispute as we had our own running water from a spring: of the remaining three members of the cast, two were from one townland and one from the other. This was the first time we had worked in this very ad-hoc kind of way. No one had time for any formal meetings; we only had two evenings of rehearsal; but it did give us a *raison d'être* – our theatrical skills and techniques suddenly had an immediate practical use. We were not taking part as 'playwrights from the outside' but all of us were improvisational performers trying to elucidate the complexities of the dilemma of the piped-water which had so far baffled all attempts at compromise. Each of us was able to contribute an insight, and each of us brought different skills. Sean Newell, a secondary-school pupil of Tonagarraun, first told us all the ins and outs of the water-controversy and acted as our chronicler of local townland politics; while Kathleen O'Shea, a small-farmer of Drumgriffin, helped by Philomena Lynch (another secondary-school pupil), was imbued with the wit and rhyming instincts, in Irish and English, of traditional storytelling, which transformed a rather arid local dispute into a kind of epic folklore struggle.

* * *

The Devil comes to Corrandulla to try and make mischief. He pours poisonous words into a woman of Tonagarraun (played by Sean) when she is pumping the water, and hoping for the speedy development of the piped scheme – a Drumgriffin woman (Kathleen) is plotting to have the new water cheaper and the whole scheme is a confidence-trick. From then on everything is brought in, all the bitterness that can still divide Irish communities, the Civil War, landlordism, clientelism, gombeen exploitation etc. The situation resolves itself when each of the women has a dream, of their years of hard work, pumping water, dying, and finally being refused entrance to heaven because they would not share water. Nor would the Devil accept them into hell, because he had too many *essential* new arrivals to deal with, political VIPs who were really wicked. So of course they do agree to compromise; and the play ended with them sitting around in heaven genteelly sharing cups of water and telling each other how foolish they had been. They wake up; and change their lives.

For a 20-minute play it had everything; expressionism, diversity of language styles, brutal realism, a filmed insert of a real funeral, and coarse comedy. The cottage-kitchen was packed to watch it, and it was an experience which we could never have had in the ordinary course of our professional theatrical life. The fluid techniques we were compelled to discover opened the way for us to complete the *The Non-Stop Connolly Show*, for which at that time we were striving hard to find a form. As for the parish itself, the people in time got their piped water and they got their community hall back.

Sean O'Scrudu

Two lecturers from Galway University, Pat Sheeran (English literature) and Des Johnson (Science), both heavily involved in the university academic staff union, the Workers' Union of Ireland, approached us in 1975 after our production of *The Non-Stop Connolly Show*. Because of the logistical problems of touring this production with its huge part-time cast, we had presented the show in Galway with a reduced company, and had had to get volunteers from the audience to fill in the gaps. Pat Sheeran was one of these and thought the whole ad-hoc improvisational atmosphere was something that could be developed further. We were then installed (unofficially and without pay) for one night a week in the university where we would meet a group of lecturers and students, let our hair down, and play games according to the theories of Viola Spolin. We called ourselves the Galway Theatre Workshop. In 1976 there was an industrial dispute in Galway – Crown Control, a multi-national manufacturer of fork-lift trucks, had sacked a shop-steward. The union at Crown was also the Workers' Union of Ireland and asked support from its membership in the university. Pat and Des were quite shocked at the response of some of their colleagues, and decided that the Theatre Workshop should make a communally-constructed play about it at the next university trade-union social.

★ ★ ★

A GUEST-LECTURER, *with a central-European accent, enters; to deliver a paper in a formal academic style.*

GUEST-LECTURER. Ladies, gentlemen, good evening. This modest dissertation I have been asked to present to you tonight is but a portion of a large and most complex analysis of the Role of the Intellectual Class, that is to say the University-graduated Class in the Developing Social Structures of ex-colonial countries throughout the world. I had intended to take Southern Africa for my prime exemplar: but due to the recent liberation of Angola, it occurred to me that conditions there were perhaps not so suitable for objective research as is Galway, *nicht wahr?* for here is no liberation-struggle, no private army, no such civil disturbance as might divert us from our true path. Very good.

Tonight we examine the way and purpose of the Trade Union as a feature of academic life! But to do this we must first expound what in fact is this 'academic life' to which so very glibly we all of us here refer. I have asked a few unattached persons to help me demonstrate. Very good. There are three historic threads to which I draw your attention. Please listen most attentively.

One. The main continental concept of the University as a home for critical and experimental thought.

Two. Out of this: the development of specifically Socialist thought in the nineteenth century, the formation of revolutionary groups and political parties, and the consequent placing of intellectual ideology at the service of the newly-formed proletarian labour organisations, such as – if you like – the Workers' Union of Ireland.

Three. The endowment of educational institutions in colonial countries by and for the benefit of the governments that ruled over them. A post-Napoleonic utilitarian measure, designed in response to the imperialist nature of the later stage of the Industrial Revolution and the need to prepare a native middle-class for the ever-increasing duties of colonial administration. A bureaucratic middle-class means in effect a crowd of yes-men; critical enquiry can therefore not be encouraged. The keynote accordingly is *anti-intellectual*. Good.

We take up our first thread, which will without interruption lead into the second. Experimental thought at all times has been opposed by vested interests: and its history is the history of the struggle of the human race out of the darkness of ignorance into the illumination of – of – *undsoweiter*, so-and-so –

Ach! let us begin in Ancient Greece!

The trial and death of SOCRATES, *in effect for the offence of* experimental thought, *is briefly enacted, and commented on by a pair of* NARRATORS; *it ends with* PLATO *announcing his conclusion that if democracy caused the martyrdom of such a man, there must be something wrong with democracy, and it should be replaced by an absolute ruler who has put himself under the guidance of the best of all legislators, a trained philosopher.*

NARRATOR 1. If therefore the trained philosopher is to be given control of the minds of those who govern us, it follows that some form of institution for training him should be established . . .

NARRATOR 2. In the Christian era, the *university* was ranked with the papacy and the Holy Roman Empire as an international force appointed by God for the direction and improvement of mankind.

The prosecution of GALILEO, *again for* experimental thought, *is briefly enacted, ending with statements by* HEGEL *and* MARX *that develop* GALILEO's *theories of astronomical time into an understanding of time as related to progress and cumulative class-struggle.*

MARX (*concluding his statement from inside his tomb*). . . . but in the end, when the time is ripe – these ideas will burst forward in the hands of men who wield control and conscious mastery of them!

Enter JAMES LARKIN.

LARKIN. The great appear great because we are on our knees –
let us arise! The employing class and the working class have
nothing in common! An injury to one is an injury to all! One
big union one big strike!

NARRATOR 1 (*confidentially whispering as everyone loudly
deprecates Larkin and his violence*). James Larkin in Ireland created
the Transport Workers' Union, and the Workers' Union of
Ireland; and – with James Connolly, the Irish Labour Party, the
only political party with the historical potential to take the gun
out of Irish politics and replace it with the full impulse of
constructive revolutionary development. At the Labour Party
Conference of 1975 the founder of this party was accorded his
deserved place in the history of the working class.

NARRATOR 2. They made Socrates drink hemlock, they made
Galileo smell fire, they made Marx hear his own voice re-echo
from enormous emptiness – James Larkin was accorded water –

NARRATOR 1. – to soften him, dilute him, dissolve him –

NARRATOR 2. – into a postage stamp!

*The recent Irish commemorative stamp-issue, bearing the head of
Larkin, is shown, to a burst of music.*

GUEST-LECTURER. James Larkin was an Irishman,
proletarian, an activist. He derived his ideology from the
continental academic tradition, *nicht wahr?* But had he sought it
from the universities in the land of his fathers, *um Gottes Willen*,
what would the good man have discovered? Thread three!
Utilitarian, imperialist, administrative, what else but the
confined breeding-house of that strange political
hermaphrodite, the notorious Castle Catholic!

Some examples. From Queen's College, Galway: Victorian
nationalist parliamentarian and journalist, Mr T. P. O'Connor.
Now in his grave, he has been interviewed with the intention
of demonstrating his characteristic contradictions . . . it may
take some time.

A pause: and then the O'CONNOR *interview is heard on tape.*

INTERVIEWER. Mr O'Connor, how do you reconcile the
Fenianism of your youth with your equally youthful aspiration
to enter the Indian Civil Service?

O'CONNOR. We were quartered on the enemy, my boy. The
fact that we were prepared to accept temporary service under a
particular form of British government did not imply that we
had sold our political principles – I can give a perfectly logical
defence of our doctrinaire Fenianism in those days.

INTERVIEWER. Well, at any rate, you gave it up for
constitutional agitation.

O'CONNOR. Yes, and see what we got for it. The
constitutional movement has been destroyed. Ireland is in a
state of chaos. The young firebrands have taken the law into
their own hands.

INTERVIEWER. Thank you, Mr O'Connor. You can go back
to sleep now. He survived until 1930, but his mind never
advanced beyond the year 1865, although his Fenian sympathies
and his hearty detestation of the English nation disguised this
fact from him.

Lord MacDonnell of Swinford –

A growl on the tape.

INTERVIEWER. He was called the Bengal Tiger by some of his
fellow-Irishmen who distrusted him –

MACDONNELL. They saw an analogy between the rigorous
but humane measures I adopted as a Civil Servant in India, and
my work in later years as Under-Secretary for Ireland. Do you
remember the fable of the old man and his ass? By trying to
please everybody, I pleased nobody in Ireland, and least of all
did I please the British Government who appointed me.

GUEST-LECTURER. If these two curiously schizophrenic
personalities were the result of an imperialist university system,
what can we look for when the nation in 1922 attains
independence; and conducts, for the first time, its own

education for its own national purposes? Already, in 1908, the last fling of colonialist legislation had created a separate university in Belfast, and had amalgamated the University Colleges of Cork, Dublin and Galway into an inevitably Catholic-dominated National University of Ireland, thereby providing the philosophical prelude to the political partition of thirteen years later.

Utilitarianism, combined now with sectarian nationalism, and claiming to foster the traditional cultural values of the native Irish people before ever the English meddled with them. Shall we see just how far they were fostered, in fact?

Senator William Magennis, of the National University, speaking for Mr De Valera's government in 1943 in a debate on censorship, had occasion to allude to a book called *The Tailor and Ansty*, the central non-fictional character of which was described by the author as follows –

NARRATOR 1. A man who has lived to the utmost within his limits. A man who has grown and learned and become wise and splendidly tolerant and full of a sense of fun. Someone whom St Francis, Montaigne, Rabelais, Shakespeare and his Falstaff would have loved. First of all, human; and the rest afterwards – Irish, Catholic, tailor . . .

GUEST-LECTURER. This same central character was described by the Senator –

MAGENNIS. The man is sex-obsessed. His wife Anastasia is what in the language of American psychology is called a moron – a person of inferior mental development who may be thirty or forty years of age, but has only the mental age of a child of four or five. There is a campaign going on to undermine Christianity. It is financed by American money. The Society that is the main agent in the endeavour to put in paganism instead of the Christian creed and practice includes Professor Joad and George Bernard Shaw.

GUEST-LECTURER. The book, of course, was banned . . .

Amongst all these contradictions, this intellectual self-devouring in a society so rapidly changing under the impact of monopoly-capitalist economy, where alcoholism and schizophrenia are notoriously prevalent chronic diseases, where a government that escorts a denounced subversive to his grave with more than one thousand men-at-arms can yet congratulate itself upon refusing to permit him a military funeral – what path upon life's pilgrimage can a young man of academic aspiration be expected to take?

Shall we see? Here is our specimen. His name is Sean O'Scrudu, and he is born of humble parents in a small rural community . . .

NARRATOR 1 (*as* O'SCRUDU *appears*). Rejoice, O young man, in thy youth; and let thy heart cheer thee in the days of thy youth –

NARRATOR 2. – and walk in the ways of thine heart, and in the sight of thine eyes.

GUEST-LECTURER. His intellectual attainments become apparent on the first stage of the assembly-line – the village national-school.

Improvised sequence showing O'SCRUDU *being good as a child at national-school: he is given a great heap of books.*

NARRATOR 1. And the child grew and waxed strong in spirit, filled with wisdom, and the race of God was upon him.

GUEST-LECTURER. His first burden is given to him: he knows how to answer questions, but not how to ask them.

Improvised sequence showing O'SCRUDU *being conscientious at secondary school: he is given an even greater heap of books.*

NARRATOR 2. And the spirit of the Lord shall rest upon him, the spirit of wisdom and understanding, the spirit of counsel and might, the spirit of knowledge and the fear of the Lord.

GUEST-LECTURER. His second burden is given to him. He knows how to accept a preconceived idea, but not how to challenge it.

Improvised sequence showing O'SCRUDU *being smug on entering the university: and receiving yet more books.*

CHORUS OF CRIES. He is the Champion!

GUEST-LECTURER. His third burden is given to him. He is now a fully trained acolyte for the monopoly-capitalist temple, and thoroughly crippled with the weight of what he must carry.

O'SCRUDU *with the three burdens can only walk with great difficulty.*

NARRATOR 1. Now I saw upon a time when he was walking in the fields, that he was reading in a book and greatly distressed in his mind. He looked this way and that way, as if he would run –

NARRATOR 2. – yet he stood still, because, as I perceived, he could not tell which way to go. And then he burst out crying –

O'SCRUDU. What shall I do to be saved!

Improvised sequence showing confusions of university society; the various contradictory lecture-courses apparently conflicting with each other and bewildering O'SCRUDU; *and the groups and activities all open for student participation. From* Opus Dei, *through the Gaelic Athletic Association,* Young Fine Gael, the Rugby Club *and* CND, *to* Sinn Fein.

GUEST-LECTURER. Contradictions inherent in the spectacle we have before us: *if* the university was set up to produce civil servants for the British Empire; and *if* the university was then used to produce unquestioning obedience to the assumed values of Catholic Nationalism; and *if* the university at the same time is expected to provide a docile personnel for the multi-national commercial enterprises which direct the economy of the country – how far can we say that the purposes of a Socrates or a Galileo are compatible with the confusion that must result? How far can experimental critical thought be pursued in an environment where the only possible resolution of all these contradictions is to be found in the exercise of an arbitrary bureaucratic authority concerned to preserve – *what?* Itself and itself alone? The *reductio ad absurdum* of the principle of Sinn Fein . . .

GUEST-LECTURER. Having joined the union, O'Scrudu is relieved of his biggest burden – he is at last a part of twentieth-century progressive thought.

Improvisation showing the dubious goings-on in the university branch of the Workers' Union of Ireland when the message is received asking for support for the Crown strike.

GUEST-LECTURER. The Workers' Union of Ireland, created by James Larkin, who derived from Karl Marx, who derived from Hegel, who derived from the northern intellectual tradition which took over where Galileo had been forced to a dead end, which in turn was because – do we dare go so far as to claim that with this union the true historical spirit of scholarly adventure and liberation of social thought has at last been brought back into Irish academia?

O'SCRUDU, *horrified by slanderous insinuations (spread among his colleagues by a professor) of violent intimidation by strikers against non-strikers, expresses his worry in an improvised speech.*

NARRATOR 1. They said nothing was too good for the working-class; and O'Scrudu went to a branch-meeting –

NARRATOR 2. – where they had a great dinner out at the Barna seafood restaurant, of laminated lobster costing around £100: and they were all so glad for what the union had done for them.

Improvisational sequence: O'SCRUDU *and the strike-pickets. He is guilty about their low rate of pay, and shows a certain humility in front of them. But then his middle-class over-enthusiasm comes into play, he has to be a leader, he lectures them on activism. And then he reproaches them (from a 'liberal' standpoint) for their attitude to the non-strikers: they are rude to him. He leaves, denying them his support.*

O'SCRUDU. But we do have to understand both sides of the question . . .

GUEST-LECTURER. Both sides of the question? By accepting that the non-strikers at Crown Control may be in the right, he has already taken sides with the management. Unlike Socrates he is frightened to ask the correct person the correct question – to enquire of the management why did they not accept the judgement of the Labour Court?

By regarding the two sets of workers at Crown Control as being potentially equally worthy of his support, he makes the mistake Galileo did not make – he has not used his observation. The action of the strikers has been recognised by the Irish Congress of Trade Unions, to which he as a trade unionist belongs. The action of the non-strikers has not.

In his conventional thinking, Brother O'Scrudu has of course accepted the judgement of the High Court – oh he is in awe of bourgeois establishment justice, but in considerably less awe of the democratic workers' organisation to which he himself belongs.

While joining a trade union to achieve benefit for himself, he at the same time rejects the entire philosophy of the movement, namely the embracement of class-struggle, and the combining together of workers upon one side of that struggle for the better advancement of the interests of *all* of them.

Nor is his thinking even that of a true Utilitarian! For he has uttered not a whisper of the damage to the national economy that this dispute at a Galway factory has brought about.

O'Scrudu, in short, has made a virtue of his own confusions. Thank goodness the strike was finally settled by the militancy of the workers and did not have to wait for the academics to provide a solution.

The future role of the intellectuals in the process of social change is one, ladies, gentlemen, I think I should leave for your further consideration, because it is for you, and only you, to determine . . . Thank you.

★   ★   ★

Sean O'Scrudu was a deliberate exercise in the academic
'disputatory' style, taken to the point of verbal knockabout. It
was uncomfortably received by many of the lecturers. They did
take the point that they must commit themselves to one side or
the other. University College, Galway, has since become one of
the most overtly utilitarian market-force-orientated institutions of
learning in the country.

The Hunting of the Mongrel Fox

After the summer of '76, Des and Pat with their academic
commitments could no longer continue with the Theatre
Workshop. The mood of the country was insecure and
demoralised because of Liam Cosgrave's Fine Gael/Labour
Coalition with its hairshirt economic policy, its refusal to listen to
pressure groups ('if you don't like what's happening, keep silence
until we offer you a general election and then you can vote for a
change!'), its obsession with *subversives* within its own ranks as
well as outside, and its consequent attacks on civil liberties; and
because of the internecine fighting that accompanied the tripartite
split within the Republican Movement. For the radical individual
it was a difficult time.

Matters came to a head when a young couple in Dublin, Marie
and Noel Murray (said to be anarchists, but claimed by no
political group), were sentenced to be hanged for shooting dead
an off-duty out-of-uniform policeman. Capital punishment had
been abolished in Ireland except for specific types of murder; this
was the first occasion since the abolition that a court decided to
impose it. There was immediate protest in the media. But before
the grass-roots could mobilise support, the authorities muzzled
the press. This seemed to frighten everyone else; and it looked as
though the hangings would be carried out with scarcely a word
raised against them. The two of us decided to test the
temperature: we put a notice in the local paper under the heading
of the Galway Theatre Workshop, asking for anyone who
thought that events were being 'swept under the carpet', and who
would like to explore this phenomenon in theatrical terms, to come
and meet us. About half-a-dozen people turned up, more women

than men. We all agreed, to start with, that as citizens we did not
wish lives to be taken in our name, and a letter was sent to the
press protesting against the death-sentences.

There was an element of urgency: this was October 1976, and it
looked as though the Murrays would be hanged before
Christmas. We decided to get a rapid play together, put it on in
the street, and so find out how people really felt. There was
disagreement within our group – some wanted a principled stand
against *all* capital punishment; others wanted to highlight the
injustices of this particular trial and to personalise support for the
Murrays. We reached a deadlock. One or two left the group, and
a consensus was then reached among the remainder: we would
use the arguments we had been having; our play should
emphasise the dilemma of the citizen confronted (a) with the fact
of capital punishment, and (b) with the suppression of protest
against it. Our resolve was strengthened by a ferocious editorial
in *The Connacht Sentinel*, saying we were not a genuine citizens'
theatre-group at all but a front for subversives.

★   ★   ★

*A very formal presentation. The cast ranged in a semi-circle, wearing
gaudy costumes and (in several cases) masks, reading out quotations from
newspapers etc., in rotation. A diversity of musical instruments, and
some interpolated songs.*

Church Scene

A BISHOP *intones a litany.*

> Love thy neighbour as thyself. (*Ora pro nobis.*)
> Life is sacred. (*Ora pro nobis.*)
> Thou shalt not kill. (*Ora pro nobis.*)
> He who giveth life alone shall take it away. (*Ora pro nobis.*)
> Blessed are the merciful for they shall obtain mercy. (*Ora pro
>   nobis.*)

Judgement Scene

1ST JUDGE. In 1964 the Criminal Justice Act abolished the death penalty for any offence other than treason, certain wartime offences, and four categories of what are termed Capital Murder. These were –

VOICE A. One. Murder of a member of the Garda Siochana acting in the course of his duty.

VOICE B. Two. Murder of a Prison Officer acting in the course of his duty.

VOICE A. Three. Murder done in the course of furtherance of an offence under Section 6, 7, 8, or 9 of the Offences Against The State Act 1939, or in the course or furtherance of the activities of an unlawful organisation within the Act.

VOICE B. Four. Murder committed within the State for a political motive, of the head of a foreign state, or of a member of the government of, or a diplomatic officer of, a foreign state.

2ND JUDGE. There were of course voices of certain politicians raised against these exceptional categories.

VOICE A. Mr Brian Lenihan of Fianna Fail. I do not mind whether a man murders a policeman or an ordinary civilian. I maintain the punishment should be the same. I suggest the Minister abolish the death penalty once and for all.

VOICE B. Mr James Tully of the Labour Party. I oppose completely any idea that capital punishment under any circumstances is right. I think it is entirely wrong for the State under any guise, or for any excuse – because I believe there is no reason for it – to take life.

VOICE A. Mr Fintan Coogan of Fine Gael. Premeditated murder is diabolical. Premeditated capital punishment by the State is equally diabolical.

2ND JUDGE. Mr Charles Haughey of Fianna Fail defended the categories. He said –

VOICE B. We are reluctantly retaining the death penalty in a very limited number of specific categories because of the right of society to protect itself.

3RD JUDGE. Mr Liam Cosgrave of Fine Gael opposed the Bill. He said –

VOICE A. I do think that the deterrent effect of the death penalty is still a powerful one. It is a mistake to abolish it: and it is difficult to justify its abolition for certain cases and its retention for others: there is no case at present for partial opposition.

1ST JUDGE. Whatever the opinions of these respected legislators, the four categories of Capital Murder were in the event maintained.

2ND JUDGE. They were retained in the name and with the full consent of the people of this Republic. They are your categories: for your security: to be only abolished through the vote of your representatives whom you yourselves have voted for.

1ST JUDGE. Prisoners at the bar! You have been found guilty of Capital Murder under Section One of the aforementioned categories. You have been found guilty by this tribunal sitting without jury in accordance with the statutory regulations of the Special Court.

3RD JUDGE. With the full consent of the people of this Republic.

2ND JUDGE. This is your court: for your security: to be only abolished through the vote of your representatives whom you yourselves have voted for.

1ST JUDGE. Prisoners at the bar! You shall hang by the neck until you are dead.

Controversy

IMMEDIATE UPROAR. Hanging! No hanging! Hanging! No Hanging! (*Etc.*)

VOICE A. The unexpected revival of the apparently abolished death sentence in the Irish Republic creates immediate political controversy – member countries of the EEC are at once reminded of the furore that greeted General Franco's decision to garotte political prisoners in Spain only last year. The situation in Ireland polarises rapidly. In favour of capital punishment –

VOICE B. The Garda Siochana Representative Body.

VOICE A. Opposed to capital punishment –

VOICE C. The Irish Council for Civil Liberties.

VOICE A. In favour –

VOICE B. The Northern Ireland Police Federation.

VOICE A. Opposed –

VOICE C. The Official Sinn Fein Party.

VOICE A. In favour –

VOICE B. The Police Federation of Great Britain.

VOICE A. Opposed –

VOICE C. The Southern Executive of the Council of Social Welfare of the Methodist Church in Ireland.

VOICE A. In favour –

VOICE B. The Rev. Ian Paisley MP.

VOICE A. Opposed –

VOICE C. The Association for Legal Justice.

VOICE A. In favour –

VOICE B. The Orange Order of Belfast.

VOICE A. Opposed –

VOICE C. Mr Mat Merrigan of the Liaison of the Left.

VOICE A. In favour –

VOICE B. Mrs Margaret Thatcher of the British Conservative and Unionist Party.

VOICE A. Opposed –

VOICE C. Senator Michael Mullen of the Irish Transport and General Workers' Union.

VOICE A. And what of the ordinary voters? Will they hold by the old doctrine of an-eye-for-an-eye and a-tooth-for-a-tooth: or do they believe that *all* life is sacred? Which way will the Catholic-thinking population of the Republic go? Today the choice is theirs!

Mary's first theme

Improvised Sequence.

MARY, *a young married woman, demonstrates her worries, approximately as follows: she didn't realise she had a choice – to hang a human being or not to hang a human being – by the neck until he is dead – if people are hanged, it will be done in her name – on the other hand, a life has been taken – but taking a life for another life will never bring the first life back – she hates violence and is frightened by violence – but is it violence to hang somebody? – she will not take the responsibility of hanging somebody – she will at least write a letter to the papers!*

Letters to the Editors

VOICE A. Editor of a national newspaper. Letter opposed to hanging. Print it.

VOICE B. Editor of a national newspaper. Letter opposed to hanging. Print it.

VOICE C. Editor of a national newspaper. Letter in favour of hanging. Print it.

VOICE A. Letter in favour. Print it.

VOICE B. Letter opposed. Print it.

VOICE C. Letter opposed. Print it.

VOICE A. Into this office on the average three letters opposed and one letter in favour. Print them.

The Muffling

THE GOVERNMENT. Dear people, as the representative of your elected representatives, I solemnly inform you that anyone attacking capital punishment is attacking the Government. Anyone attacking the Government is attacking the very roots of the foundation of the State, and thereby giving aid and comfort to the subversives whose aim is to fling open the sluice-gates of the bloodbath of civil war: thus to embroil and drown the entire population of this isle. Strong government is the only remedy; government not afraid to bring into play and indeed at times to exceed the fullest resources of the machinery of state. It is therefore my duty to use every rigour of the law to close up the loopholes through which these evil men ruthlessly infiltrate to manipulate and subvert our free institutions. To wit: the press.

1ST JUDGE. Fergus Pyle of *The Irish Times* – you printed a document critical of the democratically-instituted Special Court.

John Mulcahy of *Hibernia* – you printed correspondence suggesting grave irregularities in the handling of evidence for the prosecution before that court. We warn you that in cases of this nature the law of the land has an appropriate remedy. The editors of newspapers who connive at bringing the Irish Courts into contempt will have their papers sequestrated. Sequestrated. Sequestrated.

Bags are put over the Editors' heads.

Mary's second theme

Improvised Sequence.
MARY*'s letter has not been printed. There is total silence everywhere on the issue of the death penalty. She asks people their views. They all say, what can they do?*

She talks to her HUSBAND *about it and asks how much say and influence she and he have on the Government.*

The HUSBAND *tells her to shut up: she can vote at the general election.*

She says, she can be a pressure-group?

He says, leave it to the Government, they know what they're doing.

DONEGAN *and the* PRESIDENT *(the 'thundering disgrace') – Improvisation (See Note 1 at end of play.)*

MARY *goes to sleep in despair.*

The Sagacious Dog

The INTERNATIONAL MONETARY FUND (IMF) *enters as a circus beast-trainer, with a whip; and with the* GOVERNMENT *as a performing dog.*

IMF. Here is my dog, the Coalition Government of the Irish Republic. He will work a miracle. He will show how to make a stable economy and restore prosperity and health to the country, thus preserving an important link in the western world and saving international capitalism. The miracle will be worked if he knows how to answer all my questions correctly. Now! you have the highest inflation in Europe, you owe me £800 per minute in interest alone; and yet you pay your workers far far too much – why, you have aspirations to a standard of living equal to that of the most highly industrialised nations.

So: question one. What do you do about trade unions?

GOVERNMENT. Pull the wool over their eyes and make them accept my National Wage Agreement.

IMF. Question two. What about your individualistic trade-union rank-and-file?

GOVERNMENT. By improving technology I make them all unemployed.

IMF. Question three. What about the Labour Party?

GOVERNMENT. It's firmly on my backside and I can sit on it any time I want.

IMF. Question four. What about Conor Cruise O'Brien?

GOVERNMENT. I never let my left hand know what my right hand is doing.

IMF. Question five. What about the North?

GOVERNMENT. Conor Cruise O'Brien takes care of the North.

IMF. Question six. What about the Republican Movement?

GOVERNMENT. I lick the arse of the British Government, I let them infiltrate, assassinate and throw Republicans into gaol. The ones that are left over, if they don't jump out of window, *I* throw them into gaol.

IMF. Amend that! Why waste my money in keeping them in gaol?

GOVERNMENT. Because my gaols are terrible gaols, the worst in Europe – they're even going to bring me up over them before the Human Rights Court at Strasbourg!

IMF. Question seven. What about the Reds?

GOVERNMENT. I leave them to operate the Peaceful Road to Socialism.

IMF. Now for the Jackpot Question! The Million Million Dollar Question! If you can answer this, we will then have the miracle!

What do you do with the damned restless herd who do not
concern themselves with politics, but grumble all the time
about housing, prices, women's lib, mineral resources,
censorship, birth control, fishing rights, education, battered
wives, battered husbands, battered thundering disgraces – ?

GOVERNMENT (*highly excited, barking the answer before the
question is entirely finished*). Declaration of a State of Emergency!
To protect and enforce my State of Emergency I shall compel
them one and all into the forces of law'n'order which means
peace which means peace which means peace which means
peace . . . (*See Note 2 at end of play.*)

The IMF *retires, satisfied, for a few paces. The* GOVERNMENT
*rushes yelping and barking round and round and at last comes to rest,
in an orator's posture.*

My dear people, let me tell you: you have nothing to fear
provided that you fear! This space is for government purposes
alone and here alone is where I intend to stay – I promise you I
promise you I promise you that what I have I hold and I am not
going to be moved – the mongrel fox subversive eats up all that
we hold most dear! – where is he? can't see him, can't see
where he runs and creeps, must be able to see where he feeds
and thieves and sleeps – this space is not yet clear! Clear it!

ARMY *and* POLICE *start clearing everyone away from around him.*

Not yet clear not yet clear not yet clear – !

IMF. So make it clear.

The Fox Hunt

The GOVERNMENT (*with the* IMF's *whip*) *drives everyone into a
chaotic frenzied chase after an invisible quarry.* MARY's HUSBAND
forces her to take part.

GOVERNMENT. Make clear to all the people that the mongrel
fox is on his own – there he goes, go and catch him – tally-ho!

– so let him go – if you don't know where he is or who he is,
follow me and I will show – give a blow give a blow tally-ho –
who is he where is he smell him smell him smell – smelt and
we have his pelt!

Vortex of violence as the hunt centres on the kill.

In the heel of the hunt and the front confront the emergency
head-on and we in the van will implement the plan – red blood
for the green paper and all that we needed to do has been done!
My dear people, this is the one! The only one and he is gone
the only one and all go home. Against all forms of violence we
stand only to kill them dead and here's his head the blood runs
red!

He holds up a ghastly severed head.

Mary's third theme

MARY's HUSBAND *forces her to put her hand in the blood from the
severed head. She grabs the whip and strikes at him. She screams as he
aims a gun at her. She wakes.*

MARY (*blearily looking about her; and then, as she realises what has
happened, in a matter-of-fact voice*). Say no to capital punishment.

Concluding Slogans from Everyone

WE SAY *NO* TO CAPITAL PUNISHMENT

*and as many other slogans in favour of civil liberties, and against
repression, censorship, coercive legislation, etc., as any of the cast feel
they want to deliver to any particular audience in relation to the news of
the day . . . Similarly, if the audience has its own favourite slogans . . .*

*   *   *

The Murrays were in the end reprieved from the gallows and were sentenced to long terms of imprisonment which (1991) they are still serving – Noel in Portlaoise Prison and Marie in Mountjoy Prison, Dublin. The death-sentence has not been carried out in Ireland since; and it now looks as though it will be abolished altogether.

Notes. We kept adding to the play as we worked on it, as each new national scandal materialised; and two such topical inserts may need explanation.

1 The 'thundering disgrace': President O'Dalaigh refused to sign the death sentence on the Murrays until it was referred back to the Supreme Court. Mr Donegan, Minister for Defence, in a speech to officers of the Irish Army, referred to the President's action as a 'thundering disgrace', would neither apologise nor retract, and the President resigned.

2 The State of Emergency: this was imposed by the Government after Mr Ewart-Biggs, the British Ambassador, was murdered near his house in Dublin.

No Room at the Inn

Shortly before Christmas, 1976, while we were still performing *The Hunting of the Mongrel Fox*, the perennial problem of providing service-sites and/or housing for the Travelling Community in Galway once again became an issue: and the Galway Theatre Workshop made a play which we invited the city councillors to see. Some of them came. The play's title speaks for itself and for the season.

★ ★ ★

1

Game – 'I'm the King of the Castle, go down you dirty rascal!'
– also:

I'm a shilling looking down at sixpence
I'm sixpence looking down at three pence
I'm three pence looking down at a penny
I'm a penny looking down at a ha'penny
And I'm just a ha'penny looking down at nobody – what's
    going to happen to *me*?

2

In 1960 the Government set up a Commission to enquire into the situation of the Itinerants in Ireland. This Commission was headed by Mr Charles Haughey TD, who summed up the findings as follows:

'One over-riding consideration which dominates the entire background of this problem and is of paramount importance in

relation to it, is the simple fact that the humblest Itinerant is
entitled to a place in the sun and to a share in the benefits of our
society. Their fundamental rights as individuals and their
religious beliefs are sacred and inalienable.'

3–10

*Sequences demonstrating the alienated social position of the Travelling
Community, based on the report of the 1960 Commission, and
showing how this alienation has developed from an earlier state of
affairs when the Travellers had an accepted place in the rural economy.*

11

*In September 1976, Mr Justin Keating, Minister of Industry and
Commerce, came to Galway to open a new factory for Wilson's
Sporting Goods. Guests of honour included – The American
Ambassador, The Mayor of Galway.*

*Mr Keating saw Itinerants encamped near the Industrial Estate, and
he said: 'This is an industrial embarrassment.'*

He threw the cat among the pigeons.

*Councillor Gerald Colgan, Mayor of Galway, welcomed the
Minister's statement and said:*

'Thirty families however have been housed and thirty more
families are awaiting settlement in – A NEW ITINERANT
VILLAGE to be built at Castlegar!'

Cheers and applause.

12

Improvisation.

*US Multi-national boss calls up his Galway Factory-Manager.
The Manager passes it on to other Factory-Managers on the Industrial
Estate (situated at Castlegar and thought to have its 'security'
threatened by the ITINERANT VILLAGE).*

*The first Manager presides at a meeting of the Residents' Association.
The Residents' Association goes to demonstrate at the council-offices.*

13

Improvisation.

*City-council meeting.
Agenda of embarrassing scandals:*

1 The Leisureland *entertainment-complex scheme.
2 Oil Pollution in Galway Bay.
3 Itinerants occupying the new park-shelter in Eyre Square –
suggestions that the building be wired-up with an electric fence, or that
Itinerants be deported* en masse *to an uninhabited island off the
Atlantic coast.
4 Playing-fields* (etc.)

– all swept (literally) under the carpet.

Planning permission for the ITINERANT VILLAGE *has come
through.*

Castlegar residents demonstrate angrily; and play 'King of the Castle'.

The COUNCILLORS *sweep this protest under the carpet. They
want the goodwill of the national and local media. Publicity handout to
be prepared.*

*Meeting is closed: but –
they discover a* PRO-MAN *for the Industrialists in their midst.
Panic.*

14

PRO-MAN *reads out portions of a document which deprecate the
proximity of the* ITINERANT VILLAGE *to the factories, and
express fears of theft and vandalism.*

Improvisation.

COUNCILLORS *quarrel. The* COUNTY MANAGER *insists on continuation of agreed policy: but village plan is shelved.*

I bet if you thought these Itinerants were worth money to you, you'd have a different tale to tell!

15

Improvisation.

Christmas Eve in Galway.
A TRAVELLING-WOMAN, *begging, is kicked out of revels by boozy* COUNCILLORS *who one by one fall asleep.*

Dream-Sequence.

Arrival of mysterious ARAB *on a camel (a 'wise man from the east'), carrying a box.*
He seeks a child 'born under the stars', *the sight of whom –* 'it is written' – *will mystically provide him with the Elixir of Life.*
COUNCILLORS, *excited by the possibilities of Arabian oil-money coming into Galway, try to sell him land, and so on.*
They realise that it must be a TRAVELLER'S CHILD *that he wants. He wants to* buy *a child!*

16

Improvisation.

The council compels all the TRAVELLERS *to assemble in the Great Southern Hotel.*
The ARAB *is brought in to meet them.*
He experiences the CHILD: *and, satisfied, is about to leave. (He doesn't want to buy the child at all.)*
The COUNCILLORS *demand something from him in return.*
He refuses, denouncing their mercenary spirit.
They attack him and throw him out.
He leaves his box behind him.
The COUNCILLORS *fight over the box; and discover it contains a* Talisman. *In the struggle, the* Talisman *is accidentally rubbed.*
A GENIE *arises.*

17

GENIE. I am the Genie of the Box! You are very greedy people. I
had hoped that you would learn respect for your fellow-
creatures through a simple little parable that would give you an
opportunity to put into practice the Spirit of Christmas upon
this Christmas Eve. But you rejected it. So you must be taught
another lesson and a harsher one. So: back you go – back back
into your own history – move along there! you can't stop here!

Improvise: Galway bigotry in the 19th century.

Move along there! you can't stop here! – back you go – back!

Improvise: Galway bigotry in the 18th century.

Move along there! you can't stop here! – back you go – back!

Improvise: Galway bigotry in the 17th century.

Move along there! you can't stop here! back you go – back! – to
four hundred years ago, when your city was so great and
famous – bringing to her harbour sweet wine from the
vineyards of France and of Spain, for the nobles of the whole of
Ireland, her streets full of merchants selling silk and delicate
laces, and holding converse in a score of tongues from all
corners of the earth, her buildings of white stone decorated and
carved like caskets of ivory, the bells of her churches ringing
out their joyous peal across the waters of Galway Bay, the river
filled with salmon, the green fields outside the town alive with
the running deer – prosperity, vitality, beauty –

18

GENIE (*cont*). And where were *you*? Kept out of the gates by the
English colonial bye-laws written over them!

That no man of this town shall host or receive into their houses
at Christmas, Easter, nor no feast else, any of the Burkes,
MacWilliams, or Kellys, nor any other of the Irish, on pain to
forfeit five pounds. That neither O nor Mac shall strut nor
swagger through the streets of Galway.

Improvisation.

16th-century rural IRISH pretend to be English in order to get into the civic Christmas banquet. A friendly COLONIST-CITIZEN connives at this and is detected by his colleagues.

Fee fi fo fum
I smell the blood of an Irish man
Be he alive or be he dead
I'll grind his bones to make my bread!

A witch-hunt by loyal COLONISTS against 'Irish-loving' COLONISTS: general bigotry and racial discrimination and divide-and-rule.

19

Improvisation.

Collapse into fighting and ruin.

Happy would it have been for Ireland, had the spirit of conciliation and peace, guided by justice and tempered with mercy, actuated its rules. Its history would not now abound with the manifold and gloomy descriptions of murder, treason, and rebellion, which disgraces almost every page of it.

The COUNCILLORS wake up and remember their dreams. They repent.

If there's injustice toward even a small section of the people in this town and that injustice is not removed, the entire population will in the end suffer for it.

They resume their discussions: once the shock of the dream has worn off, the pressures of political necessity once more overcome them, and with regret (but relief) they agree to —

SWEEP THE TRAVELLERS UNDER THE CARPET!

Which is done. The WOMAN who had been begging (Sequence 15) is rolled under the carpet and left there, as they all go out of the room.

★ ★ ★

There is still a bad unresolved situation in Ireland as regards the Travelling People, and particularly in Galway: but the Travellers are now more organised, with their own confident spokespeople who stand as candidates in national elections (as for example Nan Joyce in Dublin and Margaret Sweeney in Galway).

Mary's Name

The third and last collective work of the Galway Theatre Workshop was the most difficult and it took us the longest time (several months of discussion) to work out an effective form.

The group consisted of (original members): Mary Butler and her husband Gerry, Noelle O'Hanlon, Nancy Coughlan, Margaretta D'Arcy, John Arden, Pat Cobey (who had left to go to America after *Mongrel Fox*), Anne O'Brien (who had left to go to Dublin after *No Room at the Inn*).

As well as: James Raftery, Ann Good and Ritchie Good, Eva Doherty (who all joined us after reading an account in the local paper of how a publican had thrown us out of his bar in the middle of a performance of *No Room at the Inn* because we mentioned the names of local political figures).

Mary Butler put forward the idea for the third play: the resentment she found at work and amongst her family when she decided to keep her own name after her recent marriage (which she was perfectly entitled to do under Irish law). Everyone in the group had a different view about why society so resented Mary's decision. Rather than attempt to amalgamate all these interpretations into one structure, we improvised on each one in turn, making a sort of nest of interlocking viewpoints like a chinese-puzzle. None of the script survives: we do remember that it started with *The Book of Genesis* and Adam usurping power by insisting on naming his bride – 'She shall be called Woman because she was taken out of Man.'

This was the least word-bound of our plays – much of it was in mime – and its only performance at the University Branch of the Workers' Union of Ireland (cf *Sean O'Scrudu*) aroused uproar and outrage from certain male lecturers, furious debate and fracas, which resulted in a Women's Group being immediately set up in Galway by Mary, Eva and Ann.

A Pinprick of History

The final 'intervention' of the Galway Theatre Workshop was made by three of its members, Eva Doherty, James Raftery, and M. D'Arcy, when Liam Cosgrave came to Galway on 2 June 1977 as part of his general election campaign. (By this time the Workshop had received a grant of £75 from the Irish Arts Council to help the expenses of productions that were now being taken on tour.)

Ed Berman offered D'Arcy space in his 'Almost Free' Ambience lunchtime-theatre off Leicester Square, while she and Arden were in London to defend their libel-case. She decided to devise and present *A Pinprick of History* elaboration of the Cosgrave episode, using the flexible techniques already developed by the Galway Theatre Workshop and by the readings of *The Non-Stop Connolly Show* which had been held at the 'Almost Free' the previous year – a core-cast of permanent performers; plus extra persons day-by-day, professionals and others who enjoyed this rather haphazard anarchic on-the-spot kind of theatre. The general outline and movement of the text is D'Arcy's, but many of the speeches were improvised and written by the performers who delivered them.

★ ★ ★

Cast

John Arden
Finn Arden
George Byatt
Margaretta D'Arcy
Alex Farrell
Michael Loughnan

Terence McGinity
Treasa Ní Fhátharta
Timothy O'Grady
Paul O'Keeffe
John Quinn
Linda Sheridan

*In the theatre-foyer actors in celebratory costumes welcome each member
of the audience to the Commemorative meeting of the Dialectical
Association for the Study of Pinpricks of History. It is assumed that each
new arrival has brought a delegation of performers to present a play
illuminating a selected Pinprick. Friendly debate is induced over the
merits of various aspects of twentieth-century affairs, seen as possible
Pinpricks. The atmosphere is gradually established that the date of the
show is no longer 1977 but over one hundred years further on in history
and that the Commemoration is for the Centenary of the Great World
Socialist Revolution, which finally happened at some date subsequent to
the 1970s. The purpose of the meeting is to dramatise the various
progressive Pinpricks that successively and successfully brought about this
great change in the destiny of the human race. Delegations from many
countries and cultures are assumed to be present. All is convivial,
relaxed, impregnated with jocund historical scholarship.*

*Music is heard – The Internationale, revolutionary songs from Russia,
France, Ireland, China, etc etc. An announcement is made that the stage
is now ready for the presentation of the first Pinprick, and will the first
delegation prepare their actors and make their entrance. The audience is
led into seats in the theatre. The auditorium is lavishly decorated with
garlands, slogans, exuberant banners.*

The CO-ORDINATOR *of the Commemoration begins to introduce
the first play. Suddenly she is interrupted by a complete blackout. This
lasts for two–three seconds, with silence broken only by mysterious
whisperings from the stage. When the lights come up again the actors
are all facing the audience with white hoods covering their faces
except for eye and mouth holes. They stand in a frozen pose. The*
CO-ORDINATOR *apologises. She explains that a most serious
breach of security has been discovered. A group has entered the
Commemoration who are not part of the World Socialist Celebration, as
they come from Britain – Britain being the one country in the world that
did not take part in the Great Revolution and that still is unable to
recognise her imperialist role. It is not, however, the policy of the
Association to throw people out. But on the other hand the plays to be
presented will prove incomprehensible to the British people because they
are founded on a premise that Britain has rejected. So what to do? As she
speaks, the decorations are stripped away, leaving the walls of the theatre
black and bare.*

A GERMAN DELEGATE *then announces that his delegation has a
play which might have some content attainable by a largely British
audience. He then explains his play in German. A translator supplies
the English version:*

GERMAN DELEGATE (*translation*). Epoch concluding with the Great Revolution of years following 1977. Internal contradictions of imperialist/capitalist multi-national exploitation achieve point of extreme crisis and confront puppet governments of capitalist exploitatory states with the following dilemma: how far can the forces of proletarian mass-resistance be repressed without unwittingly incorporating the lower echelons of the bourgeoisie into the ranks of the repressed? Suggested solutions – one: create fascism/racism/anti-terrorist-paranoia by means of appeals to the residual chauvinist atavism of the aforesaid lower echelons. Two: apply highly-developed techniques of security surveillance and infiltration to the residual bourgeois organs of enlightenment and cultural progressivism, thereby neutralising and subverting such organs (without their knowledge) to the purpose of the ruling class. Three: intensify the alienation between the militant proletariat of the exploitatory countries and the national liberation forces in colonial and ex-colonial territories. This cannot be done without the active assistance of the idealistic middle-class who must therefore be encouraged to divert, paternalistically, all proletarian growth of social consciousness into community projects, therapeutic welfare schemes, and committees of public protest against apparent bureaucratic obstructionism. Superficial philistine pseudo-Marxism an essential factor for this solution. The purpose of this play: to induce our world-wide comrades to redouble their efforts to capture the consciousness of the intelligentsia of Great Britain in the cause of revolution. Only through our encouragement can they eventually find the means to cast themselves free once and for all of the existing political climate in that island, the acknowledged apotheosis of extreme backwardness, abdication of confrontation, and revolutionary deadlock.

A flourish of drums. A video film commences, showing the police and strike-pickets outside the Grunwick factory in London, 1977. Tape-recorded voices transmit messages from Asian workers involved in the Grunwick strike, from Irish Revolutionists involved in the political prisoners agitation in Northern Ireland, all denouncing the apathy of the British towards their struggles, and declaring their confidence in final victory. (These messages are genuine, not spoken by actors.)

Actors read passages of prose cut up from various printed sources and arranged in a haphazard collage:

1 The other real possibility was that Captain Nairac was not dead. There was only the evidence of Captain Collett that he had not seen him again.

2 There are times when the traditional and popular solution to the problem of Ireland – to tow it into the middle of the Atlantic and sink it – commends itself almost irresistibly to anyone contemplating its condition.

3 By the holy season of Christmas there will be 300 republican prisoners men and women. They are naked twenty-four hours a day, save for a blanket. They are in solitary confinement most of the time. Some of them have been enduring these conditions for more than twelve months.

4 Babylon the great is fallen is fallen and is become the habitation of devils and the hold of every unclean spirit and a cage of every unclean and hateful bird.

5 But where do the British radicals stand upon these matters? I can remember massive demos in London protesting against American involvement in Vietnam. Two hundred Labour MPs signed a petition in support of Judith Todd, the daughter of a former Rhodesian Prime Minister, when *she* went on hunger-strike.

6 As we got closer and closer to the date when the editorial had to be written, we found that we couldn't get it done, in spite of the fact that we had tried several times and more than one draft had been written.

A verse of a traditional Irish lament is sung.

Representatives of the CIA and the IMF introduce themselves to the audience and assume menacing attitudes.

A series of fragmented acted episodes partly in mime are presented. They represent the tyranny of bureaucracy and state control over the artist and conclude with three artists being buried alive.

The next verse of the Irish lament is sung.

A second collage of prose passages:

1 It isn't difficult to see that in order to write an editorial of this nature, we would have had to have carried out already a great deal of theoretical analysis and arrived at a pretty high level of political agreement – in other words to have performed already the very tasks which the magazine itself was conceived for in the first place.

2 For Mr Van Straubenzee, the Irish constitution is negotiable; essentially of no serious moment; to be set aside with a stroke of the pen. The British constitution would, of course, be quite another matter.

3 And the kings of the earth shall see the smoke of her burning, standing afar off for fear of her torment, saying, 'Alas alas that great city of Babylon, that mighty city, for in one hour is thy judgement come.'

4 I can imagine what a din would arise in the British Parliament and press were such measures to be proposed. But evidently they would be quite all right for the Irish. In fact, I doubt if we would hear much protest from Mr Van Straubenzee, if we turned this country into a police state, as long as we didn't disturb the neighbours.

5 To advocate unity as the solution to the problems of Northern Ireland is unrealistic, unfruitful, and even mischievous, through the encouragement it gives to those who use force to achieve that undemocratic object.

6 The court should look at what Captain Nairac was engaged in – elaborate undercover work in a specially-equipped car in civilian clothes. Was he going south to pay informers, to assassinate some person, to gather information? Whatever happened that night they know that Captain Nairac's cover was broken.

All this is accompanied with rhythmical drumming.

The prose passages are repeated – this time simultaneously in a gathering cacophony, together with repetition of the tape-recorded messages. A crescendo of confused noise is reached – culminating in a general cry:

*ay, discussion continues until something is produced to satisfy the
*dience. If this vote is for the Irish play, then the IRISH
ELEGATE proceeds with her arrangements.

*he first explains that due to the natural fear of British people that
*eir every word and action is spied upon by the Police Special
ranch, the undercover detectives are asked to declare themselves. (
his is spoken in Irish, translated by the CO-ORDINATOR.) I
detectives stand up to be recognised, the IRISH DELEGATE cau
*he audience nonetheless that they should not allow themselves to
respond to the play too recklessly, as this may alert the police and g
them into trouble when they return home. She describes how unde
Prevention of Terrorism Act any person may be held by the police
seven days without access to a lawyer: and if they are Irish they ca
deported without any reason being given by the authorities. For
citizens of a country where the Rule of Law has been so badly ero
it is not possible for the theatre to be as free and open a forum of
opinion as it is in the rest of the world.

She then states that her play will contain many references to perso
and political parties important in Irish affairs in 1977: as these wi
unfamiliar to the public, she wants volunteers to represent them in
series of brief tableaux which she will immediately improvise.
Volunteers from the audience who come forward are placed in
juxtaposition, to demonstrate the relationships of the Irish politica
groupings. Various splits and assassinations among the Republica
contrived in the interest of the British Government are also
demonstrated in mime:

Billy Macmillen of the Official Republican Clubs murdered by th
   SAS
Maire Drumm of Provisional Sinn Fein murdered by the SAS
Seamus Costello of the Irish Republican Socialist Party murdered
   the SAS.

The political parties demonstrated are Fianna Fail, Fine Gael, an
Labour. It is shown that Fianna Fail under Jack Lynch is the
opposition challenging in the election the government-coalition of l
Gael under Liam Cosgrave and Labour under Brendan Corish. C
Cruise O'Brien (of Labour) is the ideologist of the Coalition
Government.

FRAGMENTATION!

A moment of silence. Followed by a pompous announcement:

The Grand Jubilee Progress of Her Majesty the Queen to
traverse in one whole year every single inch of her domain –
and the population came out to cheer and to form themselves
into the Cultural/Social/Imperial Grand Army –

to Hear See Speak No Evil –
to BUILD SUPPORT MAINTAIN the State
to BUILD SUPPORT MAINTAIN Imperialism
to BUILD SUPPORT MAINTAIN Repression.

*The Grand March comes past, saluting the Queen, whose effigy
between lighted candles, has been installed on a rostrum in the centre of
the stage. A DRUMMER in front of the Audience offers a
commentary on the marchers, chanting it to the rhythm of their
footsteps. Major-General Kitson recurs at various intervals during the
march, swirling a huge Union Jack.*

DRUMMER. The Deputy Wardens, Health Workers, Probation
Officers, Community-care and Playleaders. Psychologists,
Drama-therapists, Music-therapists, Gestalt Jungian Freudian
hypno-psychologists, and Miss Joan White, schoolteacher from
Canterbury, candidate for the National Front who welcomes
the need for paramilitary groups – *And* the mastermind and
manipulator of them all – Major-General Frank Kitson!

MARCHERS.
Hear See Speak No Evil –
BUILD SUPPORT MAINTAIN the State
BUILD SUPPORT MAINTAIN Imperialism
BUILD SUPPORT MAINTAIN Repression.

DRUMMER. And to plaster the cracks – the left-wing British
dramatists, the National Theatre, the Fringe-theatre, the
Subsidised-theatre, upstairs downstairs latenight lunchtime pub
evening cabaret street-theatre, and the Agitprop theatre. And
the new recruit to the team, Dr Conor Cruise O'Brien, critic
and playwright, editor-in-chief of the London *Observer*. *And* the
mastermind and manipulator of them all, Major-General Frank
Kitson!

MARCHERS.
    Hear See Speak No Evil
    BUILD SUPPORT MAINTAIN – (etc).

DRUMMER. The psychological-operation team from Whitehall, Lord Shackleton who is investigating the Prevention of Terrorism Act spurred on by the complaints before the Human Rights Court at Strasbourg. The telephone-tappers, letter-openers, the Irish Squad, the Special Branch, the CID, the Royal Signals, and Merlyn Rees. Colonel A –

MARCHERS. Sssh . . . !

DRUMMER. Colonel B –

MARCHERS. Sssh . . . !

DRUMMER. Who was revealed as Colonel H. A. Johnstone MBE Army Number 420864 formerly of the Royal Corps of Signals. And the mastermind and manipulator of them all – Major-General Frank Kitson!

MARCHERS. Hear See Speak No Evil (etc).

DRUMMER. Lieutenant Richard Anderson who says firefighting is very similar to Northern Ireland – the only difference is that we can't go out on patrol looking for incidents, Captain Broadbent who doesn't want to be in Northern Ireland at all, the late Captain Robert Nairac of the SAS Northern Ireland, Major Jeremy Phipps, Agee, Hosenball, Aubrey, Berry, Campbell –

MARCHERS. NO!!

DRUMMER. Our man in the North General Creasy ex-SAS under the watchful eye of his mentor Major-General Frank Kitson – the mastermind and manipulator of them all!

MARCHERS. Hear See Speak No Evil (etc).

DRUMMER. Colm McNutt was killed in revenge for Captain Nairac: Lance-Corporal Harman was killed in revenge for Colm McNutt: the Republican News printing plates have been seized in revenge for Lance-Corporal Harman. Forde and Tuzo with their bloody hands. The firemen –

MARCHERS. NO!!

DRUMMER. Peter Grimes –

MARCHERS. NO!!

DRUMMER. The Michael Collins film –

MARCHERS. NO!!

DRUMMER. The men in blue and the soldiers true, tl and their friend George Ward, Police-Constable Bre the Metropolitan Police who says: 'we stopped a Gre Goddess in London and the soldier who was driving paralytic drunk'. Lieutenant Richardson who says: 'th firefighting duty don't really like sitting around for ho nothing to do'. *And* the mastermind and manipulator all – Major-General Frank Kitson –

There is a sudden interruption by the GERMAN DELEGA who excitedly shouts out in German. The actors immediately play and take off their masks. They confer in a huddle with th GERMAN DELEGATE and the CO-ORDINATOR.

The GERMAN DELEGATE makes a rapid speech which is translated by the CO-ORDINATOR: to the general effect tha rules of the Association state that if a play is not making sense to audience, then it does not have to continue. This expressionist st too obscure and allusive and should not continue. The function o Dialectical Association is to promote understanding, not obscurity British people present would not be able to comprehend the applica of the play and it was therefore, for them, retrograde. So what to d The CO-ORDINATOR asks the Audience, perhaps can one am them think of a suitable subject for dramatisation? If someone does suggest something that seems practicable, the actors will improvise on that theme. (See Note at end of play.)

If, however, there are no suggestions, then the IRISH DELEGATE comes forward and diffidently offers a play. She explains, in Irish, that it could be a very upsetting play for the British; and she wants them to have a choice. If they do not want to be upset, then she will not present her play. There must be a nem con vote in favour of the play before she will continue with it. If there is an objection to the

The IRISH DELEGATE *reads the Argument of her play (in Irish, translated):*

This play is direct, unsophisticated, indeed naive.
Revolutionary struggle for the Socialist Republican self-determination of the Irish people posed so great a threat to the British ruling class, already in fear of their own proletariat, that they determined to smash it by all means available. Assisted in this brutal task by the incapacity of the British trade-union leadership to secure basic rights at one small London factory – Grunwick. Assisted at the same time by the vacillations of the artists and writers in the face of the corrupting policy of Arts Council subsidy for allegedly political artwork. Assisted at the same time by the treachery of running-dog elements of the Irish bourgeoisie and the political remnants of 1930s Catholic Blueshirt Hibernian Fascism. But in the year '77 came the Pinprick of History – the refusal of the Irish electorate in the 26 Counties to vote as demanded by the imperialist forces and their lickspittle Dublin associates. In spite of the perfidious attempt by the British Arts Council to influence the policy of its more recent Irish counterpart, one subsidised Irish acting group, the Galway Theatre Workshop, carried out its own pinprick in the course of the election. In the midst of the bourgeois repressive politics of the time these actors were able to fuse their Dionysiac fury with the rising tide of working-class consciousness that booted Liam Cosgrave and Conor Cruise O'Brien from the seats of power they had so long vandalised by their overweening pretensions.

Two BRITISH OFFICERS *step forward to secure the safety of their State. The Grunwick video-tape is running during this episode. People strain to hold up an (invisible) wall which threatens to burst inward as though constantly under pressure from the outside.*

FIRST BRITISH OFFICER.
You come most carefully upon your hour.

SECOND BRITISH OFFICER.
It is now struck twelve. 'Tis bitter cold
And I am sick at heart.

FIRST BRITISH OFFICER.
What, hath this thing appeared again tonight?

SECOND BRITISH OFFICER.
No no, the wall is sound. It holds – it holds.

BOTH BRITISH OFFICERS.
We hope . . .

FIRST BRITISH OFFICER.
Something is rotten in the state of England.

BOTH BRITISH OFFICERS.
Let but the wall hold: Dunkirk Dunkirk – !

SECOND BRITISH OFFICER.
Keep well the old security of the realm:
And as we stand here vigilant let us tell
Once more the roll of our advantages –
Give heart unto the citizens. You speak first.

FIRST BRITISH OFFICER.
The basic rights of all trade-unionists
Have not yet been achieved. The economy is therefore sound.

SECOND BRITISH OFFICER.
Agee and Hosenball have been successfully
Sans all resistance thoroughly banishéd.
Our freedom to conceal the truth is therefore sound.

FIRST BRITISH OFFICER.
Len Murray and the TUC well know
That should they utter in defence of such as these,
Bold Englishmen in Ireland lose their lives.
So therefore silence. The patriotism of the working-class is
    sound.

SECOND BRITISH OFFICER.
The Irish runagates and murderous rebel kerns
In English gaols are cruelly mewéd up –
All forms of law distorted and ignored to keep them safe –
Maugre their hunger-strikes and direful mutinies.
The violent Celtic fringe is therefore sound.

BOTH BRITISH OFFICERS.
Hold up the wall hold up the wall!

FIRST BRITISH OFFICER.
> Let but the jigsaw of our secret dealings
> Remain for ever scattered, none shall know
> In any time or place what 'tis we do.
> Security of our covert operations therefore sound.

SECOND BRITISH OFFICER.
> Tell Colonel A and Colonel B *we* know their names
> And hold them in our favour.

FIRST BRITISH OFFICER.
> Astride the land the firemen do renounce
> Their duties to the common-weal, but yet
> Here there and everywhere the men-at-arms,
> Brave servants of Her Majesty, soldiers, sailors, airmen, all
>   combine
> To learn th'unwonted trade of civil-service
> And so in time to rule the land when all else fails.
> So government at last shall still hold sound.

SECOND BRITISH OFFICER.
> And if it don't, do we not have – ?

SECOND BRITISH OFFICER.
> Prevention-of-the-Terrorism Act to make all safe?
> Deport, imprison, bind in chains and beat
> The living daylights out of all who murmur?
> Our judges safe and sound, inscrutable blind eye,
> Deaf ear, to men of Balcombe Street who swear "Twas I
> That left the Guildford bag when all did die!'

FIRST BRITISH OFFICER.
> With this in force, what voice will dare be raised?

SECOND BRITISH OFFICER.
> The poet's voice – still, small, a knife-i-th'heart . . . ?

FIRST BRITISH OFFICER.
> Hear then the words of the high Arts Council, thus:

Enter the ARTS COUNCIL, *to help hold the wall.*

THE ARTS COUNCIL. Artistic interest must, by the
commercial and competitive nature of the theatre, take
precedence: and any company thought to sell a rigid political

line would soon, I think, find itself publicly labelled as a *pamphleteer.*

FIRST BRITISH OFFICER.
And that, my friend, should close their mouth for ever . . .

SECOND BRITISH OFFICER.
If not, we trundle on
Bernardus Levin from the frozen steppe,
Matt Talbot redivivus in the *Sunday Times.*

Enter B. LEVIN to help hold the wall.

SECOND BRITISH OFFICER.
Seeking his Christ for ever in the words
Of lesser men who struggle to be good,
To leave all truth, political commitment,
And, above all, our Irish complications well alone –
Far off far off from their pale dramaturgy . . .

The wall seems to totter: but the WIDOW *enters and helps to hold it up.*

BOTH BRITISH OFFICERS.
Hold up the wall – !

SECOND BRITISH OFFICER.
The widow Ewart-Biggs
Now splits the power of the subversive Gaelic League
By distribution of great prizes to the commodious Irish
In the despite of all their history –

The GHOST *of Ewart-Biggs enters, armed: but does not help hold the wall – he merely wanders along inside it moaning:*

GHOST.
Revenge my foul and most unnatural murder!

FIRST BRITISH OFFICER.
Hold up the wall! Advantage still is ours!

BOTH BRITISH OFFICERS.
Hold up the wall – !

FIRST BRITISH OFFICER.
Stay stay what is that howl – ?

SECOND BRITISH OFFICER.
  It is the voice of our true lone-wolf soldiers
  Keeping the peace across the wild waste ground
  Of lacerated Ulster –

BOTH BRITISH OFFICERS.
  Hark how they howl – !

SECOND BRITISH OFFICER.
  They seek for blood blood blood and they shall have it –
  If not in Ireland, then at home: so warn the populace:
  Here here they will have blood if all do not combine
  To hold the wall and muster up our strength – ! ! !

*The wall is suddenly broken through – shouts and slogans of Irish
liberation (in Irish) – a burst of Irish music. The* BRITISH
OFFICERS *and persons holding up the wall are swept away. A
woman representing the* SPIRIT OF IRELAND *sings a song in
Irish, and announces:*

SPIRIT OF IRELAND. Ireland in the grim past!

VOICES (*in the midst of a turmoil of flashing lights and glimpses of
  confused movement*). By 1977 the vision of a country steeled with
  modern industry had been shattered. This industry was owned
  and controlled by foreigners, relied heavily upon foreign
  markets, it was an industrial base as vulnerable as a stage-set in
  a force-nine gale. Unemployment rose to 160,000: half the
  population were under twenty-five and unable to emigrate –
  conditions in Ireland were becoming dangerously unstable –

VOICES (*repeat*). Unstable, dangerously unstable.

A SINGLE DOMINANT VOICE. The British Government is
  found guilty at the European Court of Human Rights, guilty,
  of torture.

VOICES (*repeat*). Torture torture torture . . .

During the above, verses of the Connolly ballad are sung:

  Oh where oh where is our James Connolly
  Oh where oh where can that brave man be?
  He has gone to organise the union

422 IMMEDIATE ROUGH THEATRE

That workers all may yet be free.

Who carries high our burning flag
Who carries high our burning flag?
Oh who but James Connolly all pale and wounded
Carries high our burning flag. (*etc*)

COSGRAVE *and the Coalition leaders assemble for the Fine Gael
Ard Fheis (annual party conference). Fianna Fail, opposition leaders
on the other side. A COMMENTATOR describes the scene which
is enacted behind in an appropriate manner of mime and tableau.*

COMMENTATOR. Who would believe when they view the
agreeable flower-lined boulevards of Dublin today that little
more than a few short generations ago – in May 1977 – it was
the setting for the raucous and barbarous annual gathering of
the sinister forces of the Fine Gael Party, led by the grim fox-
hunting figure of the autocratic Liam Cosgrave – as he
addressed his dependent conference, the Ard Fheis as it was
then termed?

COSGRAVE *mounts the rostrum.*

COMMENTATOR. In four traumatic years of strong
government his Labour-party hatchetman Conor Cruise
O'Brien had systematically attempted to rewrite Irish history
from the very beginning, a calculated revisionism that turned
England from the hereditary enemy into the long-suffering and
devoted friend: and presented all Irish resistance against
colonialism and exploitation as the drunken ravings of a parcel
of mother-fixated thugs.

CRUISE O'BRIEN *is seen handing* COSGRAVE *material for his
speech.*

COMMENTATOR. Cosgrave had struck hard: he had terrified
his opponents with the refusal to admit that any complaint
against his government could possibly arise except from
subversive and terrorist machinations. He had declared a State
of Emergency.

The Coalition party-groups start to stamp their feet ominously.
CHARLES HAUGHEY *steps forward from the opposite side.*

COMMENTATOR. The Fine Gael Ard Fheis was compared yesterday to a Nuremberg Rally by the opposition spokesman on health, Mr Charles Haughey –

HAUGHEY. Very definite evidence of right wing militancy and hysteria. The Taoiseach's attitude to the media, the commentators, to aliens, threw civil liberties out of the window.

COMMENTATOR. For those who dared to oppose Cosgrave and who were clearly not terrorists, he had apt but brutal epithets –

COSGRAVE. Do-gooders – blow-ins!

COMMENTATOR. By blow-in he meant that they were not even Irish and as far as he was concerned they could blow out again or blow up! A clear reminiscence here of the Blueshirt Irish Fascism of the previous generation, Cosgrave's father's generation. The general election was about to be announced – if they did not vote for Cosgrave, then they were voting for subversion, and there was only one thing to do with subversives –

COSGRAVE *and* COALITION. Hunt them down, hound them out, tally-ho, and round them up – !

The COALITION *forces, led by* COSGRAVE *in his hunting-pink, gallop around until they find a fox – whooping and hallooing. (In effect, a reprise of the Galway Theatre Workshop's* Mongrel Fox *finale.) The* SPIRIT OF IRELAND *woman is chased and fallen upon.* COSGRAVE *puts his foot on her. Then a* BISHOP *and a* JUDGE *drag her out between them as* COSGRAVE *makes an announcement:*

COSGRAVE. In this democracy all subversives will be granted a fair trial. A fair trial in this community will only be fair if it thoroughly protects the community. So we don't need any jury in the special court for subversives: and their sympathisers will remain answerable to the nation-wide tribunal of well-prepared public opinion. The General Election will be held on the 16th of June 1977.

COSGRAVE *goes out, blowing his hunting-horn.*

COMMENTATOR. Bloomsday. How far does the obscure and atypical figure of James Joyce's Leopold Bloom contain a fictional parallel to the obscure and atypical figures of the Galway Theatre Workshop? Let us look at their election Odyssey. Which takes place against a background of Olympian manipulation of the mortal wanderers upon the wine-dark sea.

Enter spokesmen for the CIA *and* MI5. LYNCH *and* COSGRAVE, *as racehorses with their jockeys, stand ready for the election race.*

CIA. The Central Intelligence Agency, CIA, assigned me to this report on account of my positive profile ethnicwise, religionwise, cultural-peergroupwise. My assessment as follows: Fianna Fail, under Jack Lynch: most plausible supporters of Washington-Dublin economic concordance – maximised by reappearance in Fianna Fail top-running squad of anti-British Charlie Haughey, noted for reliable pro-American stance as of this time on IRA undercover finance projection with high level of American-Irish Catholic appeal – in two words, he paid the Provos to get rid of their Socialists and my outfit was satisfied to underwrite the investment. The British connection? Chicken-feed! My outfit not interested in outright termination of Westminster-Dublin axis: but provided Fianna Fail can deliver, we are prepared to let Callaghan twist slowly slowly in the wind.

MI5. MI5? MI6? MI8? Whichever you like, I'm not going to tell you. Colonel C, Colonel D – ? Take your choice. The chaps we put our money on are our chaps, that's all. Cosgrave: sound, loyal, silent, good fighting stock. Conor O'Brien: jolly well understands how to get inside our own lefties. Charlie Haughey: bit of a shit, what? Wouldn't invite him into the club. Hope the Irish take the hint. If they don't – chap called Nairac, always useful, cloak-and-dagger – turn him loose. What about Washington? Human rights? Damned unsound:

divisive, bad for discipline. Fine Gael and the Coalition to win, at short odds.

The Election Race begins, the COALITION *and* FINE GAEL *racing each other, with slides projected behind of newspaper headlines and pictures of the contestants. According to the sentiment on each slide, one or other of the contestants gains or drops back, or fouls the other. An improvised commentary can make this clearer over a microphone. Supporters cheer and scuffle.*

Slides:
1 ALL SET FOR ELECTION: June 16th BLOOMSDAY!
2 FINE GAEL: PROGRESS IN THE NATIONAL INTEREST.
3 KEEP THE WINNING TEAM. LET THE GOOD WORK CONTINUE. Liam Cosgrave.
4 THE FIANNA FAIL MANIFESTO. AN ACTION-PLAN FOR NATIONAL RECOVERY.
5 POLL SAYS IT'S COSGRAVE'S TEAM FOR ANOTHER TERM.
6 LYNCH SAYS JOBLESS PROSPECT 'FRIGHTENING'.
7 VOTE FIANNA FAIL. TOGETHER WE'LL GET OUR COUNTRY MOVING AGAIN.
8 ALL THOSE WHO ARE NOT FOR US ARE AGAINST US.

The GALWAY THEATRE WORKSHOP *step forward as the race runs out and round the theatre.*

GALWAY THEATRE WORKSHOP.
  Those who are not against us are for us.
  Those who are not for us are against us.

COMMENTATOR. The Galway Theatre Workshop, subsidised by the Irish Arts Council, had as its function the development of theatre as a means of commenting upon community and social affairs of public concern. In a society where the minuscule left-wing parties are splitting at the rate of twenty or thirty a day, such programmes of cultural idealistic good intention inevitably accumulate a large number of disillusioned political derelicts. The Theatre Workshop was not recognised by the Arts Council as the expression of a partisan faction.

GALWAY THEATRE WORKSHOP.
  Clear enough that a change of government
  Means community involvement.
  Clear enough the government has tried
  To stop all hostile voices being heard.
  The theatre has a voice. What shall it say?

  'Fine Gael and Fianna Fail are each as bad as the other:
  To vote at all in such a stewpot is scarcely worth the bother.'
  'Labour is associated utterly totally with reaction –
  And yet and yet they're trying to do something about
      contraception.'
  'No bourgeois vote will change this State –
  Not if Lenin himself were a candidate.'
  'No point no purpose, all is lost, too late . . .
  Cosgrave will win – it is predestinate.'

  Those who are not for us are against us. Who is in favour of a
  second term for the Coalition? But if we are not against, then
  all of us are in favour. But none of us are in favour: so therefore
  we are all against: and that's it, and we say so.

  The COMMENTATOR *describes the arrest etc of the Galway
  Theatre Workshop – the action is mimed during the narrative.*

COMMENTATOR. On June 2nd Mr Cosgrave was to address a
  Fine Gael Rally in Galway. The Theatre Workshop prepared
  themselves and their costumes to take part in the rally with a
  play. As they accoutred themselves, men came to them with
  warnings. There will be a bloodshed, they said, if the Taoiseach
  is made mock of. Look that you take your own weapons or else
  strong young men for your protection. These warnings were
  given by lawyers, who were aware of Fine Gael and the
  Blueshirts in the days of their fathers. The Theatre Workshop
  were put in fear: but at the same time they had trust in the
  working-classes of the town. They determined to show
  themselves to the people before the speeches: so their
  appearance would be made known: and bursts of rage could be
  prepared for. They mingled among the people. Upon the
  platform, Fintan Coogan, Fine Gael Deputy, a blacksmith. He
  was to introduce the Taoiseach. He took note of the Theatre
  Workshop. He said – 'There was a man shot down by bandits
  not so long ago in Galway. His blood upon the pavement is not

yet dry. Those who come before us with hoods upon their foreheads likewise carry with them the politics of the gun'. After Mr Coogan, Cosgrave. The Theatre Workshop moved forward, stood directly under the platform. As soon as he opened his mouth, they began to sing their song. They were not permitted to sing more than one bar of it. They were taken out through the crowd to the police station. The bowels of Liam Cosgrave were so conturbed by this occurrence that his speech became inchoate and his politics like a broken pot.

When he had done, he reproached Coogan: he said – 'You told me Galway was a quiet town for this election – you told me falsehood and I spurn you from my foot like the turd of a stray dog.' Word was at once heard throughout the town of what had happened.

The arrested members of the Galway Theatre Workshop have been taken behind a screen and the miming of the 'police-station' episode takes place as a shadow-show.

A drunken lawyer from his dram-shop was called to the police-station. He told the guards that they were above themselves, making arrests of ridiculous actors. A political lawyer, full of wit and poetry, was called to the police-station. He told the guards that they were ridiculous, making arrests of a few actors who were above themselves with the wine of democracy. Men from the newspapers came to the police-station. They put questions.

Improvise press questions to police, with police spokesman stonewalling and refusing to admit that an arrest has taken place.

A great crowd of strong young women and beautiful young men came together at the police-station – they raised their voices against the police: release them, release them! It must be said that never before amongst the politics of Ireland had such a thing been heard of. It must be said that the hard voices of the governors of Ireland, though indeed well-accustomed to the hard voices of opposition, were unable to repress nonsense in the open street. And out of nonsense can grow great sense: and out of sense an understanding that there is something to be done and only the people can do it. There was now a new feeling that upon the altar of the church of Cosgrave had appeared a polluting stain, neither of blood nor of excrement, but in some manner the colour of both, and it spread and it spread till the whole altar cloth became rotten. The sanctuary at last was beginning to stink.

The election horse-race continues. The MI5 spokesman appears on the sidelines behind Coalition supporters.

MI5. Situation as seen from Whitehall not at all satisfactory. Bad, in fact, bad. Civil liberties involvement should not have been raised. Cruise O'Brien, divert attention, please, to the bloodshed in Ulster. Divert attention, please, to the reputation of Charlie Haughey. Come along, come along, man: don't be so complacent – you can't *bank* on the editorship of the *Observer* if you lose . . .

CRUISE O'BRIEN *struggles across the channel and is hauled ashore panting by the MI5 man.*

MI5. In an interview with the London *Times* Dr Conor Cruise O'Brien, one of the ruling coalition's leading strategists on Ulster policy, said that –

CRUISE O'BRIEN (*handled by MI5 like a string-puppet*). The opposition Fianna Fail would turn a blind eye to the Provisional IRA activities north of the border. Dangers that might follow a Fianna Fail victory arose from the strength within the party of Mr Charles Haughey, one of the ministers dismissed after the 1970 Arms Trial, now reinstated to front bench status as health spokesman.

COMMENTATOR. Mr Haughey said in reply to this interview that –

HAUGHEY (*from the Fianna Fail side*). That Dr O'Brien should go to the London *Times* to launch a piece of character assassination against a fellow-Irishman is not surprising in view of that newspaper's role in Irish history.

COMMENTATOR. Less than a mile away from the County Mayo street-corner where Mr Cosgrave addressed an enthusiastic crowd on Wednesday the effect of his coalition's tough law'n'order policy can be seen in a sprawling hillside cemetery known as the Leigue.

Mime in the background: the Republican funeral of Frank Stagg.

COMMENTATOR. The coffin of Frank Stagg who died in Wakefield Prison remains in the family grave where he was buried February 1976 amid one of the largest security operations ever undertaken by the Irish government. Against that macabre background the Prime Minister was introduced, by Mickey Finn, a local Fine Gael candidate.

MICKEY FINN, *waving his shillelagh, bursts through the funeral group.*

MICKEY FINN. If it were not for Liam Cosgrave today, you would all be in a civil war and your country locked in strife!

The Election-race continues. JACK LYNCH *comes in way ahead of the field amidst tremendous cheering.*

Slide.
9 AND FIANNA FAIL COULD BE IN POWER INTO THE '90s!

As Lynch wins, improvise commentary to describe how NOEL BROWNE, *as an independent Socialist, surprised everyone by winning his seat in Dublin (Artane) working-class constituency. A horse and rider with a red banner surges forward to the winning post to the strains of the 'Internationale'.*

COMMENTATOR. And Fianna Fail could be in power into the '90s! There has been nothing like it in Irish electoral history. Never has there been such a swing to a political party – and never has a single party commanded so many seats in Dail Eireann. It was a rout, a devastating display of public displeasure.

COSGRAVE *staggers in at the rear of the race. Slides announce that no less than three ministers in his cabinet including* CRUISE O'BRIEN, *have lost their seats. Also* FINTAN COOGAN, *the Galway deputy.*

Slide.

10 BOWING OUT IN RIGHT STYLE: LIAM DINES WITH
   QUEEN.

COSGRAVE, *rejected by the electorate, makes servile obeisance to
the image of the Queen that was left on the stage earlier in the play.*

The two BRITISH OFFICERS *take up their places once again to
guard the (now tottering) wall. The MI5 spokesman, in a ragged
ermine cloak and battered crown, comes in and improvises in the
manner of a Shakespeare monarch. The CIA spokesman confronts
him.*

FIRST BRITISH OFFICER. Upon a platform before the castle,
re-enter two sentinels.

FIRST BRITISH OFFICER.
You come most carefully upon your hour.

SECOND BRITISH OFFICER.
Something is rotten in the state of England.

CIA (*points to slide no. 10*). Nix Biz For Pro-Brit Micks –
huh . . . ?

FIRST BRITISH OFFICER.
Peace, break thee off, look where it comes again.

SECOND BRITISH OFFICER.
Angels and ministers of grace defend us.

MI5. Out on ye, owls, nothing but songs of death? Lynch, a
sound chap, we did business with him before.

CIA. Charlie Haughey? His Provo cohorts? Well?

MI5.
Some lightfoot friend post to the streets of Belfast –
The Provos now with one called Maire Drumm are joined
A holy prophetess new risen up
Is come with a great power to raise the siege –

CIA. Don't you know what to do?

MI5. Ha – bang bang bang – ! Farewell a long farewell to all her
greatness.

Everyone joins in with bang bang bang – slide of Maire Drumm projected.

MI5.   And no-one to defend her within these walls – where are the women, Caryl Churchill, Maureen Duffy, Pam Gems – no no, no word heard – who's next? Billy MacMillen, socialist as well as nationalist of the contrary faction, kill him, lay the blame on the other contrary faction – yes yes – no word heard – bang bang bang –

Same business and slide.

MI5.   Farewell a long farewell to all his greatness. Who next, who else to shake our shaken wall – ? Did I hear Noel Browne holds vaunt and triumph over Coalition shame – ?

CIA.   He splits the Irish Labour Party, induces socialism as a longterm ideology. Possible involvement of the KGB.

MI5.   No dealings in his mind with armed republicans, leave him alone. But Costello, now Seamus Costello –

CIA.   An armed Republican, trotsky-tendency anti-capitalist, electoral support negligible: he would collect friends. So –

MI5.   So bang bang bang –

Same business with slide.

MI5.   Farewell a long farewell to all his greatness. Not a word not a word – no word heard from the left-wing dramatists – Gooch, McGrath, Howard B, Howard the other B – where were they? All blind, blind, made blind and deaf by subsidy – the whole of this most mortal world behind the wall is blind and deaf – there is no man sees what I dream and do – no voice no voice to cry against my peace – ?

CIA.   So long as you open no Watergate, my friend, the wall holds. Your abstract and brief chronicles of the time are so well used, you don't have to worry about any o'that. I hear Peter Hall has a jim-dandy little thing down at the National Theatre about how Lenin and Trotsky went wrong in 1917. They took one look at Joe Stalin and said 'that guy's chickenfeed, he'll make no more impact on history than a pinprick'. What say a bit of dinner and then down to the South Bank – if ya don't wanna bring the wife bring some sort of meaningful relationship – there just ain't nuthn you me and east-west detente are unable to contain by traditional methods.

Slide.

11 An open grave: PROVISIONALS DIG UP AND REBURY STAGG'S BODY

MI5. The wall, the wall, the wall collapses – republicanism is alive, not dead, alive alive alive.

General confusion, screaming, shouting, exeunt all in terror.

The CO-ORDINATOR *comes forward and translates the words in Irish from the* IRISH DELEGATE, *saying that there are three questions for the audience to answer for themselves, now that they have seen the Pinprick play.*

1 Should Britain leave Ireland?
2 How can they secure open access to information to enable them to answer question no. 1?
3 How can they secure themselves from the malefactions of the British legal system if they come up against it in their search for the answer of question no. 2?

Note to p. 415: This was new for all of us, and it took a couple of performances to get us relaxed and chatty enough for members of the public really to be able to feel that it was a genuine offer of participation. I remember two of these interventions vividly. One was a man who wanted to discuss Conor Cruise O'Brien's role at the United Nations. The other was an Egyptian woman who wanted some dramatisation of the background to, and meaning of, the Camp David Agreement. We could not deal with Camp David on the spot because we weren't knowledgeable enough, so she came in the following morning and we all worked together to incorporate improvisations on the subject into the show. As such suggestions continued to be made, we incorporated them day by day; we also incorporated items from the daily press. (These incidental additions are not included in this text.) – M.D'A.